THE COMPLETE IDIOT'S GUIDE® TO

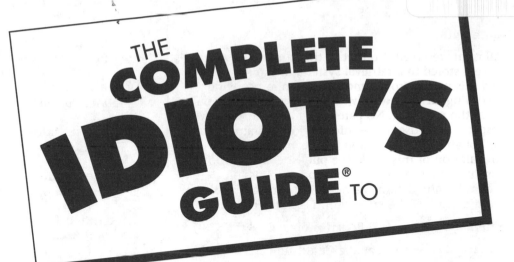

The Internet

Seventh Edition

by Peter Kent

201 West 103rd Street
Indianapolis, IN 46290

A Pearson Education Company

The Complete Idiot's Guide to the Internet, Seventh Edition

Copyright © 2001 by *Que*

...is book shall be repro-
...n, or transmitted by
...al, photocopying,
...written permission
...ibility is assumed with
...tion contained herein.
...een taken in the
...blisher and author
...rs or omissions.
Neither is any liability assumed for damages resulting from the use of the information contained herein.

International Standard Book Number: 0-7897-2523-1

Library of Congress Catalog Card Number: 00-110724

Printed in the United States of America

First Printing: *February, 2001*

01 00 99   4 3 2 1

Trademarks

All terms mentioned in this book that are known to be trademarks or service marks have been appropriately capitalized. Que cannot attest to the accuracy of this information. Use of a term in this book should not be regarded as affecting the validity of any trademark or service mark.

Warning and Disclaimer

Every effort has been made to make this book as complete and as accurate as possible, but no warranty or fitness is implied. The information provided is on an "as is" basis. The author and the publisher shall have neither liability nor responsibility to any person or entity with respect to any loss or damages arising from the information contained in this book.

Associate Publisher
Greg Wiegand

Acquisitions Editor
Stephanie J. McComb

Development Editor
Sarah Robbins

Managing Editor
Thomas F. Hayes

Project Editor
Karen S. Shields

Technical Editor
Bill Bruns

Illustrator
Judd Winick

Copy Editor
Kay Hoskin

Indexer
Chris Barrick

Interior Design
Nathan Clement

Cover Design
Michael Freeland

Proofreader
Maribeth Echard

Layout Technicians
Ayanna Lacey
Heather Hiatt Miller
Stacey Richwine-DeRome
Gloria Schurick

Contents at a Glance

Contents

11 More Internet Discussions—Mailing Lists and Web Forums   169

12 More Ways to Communicate—Net Phones, Conferences, Videoconferences   181

About the Author

Peter Kent is the author of around 45 computer and business books, including *Poor Richard's Web Site: Geek-Free, Commonsense Advice on Building a Low-Cost Web Site* (Top Floor Publishing). His work has appeared in numerous publications, from the *Manchester Guardian* to *Internet World*, the *Dallas Times Herald* to *Computerworld*, and has won him two Excellence in Journalism Awards from the Society of Professional Journalists.

Dedication

To Nick & Chris, partners in crime

Acknowledgments

Thanks to the huge team at Que (see the list of people on the Credits Page) who helped me put this book together. There's a lot more to writing a book than just, well, writing. I'm very grateful to have people willing and able to do all the stuff that comes after the words are on the computer screen. Thanks also to Eric Neyer for his assistance.

Tell Us What You Think!

As the reader of this book, *you* are our most important critic and commentator. We value your opinion and want to know what we're doing right, what we could do better, what areas you'd like to see us publish in, and any other words of wisdom you're willing to pass our way.

As an associate publisher for Que, I welcome your comments. You can fax, email, or write me directly to let me know what you did or didn't like about this book—as well as what we can do to make our books stronger.

Please note that I cannot help you with technical problems related to the topic of this book, and that due to the high volume of mail I receive, I might not be able to reply to every message.

When you write, please be sure to include this book's title and author as well as your name and phone or fax number. I will carefully review your comments and share them with the author and editors who worked on the book.

Fax: 317-581-4666

Email: feedback@quepublishing.com

Mail: Greg Wiegand
          Que
          201 West 103rd Street
          Indianapolis, IN 46290 USA

Introduction

Welcome to *The Complete Idiot's Guide to the Internet, Seventh Edition*. Seven editions in seven years—an indication of how quickly things change on the Internet. Sometimes it's hard to imagine that seven years ago few people had heard of the Internet—the average American thought that the Internet was some kind of international criminal conspiracy organized by the Russian Mafia. Even five years ago, when you'd have to be living in a cave to not have heard of the Internet, few understood what it was, beyond some kind of weird computer thing they'd heard about on television. Now it has become a necessity for many of us—it's hard to imagine life without it. And just think of the kids. Anyone younger than 15 probably has a hard time remembering the years PI (Pre Internet). Millions of people around the world have come to accept the Internet as a normal, and important, part of life.

Not for you, though. If you're reading this book, chances are you're what's known in Internetspeak as a *newbie*—a newcomer. Well, I've got good news for you. If you're just now learning about the Internet, in one way you're lucky. In 1993, even 1994, most Internet users were computer geeks, and that was okay because you needed a high degree of geekhood to get anything done on the Internet. For the average business or home computer user, getting an Internet account was like stepping into a time warp. One moment you were in your whiz bang, multimedia, mouse clicking, graphical user interface—Windows or the Macintosh—and the next minute you were back in the 1970s, working on a dumb UNIX terminal (dumb being the operative word), typing obscure and arcane—not to mention funky and strange—UNIX commands. You probably found yourself wondering, "What's this `ftp ftp.microsoft.com` thing I have to type?" or "What's *grep* all about and why do I care?" or "Why can't UNIX programmers actually *name* their programs instead of giving them two- or three-letter acronyms?" (Acronyms are so important in the UNIX world that there's even an acronym to describe acronyms: TLA, Three-Letter Acronym.)

Most Internet users today don't need to know the answers to these ancient questions. These days the majority of new users are firmly in the new century, working in the graphical user interfaces they love (or love to hate, but that's another issue). Since 1993, thousands of fancy new Internet access programs have been written. Today, it's easy to get on the Internet, and it's easy to get around after you are there.

So, Why Do You Need This Book?

Let's face it, even if you've never stumbled along the information superhighway (or "infotainment superhighway," as satirist Al Franken calls it), you've almost certainly heard of it. A recent survey found that although only 2.3 percent of American high school students could tell you the name of the countries bordering the United States, 93.7 percent knew how to get to the Penthouse Online Web site—and even more knew how to download bootleg MP3 copies of just about any band's new releases ("MP3?," you're thinking—don't worry, we'll cover that in Chapter 5).

Chances are, though, that if you've picked up this book, you are not an experienced international traveler along the highways and byways of this amazing system called the Internet. You probably need a little help. Well, you've come to the right place.

Now, I know you're not an idiot. What you do, you do well. But right now, you don't do the Internet, and you need a way to get up and running quickly. You want to know what the fuss is about, or maybe you already know what the fuss is about and you want to find out how to get in on it. Well, I'm not going to teach you how to become an Internet guru, but I will tell you the things you really *need* to know, such as

➤ How to get up and running on the Internet

➤ How to send and receive email messages

➤ How to move around on the World Wide Web (and what is the Web, anyway?)

➤ How to find what you are looking for on the Internet

➤ What this Napster thing is all about, and why the music industry is trying to close it down

➤ How to shop online—find the best deals, and not get ripped off

➤ Protecting life and limb in the information superhighway fast lane

➤ How to participate in Internet discussion groups (this could take over your life and threaten your relationships if you're not careful)

➤ How to make your fortune in cyberspace

I am, however, making a few assumptions. I'm assuming that you know how to use your computer, so don't expect me to give basic lessons on using your mouse, switching between windows, working with directories and files, and all that stuff. There's enough to cover in this book without all that. If you want really basic beginner's information, check out *The Complete Idiot's Guide to PCs* (also from Que), a great book by Joe Kraynak.

How Do You Use This Book?

I've used a few conventions in this book to make it easier for you to follow. For example, things you type, press, click, and select appear in bold like this:

type **this**

If I don't know exactly what you'll have to type (because you have to supply some of the information), I'll put the unknown information in italic. For example, you might see the following instructions. In this case, you're supplying the filename, so I made it italic to indicate that you have to supply it.

type **this** *filename*

Also, I've used the term "Enter" throughout the book, even though your keyboard might have a "Return" key instead.

Finally, Internet addresses are in a monospace type font. They'll look something like this:

```
http://www.microsoft.com/
```

In case you want a greater understanding of the subject you are learning, you'll find some background information in boxes. You can quickly skip over this information if you want to avoid all the gory details. On the other hand, you might find something that will keep you from getting into trouble. Here are the special icons and boxes used in this book.

Web Savvy

These boxes contain notes, tips, warnings, and asides that provide you with interesting and useful (at least theoretically) tidbits of Internet information.

Net Tips

The Net Tips icon calls your attention to technical information you might spout off to impress your friends, but that you'll likely never need to know to save your life.

Part 1
Connecting to the Internet

You want to start, and you want to start quickly. No problem. In Part 1, you're going to do just that. First, I'll give you a quick overview of the Internet, and then I'll have you jump right in and use the most popular Internet service, the one you've heard most about: the World Wide Web. (The Web is so important these days that many people think the Internet is the Web. I'll explain the difference in Chapter 1, "Your Connection to the Online Universe.") By the time you finish this part of the book, you'll be surfing around the Web like a true cybergeek—and you'll be ready to move on and learn about other Internet services.

Your Connection to the Online Universe

In This Chapter

➤ The obligatory "What is the Internet?" question answered

➤ What sort of information flies across the Internet?

➤ Internet services, from email to the World Wide Web

➤ The difference between the Internet and the online services

➤ Getting a connection to the Internet

➤ Connections, from fast to slow

Your journey into cyberspace begins with figuring out how to get online…which is far easier to do today than back in 1993, when I wrote the first edition of this book. Today the difficulties lie in choice, not implementation; that is, you may well spend more time figuring out which Internet service to use than getting up and running after you've decided. (You may also spend time figuring out which service you want, and then discovering that you can't *have* it, as you'll hear in a moment.) But before I help you make your choice, perhaps I should give a little background information.

What Is the Internet?

What is a computer network? It's a system in which computers are connected so they can share "information." (I'll explain what I mean by that word in a moment.) There's nothing particularly unusual about this in today's world. Millions of networks exist around the world. True, they are mostly in the industrialized world, but you won't find a nation in the world that doesn't have at least a few.

The Internet is something special, though, for two reasons. First, it's the world's largest computer network. Second, it's pretty much open to anyone with the entrance fee—and the entrance fee is pretty low, these days. Many users have free accounts and many more are paying as little as $10 to $20 a month, sometimes for "unlimited" usage. Consequently, millions of people all over the world are getting online. (By the way, *unlimited*, in Internetspeak, is a euphemism meaning "if your computer can manage to connect to the service, and if the service's computers let you stay connected, you can use it as much as you want." In other words, many Internet services are less than reliable.)

Just how big is the Internet? Many of the numbers thrown about in the past few years are complete nonsense. In 1993, people were saying 25 million. Considering that the majority of Internet users at the time were in the United States, and that 25 million is 10% of the U.S. population, and that most people in this great nation thought that the Internet was some kind of hairpiece sold through late-night infomercials, it's highly unlikely that anywhere near 25 million people were on the Internet. In fact, they weren't.

Net Tips

Cyberspace

The term *cyberspace* means the area in which you can move around online. When you are on the Internet, on an online service, or even connected to a computer BBS (bulletin board system), you are in cyberspace.

These days, estimates vary all over the place, ranging from the low hundreds of millions to the high hundreds of millions; one number I saw recently was 330 million. The truth, though, is that nobody knows how many people are using the Internet. Also, remember that many users are only infrequent visitors to cyberspace, using it just now and again, maybe once a week or so. That little bit of information might not be important to the average user, but it *is* worth bearing in mind if you plan to set up shop on the Internet, as I'll discuss in Chapter 17, "Making Money on the Internet."

One way or another, though, a whole lot of people are out there; the numbers are definitely *somewhere* in the hundreds of millions.

What Exactly Is Information?

What, then, do I mean by information? I mean anything you can send over lines of electronic communication, and that includes quite a lot these days (and seems to include more every day). I mean letters, which are called *email* on the Internet. I mean reports, magazine articles, and books, which are called *document files* on the Internet. I mean music, which is called *music* on the Internet.

You can send your voice across the Internet; you'll learn how to do that in Chapter 12, "More Ways to Communicate—Net Phones, Conferences, Videoconferences." For now let me just say that you'll find it much cheaper than talking long-distance on the phone (although most certainly not as easy), as long as you can find someone to talk to. You can also grab computer files of many kinds (programs, word-processing files, clip art, music, and anything else that can be electronically encoded—even smells) from huge libraries that collectively contain literally millions of files.

Information could also be a type of conversation. You want to talk about the tragedy in the Middle East? There's a discussion group waiting for you (whatever side you might take!). Do you want to meet like-minded souls with a passion for daytime soap operas? They're talking right now. Want to know the *truth* about the government cover up of UFOs? Plenty of people are willing to fill you in with the details.

Anything that can be sent electronically is carried on the Internet, and much that can't be sent now probably will be soon. "Such as?" you ask. How about a three-dimensional image of your face? In the next year or so, special face scanners will appear on the scene. You'll be able to scan your face, and then send a three-dimensional image of your face to someone, or use the image for your chat *avatar*. (You'll learn about avatars in Chapter 8, "Using Online Chat Rooms.")

A Word About Numbers

When I first started writing about the Internet, I tried to be specific; I might have said, "2.5 million files." However, I've given up that practice for two reasons. First, many of the numbers were made up, not by me, but by Internet gurus who were trying to be specific and made educated (and sometimes not-so-educated) guesses. Second, even if the numbers were correct when I wrote them, they were too low by the time the book got to the editor, much too low by the time the book got to the printer, and ridiculously low by the time the book got to the readers. But you can be pretty sure that at least 2,536,321 files are available for you to copy—give or take a few score million.

Oh, and those smells I mentioned a moment ago. New devices that emit odors are already available; plug them into your computer and your computer programs will be able to tell the device what stink it wants to drift across the room. Soon computer games and Web sites will become yet more realistic by adding the sense of smell to those of sight and sound. (Don't believe me? See http://www.digiscents.com/.) And we shouldn't forget the sense of touch. "Rumble" devices have been available for games for sometime, and there are now sexual devices that can be plugged into a computer to add yet another dimension. (Giving a whole new dimension to the term "reach out and touch somebody.")

The Internet Services

The following list provides a quick look at the Internet services available to you. This list is not exhaustive. Other services are available, but these are the most important ones:

➤ **Email** This is the most used Internet service. Hundreds of millions of messages—some estimates say billions (another of those completely unconfirmable figures)—wing their way around the world each day, among families, friends, and businesses. The electronic world's postal system is very much like the real world's postal system, except that you can't send fruit, bombs, or this month's selection from the Cheese of the Month club. (You can, however, send letters, spreadsheets, pictures, sounds, programs, and more.) This method is much quicker and cheaper, too. And the mailman isn't armed. Come to think of it, it's not much like the real world's postal system, but in principle it's at least similar: helping people communicate with others all over the world. See Chapter 6, "Sending and Receiving Email," and Chapter 7, "Advanced Email—HTML Mail, Voice, and Encryption," for more information about this essential service.

➤ **Chat** Chat's a bit of a misnomer. Not much chatting goes on, but you'll see an awful lot of typing. You type a message, and it's instantly transmitted to another person, or to many other people, who can type their responses right away. If you enjoy slow and confusing conversations in which it's tough to tell who's talking to whom, in which the level of literacy and humor is somewhere around fourth grade, and in which many of the chat-room members claiming to be handsome and successful businessmen are actually spotty teenage boys...you'll love chat! (Okay, maybe I'm being a little harsh; some people enjoy chat. On the other hand, some people enjoy eating monkey brains and bungee-jumping, too.) You'll learn more about chatting in Chapter 8.

The 5-Cent Email Tax

Spend enough time on the Internet, and eventually you'll hear from someone that the U.S. government is trying to impose a 5-cent per message tax on *email*. This is a complete myth, a hoax, an urban legend. It's such a common myth that Hillary Clinton declared her opposition to the tax during a political debate, but nonetheless, a myth it is.

➤ **Internet Phones** Install a sound card and microphone, get the Internet phone software, and then talk to people across the Internet. This service is not very popular today, and to be quite honest, despite all the hype, it will probably remain of use to a relatively small number of people. But if you're paying for expensive international phone calls, consider that you may be able to make those same calls free. (I've given up predicting imminent success for this service. I'll discuss some of the reasons in Chapter 12.)

➤ **FTP** The original purpose of the Internet was to simply transfer files from one place to another, and for years FTP was how it was done. FTP provides a giant electronic library of computer files; you'll learn how to use it in Chapter 19, "Downloading Files (FTP, Go!Zilla, and CuteFTP).

➤ **The World Wide Web** The Web is so popular that many Internet users think that the term *World Wide Web* is synonymous with the *Internet*. It's not, although it certainly is the pre-eminent Internet tool, one that's used for many different purposes. The Web is a giant *hypertext* system in which documents around the world are linked to one another. Click a word in a document in, say, Sydney, Australia, and another document (which might be from Salzburg, Austria) appears. You'll begin learning about this amazing system in the very next chapter.

➤ **Newsgroups** Newsgroups are discussion groups. Want to hear the latest theory about why American teenagers are arming themselves to the teeth? Want to learn an unusual kite-flying technique? Want to learn about…well, anything really? You can choose from tens of thousands of internationally distributed newsgroups, and you'll find out how to work with them in Chapter 10, "Finding and Using Newsgroups."

➤ **Mailing lists** If tens of thousands of discussion groups are not enough for you, here are hundreds of thousands more. As you'll learn in Chapter 11, "More Internet Discussions—Mailing Lists and Web Forums," mailing lists are another form of discussion group that works in a slightly different manner—you send and receive messages using your email program. You'll learn about Web forums, too, discussion groups located at Web sites. In these forums, you read and sub-mit messages using your Web browser.

Getting on the Net

So, you think the Net sounds great. How do you get to it, though? You can get Internet access in a number of ways:

➤ Your college provides you with an Internet account.

➤ Your company has an Internet connection from its internal network.

➤ You use an online service such as America Online (AOL), CompuServe, The Microsoft Network (MSN), or Prodigy.

➤ You use a small, local Internet service provider.

➤ You use a large, national Internet service provider such as PSINet, EarthLink, or SpryNet.

➤ You use a free Internet-access service.

➤ You use your cable-TV company's Internet access service.

➤ You've signed up with one of the phone companies, such as AT&T, Sprint, or MCI WorldCom, or your local phone company.

➤ You use some sort of special high-speed access system such as satellite access or microwave service.

The Internet is not owned by any one company. It resembles the world's telephone system: Each portion is owned by someone, and the overall system hangs together because of a variety of agreements among those organizations. So, you'll find no single *Internet, Inc.* where you can go to get access to the Internet. No, you have to go to one of the tens of thousands of organizations that already have access to the Internet and get a connection through it.

The Difference Between the Internet and Online Services

I often hear the questions, "What's the difference between the Internet and AOL, or CompuServe, or whatever?" and "If I have an AOL account, do I have an Internet account?" Services such as AOL (America Online), CompuServe, Prodigy, GEnie, MSN (The Microsoft Network), and so on are not the same as the Internet. They are known as *online services*. Although they are similar to the Internet in some ways (yes, they are large computer networks), they are different in the sense that they are private clubs. (They've also been around since before the Internet became popular.)

For instance, what happens when you dial into, say, CompuServe? Your computer connects across the phone lines with CompuServe's computers, which are all sitting in a big building somewhere. All those computers belong to CompuServe (well, they belong to America Online, which bought CompuServe a few years ago). Contrast this with the Internet. When you connect to the Internet, you connect to a communications system that's linked to millions of computers, which are owned by hundreds of thousands of companies, schools, government departments, and individuals. If the Internet is like a giant public highway system, the online services are like small private railroads.

However, at the risk of stretching an analogy too far (I'm already mixing metaphors, so why not?), I should mention that these private railroads let you get off the tracks and onto the public highway. In other words, although AOL, CompuServe, and the others are private clubs, they do provide a way for you to connect to the Internet. So, although the barbarians on the Internet are held at the gates to the private club, the private club members can get onto the Internet.

The online services view themselves as both private clubs and gateways to the Internet. As Russ Siegelman of The Microsoft Network stated, Microsoft wants MSN to be "the biggest and best content club and community on the Internet." So, it's intended to be part of the Internet—but a private part. In fact, although I (and many others) call these services "online services," Microsoft now refers to MSN as an "Internet Online Service."

To summarize:

➤ The Internet is a public highway system overrun with barbarians.
➤ Online services are private railroads or exclusive clubs...or something like that.

➤ Even if you use the Internet, you can't get into the online services unless you're a member of those services.

➤ If you are a member of the online services, you can get onto the Internet.

The answer to the second question I posed earlier, then, is "yes"; if you have an online-service account (at least with the services mentioned here), you also have an Internet account.

A service provider is a company that sells access to the Internet. You dial into its computer, which connects you to the Internet. The online services are, in effect, Internet service providers, too. Companies known as service providers generally provide access to the Internet and little, if anything, more, whereas online services have all sorts of file libraries, chat services, news services, and so on within the private areas of the services themselves.

Picking Your Access Provider

What does it take to get onto the infotainment superhypeway? Many of you already have Internet accounts; our high-priced research shows that most readers buy this book after they have access to the Internet (presumably because they got access and then got lost). However, I want to talk about the types of accounts (or connections) that are available because they all work in slightly different ways. This discussion will help ensure that we are all on the same wavelength before we get going.

The Best Value in Internet Access?

Let's deal with the first major question newcomers ask: Which is the best Internet service?

The best value in Internet access in North America is a bidirectional connection from a cable company. Note that there are two types of connections being sold by cable companies. The best is a system in which a network card in your computer is connected to a cable modem, which is then connected to the TV cable—all data, both uploads and downloads, travel along that cable, so it's known as *bidirectional* (two-way). However, some cable companies are using a system that requires your computer to have a modem connection at the same time. Data from your computer to the Internet passes along the phone line, while data from the Internet to your computer passes along the cable. Obviously, such a system is less convenient than bidirectional, and data won't transfer as quickly one way; but as, in most cases, most data is coming into your computer rather than out of it, such systems are still very quick.

If you can get one of the bidirectional systems, go for it. It's cheap, around $80 to install and $40 a month. You'll transfer more data per dollar on a cable system than any other Internet connection you can find. You'll get super fast connections, and it's always on—no need to log onto the Internet when you start your computer, because as soon as your computer boots up and starts its network software, it's automatically connected.

To be fair, I should point out that many people have been disappointed with these cable systems. They've found them to be slow and often nonfunctional; one problem is that you are put onto a network with your neighbors, perhaps a couple of hundred of them, so the more people in your neighborhood using the system, the slower it works. My experience with cable, though, has been different; perhaps I've just been lucky. With the exception of a few weeks when service was appalling, I've had over two years of excellent service. If your cable connection works properly, it's far better than any other connection you're likely to get.

One caveat—beware of the security problems inherent with these systems. You're connected to the same network as your neighbors—it's like being on a corporate network. So, if you turn on network file sharing, and don't password protect your directories, your neighbors can get onto your hard disk and dig around! Be sure you ask the installer how to avoid this problem. (And take a look at http://ZoneAlarm.com/ for information on fully protecting your system.)

Of course, there's another problem with cable connections—most people in North America don't live in an area in which they are being installed. (And even if you do, you might have to wait on the phone for an hour or two to get through to someone who can set up an appointment for an installation...although, I've heard recent reports that such problems are a thing of the past.)

No Cable? Try DSL

If you can't get a cable modem, you might try a DSL (Digital Subscriber Line) connection from your phone company. These connections are much faster than basic telephone-line connections, but still slower than cable, and more expensive. They're also not widely available yet, and won't be for some time. And they come from the phone company, the same people who spent several decades trying to figure out how to install ISDN connections (and not quite getting it right). I've heard bad things about DSL connections...but I know people who love them, too.

DSL provides fast connections, but generally not as fast as cable, unless you want to spend a lot of money. There are various choices, beginning at around 256Kbps (about five or six times the speed of a fast modem) and going up to 7Mbps (about 125 times faster!). Prices begin at around $40 to $60 a month (including Internet access). There's also a setup charge, and you'll have to buy a card to go into your computer.

To see whether you can get a DSL connection in your area, call your phone company, or a DSL provider advertising in your area (you may have seen billboard or newspaper ads).

By the way, to use a DSL connection, you need an Internet service provider that is set up to use DSL (most aren't). Unlike cable connections—the cable company connects your computer directly to the Internet through their own Internet service—when you get a DSL line you can connect to any Internet service provider set up to accept DSL connections. Generally, though, phone companies that provide DSL service also provide Internet service for the DSL line. Phone companies often don't make very good Internet service providers, though.

Not Quite So Good Options

Let's say you *can't* get a cable connection, and you *can't* get DSL...which, as a matter of fact, is the case for most people. There are a few moderately high-speed connections you might try to find.

ISDN

ISDN is an old Albanian acronym for "Yesterday's Technology Tomorrow—perhaps." ISDN phone lines are fast digital phone lines. This technology has been around for years, but just about the time the phone companies figured out how to install it, they decided they'd install DSL instead. (DSL is, admittedly, better.) In fact, if you call your phone company and ask for an ISDN line, they'll probably tell you wouldn't want one, that you should use DSL instead. Then they'll look up your phone number in a database, and discover that you can't get DSL in your area, and reluctantly agree to give you an ISDN line, perhaps (many areas cannot get DSL or ISDN).

Even if you can get ISDN, you may not want it. I had ISDN installed in 1997 and discovered a few oddities about this technology. It requires that large holes be dug in your yard, generally by a small group of rotund men who stand around in front of your house staring at the hole. It might

High-Speed Access for All?

Since 1995, various companies and organizations have been promising that high-speed Internet access (also known as "broadband") would be widely available soon. It wasn't, and it won't be. By late in 2000 somewhere around 5% of home users had fast access, generally cable or DSL connections. To reach a situation in which most Americans can get fast and affordable Internet access if they want it will take years. For instance, the cable companies know how much it will cost them to provide Internet access to all their customers...but currently don't have the money and don't know where it will come from.

DSL Direct from Service Providers

Some major service providers now help you set up DSL service and connect to the Internet through them. Both EarthLink and MSN charge $39.95/month.

take a dozen visits from the phone company—they might even try to install it a couple of times after they've already installed it once. It might also require the destruction of the neighbor's shrubbery. Even then, it might not work well; I eventually gave up and went back to using a normal modem, and prayed every night for a cable modem. (I've heard similar stories from other ISDN users, although now and then I come across an ISDN user who's actually happy with the service.)

Note that ISDN, while at one time thought of as a fast connection, is not—it's just a few times the speed of a normal phone modem, a fraction of the speed of a cable modem.

Again, as with DSL, if you use an ISDN line you'll probably end up using the phone company's Internet access, although you may be able to find a service provider that can work with ISDN connections.

Prices for ISDN service are all over the place. To use ISDN, you'll need a special *ISDN modem*, as it's known (more correctly, an ISDN *adapter*). That'll cost around $200 to $400, but prices are falling. Then, you pay the phone company to install the line (between $0 and $600—don't ask me how they figure out these prices), and you'll pay a monthly fee of $25 to $130. You'll have to pay both the phone company *and* the service provider an extra fee for this special service. ISDN service is actually more expensive than the much better DSL, because the phone company wants to encourage you to use DSL…which probably isn't available in your area.

Satellite

For the next few years, only one satellite service will be available in North America, the DirecPC from Hughes Network Systems (`http://www.direcpc.com/` or call 800-347-3272). Other companies plan to introduce satellite service, but the earliest such service can begin is around 2002.

Two New Ways to Use Satellite

A short time before we went to print, both MSN and AOL began selling satellite access. MSN's service is about $60/month ($300 for the equipment), whereas AOL's is around $42/month ($200 for the equipment).

It costs a little over $100 to buy the equipment, and perhaps $50 or $100 to pay someone to install it. (There's also a product called DirecDuo, which combines Internet and TV service, for around $50 more.)

DirecPC connections are at 400Kpbs, seven times faster than fast modems. Note, however, that DirecPC transmits data only *to* your computer. You still need a phone line and an Internet service provider to transmit data out (you can use Hughes's Internet access service, or use a service provider of your choice). When you connect to a Web site, for instance, the instructions to the Web server go along your phone line to the service provider; then, the data from the Web site goes up to the satellite and down to you.

The lowest rates are around $30 a month, including Internet access; that rate provides only 25 hours a month, though, with extra hours costing $1.99. You can get unlimited use for $50 a month, which is reasonable (it used to be much higher).

To get 100 hours a month you'll pay $50. Rates for businesses are higher. I've heard complaints about satellite access being unreliable. Indeed Hughes has this disclaimer on their Web site: "To ensure equal Internet access for all DirecPC subscribers, Hughes Network Systems maintains a running average fair access policy. ...To ensure this equity, customers might experience some temporary throughput limitations. DirecPC Turbo Internet access is not guaranteed."

T1 Line

This special type of digital phone line is about 10 times faster than ISDN. Having a T1 connection used to be the sign of a *real* geek, and cost thousands of dollars, but these days they're much easier to come by and cost only hundreds a month. Although this solution is okay for small businesses who really need fast access to the Internet (very few really do), it's out of the price range of most individuals. If you want one, call a local phone service (not necessarily your local phone company, but one of the new companies reselling phone service).

Microwave

Some areas that have had trouble getting fast connections, in particular wealthy rural areas, now have microwave service. Such service is pretty fast, but has some problems, being rather sensitive to weather. These are "line-of-sight" systems; that is, you have to be able to install a receiver dish that has a direct unobstructed view of the transmitter.

This service can be expensive, though. I've seen one company that charged more than $1,000 to set up the service, and from $125 to $425 a month. You may be able to find a service by looking in local computer papers and magazines, or asking at a local computer store.

Back to Basics—Your Phone Lines

For now, most of you are stuck with modems connecting your computer through the phone lines to one of the services I mentioned earlier:

➤ An online service such as America Online (AOL), CompuServe, The Microsoft Network (MSN), or Prodigy.

➤ A small, local Internet service provider.

➤ A large, national Internet service provider such as PSINet, EarthLink, or SpryNet.

➤ A free Internet access service.

➤ A phone company, such as AT&T, Sprint, or MCI WorldCom, or your local phone company.

With luck, you have a 56Kbps modem, although that doesn't mean you'll have a 56Kbps connection. The quality of the phone line affects the speed of the connection. In fact, you will *never* get the full 56Kbps, and may well get speeds *much* lower. (Someone told me, a day or two ago, that in her rural home she can never connect above 14.4Kbps, and just this morning, while calling from a hotel room, I was unable to connect faster than 19.2Kbps.)

So, how do you pick a service provider? There's no easy answer to that, unfortunately. It's rather like asking, "What makes the best spouse?" Everyone has a different answer. A service that you think is good might prove to be a lousy choice for someone else.

Basically, what you need to do is pick a service provider that is cheap, helpful, and has a reliable and fast connection to the Internet and easy-to-install software. Of course, that's very difficult to find. I've had Internet accounts with a couple of dozen providers, and I haven't found one yet that I would rave about. They've ranged from pretty good to absolutely awful.

Tips for Picking a Provider

Consider the following guidelines when you're trying to find an Internet service provider:

➤ The major online services often make it very easy to connect to the Internet: You just run the setup program and away you go.

➤ On the other hand, the major online services tend to be a bit more expensive (although their prices have dropped greatly, and the difference is no longer so significant). Some of them also have a reputation for having very slow and unreliable connections to the Internet. But then, so do many Internet service providers!

➤ There are a lot of low-priced Internet service providers (in Colorado, for example, there are about 70), and the competition is stiff!

➤ Unfortunately, many low-priced services have customer service that matches their prices—they are often not very helpful. To work on those services, you need more than a little of the geek gene inside you.

➤ On the other hand, some of these services *are* very good and will help you hook up to the Internet at a very good price.

➤ Be sure the service has a toll-free or local support telephone number—you'll almost certainly need it!

➤ A number of companies provide *free* Internet access; in general, they are funded by advertising—their software forces your computer to display ads while you are online. The two big questions about such free services are Will you be able to get online when you want to? and Will you get customer service when you need it?

➤ A number of large national Internet service providers, such as WorldNet (owned by AT&T), EarthLink, and PSINet, often have very good prices ($20-$25 a month for unlimited usage, for instance). In addition, in some areas, they might even have good service.

➤ There are no hard and fast rules! A service that is very good in one area might be lousy in another. And a service that your friend says is really good might be great right now and absolutely awful next month.

How Much Will It Cost?

Internet access is typically around $20–$25 a month. Some services charge as little as $10 a month, and some are free.

Finding a Service Provider

If you don't have an Internet account yet, but you want to find one, I can help. Here are a few ideas for tracking down service providers:

➤ Ask your friends and colleagues which local service providers are good (and which to avoid).

➤ Look in your local paper's computer section; local service providers often advertise there.

➤ Keep your eyes open for Internet-access CDs being given away in computer stores, office supply stores, and even warehouse stores and large discount stores.

➤ Look in your city's local computer publication for ads.

➤ Check the Yellow Pages' Internet category.

➤ Ask at your local computer store.

➤ Check for ads in one of the many new Internet-related magazines.

➤ Look in a general computer magazine (many of which *seem* to have turned into Internet magazines).

➤ If you know someone who has access to the World Wide Web, ask him to go Yahoo! and search for *internet service provider*. You might not know what that means, but your friend probably will (check out Chapter 15, "Finding What You Need Online," for more information). You'll find information about many service providers and even some price comparisons. (You might also try using the Web at your local library.)

➤ You might also try The List (http://thelist.internet.com/) and ISP Finder (http://ispfinder.com/), directories listing thousands of services.

19

Do You Need Speed?

Stuck with a slow connection? Don't get too jealous of people using faster connections. The Internet can be very slow at times, and even if you have a very fast connection from your service provider to your computer, you might still find yourself twiddling your fingers. For instance, when you're using the Web, the server you've connected to might be slow. Or the lines from that server across the world to your service provider might be slow. Or, your service provider's system might be clogged up with more users than it was designed to handle.

Oh, all right, I'll tell you the truth. A fast connection is fantastic—the Internet is a completely different experience. Sure, you'll run across slow servers now and then, although there seem to be fewer and fewer of them. But all of a sudden you'll find that things that make absolutely no sense over a slow modem—in particular, video—really work well. News clips at sites such as CNN (http://www.cnn.com) and The BBC (http://news.bbc.co.uk/), for instance, can be more trouble than they're worth if you're working on a phone-line modem, but over a cable connection they really work well. Before I had a cable modem, I rarely used the RealPlayer video player; these days, I routinely click on videos at new sites. Jealous? Never mind; those fast connections will be in your area soon. (Another lie; "eventually" may be more accurate.)

WebTV

Before we move on, let's consider another way to get online, WebTV. This is the first major noncomputer system to be widely available for retrieving information from the Internet. It costs from $99 to $199 to buy the equipment you'll need, plus you'll pay monthly service fees ranging from $10 to $25 a month. You'll get what is basically a little box with a modem inside and a bunch of other circuitry. (The box is made by Sony, Philips Magnavox, or Mitsubishi; the service is owned by Microsoft.)

Why a modem? Many people seem to think WebTV uses the TV cable to access the Web, but it works with a phone line. A connection is made across the phone line to the WebTV Internet service, and the box uses the TV as a screen. If you choose to use your own service provider—perhaps you're in an area that doesn't have a WebTV phone number—you'll save $10 a month on your WebTV subscription.

WebTV also comes with a remote control—this is the Internet for couch potatoes—and, optionally, a wireless keyboard. The keyboard is $50, but it's almost an essential option, as "writing" using the remote control is like eating soup with chopsticks. On the other hand, you might find an ordinary computer keyboard more comfortable—you can connect any PS2-compatible keyboard. You can also connect a printer to the system, although there's a fairly limited range of printers that will work.

I think many WebTV owners are probably a little disappointed, though. Who would have bought one? People who want the Internet because they've heard all the hype, yet don't have a computer. The Internet has been hyped in many quarters, with images of exciting video rolling across Web pages for instance. But the reality is very different, and Web pages are not TV shows. Or, perhaps there's another way to consider WebTV; it has whetted many people's appetites. Having used WebTV, they then move up to the "real thing" and get a PC.

What can WebTV do for you, then? Its basic feature is its capability to display Web pages. The WebTV box turns your TV into a Web browser. The more advanced systems, WebTV Plus and WebTV for Satellite, go much further, integrating TV and the Web in the following ways:

➤ It provides TV listings, showing what's on in your area.

➤ A feature named WebPIP (Web Picture in Picture) allows you to view a TV show and a Web page at the same time, even if your TV is not a Picture in Picture TV.

➤ TV Crossover Links provide access to Web pages designed in conjunction with TV shows. A small icon will appear at the bottom of the screen while the show is running; you can select the icon to open the related page.

➤ An IR Blaster feature allows the WebTV Plus box to control your cable box; selecting a channel on the WebTV Plus box would automatically change the cable box. Eventually, the system will allow you to program your VCR by clicking a show in the WebTV Plus listing.

➤ A 1.1GB hard drive is built into the system. It *won't* allow you to download programs in the same way you can with a computer. Rather, it's used for the Web browser's cache and will also be used for certain system enhancements. For instance, eventually you'll be able to read and write email even if you're not connected to the Internet—the email will be stored on the hard disk (right now the email is stored on the WebTV Internet server).

➤ Multimedia Email. You can grab still pictures from a TV show, from your video camera, or from your VCR, add 30 seconds of sound, and drop it into an email message.

➤ TV Pause. The satellite system comes with a feature that allows you to pause a program that you're watching, and come back and finish watching it later.

Visit http://www.webtv.com/ to get all the details.

The Drawbacks

WebTV has a number of advantages, the main one being that it provides a cheap way to connect to the Internet. However, it's not the real thing, and even the WebTV people say that it's not intended to replace computers.

It can be awkward to use, particularly if you don't have a keyboard (as one reviewer put it, "it feels very much like using DOS or one of the old IBM 3270 terminals"). You can't download and run software, and you can't use many other non-Web Internet services—Telnet and FTP, for instance. The display is low-resolution, so you can't see much of a Web page without scrolling down; small text is often very difficult to read. You can't save documents you find on the Web (although you can print them if you add a printer to the system).

The Least You Need to Know

➤ The Internet is the world's largest computer network, a huge public information highway.

➤ You can do many things on the Internet: send email, join discussion groups, grab files from electronic libraries, cruise the World Wide Web, and much more.

➤ The Internet is a public system. The online services, such as America Online, CompuServe, and The Microsoft Network, are private services with gateways to the Internet.

➤ A member of an online service can use the Internet, but an Internet user cannot use an online service unless he joins that service.

➤ There are lots of ways to connect to the Internet, but the preferred methods are generally cable or DSL...but there's a good chance these aren't available in your area.

➤ Failing those options, a few other reasonably fast methods might be available—ISDN, satellite, microwave.

➤ After that, all you have left are basic phone-line connections.

Working on the World Wide Web

The *World Wide Web* is also known as the *Web*, *WWW*, and sometimes (among really geeky company) *W3* (pronounced *double-you cubed*). In really confused company, it's called *the Internet*. The World Wide Web is not the Internet. It's simply one software system running on the Internet. Still, it's one of the most interesting and exciting systems, so it has received a lot of press, to the extent that many people believe that the terms *Web* and *Internet* are synonymous. However, the Web seems to be taking over roles previously carried out by other Internet services; at the same time, Web programs, called *browsers*, are including utilities to help people work with non-Web services. For instance, you can send and receive email with some Web browsers and you also can read Internet newsgroups with some browsers.

What's the Web?

Imagine that you are reading this page in electronic form, on your computer screen. Then imagine that some of the words are underlined and colored. Use your mouse to point at one of these underlined words on your screen and press the mouse button.

What happens? Another document opens, a document that's related in some way to the word you clicked.

That's a simple explanation of *hypertext*. If you've ever used Apple's Hypercard or a Windows Help file, you've used hypertext. Documents are linked to one another in some way, generally by clickable words and pictures. Hypertext has been around for years, but until recently, most hypertext systems were limited in both size and geographic space. Click a link, and you might see another document held by the same electronic file. Or maybe you'll see a document in another file, but one that's on the same computer's hard disk, probably the same directory.

The World Wide Web is a hypertext system without boundaries. Click a link, and you might be shown a document in the next city, on the other side of the country, or even on another continent. Links from one document to another can be created without the permission of the owner of that second document, and nobody has complete control over those links. When you put a link in your document connecting it to someone else's, you are sending your readers on a journey that you can't predict. They will land at that other document, from which they can take another link somewhere else—to another country, another subject, or another culture from which they can follow yet another link, and on and on. These kinds of connections are why we call it a Web—lots of points connected together.

The Web has no capacity limit, either. Web pages are being added every minute of the day, all over the world; the Web is pushing the growth of the Internet. Creating and posting a Web page is so easy that thousands of people are doing it, and more are joining them each day.

If you haven't seen the Web, this description might sound a little mundane. Okay, so one document leads to another that leads to another; what's the big deal? I try to avoid the Internet hype we've been inundated with over the past couple of years, but the Web really is a publishing revolution. Publishing to an international audience is now quick and simple. I don't mean to imply (as some Internet proponents seem to) that every Web page is a jewel that is widely read and appreciated (much of it is closer to a sow's ear than to silk), but it's a medium with which people can make their words available so that those words can be widely read if they have some value.

Let's Start

If you want to listen to a CD, you need a CD player. If you want to watch a video, you need a video player. If you want to view a Web page, you need a Web player: a *Web browser*.

The Web equation has two parts. First, a *Web server* is a special program running on a *host computer* (that is, a computer connected directly to the Internet). This server administers (hosts) a Web *site*, which is a collection of World Wide Web documents. The second part is the *browser*, which is a program on your PC that asks the server for the documents and then displays the documents so that you can read them.

There are two big contenders in the Web browser war (yes, there's a war going on). One is Netscape Navigator. Right now, somewhere around 40% of all Web users are working with Netscape, although in the past Netscape owned 80% of the market or higher. Netscape is available in versions for Windows 3.1, Windows 95, Windows 98, Windows NT, Windows 2000, Windows ME, the Macintosh, and various flavors of UNIX. Netscape Navigator is now part of the Netscape Communicator suite of programs. Figure 2.1 shows the Netscape Navigator Web browser.

Servers and Clients

If you hang around on the Internet long enough, you'll hear the terms server and client used over and over. A *server* (such as a Web server) is a program that provides information that a *client* program (such as a Web browser) can use in some way.

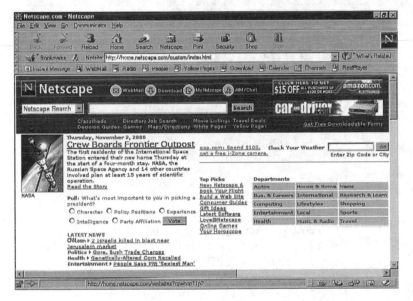

Figure 2.1

Netscape Navigator 4.76, part of the Netscape Communicator suite of programs.

The most popular browser is Internet Explorer from Microsoft (see Figure 2.2); around 60% of all Web users are working with this program. This browser is available for all flavors of Windows, and even for the Macintosh. Chances are you are using either Netscape Navigator or Internet Explorer—only a few percent of all users work with another type of browser.

Figure 2.2

Microsoft Internet Explorer 5.5, Microsoft's latest weapon in the Web war with Netscape (a war that it is winning).

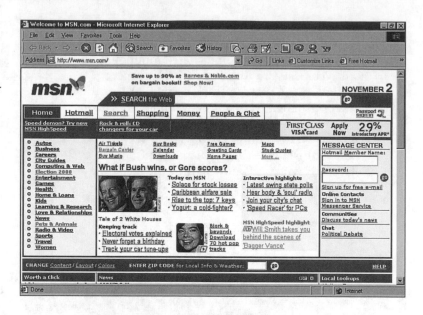

Netscape Navigator

Netscape Communications manufactures Netscape Navigator. You might think that it would be known as Navigator for short, but it's not. It's known as Netscape, mainly for historical reasons. The Netscape programmers came from the *National Center for Supercomputing Applications (NCSA)*. They originally created the first graphical Web browser, called Mosaic. Netscape was originally known as Netscape Mosaic, and the company was Mosaic Communications. Therefore, the browser was known as Netscape to differentiate it from Mosaic.

Getting a Browser

Which browser should you use? If your service provider has given you one, I suggest you start with that. You'll probably be given either Netscape or Explorer—most likely Internet Explorer these days because CompuServe, AOL, and (of course!) Microsoft Network provide that browser to their members.

Which is the better browser? Depends what sort of bugs you prefer. Each has a different set. The actual features aren't so different, although there are a few differences. I prefer Navigator's bookmarks and history list. I like the fact that I can copy images from a Web page directly into the Clipboard with Internet Explorer. I use both browsers, and switch them around depending on what I'm doing at the time.

For now, I'm going to assume that you have a Web browser installed, and that you have opened it and are ready to start. One nice thing about Web browsers is that they all work similarly, and they look very similar, too. So, whatever browser you use, you should be able to follow along with this chapter.

Browsing Begins at Home

When you open your browser, whichever page you see is, by definition, your *home page*—I'm assuming that you are already connected to the Internet, of course. (I like that kind of definition; it's easy to understand.) Ideally, the home page is a page that has lots of useful links, which take you to places on the Web where you will want to go to frequently. You can create your own home page by using something called *HTML*, the Web document language (see Chapter 13, "Setting Up Your Own Web Site") or even by using one of the fancy new customizing systems you'll find on the Web. (Both Netscape and Microsoft have systems that automatically create customized pages for you, if you have their browsers.) Go to http://www.netscape.com/custom/ for the Netscape system or http://home.microsoft.com/ for the Microsoft system (Internet Explorer 4.5 and 5 have an Internet Start button on the Links toolbar that you can click to get to this page). I'll explain how to use these *addresses* later in this chapter, in the section "A Direct Link: Using the URLs."

Moving Around on the Web

Whichever browser you are using, you'll almost certainly find links on the home page. Links are the colored and underlined words. You might also find pictures that contain links, perhaps several different links on a picture (a different link on each part of the picture). Use your mouse to point at a piece of text or a picture; if the mouse pointer changes shape—probably into a pointing hand—you are pointing at a link. (Just to confuse the issue, some pictures contain links even though the pointer doesn't change shape.)

Home Page, Start Page

Microsoft's programmers can't seem to decide whether to use the term *home page* or *start page*. The term home page originally meant the page that appeared when you opened your browser or when you used the Home button. Then, all of a sudden, everybody was using the term to mean a person or company's main Web page (the page you see when you go to that Web site), such as NEC's home page, Netscape's home page, and so on. So, Microsoft's programmers evidently thought it made more sense to rename the home page to start page. Unfortunately, they're using both terms, so Internet Explorer 3, 4, and 5 have a Home button on the toolbar; and Explorer 3 has a Go, Start Page menu option; some versions of Explorer 4 have a Go, Home Page menu option and a Home button, but mention start page in the options dialog box. Explorer 5, and the later versions of Explorer 4, seem to have completely replaced the term start page with home page.

Click whichever link looks interesting. If you are online (I'm assuming you are), your browser sends a message to a Web server somewhere, asking for a page. If the Web server is running (it might not be) and if it's not too busy (it might be), it transmits the document back to your browser, and your browser displays it on your screen.

You've just learned the primary form of Web navigation. When you see a link you want to follow, click it. Simple, eh? But what about going somewhere useful, somewhere interesting? Most browsers these days either have toolbar buttons that take you to a useful Web page or come with a default home page with useful links. For example, in Netscape Navigator 4, you can click the **Guide** button to open the Guide page, or click the **Guide** button and hold it down to display a number of options that lead you to pages that help you find your way around the Internet. In Navigator 4.5, though, they removed the **Guide** button. Instead, the Netcenter page (the page that appears each time you open your browser, unless you change your home page—which we discuss in Chapter 13), is full of options. Here are just a few:

➤ **Classifieds** This option takes you to the classifieds and auctions page.

➤ **Decision Guides** From baby strollers and mutual funds to diamonds and medical school, whenever you have a decision to make these guides can help you make your choice.

➤ **Directory** This option takes you to a directory of Web pages.

➤ **Games** If games are your thing, you'll find what you want here. Play by yourself or with others across the Internet; play free or buy game software; this option has it all.

➤ **Job Search** The Web is quickly becoming the best place to find a job. This option takes you to all the best sites.

➤ **Maps/Directions** From just about anywhere to just about anywhere else, the directions are available through this link.

➤ **Movie Listings** This link provides theater listings, times, reviews, and even directions to your favorite flick.

➤ **White Pages** This option provides links to sites that can help you track down other Internet users.

➤ **Travel Deals** This option lets you search for the best in travel for the least money.

➤ **Yellow Pages** This option displays a page from which you can select a regional Yellow Pages system and search for a business.

➤ **Netscape Search** Just enter a few keywords and press the Search button. Wherever you want to go on the Web can be found through a search. (This is fully explained in Chapter 3, "More Web Basics—Searching, Saving, and More.")

Internet Explorer 3 has a special QuickLinks toolbar (click **QuickLinks** in the Address toolbar to open the QuickLinks toolbar). In Explorer 4 and 5, this toolbar is simply named the Links bar and can be opened or closed by selecting **View**, **Toolbars**, **Links**. On this toolbar, you'll find a variety of buttons designed to take you to useful starting points. (The button names vary among versions.)

Whatever browser you are using, take a little time to explore. Go as far as you want. Then come back here, and I'll explain how to find your way back to where you came from.

Net Tips

How Does the Browser Know Where to Go?

How does your browser know which server to request the document from? What you see on your computer screen is not quite the same document that your browser sees. Open the source document (which you can probably do using the **View**, **Page Source** menu option), and you'll see what the Web document really looks like. (You'll learn more about these source documents in Chapter 13.) The source document is just basic ASCII text that contains all sorts of instructions. One of the instructions says, in effect, "if this guy clicks this link, here's which document I want you to get." You don't normally see all these funky commands because the browser *renders* the page—that is, it reads the instructions in the file and displays the text and graphics accordingly.

The Hansel and Gretel Dilemma: Where Are You?

Hypertext is a fantastic tool, but it has one huge drawback: It's easy to get lost. If you are reading a book and you flip forward a few pages, you know how to get back. You flip back, right? But with hypertext, after a few moves through the electronic library, you can become horribly lost. How do you get back to where you came from? And where did you come from, anyway?

Over the years, a number of systems have been developed to help people find their way around this rather strange freeform medium. This table explains some tools available in most Web browsers to enable you to move through the pages and sites you've seen.

Web Savvy

Link Colors

Some links change color after you click them. You won't see it right away, but if you return to the same page later, you'll find that the link is a different color. The color change indicates that the particular link points to a document that you've already seen. The used-link color does expire after a while, and the link changes back to its original color. How long it takes for this to happen is something that you can generally control with an option in your browser's Preferences or Options area.

Table 4.1 Web Page Navigation Tools

Button	Description
Back	Click the **Back** button to return to the previous Web page. In Netscape Navigator, you can also choose **Back** from the **Go** menu. In Internet Explorer 5.5, to use the menu option, you must click **View**, **Go to**, **Back**.
Forward	Click the **Forward** button or choose the **Forward** menu option (as described in Back) to return to a page you've just come back from.
Home	Click the **Home** button (or the **Start** button on some versions of Internet Explorer) to go all the way back to your home page or start page.
Bookmarks or Favorites	You can set bookmarks on pages you think you'll want to come back to (they're known as Favorites in Internet Explorer); bookmarks can be very helpful because you don't have to struggle to find your way back to the page the next time.
History	This is a list of pages you've seen previously. The **Back** and **Forward** commands take you back and forward through this list. You can also go directly to a recent history list in Netscape by selecting the **Go** menu. Your immediate history is listed at the bottom section of the menu. In Netscape 4.7, select the **Communicator** menu, **Tools**, and **History**. (In Explorer 4 and 5, click the small triangle on the **Back** button.)

Bookmarks

The bookmark system (known as Favorites in Internet Explorer) is an essential tool for finding your way around. Get to know it right away.

In most browsers, you can just click a button or select a menu option to place a bookmark. Each system works a little differently, of course. In Netscape Navigator, choose **Bookmarks**, **Add Bookmark** (Navigator 3); click the **Bookmarks** button and choose **Add Bookmark** (Navigator 4); or click the **Communicator** menu, choose **Bookmarks** from the drop-down menu, and then choose **Add Bookmark**. The bookmark is added to the bottom of the Bookmark menu (you can move it to a folder or submenu later). In Navigator 4 and later versions, you can even select which folder you want to put the bookmark in by clicking the **Bookmarks** button and then choosing **File Bookmark**.

In Internet Explorer, choose **Favorites**, **Add to Favorites**, and then click the **Create In** button and select the folder into which you want to place the bookmark.

Both systems have Bookmarks windows and an associated Bookmarks menu. (In Explorer, they're called the Favorites window and menu.) Creating a folder in the window automatically creates a submenu in the menu.

To open Netscape's Bookmarks window, choose **Bookmarks**, **Go to Bookmarks** (Navigator 3); **Bookmarks**, **Edit Bookmarks** (Navigator 4 and 4.5); or **Communicator**, **Bookmarks**, **Edit Bookmarks** (Navigator 4 and later versions). In the latest version of Explorer, you can click the **Favorites** button in the toolbar to open a Favorites panel that appears on the left side of the browser window itself.

You can even search Bookmarks or Favorites. For instance, you can search Internet Explorer's Favorites using the Windows 95 or 98 **Find** tool on the **Start** menu. In Internet Explorer 4 or 5, open the Favorites panel, and then right-click a folder in the Favorites list and choose **Find** to search the folder; see Figure 2.3.

Click the Favorites button
(rather than the Favorites menu)
to open the Favorites panel.

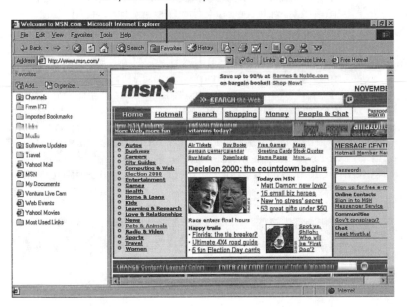

Figure 2.3

Internet Explorer's "in-browser" Favorites panel.

A Little History

The history list varies tremendously. Netscape 3's history list is not very helpful. It lists some, but not all, of the pages you've visited in the current session. Other browsers, including Netscape Navigator 4 and later, show much more, often listing pages from previous sessions. Explorer, for instance, keeps a record of up to 3,000 pages (including all the pages from the current session and earlier sessions). You can view the list in a window (see Figure 2.4) sorted by date or by name. Double-click an entry in the history list to open that Web page.

In or Out?

In Internet Explorer 2, the history window is separate from the browser window; in version 3 and later the history list is shown within the browser window. Click Internet Explorer 4 or 5's **Favorites** button, and a panel opens on the left side of the browser window to display the Favorites list. But select **Favorites, Organize Favorites** to open a separate Favorites window.

Whatever system you have, though, using the history list is simple. In Netscape Navigator, you can select an entry from the **Go** menu. To keep us on our toes, Microsoft's programmers keep moving the history list. In Internet Explorer 2, you'll find the history entries on the **File** menu; in Explorer 3 and some versions of 4, the history list is on the **Go** menu. Some later versions, and version 5, don't have a **Go** menu; instead, click the little black triangle on the right side of the Back button, and a menu drops down showing the most recent pages you've seen.

You can also open the history window to see more history entries, perhaps thousands. In versions 4 and 5 of Internet Explorer, click the **History** button in the toolbar; in version 3, choose **Go, Open History Folder**; and in version 2, choose **File, More History** (sometimes I wonder what drugs these Microsoft programmers are on). In Netscape, choose **Window, History**; or use **Communicator, History** in some later versions, depending on the operating system—and in later versions still, choose **Communicator, Tools, History**. In Netscape 4.7, you can select the number of days you want to keep history files. Select **Edit, Preferences, Navigator**. Enter the number of days you want to keep a history in the **History** section (see Figure 2.4). You also can use the **Clear History** button to clear your entire history, if you want.

Figure 2.4

With the history list found in Netscape Navigator 4 and later versions, you can go back days or even weeks in your Web travels. The list even indicates how long it has been since you visited the page and how often you've been there.

Title	Location	First Visited	Last Visited	Expiration	Visit Count
Netscape.com	http://home.netscape.com/?cp=ho...	16 hours ago	Less than one hour...	11/22/2000 11:23 ...	24
Election 2000	http://home.netscape.com/misc/snf...	Less than one hour ...	Less than one hour...	11/22/2000 11:06 ...	1
Netscape.com	http://home.netscape.com/	2 days ago	Less than one hour...	11/22/2000 11:06 ...	14
Netscape Composer	file:///C|/PROGRAM FILES/NETS...	2 hours ago	2 hours ago	11/22/2000 9:53 AM	1
Using Communicator Help	file:///C|/PROGRAM FILES/NETS...	3 days ago	2 hours ago	11/22/2000 9:52 AM	3
	file:///C|/PROGRAM FILES/NETS...	3 days ago	2 hours ago	11/22/2000 9:52 AM	20
NetHelp	file:///C|/PROGRAM FILES/NETS...	3 days ago	2 hours ago	11/22/2000 9:52 AM	3
	file:///C|/PROGRAM FILES/NETS...	3 days ago	2 hours ago	11/22/2000 9:52 AM	3
Yahoo! Mail	http://us.f105.mail.yahoo.com/ym/u...	2 hours ago	2 hours ago	11/22/2000 9:51 AM	1
Yahoo! Mail	http://us.addrss.mail.yahoo.com/y...	2 hours ago	2 hours ago	11/22/2000 9:51 AM	1
Yahoo! Mail	http://us.f105.mail.yahoo.com/ym/S...	2 hours ago	2 hours ago	11/22/2000 9:48 AM	1
Yahoo! Mail	http://us.f105.mail.yahoo.com/ym/l...	2 hours ago	2 hours ago	11/22/2000 9:47 AM	1
Welcome to Yahoo! Mail	http://mail.yahoo.com/	2 hours ago	2 hours ago	11/22/2000 9:46 AM	1
	http://my.netscape.com/mys/blank...	2 hours ago	2 hours ago	11/22/2000 9:45 AM	1
Welcome	http://my.netscape.com/welcome.t...	2 hours ago	2 hours ago	11/22/2000 9:45 AM	1
Welcome	http://my.netscape.com/welcome_f...	2 hours ago	2 hours ago	11/22/2000 9:45 AM	1
	http://my.netscape.com/welcome_a...	2 hours ago	2 hours ago	11/22/2000 9:45 AM	1
Product Registration	http://home.netscape.com/home/s...	2 hours ago	2 hours ago	11/22/2000 9:40 AM	1
Thank You	http://home.netscape.com/computi...	2 hours ago	2 hours ago	11/22/2000 9:19 AM	1
SmartDownload	http://home.netscape.com/downloa...	2 hours ago	2 hours ago	11/22/2000 9:17 AM	1
Redirect Page>	http://cgi.netscape.com/cgi-bin/ns...	2 hours ago	2 hours ago	11/22/2000 9:17 AM	1
Netscape.com - Download & U...	http://home.netscape.com/computi...	2 hours ago	2 hours ago	11/22/2000 9:17 AM	1
Internet Pictures Corp. - Visual ...	http://ipix.com/travel/ipix/boston_ai...	12 hours ago	12 hours ago	11/21/2000 11:45 ...	1
Internet Pictures Corporation	...	http://ipix.com/travel/index.shtml	12 hours ago	12 hours ago	11/21/2000 11:44 ...	1
Internet Pictures Corporation - ...	http://ipix.com/	12 hours ago	12 hours ago	11/21/2000 11:44 ...	1
Search Results - BubbleViewer	http://search.netscape.com/google...	12 hours ago	12 hours ago	11/21/2000 11:43 ...	3
Home	http://www.omnivision.com/	12 hours ago	12 hours ago	11/21/2000 11:41 ...	1
Download The IPIX Plug-In	http://www.ipix.com/cgi-bin/downlo...	12 hours ago	12 hours ago	11/21/2000 11:40 ...	3
Blank	http://www.ipix.com/blank.html	12 hours ago	12 hours ago	11/21/2000 11:39 ...	3
Internet Pictures Corporation - ...	http://www.ipix.com/sub_header.html	12 hours ago	12 hours ago	11/21/2000 11:39 ...	1
Internet Pictures Corporation - ...	http://www.ipix.com/download.html	12 hours ago	12 hours ago	11/21/2000 11:39 ...	1

A Direct Link: Using the URLs

Earlier in this chapter, I mentioned a couple of URLs. *URLs* are Web addresses, such as http://www.msn.com/ or http://www.netscape.com/. These addresses provide a direct link to a particular Web page. Instead of clicking links to try to find your way to a page, you can tell your browser the URL and say "go get this page." (Even when you do click a link, the URL is being used; point at a link and look in the browser's status bar, and you'll see the URL.)

Most browsers have a bar near the top in which you can type the URL of the page you want to go to. The bar's almost certainly already displayed; it's a long text box. If it's not there, someone must have removed it; in Netscape, use the **Options, Show Location** or **View, Show Location Toolbar** menu command to display the bar (depending on the version you're working with); in Internet Explorer, choose **View, Toolbar**, or **View, Toolbars, Address Bar**.

If you don't want the bar there all the time (after all, it takes up room that is sometimes better given to the Web pages), you can leave it turned off. If you keep it turned off, you can generally use a shortcut key to display a dialog box in which you can type a URL. In Netscape, press **Ctrl+O** to open the box (or try **Ctrl+L** if that doesn't work—earlier versions of Navigator used that shortcut; the shortcut key varies among versions); in Internet Explorer, choose **File, Open** or press **Ctrl+O**. In either case, you type the URL in the box that appears. If you prefer to use the Address or Location box at the top of the browser window, click in the box, type the address, and press **Enter**.

New History List Trick

Starting with version 4, the Internet Explorer and Netscape Navigator browsers have a handy new feature that enables you to see the history list from the **Back** and **Forward** buttons. In Navigator, click the button and hold down the mouse button; in Explorer, right-click the button, or click the little downward-pointing arrow on the button. In both cases, you'll see a list of the most recent pages that you've visited.

URL

This acronym stands for uniform resource locator, which is a fancy name for Web address.

The URL Explained

A URL consists of certain distinct parts. For example, here's a long URL:

```
http://www.poorrichard.com/newsltr/instruct/subsplain.htm
```

Each part of this URL has a specific meaning:

`http://`	This part tells the browser that the address is for a Web page. The `http://` stands for *Hypertext Transfer Protocol*, the system used on the Internet to transfer Web pages. In addition to `http://`, you might see similar prefixes for an FTP site or a Gopher menu (see Table 4.2).
`www.poorrichard.com`	This part is the hostname, the name of the computer holding the Web server that is administering the Web site you want to visit.
`/newsltr/instruct/`	This part is the directory in which the Web server has to look to find the file you want. In many cases, multiple directories will be listed, so the Web server looks down the directory tree in subdirectories. In this example, the Web server has to look in the instruct directory, which is a subdirectory of the newsltr directory.
`subsplain.htm`	This part is the name of the file you want, the Web page. These files are generally HTM or HTML files (that extension stands for Hypertext Markup Language, the coding used to create Web pages). Sometimes the URL has no filename at the end; in that case, the Web server generally sends a default document for the specified directory.

The URL is not complicated; it's just an address so your browser knows where to look for a file. The different types of URLs are identified by a different *protocol* portion of the address. The Web page URLs all begin with `http://`. This table lists some other protocols you'll see on the Internet.

Table 4.2   Other Internet Protocols

Protocol Prefix	Description
`ftp://`	The address of an FTP file library; you'll learn more about FTP in Chapter 19, "Downloading Files (FTP, Go!Zilla, and CuteFTP)."
`gopher://`	The address of a Gopher site, a little-used Internet system that predates the World Wide Web.

`news:`	The address of a newsgroup, discussed in Chapter 10, "Finding and Using Newsgroups." Note that this prefix doesn't have the // after the name; neither does `mailto:` (see the following entry).
`mailto:`	When you use this prefix, the browser's email program opens, so you can send mail. Web authors often create links using the `mailto:` URL so that when someone clicks the link, he can quickly send a message to the author.
`telnet://`	The address of a Telnet site. Telnet is a relatively little-used system for logging onto computers across the Internet.
`tn3270://`	The address of a tn3270 site. This protocol is similar to Telnet.
`wais://`	The address of a WAIS site; WAIS is a little-used database-search tool, and you probably won't run into any WAIS links. In any case, most browsers don't recognize the `wais://` protocol.

Maximizing the Web Page

Browsers have so many controls and tools that sometimes there's not enough room for the Web page. Internet Explorer 4 has a new feature. Click the **Fullscreen** button to remove almost all the controls (except a small toolbar at the top of the window), giving the Web page the maximum room. (If you're using Explorer 5, press **F11** to activate this feature—the Fullscreen button seems to have gone.) You can even remove the small toolbar using an Autohide feature similar to that used by the Windows 98 taskbar (right-click the toolbar and select **Autohide**). Actually, this feature isn't new; it's from the ancient history of the graphical Web browser (way back in 1994). It used to be called a Kiosk feature, but it disappeared for a while.

What Will You Find on Your Web Journey?

When you travel around the Web, you'll find a lot of text documents and much, much more. As a system administrator at a Free-Net once said to me, "The Web is for people who can't read!" It was a slight exaggeration, perhaps, but his point was that, on the Web, the nontext stuff is often more important than the words.

Forget *http://*

In most browsers these days (including Netscape and Internet Explorer), you don't need to type the full URL. You can omit the **http://** piece, and the browser will assume that the **http://** piece should be added. If you type something beginning with **gopher** (as in **gopher. usa.net**, for instance) or **ftp** (as in **ftp.microsoft.com**), you can omit the **gopher://** or **ftp://** part, too. Also, you can often drop the **www** (though this depends on how the Web server running the Web site has been configured). The newest browsers have an auto–fill-in feature, something you might have seen in personal-finance programs. Start typing a URL, and if the browser recognizes that you've entered it before, it will allow you to select the URL from a list of possible matches. When you select one from the list, the browser fills it in for you.

While traveling around the Web, you'll find these sorts of things:

➤ **Pictures** You'll find pictures both inside the text documents and on their own. Sometimes when you click a link (at a museum site, for example), a picture—not a document—is transferred to your browser.

➤ **Forms** These days, most browsers are forms compatible (Navigator and Explorer have always been compatible). In other words, you can use forms to interact with the Web site to send information about yourself (to sub-scribe to a service, for instance), to search for information, to buy products, or to play a game, for example.

➤ **Sounds** Most browsers can play sounds, such as voices and music. Many Web sites contain sounds. For instance, IUMA (the Internet Underground Music Archive at http://www.iuma.com/) has song clips from many new bands.

➤ **Files** Many Web sites have files you can download, such as shareware, demos of new programs, and documents of many kinds. When you click a link, your browser begins the file transfer (see Chapter 3).

➤ **Multimedia of other kinds** All sorts of strange things are on the Web: 3D images, animations, Adobe Acrobat PDF hypertext files, videos, slideshows, 2D and 3D chemical images, and plenty more. Click a link, and the file starts trans-ferring. If you have the right software installed, it automatically displays or plays the file. For instance, in Figure 2.5, you can see a BubbleViewer image. (See http://www.ipix.com/ for information about the BubbleViewer—see Figure 2.5—and Chapter 4, "Understanding Web Programs and File Types," and Chapter 5, "Web Multimedia—From Flash to Napster," to learn more about multimedia.)

Figure 2.5

A BubbleViewer image in Netscape. You can move around inside the car, viewing up, down, and all around.

Speeding Up Your Journey by Limiting Graphics

The Web started out as a very fast-moving place. The first Web browsers could display nothing but text, and text transfers across the Internet very quickly. Then things slowed down. The things I just mentioned—pictures, video, sounds, and so on—slowed down the process. Video was the slowest thing on the Web, moving at an almost glacial pace. Even pictures were a nuisance; very few sites had video, but most used static pictures. Many people today have fast Internet connections, but most do not. Connecting to the Internet at 19.2bps is not unusual, and at that speed graphic-heavy Web sites can be very slow. To load Web sites more quickly, just turn off the pictures.

Where Do I Find What I Want on the Web?

You can follow any interesting links you find, as discussed earlier in this chapter. You can also search for particular subjects and Web pages by using a Web search site, as discussed in Chapter 15, "Finding What You Need Online."

Most browsers provide a way for you to turn off the display of pictures. In Netscape Navigator, for instance, choose **Options**, **Auto Load Images**, and remove the check mark from the menu option to turn off images. In Netscape Navigator 4 and later, choose **Edit**, **Preferences**, and then click the **Advanced** category and clear **Automatically Load Images**. In Internet Explorer, you can turn off images in the Options dialog box, and you can turn off sounds and video, too. Choose **Tools**, **Internet Options** and click the **Advanced** tab, and then clear the **Show Pictures** check box in the list box below **Multimedia**. (In early versions of Explorer, you'll have to select **View**, **Options**, and might find the Show Pictures option under **General**). Because the images are no longer transmitted to your browser, you see the pages much more quickly.

Of course, you often need or want to see those images. Many images have links built into them, and although some Web pages have both graphic links and corresponding text links (for people using a browser that can't display pictures), other Web pages are unusable unless you can see the pictures. However, you can usually grab the picture you need quickly. Where there should be a picture, you'll see a little icon that functions as a sort of placeholder.

In Netscape, you can right-click the placeholder and choose **Load Image** (**Show Image** in some versions) from the shortcut menu that appears. Or you can click the **Images** button in the toolbar to see all of them. To view an image when you have images turned off in Internet Explorer, right-click the placeholder and choose **Show Picture** from the shortcut menu.

There's Plenty More!

There's a lot more to say about the Web than I've said in this chapter. In fact, one could write a book about it (I already have: *Using Netscape Communicator 4*). In the next few chapters, you'll learn a few advanced Web travel tips and all about Web multimedia.

The Least You Need to Know

➤ The World Wide Web is a giant hypertext system running on the Internet.

➤ The two best browsers available are Netscape Navigator and Microsoft Internet Explorer.

➤ The home page (sometimes called the start page in Internet Explorer) is the page that appears when you open your browser.

➤ Click a link in a document to see another document. To find your way back, use the **Back** or **Home** button.

➤ The history list shows where you've been. In Netscape Navigator 3, it includes just some of the pages you've seen in the current session; in some other browsers, including Netscape Navigator 4 and Internet Explorer, the history list includes all the pages from the current session and many pages from previous sessions.

➤ A URL is a Web address. You can use the URL to go directly to a particular Web page.

Chapter 3

More Web Basics—Searching, Saving, and More

In This Chapter

➤ Running multiple Web sessions

➤ Opening files from your hard disk

➤ All about the cache and reloading

➤ Searching documents and using the pop-up menu

➤ Copying things you find to the Clipboard

➤ Saving images, documents, and files

You've seen the basic moves; now you are ready to learn more techniques to help you find your way around the Web. In the last chapter, you learned how to move around on the Web using a Web browser such as Netscape Navigator or Internet Explorer. In this chapter, you'll find out how to run multiple Web sessions at the same time, how to deal with the cache, how to save what you find, and so on. You need to know these advanced moves to work efficiently on the Web.

Multiple Windows: Ambidextrous Browsing

These days, most browsers enable you to run more than one Web session at the same time. Why would you want to do that? There could be many reasons. While you wait for an image to load in one window, you can read something in another window. Or maybe you need to find information at another Web site but don't want to lose your place at the current one. (Yes, you have bookmarks and the history list, but sometimes it's just easier to open another window.) You can open one or more new browser windows, as shown in Figure 3.1, so that you can run multiple Web sessions. In this example, you can see two Internet Explorer windows. To make the one at the back take up the entire screen, press F11 to use the **Fullscreen** feature (earlier versions had a **Fullscreen** button), and then right-click the bar and select the **Autohide** feature (see Chapter 2, "Working on the World Wide Web").

Figure 3.1

Opening multiple windows is a good way to keep from getting lost or to do more than one thing at a time. In this illustration, one Internet Explorer sits over another that has been maximized using the Fullscreen command (press F11).

Exactly how you open a new window varies among browsers; however, most are similar. In Netscape Navigator, try these procedures:

➤ Right-click the link that you want to follow in a new window, and then choose **Open in New Window**. A new Netscape window opens, and the referenced document opens in that window.

➤ Choose **File**, **New Web Browser**, or **File**, **New**, **Navigator Window**, or press **Ctrl+N** to open a new window displaying the home page.

Internet Explorer gives you several options:

➤ Right-click the link you want to follow, and then choose **Open in New Window**. A new window opens, displaying the referenced document.

➤ Press **Tab** until the link becomes highlighted, and then press **Shift+Enter**.

➤ Choose **File**, **New Window** (or, in some versions, **File**, **New**, **Window**) or press **Ctrl+N** to open a new window that displays the same document as the one you've just viewed.

You might encounter some problems when running multiple Web sessions. Web browsers are turning into real memory hogs, so you may find that you don't have enough memory to run multiple sessions or to run more than one additional session. In addition, your modem can do only so much work. If you have several Web windows open and each is transferring things at the same time, every transfer will be slower than if it were the only thing the modem had to do.

Automatic Multiple Sessions

Now and then, windows will open automatically. If you suddenly notice that the browser's Back button is disabled, it might be that when you clicked a link, a secondary window opened and you didn't notice. Web authors can create codes in their Web pages that force browsers to open secondary or targeted windows.

Your Hard Disk As Web Server?

If you enjoy working on the Web and spend most of your waking hours there, eventually, you'll end up with HTM or HTML files on your hard disk. You'll have them in your cache (discussed next), or you may save documents using the **File**, **Save As** command. Your browser provides a way to open these HTML files—generally a **File**, **Open** command or something similar. You'll see a typical Open box from which you can select the file you want to open.

Here's a geek trick for you. If you know the exact path to the file you want to open, and if you can type quickly, click in the **Address** or **Location** text box. Then, type the entire path and filename, such as C:/Program Files/Netscape/Navigator/ownweb. htm. This trick should work in both Netscape and Internet Explorer. In some browsers, however, you might need to use the more formal (and older) method by entering the file path in this format: file:///C|/Program Files/Netscape/Navigator/ownweb. htm. Notice that in the second format, you precede the path with file:/// and replace the colon after the disk letter (in this case, C) with a pipe symbol (|).

Forward Slash or Backslash

UNIX computers use a forward slash (*/*) between directory names. DOS computers use a backslash(\\). Because the Web was developed on UNIX computers, URLs use forward slashes. Thus C:/Program Files/Netscape/Navigator/ownweb.htm is correct, even though in normal DOS notation this would appear as C:\\Program Files\\Netscape\\ Navigator\\ownweb.htm. However, you can type it whichever way you please when you're opening a file on your hard disk or a page on the Web; both Internet Explorer and Netscape will figure it out.

Turbocharging with the Cache

Have you noticed that when you return to a Web document that you've viewed recently, it appears much more quickly than when you first accessed it? That's because your browser isn't taking it from the Internet; instead, the browser is getting it from the *cache*, an area on your hard disk or in your computer's RAM (memory) in which it saves pages. The cache is handy because it greatly speeds up the process of working on the Web. After all, why bother to reload a file from the Internet when it's already sitting on your hard drive? (Okay, you may think of some reasons to do so, but I'll come back to those when I talk about the Reload command.)

When the browser loads a Web page, it places it in the cache. You can generally control the size of the cache. Not all browsers let you do so, but Netscape, Internet Explorer, and many others do. When the cache fills up, the oldest files are removed to make room for newer ones. Each time the browser tries to load a page, it might look in the cache first to see whether it has the page stored. (Whether it does depends on how you set up the cache.) If it finds that the page is available, it can retrieve the page from the cache very quickly.

Putting the Cache to Work

To take full advantage of the cache's benefits, you need to do some configuring. To configure the cache in Netscape Navigator 2 or 3, choose **Options**, **Network Preferences**, and then click the **Cache** tab. In Navigator 4 and later, select **Edit**, **Preferences**, and then open the **Advanced** category and click the **Cache** subcategory. Figure 3.2 shows Netscape's cache information.

HTM or HTML?

Depending to some degree on the operating system you use, the file extension of the HTML Web files might be .htm or .html. Originally, the Web was developed using UNIX computers, and Web files had the extension .html. Later, when Windows 3.1 machines started appearing on the Web, the .htm extension came into use because Windows 3.1 could work only with three-character file extensions, and many people were creating Web pages in Windows. Today, you'll see both extensions. Even though Windows 95 and 98 can accept four-letter extensions, not all Windows HTML-editing programs can, so people are still creating files with three-letter extensions; and many Windows users have simply become accustomed to three-character file extensions.

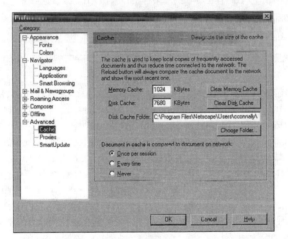

Figure 3.2

You have several options when setting up Netscape's cache.

Configure any of the available settings to meet your needs:

➤ **Memory Cache**   You can tell Netscape how much of your computer's memory you want to assign to the cache. Netscape stores a few documents in the memory so that it can retrieve them extremely quickly. The button to the right of this option enables you to remove all the pages from the memory cache.

➤ **Disk Cache**   You can also tell Netscape how large the disk cache should be—that is, how much of your disk space you want to give to Netscape. How much should you give? That all depends on how much disk space you have free. (I always say that you can never have too much hard disk space, money, or beer;

I've been proven wrong once or twice, though.) The button to the right of this option enables you to clear out the disk cache, which is handy when you finally run out of disk space.

➤ **Disk Cache Folder**   You can tell Netscape where to place the disk cache. If you have several hard disks, put the cache on the fastest disk or the one with the most room.

The Hard Disk Cache

Note that you are not reserving an area of your hard disk for the cache. For instance, if you have a 30,000KB (almost 30MB) disk cache, your browser doesn't create a 30,000KB file that prevents other programs from using that disk space. You're just telling the browser that it can use up to that much disk space for the cache if it's available—if other programs don't use up the space first. When you fill up the available cache space, the browser starts clearing out older files to make way for newer ones.

➤ **Document in Cache Is Compared to Document on Network**   Now for the complicated one. This setting tells Netscape when to verify documents. When you request a document (by clicking a link or entering a URL), Netscape can send a message to the Web server asking (basically), "Has this document changed since the last time I grabbed it?" If it has changed, Netscape downloads a new copy. If it hasn't changed, Netscape grabs the page from the cache. You can configure Netscape to ask the Web server to verify documents Once per Session (in which case, Netscape checks the first time you try to retrieve a document, but it doesn't bother after that); Every Time (so that Netscape checks every time you try to get a document, regardless of how many times you view that document in a session); or Never (in which case, Netscape doesn't even bother to check to see whether the document has been updated, unless you use the Reload command).

➤ **Allow Persistent Caching of Pages Retrieved Through SSL**   This feature is in earlier versions of Netscape (it's not in the latest versions), and it's related to Internet security. *SSL* stands for *secure sockets layer* (which probably means no more to you than SSL, so I'm not sure why I told you that). An SSL Web browser can use secure transmission of information; the information is encrypted before being transmitted. (See Chapter 18, "Staying Safe on the Internet," for a discussion of encryption.) This feature tells the browser to cache pages that were sent in a secure manner.

Figure 3.3
Internet Explorer enables you to modify the cache and view its contents directly.

Internet Explorer 5 uses a similar system. Choose **Tools**, **Internet Options**, and click the **General** tab. (As you may have noticed by now, Microsoft has to keep moving things around; in some versions of Explorer you'll need to select **View**, **Options**—or perhaps **Internet Options**—then click the General Tab, or maybe the Advanced tab.) Then, click the **Settings** button under the **Temporary Internet files** area. Although Explorer's programmers (ever the innovators) have taken to referring to the cache as Temporary Internet files, it's the same thing. Figure 3.3 shows Explorer 5.5's settings.

Near the top of the box, you can tell the browser when to check to see whether there's a newer version of the file. You can tell it to check Once per Session in Explorer 3; this option is ambiguously labeled Every Time You Start Internet Explorer in Explorer 4 and 5, but it's the same thing. Or, you can turn it off altogether (select Never). In Explorer 4 and 5, you also have the option to check Every Visit to the Page. And Explorer 5 has yet another option, Automatically. This starts off working the same as Every Time You Start Internet Explorer, but, in theory, the browser learns how often a particular page changes, and if it doesn't change often, eventually the browser stops checking quite so frequently.

You also can modify the size of the cache by dragging a slider to set the percentage of the drive you want to use (instead of by entering an MB value). You can select the cache directory using the **Move Folder** button, but notice that Explorer offers something extra: a **View Files** button. Click the **View Files** button to display a list of the files stored in the cache; you can double-click a file to open it in the browser. Explorer 5, and some versions of Explorer 4, also has a **View Objects** button, which opens a window containing ActiveX controls downloaded to your computer (see Chapter 4, "Understanding Web Programs and File Types"). You can also empty the cache; in more recent versions, there's a **Delete Files** button back in the Internet Options dialog box, whereas earlier versions had an **Empty Folder** button in the Cache Settings dialog box.

Decisions, Decisions

Which of the cache options should you use? I prefer Never because it makes my Web sessions *much* quicker. Whenever I tell a browser to go to a Web page that's already in the cache, it loads the page from the hard disk right away, without sending a verification message to the server first. Even if the browser doesn't have to retrieve the page again because the page hasn't changed, checking with the Web server can slow you down noticeably.

On the other hand, I have to remember to keep using the Reload command to be sure I'm viewing the latest version of the Web page. Some people might prefer to use the Once Per Session option to ensure that they are looking at a recent page.

What Is Reload?

Sometimes you want to get a file from the Web again. Reload is a "cure" for the cache. If you get a page from the cache, you are not getting the latest document. Sometimes getting the most recent document doesn't matter, but in a few cases, it does.

For instance, say you want to return to a site you visited several weeks ago. If you have a very large cache, that document might still be available. If you have the Never option button selected in the Preferences dialog box, your browser displays the old document, without checking to see whether the corresponding document stored on the Web has changed. Or perhaps you are viewing a Web document that changes rapidly, such as a stock quote page. Even if you viewed the page only a few minutes ago, it could already be out of date.

The cure for replacing those old, stale Web pages is to reload them. Click the **Reload** button or choose **View, Reload**. Internet Explorer's programmers, in their attempt to rename everything they can, use the term **Refresh** instead of Reload. (The fact that Reload is a term the Web has been using for several years and that Refresh has a different meaning—Netscape has a Refresh command that simply "repaints" the display using the contents of the memory cache—doesn't seem to matter to Microsoft's programmers.) Anyway, the Reload command (Refresh in Explorer) tells the browser, "Throw away the copy held in the cache and get the latest version."

You'll sometimes see a Reload Frame command, which reloads just one frame in a framed document. (Chapter 4 covers frames.) Netscape Navigator has a "super reload" command that few people know about. Holding down the Shift key and then selecting the Reload command says to Netscape Navigator, "Be absolutely sure you really do reload the page!" Navigator's Reload command has had a bug living in it for several years and in some cases it doesn't reload the page properly. (This problem seems to be related to forms and scripts not being reloaded correctly.) Holding down the Shift key ensures that the page really is reloaded.

Long Documents: Finding What You Need

Some Web pages are large. Some are positively huge—thousands of lines long with links at the top of the document that take the user to sections lower on the same page. Many Web authors prefer to create one large page than to create lots of small linked ones, the advantage being that after the page has been transferred to your browser you can use links to move to different parts of the page very quickly.

Virtually all browsers have some kind of Find command; it's generally **Edit**, **Find**, or a Find button on the toolbar. Internet Explorer's programmers (as you might guess) have a command called **Edit**, **Find (on this page)**, which I must admit is a good idea. This command tells the browser to search the current page instead of the Web; I'm sure some new users get confused about that issue. (On the other hand, Explorer's Search toolbar button is not the same as the Find command; it's for searching the Web. You'll learn how to search the Web in Chapter 15, "Finding What You Need Online.")

The Find command works in a way that's very similar to what you've probably used in other programs (in particular, in word processors). Click the **Find** button, or choose **Edit**, **Find**, and the Find dialog box opens. Type the word or words you are looking for, choose **Match Case** (if necessary), and then click **Find Next**. The browser moves the document so that the first line containing the word or words you are searching for is at the top of the window.

Remember to Right-Click

Remember to use the shortcut menus that appear when you right-click on items. Both Netscape and Internet Explorer use them, as do other browsers. The shortcut menu is a new toy in the programmer's toy box—and a very nice one at that. (The Macintosh mouse has only one button; on Macintosh browsers, you might be able to access a pop-up menu by pressing the button and holding it down.) Experiment by right-clicking links, pictures, and the background, and you'll find all sorts of useful commands, such as those listed here:

➤ **Copy Shortcut or Copy Link Location** This command copies the URL from the link to the Clipboard.

➤ **Open** This command opens the related document, just as if you had clicked the link.

➤ **Open in New Window** This command opens a new window and loads the document referenced by the link you clicked.

➤ **Save Target As or Save Link As** This command transfers the referenced document and saves it on your hard disk without bothering to display it in the browser first.

➤ **Add Bookmark or Add to Favorites** This command places an entry for the document referenced by the link in the Bookmark or Favorites system.

Look to see which other commands are available. You'll find commands for moving back through framed documents, saving image files, saving background images as your desktop wallpaper, adding wallpaper, sending the Web page in an email message, and so on. (Which reminds me, maybe you should learn how to save such things from the Web, eh?)

Is It Worth Saving?

A lot of it is. Yes, I know that multimedia consultant and author William Horton has called the Web a GITSO (Garbage In, Toxic Sludge Out) system. Although there *is* a lot of sludge out there, it's not *all* sludge. Much of it is worth saving. And now and then that's just what you'll want to do: Save some of it to your hard disk. Let's look at two aspects of saving in particular: how to save and what you can save.

You can save many things from the Web. Most browsers work in much the same way, although one or two have a few nice little extra "save" features. Here's what you can save:

➤ **Save the document text**   You can copy text from a browser to the Clipboard and then paste the text into another application. Or you can use the **File, Save As** command, which enables you to choose to save the document as plain text (that is, without all the little codes used to create a Web document; you'll look at those in Chapter 13, "Setting Up Your Own Web Site").

It's Not Yours

Remember that much of what you come across on the Web is copyrighted material. Unless you are sure that what you are viewing is not copyrighted, you should assume that it is. That means you have no right to take and republish the material (such as placing it on your Web site), and could even be prosecuted for doing it.

➤ **Save the HTML source document**   The source document is the HTML (Hypertext Markup Language) document used to create the document that you see in your browser. The source document has lots of funky little codes, which you'll understand completely after you read Chapter 13 (perhaps not completely, but at least you'll understand the basics). After you begin creating your own Web pages (you are planning to do that, aren't you? Everyone else and his dog is), you might want to save source documents so you can "borrow" bits of them. Use **File, Save As** and choose to save as HTML. The problem with saving a Web page in this manner, though, is that the images are not saved. To save them, you'll need to use the following method.

➤ **Save the entire document, pictures and all**   Recent versions of Internet Explorer provide two more save options when you use the **File, Save As** command: **Web Page, complete,** and **Web Archive, single file.** The first, **Web Page,**

complete, saves the images in a directory, and then saves the Web page itself and changes all the image references to point to the saved images. The second method, **Web Archive, single file**, saves the page and images in a special archive file with the file extension MHT.

➤ **Save the text or HTML source for documents you haven't even viewed**   You don't have to view a page before you save it (although to be honest, I haven't yet figured out why you would want to save it if you haven't seen it). Right-click the link and choose **Save Target As** or **Save Link As** from the shortcut menu.

➤ **Save inline images in graphics files**   You can copy images you see in Web pages directly to your hard drive. Right-click an image and choose **Save Image As** or **Save Picture As**.

➤ **Save the document background**   Internet Explorer even lets you save the small image that is used to put the background color or pattern in many documents. Right-click the background and choose **Save Background As**.

➤ **Create Windows wallpaper**   Internet Explorer also lets you quickly take an image or background from a document and use it as your Windows wallpaper image. Right-click the picture or the background and choose **Set As Wallpaper**.

➤ **Copy images to the Clipboard**   With this neat Explorer feature, you can copy images and background images directly to the Clipboard. Right-click the image, and then choose **Copy** or **Copy Background** from the shortcut menu.

➤ **Print the document**   Most browsers have a File, Print command and maybe even a Print button. Likewise, you'll often find a Page Setup command that lets you set margins and create headers and footers.

➤ **Save URLs to the Clipboard**   You can save URLs to the Clipboard so that you can copy them into another program. Copy the URL directly from the Address or Location text box, or right-click a link and choose **Copy Shortcut** or **Copy Link Location**. Some versions of Netscape also allow you to drag a link onto a document in another program; the link's URL will then appear in the document.

➤ **Grab files directly from the cache**   Remember that the cache is dynamic; the browser is constantly adding files to and removing files from it. If you have something you want to save, you can copy it directly from the cache. Internet Explorer makes this process easy; simply click the **View Files** button in the Options dialog box. With Netscape, you can view the directory holding the files. However, Netscape renames files, making them hard to identify. (Explorer names each file with its URL.) You can also find special programs that will help you view and manage files in your cache; see Appendix C, "All the Software You'll Ever Need," for information about tracking down software.

➤ **Save computer files referenced by links**   Many links do not point to other Web documents; they point to files of other formats, which opens a whole new can of worms that we'll explore right now.

Grabbing Files from the Web

I like to group nondocument files into the following two types:

➤ **Files that you want to transfer to your hard disk**   A link might point to an EXE or ZIP file (a program file or a ZIP archive file) that contains a program you want to install on your computer. Chapter 4, "Understanding Web Programs and File Types," deals with file formats. (See Appendix C for information about sources of shareware programs, which would fall into this category.)

Files Can Be in Both Categories

Files can be in both the first and second categories. What counts is not so much the type of file, but what you want to do with the file and how your browser is configured. If you want to save the file on your hard disk, perhaps for later use, it would fall into the first category: save on your hard disk. If you want to view the file right now, it would fall into the second category: view in a viewer or plug-in.

Which category a file fits into also depends on the manner in which the file was saved. In its normal format, for instance, an Adobe Acrobat file (a PDF file) could fall into either category. In some compressed formats, it would fall into the first category only because you'd have to save it to your hard disk and decompress it before you could view it. (Compressed formats are explained in Chapter 4.)

➤ **Files that you want to play or view**   Other files are not things you want to keep; instead, they are files containing items such as sounds (music and speech), video, graphics, or word processing documents that are part of the Web site you are viewing.

Both types of files are the same in one way: Whatever you want to do with them—whether you want to save them or play them—you *must* transfer them to your computer. However, the purpose of the transfer is different, and the way it's carried out is different. When you want to play or display a file, you might have to configure a special viewer, helper application, or plug-in so that when the browser transfers the file it knows how to play or display it. Chapter 5, "Web Multimedia—From Flash to Napster," covers such things in detail. For now, we're interested only in the first type of file—a file that you want to transfer and save on your hard disk.

Web authors can distribute computer files directly from their Web documents. Several years ago, pretty much the only file libraries were FTP sites (covered in Chapter 19). Now many Web sites have links to files. Companies that want to distribute their programs (shareware, freeware, or demo programs) and authors who want to distribute non-Web documents (PostScript, Word for Windows, Adobe Acrobat, and Windows Help documents, for example) can use Web sites to provide a convenient way to transfer files.

Save It

To see how you can save a file, go to TUCOWS (The Ultimate Collection of Winsock Software) at http://www.tucows.com/. (Its logo is two cows.) This site contains a fantastic library of Internet software for Windows and Macintosh computers.

Suppose you find a link to a program that you want to transfer. You click it as usual, and what happens? If you're using Netscape, and if the file is an EXE or COM file, you'll probably see a File Save box. If so, choose the directory into which you want to save the file (download directories are discussed in Chapter 4). Or, you might see the Unknown File Type dialog box (shown in Figure 3.4). This box appears whenever Netscape tries to transfer a file that it doesn't recognize; Netscape wants you to tell it what to do. You can click the **Save File** button to get to the Save As dialog box, and then you can proceed to tell your computer where you want to save the file.

Winsock?

What's this Winsock thing? Winsock is a contraction of *Windows Sockets*, the name of the TCP/IP driver used to connect Windows programs to the Internet's TCP/IP system. Just as you need a print driver to connect a Windows program to a printer, you also need a special driver to connect a program to the Internet. The term Winsock refers to programs that can connect to a TCP/IP network.

Explorer uses a slightly different method. First, it displays a dialog box showing that a file is being transferred. After a moment or two, you'll see another dialog box (similar to the one in Figure 3.5).

Figure 3.4

Netscape doesn't know what to do with this file type, so you have to tell it.

Figure 3.5

Internet Explorer uses a slightly different method for managing file transfers.

You now have two choices:

➤ You can tell Explorer to open it, in which case Explorer transfers the file to your desktop and runs the file. This is a pretty lousy idea, for a couple of reasons. First, if the file is a compressed archive file, you'll be expanding all files held by the archive onto the desktop, making a huge mess and mixing them in with all the other files already there. Second, the file may be a program file that will run automatically. If it contains a virus, you could be in trouble. You should check program files with virus-check software before running them. (You'll learn more about that subject in Chapter 18.)

➤ You can save it to disk. This is the preferable option. Choose this option and click **OK**, and the transfer will continue. After the file has been transferred to your hard disk, you'll see a Save As dialog box in which you can choose where to place the file.

Notice the check box titled Always Ask Before Opening This Type of File. If you clear the check box, the next time you download a file, Explorer will automatically transfer it and open it, even if you chose the **Save It to Disk** option button the first time. (To recheck this check box, go to Windows Explorer, and then choose **View**, **Options**—or **View**, **Folder Options**—and click the **File Types** tab. Then, click the file type in the list box, click **Edit**, click **Confirm Open After Download**, and click **OK**.)

The Least You Need to Know

➤ If your computer has enough memory, you can open a second Web document in a new window and keep the current window open.

➤ You'll probably end up saving Web documents on your hard disk; you can reopen them using the **File**, **Open** command.

➤ The cache stores documents you've seen on your hard disk. The browser can get those documents from the cache the next time you want to see them, which speeds up work tremendously.

➤ The Reload command (or Refresh in Internet Explorer) throws away the version of the page held in the cache and grabs a new one from the Web site. You can configure the cache to do this automatically once every session.

➤ You can copy, print, and save all sorts of things from the Web: document text, the document source file, images, background images, and more.

➤ If you click a link to a nondocument file, your browser might ask you what to do with it. You can save it to your hard drive if you want.

Chapter 4

Understanding Web Programs and File Types

In This Chapter

➤ Unexpected things you'll run into on the Web

➤ Using tables and forms

➤ Getting into password-protected sites

➤ Using frames and secondary windows

➤ Web programming: Java, JavaScript, and ActiveX

➤ Pushing, pulling, and multimedia

➤ About the directory (folder) system

➤ File extensions and file types

➤ File types you'll run into

Not so long ago, the Web was filled with static documents that contained pictures and text—originally Web documents didn't even have pictures. But the Web has changed and is still changing; no longer is it just a static medium that you read. In this chapter, you're going to take a quick look at some weird and wonderful things you might find on the Web, such as tables, forms, password-protected sites, secondary or targeted windows, and frames. You'll learn about Java, JavaScript, and ActiveX applets, as well as push and pull commands and multimedia. We will also take a look at directories and file types.

Working with Tables

A *table* is...well, you know, a table. It's a grid made up of a set of columns and rows in which you organize text and (sometimes) pictures. Virtually all popular browsers these days can display tables. So, if you are using a recent one (such as Netscape or Internet Explorer), you'll have no problems. Tables are often used to display tabular data (go figure), but they can also be used as a simple page layout tool to get pictures and text to sit in the correct places, as you can see in Figure 4.1) Recent improvements to the way that browsers handle tables enable Web page authors to use different background colors and different border colors in each cell.

Figure 4.1

The Discovery Channel (http://www.discovery. com/) page formatted using the table feature.

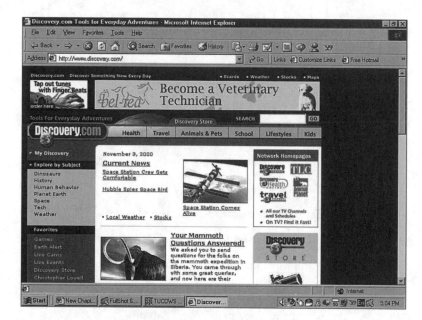

Interactive Web Pages: Using Forms

A *form* is a special *interactive* Web document. It contains the sorts of components that you've become familiar with while working in today's graphical user interfaces: text boxes, option buttons (also known as radio buttons), command buttons, check boxes, list boxes, drop-down list boxes, and so on. You'll find forms at the search sites (see Chapter 3, "More Web Basics—Searching, Saving and More"). You use them just as you would a Windows or Macintosh dialog box: You type a search word into a text box, select any necessary options by clicking option buttons and check boxes, and then click a command button.

Forms are also used to collect information (you might have to enter your name and address when downloading demo software, for instance) and make sales. You can choose the products you want to buy and enter your credit card information into a form. Figure 4.2 shows an order form at a Web site.

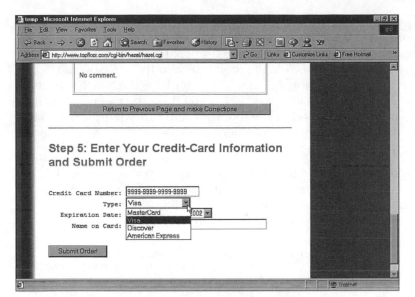

Figure 4.2

Enter all the required information, select options from the drop-down list boxes, and then click the Submit Order button.

Playing It Safe: Secure Sites

When you enter information into a form and send that information back to the Web server, there is a slight chance that it could be intercepted by someone and read. (It's not very *likely* that your information will be intercepted, but that's another story—which I'll get to in Chapter 18, "Staying Safe on the Internet.") Netscape, Internet Explorer, and some other browsers provide a way to send information *securely*. If the form you are viewing comes from a special `https://` server (a secure server), the information is *encrypted* before it's sent back from the form to the server. When the server receives the information, it decrypts the information. While the encrypted data is between your computer and the server, the information is useless; anyone who intercepted the information would end up with a load of garbled rubbish.

In most browsers, you know when you are at a secure site. In Internet Explorer, the little padlock icon in the lower-right corner is locked (in some versions of Explorer, no lock appears until you're displaying a secure page; in others, the lock's

Just a Little Different

Forms in Web pages do function just a little differently from forms in other programs. For a start, you must click directly on an option button or check box to select it, not just on the label; in some operating systems—Windows, for instance—clicking the label will select the option or box. Although you can press **Tab** to move to the next field in a form in most browsers (or **Shift+Tab** to move to the last), this keystroke doesn't work in all browsers.

always there, but it's open when you're at a page that is not secure). Some versions of Netscape Navigator have a key in the lower-left corner of the window; the key is whole at a secure page (it's broken on pages that are not secure). These versions of Navigator also display a blue bar just below the toolbars when the site is secure. Some recent versions of Navigator (Versions 4, 4.5, and 4.6) don't have the blue bar or the key. Instead, they use a padlock icon, which is closed. You'll see the padlock icon in the lower-left corner of the browser and in the toolbar; the Security button is a padlock that changes according to the type of document displayed. Other browsers use similar but slightly different methods to indicate that you are at a secure page.

One indicator of a secure site is visible in any Web browser. As you can see in the Figure 4.3, the URL of a secure Web page begins with `https://` instead of `http://`. If you send information to this site or receive information from it, you can be sure that the information will be transmitted in a secure, encrypted manner.

Figure 4.3

Browsers use various indicators to show that a site is secure.

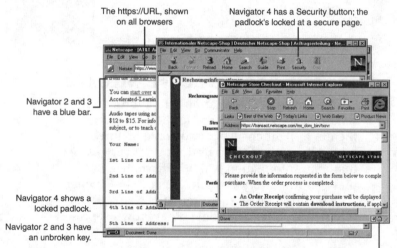

The https://URL, shown on all browsers

Navigator 4 has a Security button; the padlock's locked at a secure page.

Navigator 2 and 3 have a blue bar.

Navigator 4 shows a locked padlock.

Navigator 2 and 3 have an unbroken key.

Internet Explorer shows a padlock here.

For Your Eyes Only: Password-Protected Sites

Many Web sites are password-protected or have an area that is password-protected. You can't enter a password-protected Web site or area unless you enter a password, which is given to you when you go through a registration process (which often, although not always, includes payment of some kind).

Why do sites use passwords? They may be selling information or some other kind of data (the single most common form of sold data, and in general the most profitable, is pornography). They may have private areas for employees of a particular company or members of a club or association. But sometimes free sites that are open to the public require that you log in. This requirement is often because these sites create an account for you and save information about you. To access that account, you have to log in (see the Figure 4.4). For instance, Expedia (`http://expedia.com/`), Microsoft's travel Web site, creates accounts for people that save information about them: their email address, ZIP code, the airport they generally fly from, and a subscription to an email notification of travel promotions.

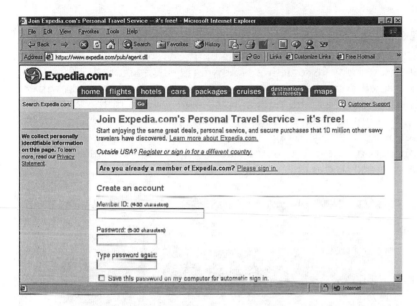

Figure 4.4

Microsoft Expedia is free, but you have to set up an account—with an account name and password—if you want to use it.

Dealing with Secondary Windows

I should know better, but once or twice I've been confused when I've suddenly discovered that Netscape Navigator's history list has disappeared. What happened? I clicked a link and then looked away for a moment. While my eyes were averted, another browser window opened automatically. I continued, unaware of what had happened.

Web authors can set up a link so that when you click it, a new window opens, and the referenced document appears in that window. It's a very handy feature when used properly. These windows are called *targeted* windows. (I prefer to use an older hypertext term: *secondary* windows; sometimes they're called pop-ups.)

When a targeted window opens in Netscape Navigator, the history list disappears from the previous window because the history list is linked to a particular window. In newer versions of

Web Savvy

Public Letter to Web Authors

Dear Web authors: It's bad interface design to open a secondary window full-screen. Please open your windows slightly less than full screen, so it's obvious to your users what's going on! Signed, Confused in Denver. (Unfortunately, browsers aren't very helpful. In many cases, the Web author can't determine the screen size.)

Navigator, you *can* still use the history list from the Go menu, although the Back button won't work. That's how it works in all versions of Internet Explorer—although the Back and Forward commands stop working in that browser, you can still access the full history list and get back to a previous page.

Panes or Frames

Another new feature you might find while browsing on the Web is *frames*. (In other earlier hypertext systems, these were sometimes known as *panes*.) Figure 4.5 shows an example of frames. A framed document displays two or more documents, each within its own pane. The frames around each document might be movable (if the author set them up that way), and you might have scrollbars in each pane. Why put documents in frames? Frames can be a good way to organize a lot of information. For example, you might find a table of contents in one frame; clicking a link in the table of contents would load the specified document into the other frame.

Figure 4.5

The Continental Airlines page shows two framed documents. You can enter desired flight information in the left frame or read news and information in the right. Each frame has a scrollbar so that it moves independently of the other.

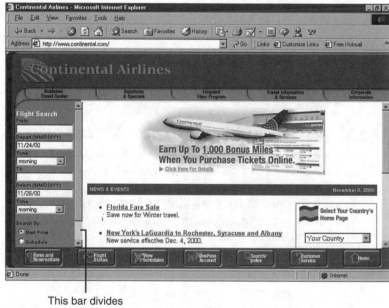

This bar divides
the frames.

Some browsers have a special reload command for frames: Click inside a frame and then choose **View**, **Reload Frame** to reload the contents of that one frame. Some versions of the Netscape browser also have a **Back in Frame** command with which you can move back to the previously viewed document within the frame. Navigator Version 2 had a real problem with frames, though; using the Back command took you all the way out of the frames, perhaps many steps back, rather than showing you the previous document you viewed within the frames. Internet Explorer and the more recent versions of Navigator (Navigator Version 4) have no Back in Frame command; instead, they assume that if you're using the Back command, you want to go back step by step, not all the way out of the frames.

Frames are one of the most hated features on the Web. Although they can be very useful when designed properly, too many Web authors misuse them; they put too many frames into a window or lock frame contents so you can't scroll down the page within the frame. Such authors are often working with very high-resolution monitors on which everything works fine, but things get totally messed up on lower-resolution monitors.

Animated Icons

Animated icons are becoming popular these days. These little pictures embedded into Web documents appear to be in motion. They are relatively easy for Web authors to create, so you can expect to see many more of them appearing on the Web. They add a little motion to a page (this is known in Web jargon as "making a page more compelling") without causing a lot of extra stuff to be transmitted to your computer. Unfortunately, such animations can be extremely irritating, as user research has shown. Many authors throw in animations because they're cool, without realizing that they sometimes make the page harder to read.

If you find large and complicated things in motion, you've stumbled across some kind of video or animation file format (see Chapter 5, "Web Multimedia—From Flash to Napster") or perhaps a Web program created in Java or ActiveX, which we'll look at next.

Web Programs: Java, JavaScript, and ActiveX

You might have heard of Java by now. I'm not talking about a chain of coffee bars; I'm talking about a new programming language that will (if you believe the hype) make the Web more exciting, make every appliance from toasters to dishwashers talk to you in Swahili, bring about world peace, and lead to a complete and total eradication of body odor.

Java has been hyped for a couple of years, but I think it's finally becoming useful. A number of sites now have Java applets that do something useful (in the early days Java was a toy, and the average Java applet was nothing more useful than a picture of bouncing heads). The Expedia site mentioned earlier, for instance, has Java-based maps. You can select an area to see a map showing a few hotels, and then zoom in on a particular area, or find information about one of the hotels. Java is also used to create moving banners, automatically scrolling text boxes, chat programs (see Chapter 8, "Using Online Chat Rooms"), and many other useful and not-so-useful things.

Net Tips

Java Interpreters

Java-compatible browsers are Java "interpreters." In effect, an interpreter is a program that can run another program, coordinating between the computer's operating system and the program. So, a Java applet can run on any operating system (Windows 3.1, Windows 95, Macintosh System 7, and UNIX of various flavors) as long as there is an interpreter created for that operating system. Both Netscape Navigator and Internet Explorer are Java interpreters.

For these programs to work, you must be using a Java-compatible Web browser—and even then they might not work. Netscape 2.0 and later versions, and Internet Explorer 3.0 and later versions, are Java-compatible. The later the version, the more likely that the Java applet will function (Netscape Navigator 2, for instance, doesn't handle Java applets very well). But even if you have the very latest browser, you might still run into problems.

When you reach a Web page that has an embedded Java applet, the Java program is transmitted to your computer, and the browser then runs the program. The program might be a game of some sort, a multimedia display, a financial calculator of some kind, or just about anything else. Figure 4.6 shows one of the Java maps at Expedia.

Figure 4.6

Expedia's Java maps help you find a hotel.

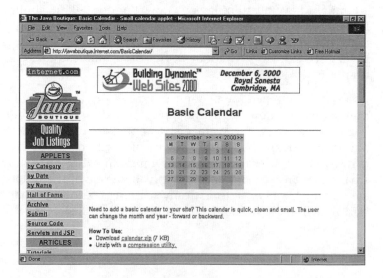

For all the overblown projections, many Java applets are rarely used, and remain unreliable and slow (and all too often pointless). Searching for interesting or useful Java applets has been an experience in frustration and disappointment for some time. The situation is improving, though, with truly useful Java applets becoming more common and more reliable.

What About JavaScript and ActiveX?

JavaScript is Java's baby brother. It's a scripting language in which programs are written within the Web page. In other words, a JavaScript-compatible browser reads the Web page, extracts the JavaScript commands, and runs them. JavaScript is not as powerful a programming language as Java, but it's easier to create programs using JavaScript, so it's more common. You can find loads of JavaScript programs at Developer.com (http://www. developer.com/) as well as some useful tutorials. Figure 4.7 shows an example of a JavaScript application, taken from a book I wrote on the subject.

Applications Across the Net

You might have heard the theory that pretty soon, instead of buying software and installing it on your hard drive, you'll "rent" programs across the Internet, paying for the time you use. If this *ever* happens (and there are good reasons to suspect it won't), it will be a very long time from now. Internet connections are currently about as reliable and efficient as a drunk at a beer tasting, and until they are as reliable as the electricity supply, this system won't work. I've added this projection to my "yeah, right, don't hold your breath" list.

A competitor to Java, ActiveX is a system from Microsoft, designed to enable Web authors to easily incorporate multimedia and programs into their Web pages. Currently, the only ActiveX browser is Internet Explorer, and you can probably expect it to stay that way for a while.

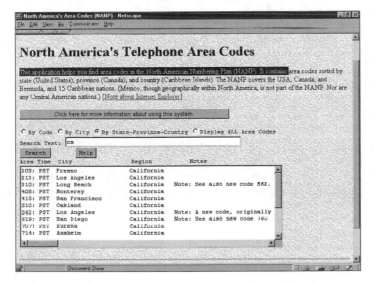

Figure 4.7

My Area Code program, written in JavaScript (http://TopFloor.com/ javascript/areacode.htm).

The Latest Programmer's Toy, Dynamic HTML

There's another way to make Web pages move, and that's with a new toy called Dynamic HTML (also called DHTML) and layers. A Web designer can now create different layers of information—pictures and text—and then shuffle these layers around on the page, making them visible and then invisible, to create an animation effect and even let people move things around on the page (see the alien head in the following illustration). People define Dynamic HTML differently; layering is a feature that's often used in conjunction with Dynamic HTML, although the purists may say it's a different thing. Microsoft and Netscape regard Dynamic HTML and layers as different things, too.

Dynamic HTML means Dynamic Hypertext Markup Language. You might remember from Chapter 2, "Working on the World Wide Web," that HTML is Hypertext Markup Language and is the coding used to create Web pages—you'll see it in action in Chapter 13, "Setting Up Your Own Web Site." So, DHTML is sort of like HTML in motion. That's the theory, but advanced DHTML also requires programming skills, not just Web-authoring skills.

Often DHTML is used as nothing more than a programmer's toy (you can see an example in Figure 4.8), but it's also becoming a very popular tool for adding program interactivity to Web sites—making Web pages operate more like computer programs. However, incompatibilities between browsers, particularly older browsers, mean that DHTML can often be unreliable.

Figure 4.8

Create your own alien head through the wonders of DHTML. (You'll have to use Internet Explorer, though.)

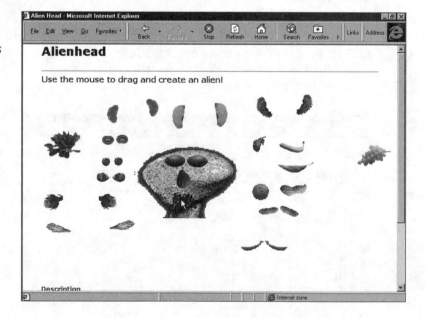

Just a Little Shove: Pushing and Pulling

Information generally arrives at your screen because you've directly requested it by clicking a link or entering a URL. However, Web authors can set up their Web pages to use server push and client pull so you can get information without doing a thing.

The first of these, *server push*, occurs when the Web server continues sending information even though you haven't requested it. Suppose you click a link to display a Web page, and just a few minutes later, the Web page changes. Even if you don't request more information, the server sends updated information and continues to send periodic updates until you close the page.

Client pull is similar, except that the request for updates comes from the browser. For instance, you open a page. At the same time the server sends the page, it sends a special program (you don't see this; it all happens in the background). This program tells the browser when to request updates. After the defined interval, the browser sends a request to the server asking for the information. Again, these updates will continue until you leave the page.

These systems work so similarly that you usually won't know which method is being used. They are very useful when you're viewing information that changes rapidly, such as stock quotes, weather reports, news headlines, or auctions.

The Multimedia Experience

You'll find all sorts of file formats on the World Wide Web, including still pictures, video and animations, sounds, electronic documents, and 3D images. Any file format that you can play or display on your computer can be linked to a Web page.

When you click a link that takes you to one of these file formats, your browser handles the file, if it can. It displays the document or picture in the window in the normal way. If the file is a format that your browser can't handle, it has two options. Your browser may send the file directly to a program that *can* handle it (known as a *plug-in*, *viewer*, or *helper*), or it might ask you what to do. Chapter 5 deals with this topic.

The Web Gets More Complicated

As you'll see in Chapter 13, creating a simple Web page is quite easy; even many of the more advanced Web-authoring techniques are not particularly complicated. Sure, there are special codes to learn, but it's all reasonably straightforward.

But the latest technologies are things that the average Web author will find much more complicated to use. Technologies such as Java, JavaScript, ActiveX, and Dynamic HTML require programming skills. As a result, it's becoming harder for Web authors to keep up with the Joneses (technologically speaking), which might be a good thing. Now they can concentrate on function instead of form, forget about the glitz, and compete by making their Web sites interesting and content-rich instead of just trying to be cool.

Before I move on, though, here's a quick thought related to this issue:

The Internet is not a multimedia system!

Remember that, and you'll be saved from a lot of frustration. This statement might seem a little strange after you've been bombarded by several years of advertising and media hype about the Internet. We've all seen the TV ads in which video rolls across a computer screen within a Web browser, as quickly as if it were being displayed on a TV screen. But the Internet does *not* work that quickly, and many of its problems seem to arise from people trying to treat it as if it does.

As a multimedia system, the Internet is primitive, mainly because it's so slow. If it's "lights, cameras, action" that you're after, use the TV or go see a movie; the Internet can't compete. The Internet, despite what you might have heard, is primarily a text-based system. (What's the fastest growing area on the Internet? Email publishing!) Even the Web is primarily text. All the hype in the world won't change that. What will change that is much faster connections from people's homes to the Internet, faster Web servers, and faster and more reliable backbone connections across the Internet. But don't hold your breath, because although some of you already have fast connections, and some will get them soon...most of you will turn blue before you get fast connections in your homes.

What on Earth Are All Those File Types?

It's possible to work with a computer for years without really understanding directories and file types. I know people who simply save files from their word processor (the only program they ever use) "on the disk." *Where on the disk?* Well, you know, on the hard disk. *Yes, but where? Which directory?* Well, you know, where the program saves the files.

You can get away with this lack of knowledge if you use only one program and don't use it too much. But if you plan to spend any time on the Internet and plan to make the most of your time there, you'll need to understand a bit more about files and directories. You'll come across a plethora of file types, and it helps if you understand what you are looking at.

About Download Directories

I don't want to spend a lot of time explaining what a directory is. This is very basic computing stuff, and if you don't understand it, you should probably read an introduction to computing (such as *The Complete Idiot's Guide to PCs* by Joe Kraynak). However, I'll quickly explain it, and that might be enough.

You can think of a directory as an area on your hard disk that stores computer files. You might think of it as a file folder in a filing cabinet. The hard disk is the filing cabinet, holding dozens, maybe hundreds, of folders (directories). In some graphical user interfaces, such as recent versions of Microsoft Windows and the Macintosh, directories are actually called *folders*. (But I've been using the term *directory* too long to give it up now.)

If you look inside a filing cabinet and open a file folder, what do you find? Documents—those are the individual files. You might also find another folder within the first folder. That's a *subdirectory*. So, directories can contain files and other directories, and those directories can contain more files and more directories (more subdirectories), and so on. Therefore, you have what is known as the directory tree. (Figure 4.9 shows what this "tree" looks like.) The point of this system is to help you organize your files. It's not uncommon for today's computers to have thousands of files, tens of thousands even. If you don't organize this lot logically, you'll end up with a mess that will make the Gordian knot look simple.

Directories Are Not Areas of the Hard Disk!

Before you email me saying that a directory is *not* an area on your hard disk, let me say *I know that!* It just *appears* to be an area on your hard disk. Computer files are spread across the disk in an apparently illogical and disorganized manner—a piece of a file here, a piece there. The directory system is a visual way to organize the files to make the hard disk easier to use.

The disk says, "I have a directory here that contains these files." But that's a lie, because the files are scattered all over the place. But it doesn't matter. It's rather like a child who *swears* that he has tidied up his room, that his socks are in the dresser and his shoes are in the closet. They're not, of course; everything's scattered over the floor. But you really don't want to look inside because it will just upset you. So, you accept it and think in terms of where things *should be* within the room, without wanting to see the truth. Don't worry about the technical details; directories contain files, and that's all you need to know.

A *download directory* is a directory into which you download a file. Let's say that you are using your Web browser to download a shareware program from one of the libraries listed in Appendix C, "All the Software You'll Ever Need." Where is that file saved? By definition, it's downloaded into the download directory. What is the download directory named? It might be called DOWNLOAD, but it could be anything; the download directory is whichever directory you tell the program to put the file in.

Figure 4.9

Folders within folders within folders make up the directory tree, shown here in Windows ME Explorer.

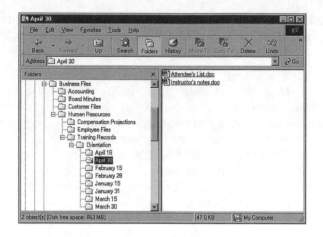

The directory chosen by the browser as the download directory is not always the best place to put the file. In many cases, it's a lousy choice. Internet Explorer, for instance, wants to place downloaded files on the Windows *desktop*. (In Windows 95, 98, and NT, the desktop is a special subdirectory of the WINDOWS or WINNT directory; anything placed inside that directory will appear on the desktop, which is the area of your computer screen that is visible when all the programs have been closed.) That's often a bad place to put it; if you download a lot of things, your desktop will soon be as cluttered as my office. (And believe me, that's not good.) Of course, you can always move the file to another directory later, but in that case, why not put it where you want it in the first place?

Also, many of the files that you will download are archive files; these files are sort of file "containers." Although an archive file is a single file, it has other files within it, perhaps hundreds of them. When you extract those files, they are generally placed in the same directory. After you extract those files, you no longer have one easily recognized file on your desktop (or in whichever download directory the program chose). You now have dozens or more new files there. Do this with several download files, and you'll soon become confused; which file came from which archive?

Pick a Download Directory Sensibly

When you download files from the Web, FTP, your online service, or wherever, think sensibly about where you place the files. Many users create a special directory called *download*. Some programs even do this automatically: Many FTP programs, for instance, create a directory called *download* to be used as the default location for downloaded files. You can place all the downloaded files directly into that directory. Later you can decide what you want to do with each file.

I prefer to go one step further. When I download a file, I think about where I'll eventually want the file. For instance, if it's a document file related to a book I'm working on, I save it directly into one of the directories I've created to hold the book. If it's a program file, I'll have to create a directory to hold the program at some point, so why not create a directory for the program right now and download the file directly into that directory? (Depending on which operating system and program you are using, you might be able to create the directory while you are telling the program where to save the file; or you might have to use some kind of file-management program to create the directory and *then* save the file.)

Learn about directories. Be sure you understand how to find your way around the directory tree (or folder system, as it's known in some operating systems). And be sure you save files in such a manner that you can find them when you need them.

A Cornucopia of File Formats

Many computer users don't understand the concept of file formats because they never really see any files. They open their word processors, do some work, and then save the file. They might notice that when they give the file a name, the program adds a few letters such as .doc or .wpd at the end, but they don't think much about it. If you're going to be playing on the Net, though, you need to understand just a little about file formats because you'll have to pick and choose the ones you want.

All computer files have one thing in common: They all save information in the form of zeros and ones. The difference between a file created by one word processor and another, or between a file created by a word processor and one created by a graphics program, is in what those zeros and ones *mean*. Just as two languages can use the same basic sounds and string them together to create different words, different programs use the zeros and ones to mean different things. One program uses zeros and ones to create words, another to create sounds, another to create pictures, and so on.

Hidden File Extensions

Microsoft Windows, in Windows 95 and later, hides the file extensions from you. I think this is particularly stupid, but then, Microsoft didn't ask me before deciding to do this. To see file extensions in Windows 95 open Windows Explorer and select **View**, **Options**. Then, under the **View** tab, clear the check box labeled **Hide MS–DOS File Extensions for File Types That Are Registered**. In Windows 98, select **View, Folder Options**. Then, under the **View** tab, clear the check box labeled **Hide File Extensions for Known File Types**. Windows 2000 and Windows ME change the location again, of course; you'll find it under **Tools, Folder Options**.

The File Extension

How, then, can computer programs identify one file from another? They can often look for a familiar sequence of zeros and ones at the beginning of a file; if they find it, they know they have the right file. But there's also something called a *file extension* that identifies files, and it has the added advantage of being visible to mere mortals. A file extension is a piece of text at the end of a filename, preceded by a period, which is used to identify the file type. For example, look at this sample filename:

```
THISDOC.TXT
```

Different Extensions, Same Format

Some files are identified by two or more file extensions. For instance, the .jpeg extension is often used on UNIX computers to identify a form of graphics file commonly used on the Web. But because Windows 3.1 and DOS can't display four-character extensions, this type of file is often seen with the .jpg extension, different extension, but the same file format. You'll also find HTM and HTML files, TXT and TEXT files, and AIF and AIFF files (sound files).

The extension is the TXT bit. This extension means the file is a plain text file; any program that can read what is known as ASCII text can open this file and read it.

Now, in most operating systems (including DOS and Windows), file extensions are three characters long; on some operating systems, extensions are three or four characters. Normally, each file has only one file extension. Some operating systems, such as UNIX and Windows 98, for example, allow multiple extensions and extensions with more than three characters, such as THISDOC.NEWONE.TEXT. However, this sort of thing is becoming rare on the Internet these days, and you generally run into only simple three- and four-character extensions.

Macintosh files, by the way, don't require a file extension; rather, an identifier is built into the file, visible to the computer but not to the computer operator. However, note that Macintosh files stored on the Internet often *do* have an extension—.hqx or .sea, for instance. This extension is to make them readily identifiable as Macintosh files by human beings. (I find it amusing that the Mac's programmers, for all the talk of making their computers easy to use, didn't realize how important file extensions are to mere humans.)

You might be thinking that there are probably three or four file formats you need to know about. No, not quite. Try four or five dozen. Table 15.1 gives you a list to get you started.

Table 15.1   File Formats You Should Know

File Format	Type of File It Identifies
ARC	A PKARC file (a DOS compression file).
AU, AIF, AIFF, AIFC, SND	Sound files often used on Macintosh and UNIX systems; Netscape and Internet Explorer can play these sounds.
ASP	Active Server Page, a page containing special scripts run by a Web browser.
AVI	Video for Windows.
BMP, PCX	Common bitmap graphics formats.
CSV	Comma Delimited Data file, containing information that can be imported into a database program.
DOC	Microsoft Word files, from Word for the Macintosh, Word for Windows, and Windows WordPad.
EPS	A PostScript image.

Table 15.1   File Formats You Should Know CONTINUED

File Format	Type of File It Identifies
EXE	A program file or a self-extracting archive file.
FLC, FLI, AAS	Autodesk Animator files.
GIF	Graphics files often found in Web pages.
.gzip and .gz	UNIX compressed files.
HLP	Windows Help files.
HTM, HTML	The basic Web document format.
HQX	A BinHex file, a format often used to archive Macintosh files. Programs such as StuffIt Expander can open these files.
JPG, JPEG, JPE	JPEG graphics files, also often found in Web pages.
JFIF, PJPEG, PJP	A few more variations of the JPEG file format.
MID, RMI	MIDI (Musical Instrument Digital Interface) sounds.
MMM	Microsoft Multimedia Movie Player files.
MOV, QT	The QuickTime video format.
MP2	An MPEG audio format.
MP3	A music format that has the music business terrified. It's CD quality, yet takes up only around 1MB for each minute of sound. MP3 files can also include images (CD cover art, for instance), lyrics, artists' bios, and so on.
MPEG, MPG, MPE, M1V	The MPEG (Moving Picture Experts Group) video formats.
PDF	The Portable Document Format, an Adobe Acrobat hypertext file. This format is becoming a very popular means of distributing electronic documents.
PHP	A file containing scripts that are run by the Web browser. Although PHP used to mean Personal Home Page, it's no longer used as an acronym; PHP is simply the name of the script language.
.pit	The Macintosh PackIt archive format.
PS	A PostScript document.
RAM, RA	RealAudio. This sound format plays while it's being transmitted. Click a link to a RealAudio file, and it begins playing within a few seconds (you don't have to wait until the entire file is transferred).
RTF	Rich Text Format. These word processing files work in a variety of Windows word processors.
.sea	A Macintosh self-extracting archive.
SGML	A document format.
.shar	A UNIX shell archive file.
SIT	The Macintosh StuffIt archive format.

Table 15.1   File Formats You Should Know CONTINUED

File Format	Type of File It Identifies
TAR	A UNIX tar archive file.
TIF, TIFF	A common graphics format.
TSP	TrueSpeech, a sound format similar to RealAudio.
TTF	Windows TrueType font files.
TXT, TEXT	A text file.
WAV	The standard Windows "wave" sound format.
WPD	A WordPerfect document file.
WRI	Windows Write word-processing files.
WRL	A VRML (Virtual Reality Modeling Language) 3D object.
XBM	Another graphics file that can be displayed by Web browsers (although it's not used very often these days).
XDM	The StreamWorks WebTV and WebRadio format. This is similar to RealAudio,but it allows the real-time playing of video in addition to sound.
XLS	A Microsoft Excel spreadsheet file.
Z	A UNIX compressed file.
z	A UNIX packed file.
ZIP	A PKZIP archive file (a DOS and Windows compression file), used by many Windows (and even some Macintosh) compression utilities.
.zoo	A zoo210 archive format available on various systems.

Is It Possible?

This is similar to Dr. Who's Tardis, which has much more space *inside* than would be allowed within a box of that size according to normal physics. And, no, I don't plan to explain how it's done. Suffice it to say that, thanks to a little magic and nifty computing tricks, these programs make files smaller.

Is that all? By no means! There are all sorts of file formats out there; to be honest, though, you'll run across only a few of them. You might never even run across some of the ones I included in the table; for instance, the ARC format, which used to be very common in the shareware world, is now quite rare.

File Compression Basics

As you can see from the preceding table, a number of these file formats are archive or compressed formats. These are files containing other files within them. You can use a special program to extract those files; or in the case of a "self-extracting archive," the file can automatically extract the files within it.

Why do people bother to put files inside archive files? Or even, in some cases, a single file within an archive file? Two reasons. First, the programs that create these files often compress the files being placed inside, so the single file is much smaller than the combined size of all the files inside. You can reduce files to as little as 2% of their normal size, depending on the type of file and the program you use (although 40% to 75% is probably a more normal range). Bitmap graphics, for instance, often compress to a very small size; program files and Windows Help files can't be compressed so far. If you want to transfer a file across the Internet, it's a lot quicker to transfer a compressed file than an uncompressed file.

The other reason to use these systems is that you can place files inside another file as a sort of packaging or container. If a shareware program has, say, 20 different files that it needs in order to run, it's better to wrap all these into one file than to expect people to transfer all 20 files one at a time.

Which Format?

Most compressed DOS and Windows files are in Zip format, a format often created by a program called PKZIP (but the file format is not owned by anyone, so other programs create Zip files, too). There are other compressed formats, though; you might also see ARJ (created by a program called ARJ) and LZH (created by LHARC) now and again, but probably not very often. PKZIP won the compression war.

Archive Versus Compressed

What's the difference between an archive file and a compressed file? They're often the same thing, and people (including me) tend to use the terms interchangeably. Originally, however, an archive file was a file that stored lots of other files: It archived them. An archive file doesn't have to be a compressed file; it's just a convenient place to put files that you are not using. A compressed file must, of course, be compressed. These days, archive files are usually—although, not always—compressed files, and compressed files are often used for archiving files. So, there's not a lot of difference between the two anymore. There's one notable exception, though. The .tar files you might run across, UNIX tape archive files, are *not* compressed. However, .tar archive files are often compressed using the .gzip format (you'll see something such as filename.tar.gz).

In the UNIX world, .Z, .gz, and .tar files are common archive formats. On the Macintosh, you'll find .sit (StuffIt) and .pit (PackIt) compressed formats, as well as .hqx (BinHex) archive files. This table gives you a quick rundown of the archive formats you'll see.

Table 15.2   Common Compressed and Archive File Formats

Extension	Program That Compressed or Archived It
.arc	DOS, PKARC (an older method, predating PKZIP and rarely seen these days)
.exe	A DOS or Windows self-extracting archive
.gz	Usually a UNIX gzip compressed file (although there are versions of gzip for other operating systems, they're rarely used)
.hqx	Macintosh BinHex
.pit	Macintosh PackIt
.sea	A Macintosh self-extracting archive
.shar	UNIX shell archive
.sit	Macintosh StuffIt
.tar	UNIX tape archive
.Z	UNIX compress
.z	UNIX pack
.zip	PKZIP, WinZip, and many others
.zoo	zoo210 (available on various systems)

It goes without saying (but I'll say it anyway, just in case) that if you see a file with an extension that is common on an operating system other than yours, it might contain files that won't be good on your system. Macintosh and UNIX software won't run on Windows, for instance. However, that's not always true. The file might contain text files, for instance, which can be read on any system. So, there are cross-platform utilities; for example, some Macintosh utilities can uncompress archive files, such as Zip files, that are not common in the Macintosh world, and some Zip utilities running in Windows can extract files from .gz and .tar files. For instance, some versions of StuffIt Expander, a Macintosh utility, can open Zip files, and WinZip, a Windows program, can open .gz and .tar files.

In the Meantime

How can you download and extract one of these compression utilities from a shareware library before you have a program that will extract an archive file? Don't worry; the programmers thought of that! These utilities are generally stored in self-extracting format, so you can download them and automatically extract them by running the file.

Those Self-Extracting Archives

Various programs, such as PKZIP and ARJ, can create files that can be executed (run) to extract the archived files automatically. These files, called self-extracting archives, are very useful for sending a compressed file to someone when you're not sure whether he has the program to decompress the file (or would know how to use it). For instance, PKZIP can create a file with an .exe extension; you can run such a file directly from the DOS prompt just by typing its name and pressing

Enter or by double-clicking the file in the Windows Explorer file-management program. When you do so, all the compressed files pop out. In the Macintosh world, .sea (self-extracting archive) files do the same thing. Double-click a .sea file, and the contents are automatically extracted.

If you find a file in two formats, ZIP and EXE for instance, you might want to take the EXE format. The EXE files are not much larger than the ZIP files, and you don't need to worry about finding a program to extract the files. If you take a ZIP file, you must have a program that can read the ZIP file and extract the archived files from within. You might already have such a program. Some Windows file-management programs, for instance, can work with ZIP files. Otherwise, you'll need a program that can extract from the compressed format. See Appendix C for information about file libraries where you can download freeware and shareware that will do the job.

Your Computer Can Get Sick, Too

Downloading all these computer files can lead to problems: computer viruses. File viruses hide out in program files and copy themselves to other program files when someone runs that program. Viruses and other malevolent computer bugs are real, and they do real damage. Now and then you'll even hear of service providers having to close down temporarily after their systems become infected.

Unfortunately, security on the Internet is lax. The major online services have strict regulations about virus checks. Members generally cannot post directly to public areas, for instance; they post to an area in which the file can be checked for viruses before it's available to the public. But on the Internet it's up to each system administrator (and there are hundreds of thousands of them) to keep his own system clean. If just one administrator does a bad job, a virus can get through and be carried by FTP, the Web, or email all over the

Viruses Under the Microscope

The term *virus* has become a catchall for a variety of digital organisms, such as

➤ Bacteria, which reproduce and do no direct damage except using up disk space and memory.

➤ Rabbits, which get their name because they reproduce very quickly.

➤ Trojan horses, which are damaging programs embedded in otherwise useful programs.

➤ Bombs, which are programs that just sit and wait for a particular date or event (at which time they wreak destruction); these are often left deep inside programs by disgruntled employees.

➤ Worms, which are programs that copy themselves from one computer to another, independent of other executable files, and clog the computers by taking over memory and disk space.

world. The large shareware archives are probably quite careful, but there are tens of thousands of places to download software on the Internet, and some of those are probably a little careless.

However, having said all that, I also must say that the virus threat is overstated—probably by companies selling antivirus software. We've reached a stage where almost any confusing computer problem is blamed on computer viruses, and technical support lines are using it as an excuse not to talk with people. "Your computer can't read your hard disk? You've been downloading files from the Internet? You must have a virus!" Most computer users have never been "hit" by a computer virus. Many who think they have probably haven't; a lot of problems are blamed on viruses these days. So, don't get overly worried about it. Take some sensible precautions, and you'll be okay.

Rule of Thumb

Here's a rule of thumb to figure out whether a file is dangerous: "If it does something, it can carry a virus; if it has things done to it, it's safe." Only files that can carry out actions (such as script files, program files, and word-processing files from the fancy word processors—such as Word for Windows—that have built-in macro systems) can pose a threat. If a file can't do anything—it just sits waiting until a program displays or plays it—it's safe. Pictures and sounds, for instance, might offend you personally, but they won't do your computer any harm. (Can self-extracting archives carry viruses? Absolutely. They're programs, and they run—you don't know that they're self-extracting archives until they've extracted, after all.)

Tips for Safe Computing

If you are just working with basic ASCII text email and perhaps FTPing documents, you're okay. The problem of viruses arises when you transfer programs, including self-extracting archive files, or files that contain mini "programs." (For instance, many word-processing files can now contain macros, special little programs that might run when you open the file.)

If you do plan to transfer programs, perhaps the best advice is to get a good antivirus program. They're available for all computer types. Each time you transmit an executable file, use your antivirus program to check it. (Some programs can even be installed as browser "plug-ins," so they automatically check files that you download through your browser.) Also, be sure you keep good backups of your data. Although backups can also become infected with viruses, if a virus hits, at least you can reload your backup data and use an antivirus program to clean the files (and some backup programs check for viruses while backing up).

The Least You Need to Know

➤ The Web is far more diverse than it was a year or two ago; it's much more than just text with pictures.

➤ You'll find lots of tables and forms.

➤ Framed documents allow an author to split a document into multiple pieces, each of which is displayed in its own frame.

➤ Java, JavaScript, and ActiveX are Web programming languages that enable authors to bring their pages to life. The new programmer's toy is Dynamic HTML.

➤ Client pull is a system by which a browser automatically requests updates to a page. Server push is a system by which a server automatically sends updates.

➤ A wide range of multimedia formats must be displayed in viewers or plug-ins; you'll learn about those in Chapter 5.

➤ Don't transfer files to your computer without thinking about *where* on your hard disk they should be. Create a download directory in a sensible place.

➤ Files are identified by the file extension, typically a three-character (sometimes four-character) "code" preceded by a period.

➤ The virus rule of thumb is this: "If it does something, it can carry a virus; if it has things done to it, it's safe."

Web Multimedia—From Flash to Napster

As the Web gets older, and as people start using it more, it's storing more and more types of computer files. You'll find animations, videos, pictures of various formats, sounds that play after they've transferred to your computer, sounds that play *as* they transfer to your computer, "slide" presentations, and all sorts of other weird and wonderful things. Think of these formats as the *multimedia* content of the Web—literally "multiple media." For some of us, those with fast connections, the Internet is finally turning into a true multimedia system; that is, one that can work with various types of media without causing great frustration.

For most of us still accessing the Internet through slow modem lines, the full potential has yet to be reached! If *you* are still stuck with a slow connection, some of the things I'll talk about in this chapter will be things you might try now and then, but won't want to put up with very often.

What do I mean by slow connections? Pretty much any kind of telephone modem—it really doesn't whether it's a "fast" modem (a 56kbps modem, for instance), all phone modems are slow. It's not until you have the speed of a cable, DSL, or satellite connection—or faster—that you'll find multimedia works well.

How Browsers Deal with Different Files

Today's Web browsers are designed to handle *any* computer file format. When you click a link to a file, that file is transferred to your computer, and your browser can then use it in one of three ways:

➤ **On its own**   The file format might be one that the browser can handle directly. Web browsers can display or play Web pages (HTM or HTML files), text documents (TXT), some graphics formats (GIF, XBM, JPG, JPEG, and PNG), and some sound formats (WAV and SND).

➤ **With a plug-in**   The browser might open a *plug-in*, a special add-on program that plays or displays the file within the browser window.

➤ **With a viewer (or helper)**   The browser might send the file to a *viewer* or *helper*, which is a separate program that recognizes the file format. That program then opens a window in which the file is played or displayed.

In effect, a plug-in extends the capabilities of the browser, allowing it to work with a file type that it couldn't use before. A viewer, on the other hand, is a completely separate program; the Web browser remains at the previous Web page while the multimedia file is sent to, and "played" by, the viewer. Note, however, that some programs can work both ways, depending on how the Web author has linked to the media file. RealPlayer and Windows Media Player, for instance, can both run as "standalone" programs, or can run within a browser window.

If you buy a brand-new computer, the browser will probably recognize most of the file formats you'll encounter. That's not the case with older systems that have not been upgraded. Still, old or new, when your browser comes across a file format that it doesn't recognize, it will ask you what to do; you can then install a new plug-in or viewer to handle that file type, or simply save the file on your hard disk.

Two Types of Multimedia Inclusions

There are basically two ways to include a multimedia file in a Web page. The author might include the file as an *embedded* (sometimes known as *live* or *inline object*), a file that is automatically transferred to your computer along with the Web page. For instance, an embedded file might play a background sound or display a video within the Web page. On the other hand, the author can include the file as an *external file*; you click a link, and that file alone (without a Web page) is transferred to your computer.

What's Available?

Scores of plug-ins and viewers are available; you just have to know where to find them. A good starting point for Netscape Navigator plug-ins is the Netscape Navigator Components page; select **Help**, **About Plug-Ins**, and then click the **For More Information on Netscape Plug-Ins**, **Click Here** link near the top of the page; or go directly to http://home.netscape.com/plugins/. For Internet Explorer, use the **Help**, **Product Updates** command if you're working with an old version, or visit the Windows Updates site (click your **Start** button, and then select **Windows Update**). You can also find many viewers at the sites discussed in Appendix C, "All the Software You'll Ever Need."

Which Do You Need? Which Do You Want?

You don't need all the available viewers and plug-ins. There are hundreds already— a few years ago Netscape claimed there were almost 180 plug-ins for Netscape Navigator, but they seem to have stopped counting. So, unless you are independently wealthy and don't need to waste time working, you probably won't have time to install them all (and you probably don't have the disk space you'd need). To help you determine which plug-ins and viewers you should get, I've broken them down into a few categories and the most common file formats. You might not want to get them until you need them, though—I'd recommend that you simply wait until you need one, and then go find it. (In most cases, a Web site will provide a link to the plug-in/viewer's download site.)

Music and Voice (Very Useful)

Some of the most useful plug-ins and viewers are those for music and voice. In particular, you might want RealPlayer, the most popular "streaming media" tool (http://www.Real.com/) and Windows Media Player, which comes with Microsoft Windows.

Streaming media has become popular only in the last few years. Until streaming media, a file would have to transfer completely to your disk drive before it could be played. For instance, let's say you're transferring a 5MB video file. You'd twiddle your thumbs for a long time—perhaps go for coffee or take a nap. After the file had been fully transferred, it would be loaded into a player and begin playing.

Streaming media files begin playing soon after they begin transferring; the parts of the file already transferred are played while the rest of the file is still coming across the Internet to your computer.

There used to be many different streaming media players, but RealPlayer and Windows Media Player are the two most popular now, and indeed Real Networks, the owner of RealPlayer, seems to have subsumed some of the others. StreamWorks (http://www.StreamWorks.com/) was common a year or two ago, but it's been merged with Real Networks. There's another popular streaming video player, Vivo (http://www.Vivo.com/), although I suspect it's used mainly in porno sites. But it's no longer developed, so will probably die out soon...and the URL takes you to the Real Networks site. Then, there's TrueSpeech, another popular format that seems to have simply disappeared. That's the way it works on the Internet.

What, then, is streaming media used for? (In addition to pornography, that is?) A lot of radio stations and music libraries use them, for example, so you can listen to the news from National Public Radio (http://www.npr.org) or music from the Internet Underground Music Archives (http://www.iuma.com). Many news sites, use them, too—in fact, just about any site that wants to transfer any kind of video or sound. And many movie sites use them to display trailers and clips.

You Already Have Viewers

In many cases, you might already have viewers for certain file formats. For instance, if you use Windows, you can use the Windows Media Player as a viewer for MIDI files, MPG, and AVI video files, MP3 music files, CDA (CD Audio) tracks, and so on; if you have installed Microsoft Word, you can use Word as the viewer for Word DOC files; if you use Windows, Microsoft Paint can be used to display BMP files, and so on. In fact, if you use Windows, you'll probably find a huge range of viewers and plug-ins already installed; all the Microsoft Office programs, for instance, will work as plug-ins in Internet Explorer—while if you're using Netscape Navigator they work as viewers. For instance, open an Excel spreadsheet file in Internet Explorer, and the file appears within the browser. Open it in Netscape Navigator and the browser opens Excel and loads the file into that program.

During your Internet travels, you are likely to come across these other sound formats:

➤ **AU**, **AIF**, **AIFF**, **AIFC**, and **SND**   These common sound formats are used on UNIX and on the Macintosh. Your browser can probably play these formats without an additional plug-in or viewer. (These formats are dying out, however, being replaced by others.)

➤ **WAV**   This is the Windows sound format. Your browser can probably play files in this format without an additional plug-in or viewer.

➤ **MID** and **RMI**   These are MIDI (Musical Instrument Digital Interface) formats. You might need to add a plug-in or viewer for these. (Netscape Navigator, since version 3, comes with a preinstalled plug-in that will work with MIDI files; if you use Windows, Windows Media Player will handle these.)

The MIDI formats are not common, but they are of interest to people who, well, are interested in MIDI. Many MIDI sites on the Web have sound clips. (MIDI is a system used to create music using computers and other electronic toys.)

MP3

MP3 is an important sound format that needs a little more explanation. What's so special about MP3? Well, MP3 files are CD-quality, and take up relatively little room. One minute of music takes up just 1MB, more or less, of disk space (the format used on audio CDs requires almost 10MB for each minute). MP3 is very popular, and it has the music business terrified; in fact, the Recording Industry Association of America has even tried to have an MP3 player banned. You can see one of the most popular players, MusicMatch, in Figure 5.1.

Figure 5.1

MusicMatch, one of the top MP3 players.

MP3 can be used in many different ways. You can store all your music on your computer, and then create playlists. Having a weekend party? Set up a playlist to run all weekend, click the start button, and forget about the music for the next 72 hours.

You can also create custom CDs. Pick the tracks you want, convert them to audio CD, and cut your own CD. Or, play the music through an MP3 player, such as Rio from Diamond Multimedia—plug the player into your computer, load the music, and away you go. Create custom cassette tapes and DAT tapes. Send your friends tracks across the Internet, and so on. The music business is terrified.

The two most popular MP3 players are Winamp (`http://www.Winamp.com/`) and MusicMatch (`http://www.MusicMatch.com`). MusicMatch has the advantage of including a "ripper," software that can take tracks off your audio CDs and save them in MP3 format (Winamp may include a ripper soon, too).

To find music, and learn about all the neat MP3 tools, visit MP3.com (`http://www.MP3.com`, of course), or one of these sites:

> Songs.com
> `http://www.songs.com`
>
> MP3 2000
> `http://www.mp3-2000.com`
>
> MPEG.ORG
> `http://www.mpeg.org`
>
> Dimension Music
> `http://www.dmusic.com`

Oh, and don't forget to check out a couple of books I've just published, *MP3 and the Digital Music Revolution: Turn Your PC into a CD-Quality Digital Jukebox*, and *MP3 for Musicians* (`http://TopFloor.com/`). Both come with the MusicMatch software and hours of music.

What's the music business doing about all this? They're trying to come up with their own sound formats, such as Liquid Audio and A2B (which comes from AT&T, of all places). Of course, the problem is that most people won't want to use these sound formats, because the entire purpose of these formats is to make moving your music around *inconvenient*, to discourage piracy. But if it's inconvenient for software pirates (the music business has finally come to the realization that music is a form of software), it's inconvenient for the rest of us, so the music business will find it hard to get people to switch.

Try this test; visit AltaVista, a search site we discuss in Chapter 15, and search for the word MP3. Look for the count, showing you how many pages have been found—it may be hidden away at the bottom of the page. When I did the search a moment ago, AltaVista found 9,728,239 pages. Then, search for "Liquid Audio"; you'll quickly see which is the more popular! (I just found 94,306 pages.)

Don't Forget Napster

Well, I'd better mention Napster (`http://www.Napster.com/`), which will probably still be in business by the time you read this. However, perhaps not. Napster is a system that allows you to view music collections on hundreds of thousands of users' computers around the world.

It works like this. You begin by downloading and installing the Napster software (available for Windows and the Mac). Now, let's say you want to find music by Smash Mouth. Use the Napster program to search, and the Napster server will create a list of other computers that contain MP3 files containing Smash Mouth music; you can then download tracks from those computers. (And other users can see which MP3 files you've put into your Napster file directory, and copy them from there.) Check out Figure 5.2 to see what Napster looks like.

Of course, this has the music business worried. Why buy music if you can just grab it from someone else's computer? You can copy it onto a CD, or play it on one of the many new MP3 players, or just leave it on your computer and play it through your stereo system.

There are two main arguments revolving around Napster. Supporters say that the ability to get music you've never paid for will actually lead to more music sales, as people hear things they would never have heard otherwise. Detractors say that this is nonsense—that people are downloading music that they want, not merely experimenting with new sounds and bands, and they're *not* buying CDs they would otherwise buy. (In fact, there are reports of music stores close to U.S. colleges going out of business because of a decline in music sales.)

There's definitely a chance Napster will be forced out of business by the courts. On the other hand, at the time of writing, Napster had announced an agreement with Bertelsmann, the owner of the BMG music label, which sells around 15% of all music in the U.S. Reportedly, the agreement calls for Napster to convert its free service into a for-pay service (probably $4.95/month), and use the fees to pay royalties to music producers and artists. It remains to be seen whether the other music labels will stop their lawsuits against Napster.

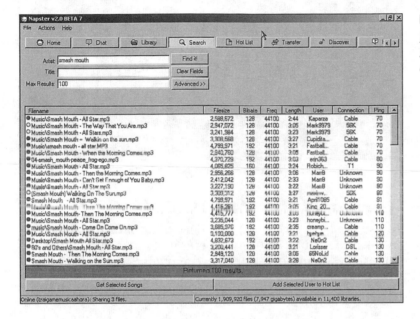

Figure 5.2

Napster. Pick a song, any song, and it's probably out there somewhere.

Flash and Shockwave

There are two very popular media formats that you're almost certain to run into: Flash and Shockwave, from Macromedia. You might think of Flash as Shockwave's little brother. Shockwave has been around for a few years, and can be used for interactive games, animations, and applications. Flash is not quite as flexible as Shockwave, but very popular for animations. There are two players for these programs; you can install the Flash Player, or the Shockwave Player, which also includes the Flash Player (http://www.Macromedia.com/).

Macromedia claims that 96% of all Internet users have the Flash Player installed, and certainly many Web designers are integrating these formats into their Web sites. If you would like to take a quick look at what Flash—and Shockwave—can do, visit http://www.Flash.com/.

Figure 5.3

The Snacktreat Boys singing, "I Want a Fat Babe," in a Flash Back Street Boys satire. (Sung to the tune of "I Want It That Way," of course.)

Other Document Formats (Also Very Useful)

Viewers and plug-ins are also available for a number of document formats that you'll find on the Web. In particular, the Adobe Acrobat Reader is useful. You'll also find viewers and plug-ins that display Microsoft Word, Envoy, and PostScript documents.

Adobe Acrobat is a hypertext format that predates the Web. It enables an author to create a multipage hypertext document that is contained in a single PDF file and that can be read by any Acrobat Reader, regardless of the operating system it is running on. Many authors like to use Acrobat because it gives them more control over the layout than they get when creating Web pages. It's also often used by companies that want to allow people to download forms from their Web sites; you can open the form in Adobe Acrobat Reader and then print it, and it will look exactly as the company intended (it's difficult to create high-quality forms using Web pages). For instance, most Internal Revenue Service forms are available in PDF format. You can see an example of an Acrobat file in Figure 5.4.

VRML

These 3D images are in a format known as VRML: Virtual Reality Modeling Language.

3D Worlds (Greatly Overrated!)

There are a number of viewers and browsers that display 3D (three-dimensional) images. Netscape Navigator has a plug-in called Live3D or Cosmo Player (depending on the version of Navigator that you are using), which might have been installed when you installed the browser. Internet Explorer has a plug-in called Microsoft VRML Viewer, which probably won't be installed with the browser—you'll have to add it later. You can download other 3D plug-ins or viewers, too.

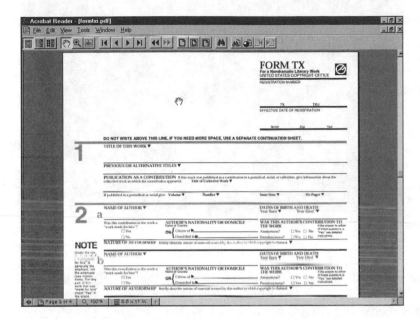

Figure 5.4

A form from the United States Copyright Office saved in an Adobe Acrobat file and displayed in the Adobe Acrobat viewer.

Do you need a 3D plug-in or viewer? Probably not. After you've seen a couple of 3D sites, the novelty will quickly wear off. This is another of those much-touted technologies that hasn't yet lived up to the hype. Five years ago or so it was supposed to be "the next big thing." We're still waiting. Three-dimensional images load slowly and move slowly. They are, in my opinion, unnecessary gimmicks. Perhaps one day they'll be an integral part of the Web, but for now they're little more than toys. (You can see an example in Figure 5.5.)

Still, if you want to experiment, visit one of the following sites, download a viewer, and play...

The VRML Depository: http://www.web3d.org/vrml/vrml.htm

VRMLSite Magazine: http://www.web3d.org/vrml/vrml.htm

Proteinman's Top Ten VRML2.0 Worlds:
http://www.virtpark.com/theme/proteinman/

Aereal Instant VRML Home World: http://www.aereal.com/instant/

Figure 5.5

You can walk around these buildings and maybe even into them. This technology is cute, but slow (and not terribly exciting after you've done it once or twice).

GIF Animations

Another very common form of animation is GIF animation. In fact, probably the singlemost common form of animation; those little moving pictures and icons you see are generally GIF animations. The GIF format is one of the basic image formats used on the Web, and GIF animations are created by layering several images, and the browser simply displays one image after another. These animations require no plug-in or viewer; if a browser can display images, it can probably display GIF animations. In Figure 5.6, you can see perhaps the most famous example of GIF animation on the Web.

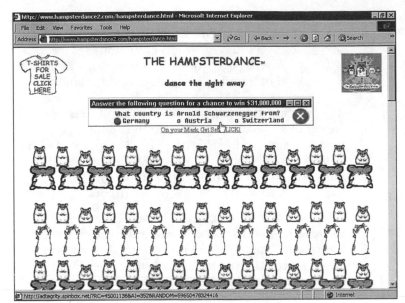

Figure 5.6
*The original
Hampsterdance*
(http://www.
hampsterdance2.com/
hampsterdance.html), *an
example of the wonders
of GIF animation!*

Other Weird File Formats

You'll find plug-ins and viewers available for all sorts of unusual file formats. Some plug-ins are not programs designed for handling particular file formats that you might come across while cruising the Web—they are more like special utilities designed to extend the features of the Web browser. For instance, there are Netscape plug-ins available for these tasks:

➤ **Internet Postage**   From Stamps.com, this plug-in lets you print postage stamps from your computer.

➤ **Carbon Copy**   This Netscape plug-in lets you control a PC across the Internet.

➤ **Chemscape Chime**   This is a plug-in for 2D and 3D chemical models.

➤ **EarthTime**   This plug-in displays eight different times from cities around the world.

➤ **ISYS Hindsight**   This plug-in keeps a record of every Web page you've seen and even allows you to search the text in those pages.

➤ **Post-it Notes**   Lets you view and drag Post-it Notes attached to Web pages and drop them onto your desktop. Clicking a Post-it Note later will open your browser and load that page. Very useful, except that you're very unlikely to run into many pages with Post-it Notes attached.

➤ **Look@Me**   This plug-in allows you to view another user's computer screen across the Web and see what's going on (assuming that person *wants* you to see what's going on, of course).

➤ **Net-Install**   This plug-in is designed to automate the transfer and installation of software across the Internet.

➤ **Cryptolink Agent** "Enables developers working with Dallas Semiconductor's Java- or Crypto-iButtons the ability to write interfaces in Java and JavaScript; access iButton's low-level functionality from your Web page, allowing you to easily build any kind of interface you desire." Understand?

Looking for Samples?

A good place to find samples of these various multimedia formats is the Netscape plug-ins page that I mentioned earlier. For each plug-in or viewer, you'll find links to Web sites using the file format handled by that program.

As I mentioned earlier, any file type can be sent to a viewer of some kind. However, only a handful of file types are commonly used (the ones I mentioned earlier as the common formats). You'll want to install other plug-ins and viewers only if the particular file type happens to be used at the Web sites that you frequent.

You don't necessarily need to install these plug-ins or viewers right away. You can wait until you stumble across a link to one of the file formats. If your browser doesn't recognize the format, it will ask you what to do with the file. If you want to access the file, you will need to install the appropriate viewer or plug-in at that time.

Automatic Installations of Plug-Ins

Installing a browser plug-in can be very simple. If you try to load a file type that your browser cannot handle, you may simply have to follow a series of quick steps to automatically install it. If you're lucky, you'll see something like the box in Figure 5.7, asking whether you want to install and run the plug-in. All you need to do is click the **Yes** button and the plug-in is installed. (It's up to you to decide whether you want to take the security risk implied by the message in the dialog box. There's no easy answer here; all I can say is that in the vast majority of cases it's going to be safe to download and install the software—but that doesn't mean it isn't possible for someone to create a plug-in that is designed to do bad things to your computer!)

Unfortunately, installing plug-ins and viewers is not always this simple. Although it doesn't have to be rocket science, it often takes a few more steps.

Figure 5.7

Installing the BubbleViewer (`http://www.ipix.com/`) was as easy as clicking the Yes button.

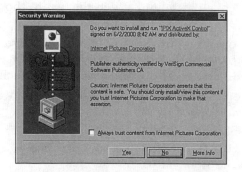

Installing a Plug-In

Installing a plug-in the "hard" way is still pretty easy. In some cases, you may have to transfer and install the plug-in. Transfer the installation file from the Web and place it in a download directory (see Chapter 15, "Finding What You Need Online"). Then, run the file (double-click it, for instance) to run the installation program. The installation program might run immediately, or you might find that a series of files are extracted from the one you downloaded, in which case you have to run a SETUP.EXE file to start the installation program. Follow the instructions to install the file. After you have installed the plug-in, your browser will be able to automatically call the plug-in anytime it needs it.

By the way, your browser might sometimes tell you when you need a plug-in. For instance, if you see the dialog box shown in Figure 5.8 (or something similar), you have displayed a Web page with an embedded file format that requires a plug-in. You can click the **Get the Plugin** button, and the browser will open another window and take you to a page with information about plug-ins.

Figure 5.8

This Netscape dialog box opens when you click a link that loads a file requiring a plug-in you don't have.

Installing a Viewer

Installing a viewer is a little more complicated than installing a plug-in, but it's still not rocket science. There are generally two different types of viewer installations. One is the type used by the early versions of Netscape and by the Macintosh and UNIX versions of Netscape. In this type of installation, you tell the browser which viewer to work with for each file type. You also add information about a particular viewer to a list of viewers that the browser refers to when it needs to handle the appropriate file type.

The other method is that used by the Windows versions of Internet Explorer and by the Windows versions of Netscape Navigator 4 and later. These use the Windows file associations to set up viewers. For instance, by default, Windows associates WAV files with the Sound Recorder program. That means if you double-click a WAV file in File Manager, Sound Recorder opens and plays the file. Internet Explorer and Navigator 4 and 4.5 use the same systemwide file-association system to determine which program should be used when it comes across a file type.

The next section gives you a look at installing a viewer in a Windows version of Internet Explorer, which is very similar to what you would do in the Windows version of Netscape Navigator 4 or 4.5. The section after that covers installing a viewer in a Windows version of Netscape Navigator 3, which is similar to the way installation is handled in other, non-Windows versions of Navigator and in some other browsers.

Installing a Viewer in Internet Explorer

When you install a viewer in Internet Explorer, you're not merely modifying Internet Explorer's internal settings; you are modifying the Windows file-association settings. When you click a file type that Internet Explorer doesn't recognize, it opens the dialog box shown in Figure 5.9. (This dialog box is similar to what you saw from Netscape.) Because Explorer doesn't recognize the file type, you have to tell it what to do. Click the **Open It Using an Application on Your Computer** option button, and then click **OK**. Explorer transfers the file and then tries to open it.

Figure 5.9

If Explorer doesn't recognize a file, you will see this dialog box.

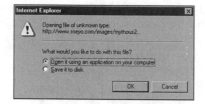

You'll then see the Open With dialog box, shown next in Figure 5.10. Type a name for this type of file into the text box at the top. Then, if you can find the viewer you want to use in this list, click it and click **OK**. If you can't find it, click the **Other** button. In the Open dialog box that appears, select the viewer you want to use.

Figure 5.10

Enter a name for the file type, and then choose the application you want to use as a viewer.

Installing a Viewer in Explorer Beforehand

You can also install an Internet Explorer viewer before you need it. You do this using the File Types system, which you can access from the Windows Explorer file-management utility or, in some versions of Internet Explorer and in Netscape Navigator 4, from within the browser.

Open Windows Explorer, and then select **View**, **Options** (or **View**, **Folder Options** in some versions of Windows), and then click the **File Types** tab. You'll see an Options dialog box similar to that shown in Figure 5.11. In Netscape Navigator 4 for Windows, select **Edit**, **Preferences**, and then open the **Navigator** category and click the **Applications** subcategory. The Navigator dialog boxes will be slightly different from those shown here, but similar enough for you to be able to follow along.

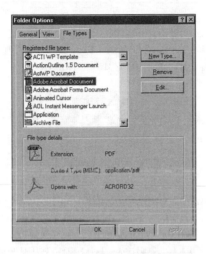

Figure 5.11

You can add viewers to Internet Explorer using the Options dialog box.

To add a new viewer, click the **New Type** button, and then fill in all the information in the dialog box that appears. Enter the description (whatever you want to call it), the file extensions used by that file type, and the MIME type. Click the **New** button and type **open** in the first text box you see. Then, click the **Browse** button and find the application you want to use as the viewer.

What's MIME?

MIME stands for multipurpose Internet mail extensions. Although originally intended for email transmission of files, MIME is used on the Web to identify file formats. You can find detailed information about MIME and a large list of MIME types at http://www.cis. ohio-state.edu/hypertext/faq/usenet/mail/mime-faq/top.html or at http://home.netscape.com/assist/helper_apps/mime.html.

Installing a Viewer in Netscape 3

This section explains how to configure a viewer in the Windows version of Netscape Navigator 3. The process is similar in earlier versions of Netscape and even in other browsers. Rather than modifying the list of Windows file associations, you're modifying a list belonging to the browser. (For Windows versions of Netscape 4 and 4.5, go back and read the Internet Explorer instructions; these versions of Netscape use a similar method.)

Suppose you came across a link that looked interesting, and you clicked it. Netscape displayed the Unknown File Type dialog box, shown in Figure 5.12. This means that Netscape doesn't recognize the file, so you have to tell it what to do.

Figure 5.12

The Unknown File Type dialog box opens if you click a link to a file that Netscape doesn't recognize.

If you want, you can click the **More Info** button. Netscape will open another browser window and display an information document with a link to a page from which, perhaps, you can download a plug-in. Let's assume that you already know there is no plug-in for this particular file type or that for some other reason you want to configure a viewer. Click the **Pick App** button, and you'll see the dialog box in Figure 5.13.

Figure 5.13

The Configure External Viewer dialog box lets you define which viewer should handle the file type.

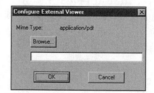

Click the **Browse** button and then find the program that you know can handle this type of file. (Remember, you can find viewers at the sites listed in Appendix C.) Double-click the program, and it is placed into the Configure External Viewer dialog box. Then click **OK**. That's it! You've just configured the viewer. The file referenced by the link you clicked will now be transferred to your computer and sent to the program you defined as the viewer. The viewer will then display the file (assuming, of course, that you picked the right viewer).

Setting Up Netscape Navigator Beforehand

You can also set up Netscape Navigator's viewers before you ever get to a site that uses unusual file formats. Choose **Edit**, **Preferences**, and then open the **Navigator** category and click the **Applications** subcategory. Or, if you're using an early version of

Navigator, choose **Options**, **General Preferences**, and then click the **Helpers** tab. You'll see the dialog box shown in Figure 5.14.

What's That Button For?

In case you're wondering, the **Unknown: Prompt User** option button is the default setting for formats that haven't been set up with a viewer. If you click a file for which you've configured this setting, Netscape will ask you what to do with the files of this type when they are transferred to your browser.

The big list shows all the different file types (well, most of them; you can add more using the **Create New Type** button). To configure a viewer for one, click it in the list and then click one of the **Actions**. You can tell Netscape to **Save to Disk** if you want, but if you intend to configure a viewer, click **Launch the Application** instead. Then click the **Browse** button to find the application you want to use as the viewer.

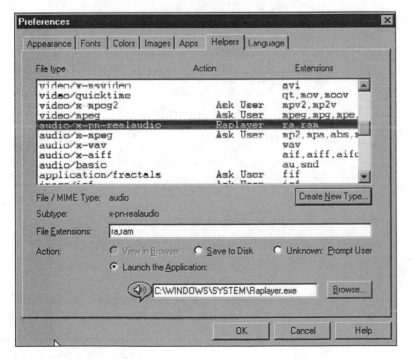

Figure 5.14

You can preconfigure viewers in Netscape's Preferences dialog box.

The Least You Need to Know

➤ A browser can handle many file formats: HTML, text, graphics, and sounds of various kinds. If a browser encounters a file format that it can't handle, it tries to pass the file to a viewer or plug-in.

➤ Viewers and plug-ins are designed to play or display file types that browsers can't handle. The difference between the two is that a plug-in temporarily converts the browser window into a viewer, but a viewer is a completely separate program that opens without changing the browser window in any way.

➤ If you are using Microsoft Windows, you'll find that most of the file types you'll run across can be handled by existing viewers.

➤ Some of the most common media types you'll run across are Flash, Shockwave, MP3, and video and audio files that can be played by RealPlayer or Windows Media Player.

➤ There are hundreds of viewers and plug-ins for scores of file types. Most of these file types are rarely used, however.

➤ If your browser comes across a file type that it doesn't recognize, it asks you what to do. You can then install a plug-in or specify a viewer.

➤ In many cases a plug-in can be installed with a single mouse click.

Part 2
Communicating

What is the Internet if not a communications tool? In this part of the book, you'll learn how to communicate directly with others online. I'll begin by explaining how to use email, the single most important communication tool online.

You'll also learn about a system called chat. No, it's not really chat—instead of talking, you type—but many people find it to be a great way to while away an hour or ten. And then there's instant messaging, a system that has brought many friends and families into almost continual communication; people leave their instant messenger windows open whenever their computers are on, just waiting for someone to say something.

I'll tell you about the Internet's hundreds of thousands of discussion groups, too (newsgroups, bulletin boards, and mailing lists); about other strange systems that let you speak to people anywhere in the world for next to nothing, or carry out videoconferences across the continents. And I'll even show you how to get your message out on the Web, by creating your own Web pages.

Chapter 6

Sending and Receiving Email

In This Chapter

➤ Which email program are you using?

➤ All about email addresses

➤ Setting up your email program

➤ Sending a message

➤ Retrieving your messages—then what?

➤ Sending files across the Internet

➤ Avoiding fights

Although email might not be as exciting, cool, or compelling as some other Internet tools, it is the most popular; and, in many ways, the most useful Internet service. More people use email on any given day than use any other Internet service. Tens of millions of messages fly across the wires each day. According to *Wired* magazine, publishing via email—newsletters, bulletins, even small books—is growing very quickly, perhaps more quickly than publishing on the World Wide Web.

Despite all the glitz of the Web (you learned about that glitz in Chapters 2 through 5, the chapters about the World Wide Web), the potential of Internet phone systems (Chapter 12, "More Ways to Communicate—Net Phones, Conferences, Video-conferences."), and the excitement—for some—of the many chat systems (Chapter 8,

"Using Online Chat Rooms"), email is probably the most productive tool there is. Email is a sort of Internet workhorse, getting the work done without any great fanfare.

After spending huge sums of money polling Internet users, we've come to the conclusion that the very first thing Internet users want to do is send email messages. Sending email messages is not too threatening, and it's an understandable concept: You're sending a letter. The only differences are that you don't take it to the post office and that it's much faster. So, that's what I'm going to start with: how to send an email message.

Start with What You Were Given

I suggest you start off using the email program that you were given when you set up your account. You might be able to use something else later. If you'd like to try Eudora later, go to **http://www.Eudora. com/**. Free versions of Eudora are available for the Macintosh and Windows, you just have to put up with some advertisements. You can find Pegasus at **http://www.PMail. com/**.

Which Email System?

Which email system do you use? If you are a member of an online service, you have a built-in mail system. But if you are not a member of one of the major online services, who the heck knows what you are using for email! I don't. For that matter, even with an online service, there are different options; CompuServe, for instance, offers a number of different programs you can use.

Basically, it all depends on what your service provider set you up with. You might be using Netscape, a World Wide Web browser (discussed in Chapter 2) that has a built-in email program. Or perhaps you're using Microsoft Exchange, which comes with Windows 95 and NT4, or if you are working with a very recent version of Windows 95 or subsequent Windows versions, you might be using Outlook Express. If you are a Microsoft Office user, you may be using Outlook. You could be using Eudora, which is one of the most popular email programs on the Internet, or perhaps Pegasus. Or you might be using something else entirely. Luckily, the email concepts are all the same, regardless of the type of program you are using—even if the buttons you click are different.

To POP or Not to POP

POP (Post Office Protocol) is a very common system used for handling Internet email. A POP server receives email that's been sent to you and holds it until you use your mail program to retrieve it. However, POP's not ubiquitous; some online services and many companies do not use POP.

Why do you care what system is used to hold your mail? After all, all you really care about is the program you use to collect and read the mail, not what arcane system your company or service provider uses. However, the POP issue becomes important if you want to change mail programs. In general, the best and most advanced email programs are designed to be used with POP servers. So, if you need some specific email features and have decided you want to switch to another mail program, you might find you can't do so.

Suppose that you have an America Online or CompuServe account. The mail programs provided by these systems are quite basic. They lack many features that programs such as Eudora have, such as advanced filtering. (Filtering allows you to automatically carry out actions on incoming email depending on the characteristics of that mail. For instance, you could set up the program to automatically delete all the email messages received from your boss. That way you won't be lying when you tell him you didn't receive his message.) But you might be stuck with what you've got. At the time of this writing, you could not use a POP program with an America Online account, so you couldn't install Eudora or any other POP program. On the other hand, CompuServe now does provide POP mail, but you have to sign up for this optional service (it's free; use **GO POPMAIL** to find more information). On the other hand, CompuServe 2000, the brand-new CompuServe software release, does not have a POP system, for some bizarre reason. This is a classic case of a software upgrade introducing new bugs. (This sort of design screwup is sometimes called a "buglike feature.")

Another common mail system, IMAP (Internet Message Access Protocol), is generally used by corporate networks, not Internet service providers. If you're using a corporate network, you probably won't have much choice about which mail program you can use.

You Have a New Address!

I recently discovered how to spot an absolute beginner on the Internet: He often talks about his email number, equating email with telephones. They are both electronic, after all. However, you have an *email address*. That address has three parts:

➤ Your account name

➤ The "at" sign (@)

➤ Your domain name

What's your account name? Usually it is the name you use to log on to your Internet account. For instance, when I log on to my CompuServe account, I have to type 71601,1266. That's my account name. When I log on to MSN, I use CIGInternet, and on AOL, I use PeKent. (Note that the CompuServe account name is a special case; when using this account in an email address, I have to replace the comma with a period, such as this: 71601.1266@compuserve.com.)

After your account name, you use the @ sign. Why? How else would the Internet mail system know where the account name ends and the domain name starts?

Finally, you use the domain name, which is the address of your company, your service provider, or your online service. Think of it as the street part of an address: One street (the domain name) can be used for thousands of account names.

Net Tips

Account Names: They're All the Same

CompuServe calls the account name a *User ID*, MSN calls it a *Member Name*, and AOL calls it a *Screen Name*. In addition, you might hear the account name called a *username* or *logon ID*. All these names mean the same thing: the name by which you are identified when you log on to your account. However, I discovered that some large service providers (mainly the phone companies, for some reason, who "don't quite get it") do something a little odd. You get some strange number as the account name, and you get another name to use when accessing your email. Someone at AT&T's WorldNet gave me a flip answer as to why they do this, using a sort of "well, of course, we *have* to do this, but you probably wouldn't understand" tone of voice; I wasn't convinced.

Where do you get the domain name? If you haven't been told already, ask the system administrator or tech-support people. (Later in this chapter, you learn the domain names of the larger online services.)

Web Savvy

Pronouncing Your Email Address

Here's the correct way to say an email address out loud. You say "dot" for the periods and "at" for the @ sign. Thus, **pkent@topfloor. com** is "p kent at topfloor dot com."

A Word About Setup

You might need to set up your email system before it will work. In many cases, this setup has already been done for you. If you are with one of the online services, you don't need to worry—it's done for you. Some of the Internet service providers also do all this configuring stuff for you. Others, however, expect you to get into your program and enter some information. It doesn't have to be difficult. Figure 6.1 shows some of the options you can configure in Netscape Messenger, the email program that comes—along with Navigator—as part of the Netscape Communicator package, but the options will be similar in other programs.

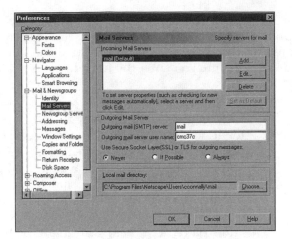

Figure 6.1

*One of several mail-
related panels in Netscape
Messenger's Preferences
dialog box, in which you
can configure the mail
program before you use it.*

Whatever program you have, you might have to enter the following information:

➤ **Incoming Mail Server**   This is usually a POP account, although if you're on a corporate network it might be an IMAP (Internet Message Access Protocol) account. When you connect to your service provider, your email program needs to check with the mail server (a program running on your service provider's system) to see whether any mail has arrived. This mail server holds the messages that arrive for you until your mail program asks for them. Your account name is usually the same as the account name that you use to log on to your service. You might need to enter the full account name and the server hostname (for instance, in Netscape Messenger, I enter pkent, my account name, in the Mail Server User Name box, and then enter the server name—topfloor.com—in the Incoming Mail Server text box, and click the **POP** option button). On some systems, such as Eudora, you might have to enter the account name and server name all together in one box.

➤ **SMTP (Simple Mail Transfer Protocol) Server**   This mail program is used to send mail. While the POP account holds your incoming mail, the SMTP server transmits your messages onto the Internet. This time you'll enter a hostname (mail.usa.net, for instance) or maybe a number (something such as 192.156.196.1) that your service provider has given to you.

➤ **Password**   You'll need to enter your password so the email program can check the POP for mail. This password is generally the same one you use to log onto the system. Some programs, however, don't request your password until the first time you log on to retrieve your mail.

➤ **Real Name**   This is, yes, your actual name. Most mail programs will send your name along with the email address when you send email in the From line of the message.

➤ **Return or Reply To Address**   You can make the email program place a different Reply To address on your messages. For instance, if you send mail from work but want to receive responses to those messages at home, you'd use a different Reply To address. If you do this, be sure you enter the full address (such as pkent@topfloor.com).

➤ **All Sorts of Other Stuff**   You can get a good mail program to do all sorts of things. You can tell it how often to check the POP to see whether new mail has arrived, choose the font you want the message displayed in, and get the program to automatically include the original message when you reply to a message. You can even tell it to leave messages at the POP server after you retrieve them. This might be handy if you like to check your mail from work; if you configure the program to leave the messages at the POP, you can retrieve them again when you get home, using the program on your home machine. You can also define how the program will handle attachments, but that is a complicated subject that I'll get to in the later section "Sending Files Is Getting Easier."

What Else Can I Do with My Mail Program?

You might be able to do lots of things. Check your documentation or Help files, or browse through the configuration dialog boxes to see what you can do. Note, however, that the online services' email programs generally have a limited number of choices. Email programs such as Eudora, Pegasus, and those included with Netscape Communicator and Internet Explorer have many more choices.

There are so many email programs around; I can't help you configure them all. If you have trouble configuring your program, check the documentation or call the service's technical support. As I've said before, if your service doesn't want to help, find another service!

Sending a Message

Now that you understand addresses and have configured the mail program, you can send a message. So, to whom can you mail a message? You might already have friends and colleagues whom you can bother with your flippant "Hey, I've finally made it onto the Internet" message. Or mail me at testmail@topfloor.com, and I'll send a response back to you. (To do that, I'll use something called an *autoresponder*, a program that automatically replies to messages that it receives.)

So, start your email program, and then open the window in which you are going to write the message. You might have to double-click an icon or choose a menu option that opens the mail's Compose window. For instance, in Eudora, after the program is open, you click the **New Message** button on the toolbar or choose **Message, New Message**.

In all the email programs, the Compose window has certain common elements. Some programs have a few extras. Here's what you might find:

➤ **To**   This line is for the address of the person you are mailing to. If you are using an online service and you are sending a message to another member of that service, all you need to use is the person's account name. For instance, if you are an AOL member and you're mailing to another AOL member with the screen name of PeKent, that's all you need to enter. To mail to that member from a service other than AOL, however, you enter the full address: pekent@aol.com. (I'll explain more about mailing to online services later in this chapter, in the section "We Are All One: Sending Email to Online Services.")

➤ **From**   Not all mail programs show this line, but it shows your email address, which is included in the message header (the clutter at the top of an Internet message). It lets the recipient know whom to reply to.

➤ **Reply To**   You might have both a From address (to show which account the message came from) and a Reply To address (to get the recipient to reply to a different address).

➤ **Subject**   This line is a sort of message title—a few words summarizing the contents. The recipient can scan through a list of subjects to see what each message is about. (Some mail programs won't let you send a message unless you fill in the Subject line; others, perhaps most, don't mind if you leave it blank.)

➤ **Cc**   You can enter an address here to send a copy to someone other than the person whose address you placed in the To line.

➤ **Bc**   This means "blind copy." As with the Cc line, a copy of the message will be sent to the address (or addresses) you place in the Bc (or Bcc) line; however, the recipient of the original message won't be able to tell that the Bcc address received a copy. (If you use Cc, the recipient of the original message sees a Cc line in the header.)

Online Services

If you are working in one of the old CompuServe programs, choose **Mail**, **Create New Mail**. With CompuServe 2000, click the big **Create Mail** button in the toolbar. In AOL, choose **Mail**, **Compose Mail**. In MSN, you open the **Communicate** menu and select **Send or Read Email**. (If you're still working with the old version of the MSN software, click the big **Email** bar in MSN Central.) If you are using Netscape's email program, there are all sorts of ways to begin: Select **File**, **New**, **Message**, for instance.

Don't Cc to a List!

If you want to mail a message to a large list of people, don't put all the addresses into the Cc line. Addresses in the Cc line will be visible to all recipients, and most people don't like the idea of their email address being given away to strangers. Instead, put the list into the Bcc line. Addresses in the Bcc line will not be displayed anywhere in the email message.

103

➤ **Attachments**   This option is for sending computer files along with the message. (Again, I'll get to that later in this chapter, in the section "Sending Files Is Getting Easier.")

➤ **A big blank area**   This area is where you type your message.

Email programs vary greatly, and not all programs have all these features. Again, the online service mail programs tend to be a bit limited. Figures 6.2 and 6.3 show the Compose window in two very different mail programs.

Figure 6.2

This is Eudora, one of the Internet's most popular mail services.

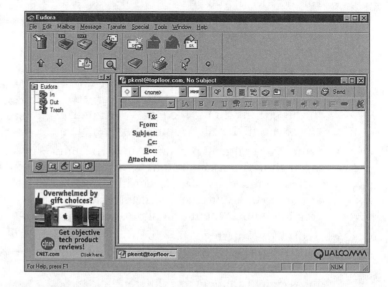

Figure 6.3

This is CompuServe 2000's mail composition window.

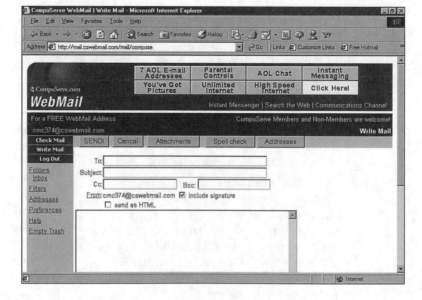

Go ahead and type a To address; Email testmail@topfloor.com, and you'll get a response. Or email to your own address. If you use an online service, you might as well use the entire Internet address (for instance, on AOL type name@aol.com). The message will probably go out onto the Internet and then turn around and come back to you. I'll explain those online service addresses in the next section.

We Are All One: Sending Email to Online Services

One of the especially nice things about the Internet, from an email point of view, is that because all the online services are now connected to the Internet, you can send email between online services. (Not so long ago the online services were completely separate; you could email someone on a service only if you had an account with that service.) Perhaps you have an America Online account because AOL sent you a disk in the mail. Perhaps your brother has a CompuServe account because he's a geek, and that's where the geeks have been hanging out for years. (Before you email me to complain, I've had a CompuServe account for almost 15 years.) You can send email to one another, using the Internet as a sort of bridge. How? You just have to know the other person's account name on that service and that service's domain name.

For instance, CompuServe has this Internet domain name: compuserve.com. Say you want to send an email message to someone at CompuServe who has the account name (or User ID as it's called on CompuServe) of 71601,1266. You add the two together with the @ in the middle. Then, you have 71601,1266@compuserve.com. However, you can't have a comma in an Internet address. So, you replace it with a period, and you end up with 71601.1266@compuserve.com. (Some CompuServe users have "proper" email addresses, names instead of numbers. If you use CompuServe and want one of these real addresses, use **GO REGISTER**.) The following table lists a few services and tells you how to send email to them.

Table 6.1   Sending Email to Other Services

Service	Method of Addressing
America Online	Add @aol.com to the end of an America Online address.
CompuServe	In the User ID, replace the comma (,) with a period (.), and then add @compuserve.com to the end (these days many CompuServe members have Internet-style addresses, although probably most still have the old style, such as 71601,1266, which would be written as 71601.1266@compuserve.com).
MCImail	Add @mcimail.com to the end of an MCImail address.
Microsoft Network	Add @msn.com to the end of the MSN Member name.
Prodigy	Add @prodigy.com to the end of the user's Prodigy address.

These addresses are quite easy. Of course, there are more complicated Internet addresses, but you'll rarely run into them. However, if you have trouble emailing someone, call and ask exactly what you must type as his email address. (There's no rule that says you can't use the telephone anymore.)

Write the Message

Now that you have the address onscreen, write your message—whatever you want to say. Then, send the message. How's that done? There's usually a big **Send** button, or maybe a menu option that says **Send** or **Mail**. What happens when you click the button? That depends on the program and whether you are logged on at the moment. Generally, if you are logged on, the mail is sent immediately. Not always, though. Some programs will put the message in a queue and won't send the message until told to do so. Others will send the message immediately, and if you are not logged on, they will try to log on first. Watch closely and you'll usually see what's happening. A message will let you know whether the message is being sent. If it hasn't been sent, look for some kind of **Send Immediately** menu option or perhaps **Send Queued Messages**. Whether the message should be sent immediately or put in a queue is often one of the configuration options available to you.

Where'd It Go? Incoming Email

You've sent yourself an email message, but where did it go? It went out into the electronic wilderness to wander around for a few seconds or maybe a few minutes. Sometimes email messages can take a few hours to reach their destinations. Very occasionally, it even takes a few days. (Generally, the message comes back in a few minutes, especially if you're sending yourself a message, unless you mistyped the address, in which case you'll get a special message telling you that it's a bad address.)

Now it's time to check for incoming email. If you are using an online service, as soon as you log on you'll see a message saying that email has arrived. If you are already online, you might see a message telling you that mail has arrived, or you might need to check periodically; you might find a Get New Mail menu option. If you are working with an Internet service provider, you generally won't be informed of incoming mail; rather your email program has to go and check. Either you can do that manually (for instance, in Eudora, there's a **File**, **Check Mail** command), or you can configure the program to check automatically every so often.

What Now?

What can you do with your incoming email? All sorts of things. I think I'm pretty safe in saying that every email program allows you to read incoming messages. Most programs also let you print and save messages (if your program doesn't, you need another). You can also delete them, forward them to someone else, or reply directly to the sender. These commands should be easy to find. Generally you'll have toolbar buttons for the most important commands, and more options will be available if you dig around a little in the menus, too.

Fancy Fonts

Some of the online services allow you to use fancy text formatting features. For example, MSN and AOL let you use colors, indents, different fonts, bold, italic, and so on. But in general these features work only in messages sent *within* the online services. Internet email is plain text—nothing fancy. Don't bother getting fancy in your Internet email because the online service's email system will strip out all that attractive stuff when the message is sent out onto the Internet. However, there is a system you can use to send formatted email, if both you and the recipient have the right type of mail program— HTML Mail. We'll take a quick look at HTML Mail in Chapter 7, "Advanced Email—HTML Mail, Voice, and Encryption."

A Word About Quoting

It's a good idea to quote when you respond to a message. This means that you include part or all the original message. Some programs automatically quote the original message. Different programs mark quoted messages in different ways; usually, you'll see a greater than symbol (>) at the beginning of each line. Figure 6.4 shows a reply message that contains a quote from the original message.

You aren't required to quote. But if you don't, the recipient might not know what you are talking about. I receive scores of messages a day and I know people who get hundreds. (Of course, the radiation emitted from their computer screens is probably frying their brains.) If you respond to a message without reminding the recipient exactly which of the 200 messages he sent out last week (or which of the five he sent to you) you are responding to, he might be slightly confused. Quoting is especially important when sending messages to mailing lists and newsgroups (discussed in Chapter 10, "Finding and Using Newsgroups"), where your message might be read by people who didn't read the message to which you are responding.

Figure 6.4

Quote the original message when responding to remind the sender what he said.

```
Re: Confused - Message (HTML)                                    _ □ X
File   Edit   View   Insert   Format   Tools   Actions   Help    Type a question for help.  ▾
Send  🖫 🖨 ✂ 🗎 🗎 ! ↓ ▾ Follow Up... ⬚ Options... ❓  » Courier New  ▾ »

To...    Loyal Fan <LF@xyz.com>
Cc...
Subject: Re: Confused

Dear Fan:

At 08:02 PM 04/4/2001 -0800, the sender wrote:
>Peter:
>
>I am enjoying your book. However, would you please
explain why some repeat my words back to me in my emails.
It confuses me.

It is a good idea to quote part or all of the original
message (as I am doing here) when you respond to a message.
Some people get hundreds of email messages each day.
This practice puts your reply in a frame of reference.

Look for the greater than symbols (>) that separate the
quoted message from the reply.

Hope this ends your confusion. I'm glad that my book is helpful.

Peter
```

In the Old Days

There used to be four ways to send files. Using **MIME** (Multimedia Internet Mail Extensions); **uuencode** (the file was converted to plain ASCII text); **BinHex** (a system similar to uuencode, used by Macintosh computers); and various methods used by different online services. These days the situation is much improved and you can let your email program figure out how to transmit files.

Sending Files Is Getting Easier

I used to hate sending files across the Internet. Not because it was so difficult to send files (although it was), but because it was sort of embarrassing to admit how difficult it was. I recall, for instance, the incredible problems I had transferring computer files to *Internet World*, of all magazines, early in 1995. It didn't matter what transmission format I used, or what program I was working with; the staff at the magazine couldn't seem to open those files. Today the situation is much improved, and the problems inherent in file transfers are, for many users, a thing of the past.

I'll assume you're working with decent software. Most programs these days can transmit and receive files. You can email files from Outlook to Eudora, from Eudora to CompuServe, from CompuServe to AOL, from AOL to Pegasus, and so on.

Your program will have some kind of command that enables you to insert or attach a file. For instance, in Eudora choose **Message, Attach File**. In AOL, click the **Attach** button; in CompuServe (see Figure 6.5), use the **Write Mail** button in the main window and then click the **Attachment** button in the Web Mail window.

Figure 6.5

Sending a file with your email is usually as simple as clicking a button and selecting the file.

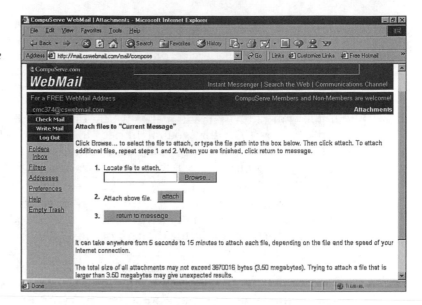

Cool Things You Can Do with Email

After you understand your email system and realize that it won't bite, you might begin to enjoy using it. The following list contains suggestions of some things you might want to do with your email program:

➤ **Create a mailing list**   You can create a special mailing list that contains the email addresses of many people. For instance, if you want to send a message to everyone in your department (or family, or club) at the same time, you can create a mailing list. Put all the addresses in the list, and then send the message to the list. Everyone on the list receives the message, and you save time and hassle. Some programs will have a mailing list dialog box of some sort; others let you create a nickname or alias for the mailing list and then associate the addresses with it.

➤ **Create an address book**   Virtually all email systems have address books, and they're usually quite easy to use. You can store a person's complicated email address and then retrieve it quickly using the person's real name.

➤ **Use aliases**   An alias, sometimes known as a *nickname*, is a simple identifier you give to someone in your address book. Instead of typing peter kent or pkent@topfloor.com, for instance, you could just type a simple alias such as pk to address a message to that person.

➤ **Work with mail while you're offline**   Most programs these days let you read and write email offline. The program quickly logs on to send and retrieve messages, and then logs off again automatically. This feature is of particular importance with services that charge you for the amount of time you are online.

➤ **Forward your mail**   After being on the Internet for a while, there's a risk of attaining real geekhood by getting multiple Internet accounts, such as one with your favorite online service, one at work, one with a cheap service provider, and so on. (Right now, I have about eight, I think.) That's a lot of trouble logging on to check for email. However, some services let you forward your email to another account so that if a message arrives at, say, the account you use at home, you can have it automatically sent on to you at work. Ask your service provider how to do this; you might need to log on to your shell account to set this up (discussed in Chapter 22, "21 Questions—The Complete Internet FAQ"). Although most Internet service providers let you do this, the online services generally don't.

➤ **Create a vacation message**   When you go on vacation, your email doesn't stop. That's why so many cybergeeks never go on vacation, or take a laptop if they do: They can't bear the thought of missing all those messages. Still, if you manage to break away, you might be able to set a special vacation message, an automatic response to any incoming mail that says basically, "I'm away, be back soon." (You get to write the response message.) Again, ask your service provider. The online services generally don't have this service.

➤ **Filter your files**   Sophisticated email programs have file-filtering capabilities. You can tell the program to look at incoming mail and carry out certain actions according to what it finds. You can place email from your newsgroups into special inboxes, grab only the message subject if the message is very long, delete mail from certain people or organizations, and so on.

Caution: Email Can Be Dangerous!

The more I use email, the more I believe that it can be a dangerous tool. There are three main problems: 1) People often don't realize the implications of what they are saying, 2) people often misinterpret what others are saying, and 3) people are comfortable typing things into a computer that they would never say to a person face-to-face. Consequently, online fights are common both in private (between email correspondents) and in public (in the newsgroups and mailing lists).

The real problem is that when you send an email message, the recipient can't see your face or hear your tone of voice. Of course, when you write a letter, you have the same problem, but email is replacing conversations as well as letters. The U.S. Post Office is as busy as ever, so I figure email is mainly replacing conversations. That contributes to the problem because people are writing messages in a chatty conversational style, forgetting that email lacks all the visual and auditory "cues" that go along with a conversation.

In the interest of world peace, I give you these email guidelines to follow:

➤ **Don't write something you will regret later**   Lawsuits have been based on the contents of electronic messages, so consider what you are writing and whether you would want it to be read by someone other than the recipient. A message can always be forwarded, read over the recipient's shoulder, printed out and passed around, backed up onto the company's archives, and so on. You don't have to use email—there's always the telephone.

➤ **Consider the tone of your message**   It's easy to try to be flippant and come out as arrogant or to try to be funny and come out as sarcastic. When you write, think about how your words will appear to the recipient.

➤ **Give the sender the benefit of the doubt**   If a person's message sounds arrogant or sarcastic, consider that he might be trying to be flippant or funny! If you are not sure what the person is saying, ask him to explain.

➤ **Read before you send**   It will give you a chance to fix embarrassing spelling and grammatical errors and to reconsider what you've just said. (Some mail programs have spell checkers.)

➤ **Wait a day...or three**   If you typed something in anger, wait a few days before sending it and read the message again. Give yourself a chance to reconsider.

➤ **Be nice**   There's no need for vulgarity or rudeness (except in certain newsgroups, where it seems to be a requirement for entrance).

➤ **Attack the argument, not the person**   I've seen fights start when someone disagrees with another person's views and sends a message making a personal attack upon that person. (This point is more related to mailing lists and newsgroups than email proper, but we are on the subject of avoiding fights.) Instead of saying, "Anyone who thinks *Days of Our Lives* is not worth the electrons it's transmitted on must be a half-witted moron with all the common sense of the average pineapple," consider saying, "You might think it's not very good, but clearly many other people find great enjoyment in this show."

➤ **Use smileys**   One way to add some of those missing visual and auditory cues is to add smileys—keep reading.

You're Being Baited

Some people send rude or vicious messages because they *enjoy* getting into a fight like this—where they can fight from the safety of their computer terminals. Avoid conversations with people who are obviously baiting you.

Share the Smiles

Many people call these character faces "smiley faces." But if you'd like to impress your friends with a bit of technobabble, you can call them *emoticons*. If you really want to impress your colleagues, visit Dave Barry's Emoticons library, at `http://www.randomhouse.com/features/davebarry/emoticon.html`, which contains thousands of entries.

Smile and Be Understood!

Over the past few years, email users have developed a number of ways to clarify the meaning of messages. You might see <g> at the end of the line, for example. This means grin and is shorthand for saying, "You know, of course, that what I just said was a joke, right?" You might also see :-) in the message. Turn this book sideways, so that the left column of this page is up and the right column is down, and you'll see that this symbol is a small smiley face. It means the same as <g>, "Of course, that was a joke, okay?"

Emoticons Galore

Little pictures are commonly known as *smileys*. But the smiley face, although by far the most common, is just one of many available symbols. You might see some of the emoticons in the following table, and you might want to use them. Perhaps you can create a few of your own.

Table 6.2   Commonly Used Emoticons

Emoticon	Meaning
:-(	Sadness, disappointment
8-)	Kinda goofy-looking smile, or wearing glasses
:->	A big smile
;-)	A wink
*<|:-)	Santa Claus
:-&	Tongue-tied
:-o	A look of shock
:-p	Tongue stuck out
=:o]	Bill Clinton
,:-) or 7:^]	Ronald Reagan

(For a handy reference to smileys, see `http://www.parscom.cz/clients/smilies/index.html`.) Personally, I don't like smileys much. They strike me as being just a *tiiiny* bit too cutesy. However, I do use them now and again to make absolutely sure that I'm not misunderstood!

Message Shorthand

There are a couple of other ways people try to liven up their messages. One is to use obscure acronyms such as the ones in this table.

Table 6.3 Online Shorthand

Acronym	Meaning
BTW	By the way
FWIW	For what it's worth
FYI	For your information
<G>	Grin
IMO	In my opinion
IMHO	In my humble opinion
LOL	Laughing out loud (used as an aside to show your disbelief)
OTFL	On the floor, laughing (used as an aside)
PMFBI	Pardon me for butting in
PMFJI	Pardon me for jumping in
RTFM	Read the &*^%# manual
ROTFL or ROFL	Rolling on the floor laughing (used as an aside)
ROTFLMAO	Same as above, except with "laughing my a** off" added on the end. (You didn't expect me to say it, did you? This is a family book, and anyway, the editors won't let me.)
TIA	Thanks in advance
YMMV	Your mileage might vary

The real benefit of using these is that they confuse the average neophyte. I suggest that you learn them quickly, so you can pass for a longterm cybergeek.

You'll also see different ways of stressing particular words. (You can't use bold and italic in most Internet email, remember?) You might see words marked with an underscore on each side (_now!_) or, perhaps frequently, with an asterisk (*now!*).

The Least You Need to Know

➤ There are many different email systems, but the basic procedures all work similarly.

➤ Even if your online service lets you use fancy text (colors, different fonts, different styles) within the service, that text won't work in Internet messages (see Chapter 7 for information on HTML Mail).

➤ Sending files across the Internet is much easier now than it was just a year or so ago, but problems still arise; sending files within the online services is always easy.

➤ On the Internet, the most common file-transfer method is MIME; uuencode is also used now and then. These often are built into mail programs, or you can use external utilities to convert the files.

➤ In most cases these days, you can just attach a file and send it—it'll probably get through okay. But things can go wrong now and then, especially if the sender or recipient is using an old program.

➤ Get to know all the neat little things your email program can do for you, such as create mailing lists and filter files.

➤ Be careful with email; misunderstandings (and fights) are common.

Chapter 7

Advanced Email—HTML Mail, Voice, and Encryption

In This Chapter

➤ HTML Mail: An end to plain old text messages?

➤ Email encryption

➤ Public-key encryption and how it works

➤ Digitally signing your messages

➤ Why key length makes a difference

➤ Using your voice in emails

➤ Faxes, voice messages, and more

Email has changed quite a bit over the past year or so and will continue to change dramatically over the next year or so, thanks to two important systems: HTML Mail and encryption.

The first of these, HTML Mail, livens up email a little—in some cases, quite a lot. HTML Mail enables you to use different colors for the text in your messages, to work with different font sizes and styles, to create bulleted lists and centered text, and even to insert pictures and sounds.

Although encryption has been available for a few years, it was too complicated to catch on. Now email encryption—the ability to encrypt, or scramble, email messages to make them unreadable to all but the recipient—is being built into email programs, which makes it easier to use. I used to predict that everyone would be using encryption pretty soon, but I've given up on that prediction. Most people just don't seem to care. Still, the systems are available if you need them, so I'll explain what encryption can do for you and how to use it.

Banish Dull Email with HTML Mail

HTML Mail is a system in which HTML tags can be used within email messages. *HTML* means Hypertext Markup Language, and as you learned in the World Wide Web chapters of this book (Chapters 2 to 5, and Chapter 13), HTML is used to create World Wide Web pages. HTML tags are the codes inserted into a Web page that tell a Web browser how to display the page. These tags can be used to modify the manner in which text appears on the page—its color, size, style, and so on—and where the text appears on the page. They can be used to create tables, insert pictures and Java applications, and plenty more. Now that HTML is coming to email, email messages can be far more than just plain text.

To use HTML Mail, you need two things. First, you need an HTML Mail program. Second (but just as important), you need to ensure that the recipient has an HTML Mail program. If you send an HTML Mail message to someone who doesn't have an HTML Mail program, that person won't see all the formatting you've added to the message. Worse, depending on the program you've used, the message the person receives might be very difficult to read because it will be full of HTML tags. (Some HTML Mail programs insert a plain-text version of the message at the beginning of the message, so a recipient who isn't using an HTML Mail program can still read the message.)

Finding an HTML Mail Program

Most recent mail programs can work with HTML Mail in some form or other. If you're working with Netscape Messenger or Microsoft Outlook, the two most commonly used programs on the Internet, you have an HTML Mail–capable program. Most other major programs also work with HTML Mail, too—Eudora and Pegasus, for instance. You can see a couple of these HTML programs at work in Figures 7.1 and 7.2. Unfortunately, some of the online services' email systems use a different method. CompuServe 2000, for instance, allows you to format your messages with colors, bolding, and so on, and even to insert images. But they're not using HTML Mail, so people receiving the messages in an HTML Mail program won't be able to view them properly. If people with HTML Mail programs send formatted mail to CompuServe 2000, it won't be received in the correct format.

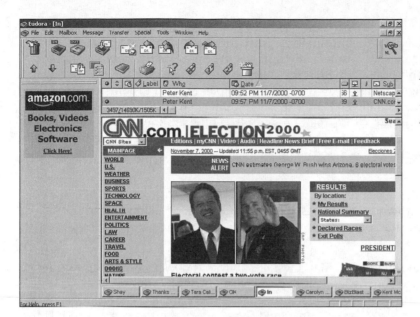

Figure 7.1

This is a Web page transmitted to a Eudora email program. Because Eudora works well with HTML Mail, it can display the page inside the message.

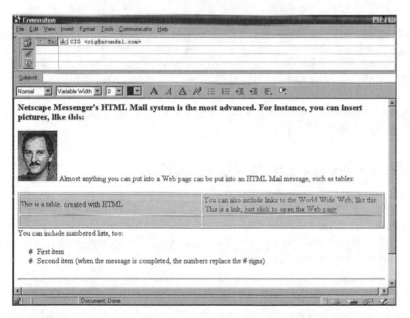

Figure 7.2

Netscape Messenger, the program that introduced HTML Mail to the world.

Different Programs, Different Abilities

Just because an email program supports HTML Mail doesn't mean that it supports it well or in the best way. Some programs can handle a few simple things, but not the more complicated processes involved with HTML Mail.

Suppose you insert an image into a message using Netscape Messenger. That image will be transferred along with the email message. If the recipient has Netscape Messenger, the image will be displayed within the message exactly where it should be. If the user has another HTML Mail program, though, the image might not be displayed in the message; it might be saved on the recipient's hard disk instead. Some HTML Mail programs won't even send the inserted image with the message. The early HTML Mail versions of Netscape's mail program (the program included with Netscape Navigator 3) inserted a link to the image instead of transferring the image itself. That caused problems, of course, because the image might be on the user's hard disk and unavailable to the recipient.

Some HTML Mail programs might be unable to display some forms of HTML Mail messages, too, and other idiosyncrasies abound. Eudora 5, for example, can display HTML Mail messages, but for some reason doesn't seem able to *forward* them in HTML Mail form.

You might be able to send HTML Mail messages, but that doesn't mean the recipients can view the message properly, even if they do have an HTML Mail program. Is anyone really using HTML Mail? Yes, but a surprising number are *not*. People using older computers, who quite likely haven't upgraded their software, often can't view HTML Mail messages, so don't like to receive them.

Many people use HTML Mail all the time, not realizing that many recipients can't see the formatting. Many long-term Internet users do not use HTML Mail at all. I'm a newsletter publisher myself, with over 30,000 subscribers (visit `http://PoorRichard.com/newsltr/`), and I certainly don't use HTML Mail, nor have I felt much pressure from my subscribers to do so. However, advertisers like HTML Mail, because it allows them to insert banners and other graphical ads into the mail, so many newsletters have gone to HTML Mail to please the advertisers.

Keep Away Prying Eyes with Encryption

The other major change coming to email is the capability to encrypt messages. In other words, messages can be scrambled so that they can't be read if intercepted. Before a scrambled message can be read, it must be decrypted—that is, converted back to its original form. Then, it will be legible. If all goes well, the only person who can decrypt the message is the intended recipient.

There was a great deal of interest in data encryption late in 1994 and early in 1995. Most of this interest centered around a program called *PGP* (Pretty Good Privacy). This program is able to encrypt a message so solidly that it's essentially unbreakable. It's almost certainly impossible to break a PGP-encrypted message using current computer technology, and even when technology improves a little, breaking such a message might remain prohibitively expensive. (As I'll explain, there are different levels of encryption; although it's possible to break messages encrypted using the low levels, the most secure messages cannot be broken.) For instance, breaking into a message to your Aunt Edna explaining when you're going to arrive for Christmas dinner would probably cost the CIA more than engineering a coup in a midsize Central American republic. Therefore, your mail will likely remain completely safe. (This, of course, upsets the U.S. government, along with many other governments around the world.)

I know exactly when this intense interest in PGP occurred because I made a shameless attempt to cash in on the interest by writing a book about PGP. I also know exactly when this interest subsided—about three days before my book was published. Why the sudden decline in interest in a technology that could be so useful? Because it's so hard to use.

I wrote my book based on an application called WinPGP, a Windows program that insulates the user from many of the intricacies of using PGP. Still, even using a front end such as WinPGP, PGP remained a little complicated, and I told anyone who would listen to me that "encryption won't be popular until it's built into email programs and is as easy to use as clicking a button." I'd like to say that everyone took my advice and immediately began work on email programs with built-in encryption, but actually few people listen to me (except my family, and I suspect they're just pretending). Nonetheless, such email programs have begun appearing on the scene, most notably Netscape Messenger, the email portion of Netscape Communicator. Encrypting email messages is still a little more complicated than clicking a button, but it's certainly much simpler than it all used to be.

Why Encrypt Your Email?

Email can get you in a lot of trouble. It got Oliver North in hot water, and people have lost their jobs or been sued over things they've said in email. Several things can go wrong when you use email:

➤ The recipient might pass the email on to someone else.

➤ The message can be backed up to a backup system and later read by someone other than the recipient.

➤ Someone could spy on you and read your email looking for incriminating comments.

➤ Your boss might decide to read your email, based on the idea that if it's written on company time and company equipment, it's company property (and the courts will almost certainly back him up).

The most likely scenario is that the recipient intentionally or thoughtlessly passes your message to someone who you didn't count on seeing it. Unfortunately, encryption can't help you with that problem. The second problem—that the message could be copied to a backup system— has gotten many, many people into trouble. Even if you delete a message and the recipient deletes the message, it might still exist somewhere on the network if the system administrator happened to do a backup before it was deleted. So, if you are ever the subject of some kind of investigation, that message could be revived. This is more of a problem on the Internet because a message goes from your computer, to your service provider's computer, to the recipient's service

119

provider's computer, to the recipient's computer—at least four places from which it could be copied. Finally, someone might be out to get you. Internet Email is basic text, and a knowledgeable hacker with access to your service provider's system (or the recipient's service provider's system) can grab your messages and read them.

What do you do, then? The simplest solution is to avoid putting things in email that you would be embarrassed to have others read. The more complicated solution is to encrypt your email.

Public-Key Encryption: It's Magic

Email encryption systems depend on something known as *public-key encryption*. I'd like to give you a full and detailed description of exactly how it works, but I don't know exactly how it works (I'm no mathematician, and encryption is done using the sort of math that only a geek could love), so I'll give you the simple answer: It's magic. Perhaps that's insufficient; I'll endeavor to explain a little more without getting more complicated than necessary.

First, let me describe *private-key encryption*, which you might have already used. A computer file can be encrypted—turned into a jumble of garbage characters that makes it useless—using a program that works with a *private key* (also known as a *secret key* or even simply called a *password*). The private key is a sort of code word. Tell the program the name of the file you want to encrypt and the private key, and the program uses a mathematical algorithm to encrypt the file. How can you decrypt the file? You do the same thing: Give the program the name of the encrypted file and the private key, and it uses the algorithm to reverse the process and decrypt the file. You might have used private-key encryption already, because many computer programs use it. For instance, if you use the Protect Document command in Word for Windows, you are using private-key encryption. The password that the program asks you for is, in effect, the private key.

Public-key encryption is where the process starts to get a little weird. Public-key encryption uses two keys: a private key and a public key. Through the wonders of mathematics, these keys work together. When you encrypt a file with one key (the public key, for example), the file can be decrypted only with the other key! You can't decrypt the file with the key you used to encrypt it; you must use the other key. Sounds a little odd, but that's how it works. (Okay, this is where my knowledge breaks down. Don't ask me how the mathematics work; as far as I'm concerned, it's magic!)

Public-Key Encryption and Your Email

How, then, does public-key encryption apply to email encryption? An email program with built-in encryption uses public-key encryption to encrypt your email message before it sends it. When you want to send an encrypted message to someone, you have to get that person's public key. These keys are often posted—yes, publicly—on the Internet. There's no need to worry about who has the public key because it can't be used to decrypt an encrypted message. Using the recipient's public key, you encrypt a message and send it off. The recipient then uses his private key to decode the message.

Where do you find someone's public key? It used to be complicated; you might have to go to a *key server*, a Web site or FTP site that stored thousands of public keys. Or you could ask the person to send you the key. A new system is greatly simplifying the task. Some new email programs, such as Netscape Messenger, enable a user to include a digital "certificate," containing his public key, in what's known as a *Vcard*, a special block of information that can be tacked onto the end of an email message. The user can set up Messenger so that every time it sends a message it includes the Vcard, which includes the public key. The email program receiving the message can then extract the public key and place it into a directory of public keys (assuming, of course, that the email program can work with Vcards, and currently most can't). Netscape Communicator's Messenger email program will automatically extract certificates from incoming email. With another program, you might have to choose to save the certificate.

Outlook Express, the new program starting with Windows 95, handles certificates a little differently. It doesn't use a Vcard, but it does attach the certificate containing the public key to a message. If you receive an email message containing a digital certificate, you can add the certificate to your address book by selecting **File**, **Properties**, clicking the **Security** tab, and clicking the **Add Digital ID to Address Book** button.

So, here's how it works:

1. Someone sends you an email message. She's using a Vcard-enabled program and has a public key in the Vcard.

2. When your email program receives the message, it extracts the sender's public key and saves it.

3. Later, you decide that you want to send a private message back to this person, one that's so sensitive it must be encrypted. So, you write the message, and then click the **Encrypted** check box. (Netscape Messenger has an Encrypted check box; other programs might have a button or menu command.)

4. You click the **Send** button, and the mail program sees that you want to encrypt the file. The program looks through its list of public keys, searching for one that is related to the recipient's email address. When it finds the public key, it uses the key to scramble the message, and then it sends the message across the Internet.

5. The recipient's email program receives the message and sees that it has been encrypted. It takes a closer look and sees that it has been encrypted with the recipient's own public key, so it uses the matching private key to decrypt the message. The recipient can now read the message.

What happens if someone other than the intended recipient receives the message? The recipient won't be able to decrypt the message because the recipient won't have the correct private key. Well, you assume he won't, but that's a weakness of the system. If the private key is stolen, the security is compromised. Where the system breaks down completely is that just because the message is encrypted doesn't mean the recipient won't decrypt it and then share it with someone else.

121

Digital Signatures

You can encrypt messages with either the public or private key. Encrypt with one key, and only the matching key can decrypt it. Of course, it wouldn't be a good idea to secure a message by encrypting it with your private key. Remember, a message encrypted with your private key can be decrypted with your public key, and the public key is, well, public. However, if the message can be decrypted with your public key, it means that it must have been encrypted with the corresponding private key, your private key. If you assume that only you have access to the private key, you've just signed the message. In other words, you can sign messages by encrypting them with your private key. As long as your private key remains secure, then the recipient can be sure that the message came from you.

Just to clarify all this, remember these key points:

➤ To send an encrypted message to someone, use that person's public key.

➤ To send a signed message to someone, use your private key.

➤ To send an encrypted message to someone and sign it, use your private key and the recipient's public key.

You don't have to remember all this—an email program will handle it for you. In Netscape Messenger, for instance, if you want to sign a message, click the **Signed** check box. The program will automatically encrypt your message using your private key. In Figure 7.3, you can see Microsoft Outlook Express's encryption features.

Figure 7.3

Microsoft Outlook Express, the mail program in recent versions of Windows, enables you to encrypt and sign email messages.

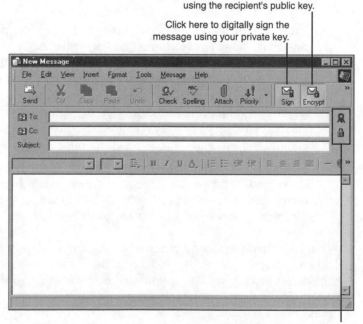

Click here to encrypt the message using the recipient's public key.

Click here to digitally sign the message using your private key.

These icons indicate that the message is signed and encrypted.

I'm Sold; Where Do I Get My Keys?

Keep in mind that there are two types of email encryption in use. Some email programs use PGP encryption. To work with this type of encryption, you have to download PGP and create your public and private key pairs. Working with PGP can be complicated, though; if you want more information, search for PGP at one of the Web search sites (see Chapter 15, "Finding What You Need Online"), or go to http://www.nai.com/.

Probably the most common system—the system that will win the encryption war—is the one being used by Netscape Communicator in the Netscape Navigator and Netscape Messenger programs and, recently, by Microsoft in Outlook Express. This system doesn't use PGP. Rather, you must get a *personal certificate*, a special digital certificate that contains your private and public keys.

Where do you get your certificate? From a *key server*, a site with the necessary software to issue certificates. There are both public- and private-key servers. You can get a certificate from a variety of places, the two most commonly used being VeriSign (http://www.verisign.com/) and Thawte (http://www.thawte.com/). Install the email program you've chosen, and then go to one of these sites and follow the instructions for creating and installing the personal certificate (called a Digital ID by VeriSign) in the program. (I'd recommend Thawte; they give certificates away, whereas VeriSign charges $9.95 a year.)

Of course, to use this system, you'll need a mail program that supports it. Here are a few:

Netscape Messenger (http://www.netscape.com/)

Microsoft Outlook and Outlook Express (http://www.microsoft.com/)

Email Connection (http://email-connection.com/)

Frontier Technologies Email (http://www.frontiertech.com/)

Opensoft ExpressMail (http://www.opensoft.com/)

Tumbleweed MMS (http://www.tumbleweed.com/)

TrustedMIME: (http://www.sse.ie/)

I thought that many more would soon join the fray, but this list has remained the same size for more than a year.

Different-Size Keys

The size of the keys determines the security of the encryption system. For instance, the Netscape Messenger security software comes in two versions: a 40-bit version and a 128-bit version. These numbers refer to the length of the key (the code) that is used to encrypt data. The longer the key, the more secure the transmission. The 128-bit software is built into most recent versions of the Netscape programs, originally intended just for customers within the United States. The 40-bit software was built

123

into Netscape programs that sold to customers outside the United States. These restrictions were because of draconian U.S. laws governing encryption products. In recent months this has changed, and now almost anyone, anywhere in the world—with the exception of a few restricted countries—can download the full-encryption version of the software.

How Much Stronger Is 128-Bit Encryption?

Much, much stronger. For instance, Pretty Good Privacy, Inc. says that the 128-bit PGP software creates messages that are 309,485,009,821,341,068,724,781,056 times more difficult to break than 40-bit messages. They also quote a U.S. government study that found it would take "12 million times the age of the universe, on average, to break a single 128-bit message encrypted with PGP." (That's just an average, so your mileage might vary.)

The Law Was Absurd

ITAR, the U.S. government's International Traffic in Arms Regulations, was used to regulate encryption software. Encryption software using keys more than 40 bits long was, as far as ITAR was concerned, on a par with armaments (SAM missiles and the like) and could not be exported. The law was absurd.

Phil Zimmermann, the designer of the PGP encryption software, demonstrated how ridiculous the law was by exporting the program in a legal manner—in the form of printed text. It was then scanned in another country and converted back to computer code. The law changed, as the absurdity of the law became apparent.

Realistically, it made little difference whether you were using a 40-bit or 128-bit version. 40-bit software is strong enough for all but the most critical of applications. A government department using the Web to transfer information throughout the world would probably want to use 128-bit encryption, ensuring that the message is unbreakable. But for most uses, 40-bit keys are fine. Still, 40-bit keys are much weaker and could be broken by someone with the available computing resources. (The cost might be in the tens of thousands of dollars to break a message; if you think someone's willing to spend that to see what you're saying, you need stronger encryption!)

Sending Voice Messages

It's possible—although perhaps not desirable—to send voice messages in your email messages. Quite frankly, this is a technology that is barely used right now. I've *never* received a voice message inside an email message. And there are problems—if you're communicating with people who are using slow modem connections, they may not want to receive voice messages because of the size.

Still, if you want to play with voice, try a program such as Eudora (http://www. Eudora.com/), which has a built-in voice attachment system, or Voice E-Mail from Bonzi (http://www.bonzi.com/).

Another, perhaps minor, problem with voice annotated email; the recipient must have some kind of player. In the case of Bonzi's Voice E-mail, for instance, you can send the recipient a player, so that even if he doesn't have the same program he can still hear your message. But such players are sometimes a nuisance. In the case of Eudora, for example, the Windows version of the player is 1.32MB.

Finally…are you sure the recipient's computer is properly configured to play sounds? Thanks to the vagaries of Windows, a large number of machines that, in theory, should be able to play sounds, in fact, can't. And many older machines simply aren't properly equipped with a sound card and speakers.

Really Fancy Mail

Email is becoming, well, more than just email. There are now fancy programs that play all sorts of neat tricks, such as faxing you your email messages. Or emailing you your fax messages. One of the more popular of these systems is J2 (http://www.j2.com/). With a J2 account, you can receive faxes and voice messages by email. The faxes are converted to image files, and the voice messages are saved as sound files. So, when you receive them, you can view or listen to them. You can then forward them, save them, mark up and print the faxes, and so on.

You can send faxes, too. You simply send an email to @j2send.com, preceding the @ with the phone number to which you want to send the fax. J2 will then fax it out for you (they charge 5 cents per page, and a monthly fee of $12.50).

Free Toll-Free Numbers

I recently began using a service called uReach.com. They'll provide a toll-free number at no charge (up to 30 minutes use, then from 8 to 10 cents a minute), and allow you to receive faxes and voice messages. Although these are not sent to you through email, you will receive a notification email message, and can quickly go to the uReach.com Web site to view your faxes or hear your messages.

There's more. How about listening to your email? J2 has a service that allows you to call in and have a computer read the message to you. You can then forward the messages to a fax machine...(just don't get your fax numbers mixed up and fax it to your email account). Of course, you might waste a lot of time listening to messages such as "$$$ One Year Guarantee!! $$$ L@@K NOW $$$ Easy Home Business. All you do is send out this exact email!" (I wonder how you pronounce L@@K...)

Some of these J2 services are free, by the way; you can receive faxes in your email for free, for instance (you'll need to pay if you want to send them, though, and for various other features).

There are paging systems integrated with email, too. You can email messages to alphanumeric pagers, by mailing them to a particular address and providing the pager number you want to reach. There are services that send weather information, reminders, and sports scores to your email. There are programs that make it easy to send voice messages in email, too, so you can give up typing and just speak your messages. Imagine any kind of mix of email and just about anything else, and somebody has probably already created it. (If not, start looking for venture capital and you, too, can be part of the Internet start-up craze.)

To find these sorts of email integration services, visit a search engine (which we'll discuss in Chapter 15), and search for *email fax, email pager*, and so on. As email takes over our lives (I've reached the point at which I simply don't have time to respond to all the mail I receive), we'll see more neat tricks being played with email, and more ways for email to extend its stranglehold.

The Least You Need to Know

➤ HTML Mail enables you to create email messages with colors, special fonts, pictures, tables, and more.

➤ Both the sender and recipient must have HTML Mail-compatible programs, or the system won't work. For the moment at least, the online services don't work with HTML Mail.

➤ Mail is getting pretty weird; you can now mail your voice and receive faxes in email.

➤ Email encryption uses a system called public-key encryption; you'll need to get a personal certificate and install it in a compatible email program.

➤ Email programs that allow encryption also allow you to digitally sign messages, proving that they've come from you.

➤ Encryption is not legal everywhere. Some versions of the email software can be sold only in the United States.

➤ The longer the key, the safer the encryption, but even 40-bit keys are safe enough for most everyday use.

Chapter 8

Using Online Chat Rooms

In This Chapter

➤ What are chat and talk?

➤ Chat sessions and public auditoriums

➤ Using the online service chat rooms

➤ Using a graphical chat program

➤ Working with IRC (Internet Relay Chat)

➤ Real uses for chat

One of the most important—yet least discussed—systems in cyberspace is chat. It's important because its immense popularity has been a significant factor in the growth of online services (not so much the Internet as a whole). It is, perhaps, the least discussed because the fact is that many people use the chat systems as a way to talk about sex and even to contact potential sexual partners. In this chapter, you'll take a look at chatting in cyberspace, using a variety of different chat systems, both Internet-based and online-service systems. You'll also learn that there's plenty more than sex-related chat.

Chatting and Talking

What is chat? Here's what it's *not:* a system that allows you to talk out loud to people across the Internet or an online service. That sort of system does exist (see Chapter 12, "More Ways to Communicate—Net Phones, Conferences, Videoconferences"), but a chat system does not use voice; it uses the typed word. Communications are carried out by typing messages.

What's the difference between chat and email, then? With email, you send a message and then go away and do something else. You come back later—maybe later that day, maybe later that week—to see whether you have a response. Chat is quite different: It takes place in *real-time*, to use a geek term. (What other kind of time is there but real-time, one wonders.) In other words, you type a message, and the other party in the chat session sees the message almost instantly. He can then respond right away, and you see the response right away. It's just like, yes, a chat—only you are typing instead of talking.

Chat Can Have Voice

The problem with the Internet is that you make a statement today, and tomorrow it's wrong. Right now the use of voice in chat sessions is rare. Voice *is* being added to chat, though, and you can expect chat sessions to gradually come to resemble the real thing, as people type less and talk more. However, as wonderful as that might sound, it presents a problem. Many chat users are working at big companies, sitting in their little cubicles, typing away and looking busy. Their bosses might think they are working hard, but they are actually gabbing away in one chat system or another, and voices would just give away the game!

There's also an Internet system once known as *talk*, which also isn't talking. Talk is a system in which one person can "call" another on the Internet and, after a connection has been made, can type messages to the other person. You probably know this by its more recent name, *instant messaging*. It's very similar to chat after the two parties are connected, but the manner in which you connect is different. With chat, you have to go to a chat "room" to chat with people; with talk—instant messaging—you simply open the talk program, enter the address of the person you want to connect to, and click a button to call that person (who might not be available, of course). We'll look at these instant-messaging systems in Chapter 9.

To further complicate the issue, some Voice on the Net programs (discussed in Chapter 12) incorporate these talk programs, but they sometimes call them *chat* systems! For instance, Netscape Communicator's Conference program (known as CoolTalk in earlier versions of Netscape Navigator) has a little program that you can use to type messages to another person, but it's called the Chat tool.

Chat is one of those love it or hate it kind of things. Many people just love it; they even find it addictive, spending hours online each night. Personally, I can do without it. It's an awkward way to communicate. I can type faster than most people, yet I still find chat rather clunky. I've been the guest in chat question-and-answer sessions in both MSN and CompuServe and at a Web site called TalkCity, and quite frankly my experiences with chat sessions have not exactly been the high points of my life. The sessions tended to be chaotic at worst, simply slow at best. You run into too many people trying to ask questions at once (some chat systems are not designed to allow someone to control the flow of questions very well), lots of typos, long pauses while you wait for people to type and they wait for you, and so on. I'm no chat fan, but chat certainly appeals to millions of people.

Two Types of Sessions

Chat sessions are categorized into two types: private and group. Generally, what happens is that you join a *chat room*, in which a lot of people are talking (okay, typing) at once. Then, someone might invite you to a private room, where just the two of you can talk without the babble of the public room. These private rooms are often used for cybersex sessions, although, of course, they can also be used for more innocent purposes, such as catching up on the latest news with your brother-in-law in Paris, discussing a project with a colleague, or talking about a good scuba-diving spot in Mexico.

Public chat rooms are often used as a type of auditorium or lecture hall. A famous or knowledgeable person responds to questions from the crowd. Michael Jackson and Buzz Aldrin, for instance, have been guest "speakers" in chat forums, as have many other world-famous people.

Web Savvy

Sex?

Should I be talking about sex in this book? My editors have suggested that I avoid sexual subjects for fear of offending people. Chat, however, is a case in which it's hard to avoid the sexual. Certainly, many people go to chat rooms for non-sexual purposes. But be warned that many (possibly most?) are there to meet members of the opposite sex (or the same sex in some cases) for sexual purposes, both real and imagined. (Imagined sex is known, on the Internet, as cybersex. Real sex is known as sex.)

Score One for the Online Services

I'm going to mostly discuss the online services in this chapter because they generally have the most popular, and in some ways the best, chat systems. Chat has been extremely important to the growth of the online services, so they've made an effort to provide good chat services. Chat out on the Internet, though, is still relatively little used and in many ways not as sophisticated. That's changing as many new chat programs designed for the Internet, often running through the Web, are being introduced. And the line between online-service chat and Web chat is starting to blur, as the online services move out onto the Web. Both MSN and CompuServe, for instance, now provide its chat rooms through Web-based software, accessible to anyone.

Chatting in AOL

In AOL, click the **People** button, and then select **People Connection** from the menu that opens (if you're not using the latest version of the software, you might have to use the keyword **chat**, or click the **People Connection** button in the Welcome window). You'll see a window where you can "Find a Chat" or "Chat Now!" (see Figure 8.1). Use the **Find a Chat** button to see all the available chat categories. There are about a dozen categories and hundreds of individual rooms.

Figure 8.1

AOL's chat room system: lots of glitz, very busy.

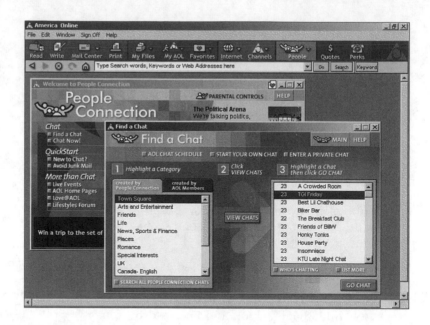

AOL's system enables you to create private rooms so that you and your friends (or family or colleagues) can use that room without interference. If you want to talk to only one person, you just double-click the person's name in the People Here box and click the **Send Message** button. If the person responds, you get your own private message window for just the two of you. You can see in the Figure 8.2 that this message box has special buttons that allow you to modify the text format.

Figure 8.2

AOL provides you with a little message window in which you can carry on private conversations.

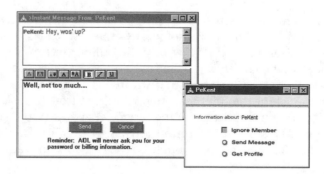

CompuServe's Chat Rooms

To use a CompuServe chat room, you can go to just about any forum or to the Chat forum, where you'll find loads of chat sessions. Most forums have a number of conference rooms, but unless some kind of presentation has been scheduled, they might all be empty. You can be sure to find people to chat with in the Chat forum, though (**GO CHAT**, or click the **People & Chat** button in the main menu). You can also go directly to the Chat area in a Web browser, using `http://member.compuserve.com/chat/`. You'll also find chat rooms in the CompuServe forums; near the top of the page you'll see a **Chat** button.

You can sometimes enter Chat rooms directly from a link—clicking on a link opens the program and drops you into the room directly. But in some cases a list of available rooms opens (see Figure 8.3).

Figure 8.3

Pick a chat room, any chat room...then click ***Enter*** *or* ***Eavesdrop***.

Double-click a room to open the chat window, or click a room and then click the **Enter** or **Eavesdrop** button to take part in the chat room's discussion or just "listen in." The list of rooms shows you how many people are in each room; this might be helpful if you want to pick a quiet one or get right into the action. As you can see in the previous figure, you can listen by reading other people's messages. Whenever you want to jump in, you can type your own message in the lower panel of the window; press **Enter** to send the message, or click the **Send** button. You can invite people to private rooms, too; just double-click on the name of a participant in the right pane, and a little message window opens up into which you can type a private message (see Figure 8.4).

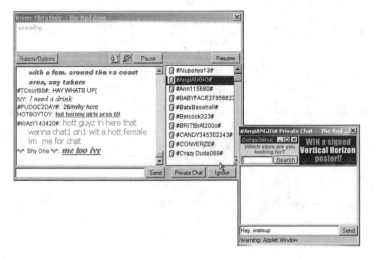

Figure 8.4

CompuServe's chat system. Nobody said it was going to be intellectually demanding.

Microsoft Chat

If you have Windows 98, you'll find that Microsoft Chat may actually be installed on your computer and accessible through a Start menu option (**Start**, **Programs**, **Internet Explorer**, **Microsoft Chat**). However, this program no longer functions, having been superceded by a Chat program that is installed from the Web site into your Web browser.

Microsoft Chat and MSN

If you use The Microsoft Network (http://www.msn.com/), you'll find chat rooms scattered all over the place; almost every forum (or Community as they're known in MSN-speak) has a chat room. In addition, you'll probably find a **People & Chat** link near the top of the main MSN page in your browser. To go directly to MSN's Chat site, go to http://chat.msn.com/.

Click the chat link and either Microsoft Chat will open, or, if it's not yet installed on your machine, an installation program appears—follow the instructions to download and install the chat program, a two-minute task if everything works correctly (which it doesn't always). You can see the MSN chat window in Figure 8.5.

Figure 8.5

MSN's chat system—just as goofy as the others.

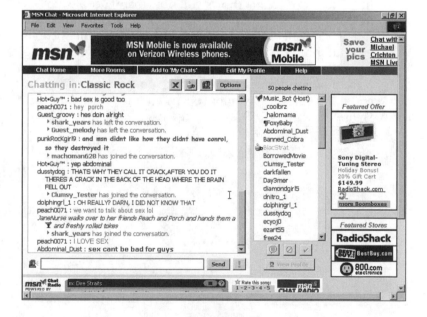

Commands to Look For

Although the details for using each chat system differ, a number of features are similar in most systems. For example, these features are generally similar (even though the names might vary):

➤ Who or People Here shows a list of people currently participating in the chat session.

➤ Invite enables you to invite a participant in the current chat to a private chat room.

➤ Ignore or Squelch enables you to tell the program to stop displaying messages from a particular user. This command is very useful for shutting up obnoxious chat-room members. (You'll find a lot of them!) It's also a good tool for "tuning out" conversations you don't want to hear.

➤ Profile allows you to view information about a particular participant, including whatever information that person decided to make public. Some systems allow more information than others, but the information might include a person's email address, interests, real name, and even phone number and address in some systems (although most participants choose *not* to include this information).

➤ Change Profile or Handle gives you access to the place where you'll change your own information. Some systems let you change your profile from within the Chat program, but on others you might have to select a menu option or command elsewhere.

➤ Record or Log or Capture usually lets you record a session. (Of course, in most cases you'll want to forget the drivel—oh, there I go again!)

➤ Preferences enables you to set up how the system works: whether to tell you when people enter or leave the room, for example.

➤ Kick or Ban is available on some systems if you set up the chat room yourself. Kick allows you to remove someone from the chat room; Ban stops the person from getting back in.

No matter which chat system you use, read the documentation carefully so you can figure out exactly how to get the most out of it.

Pick Your Avatar

The latest thing in chat is the use of graphical systems in which you select an *avatar*, an image that represents you in the chat session. Figure 8.6 shows a room with several avatars, each representing a real-life person, in Club Chat (http://www.ClubChat.com/). Selecting an avatar is a simple matter of clicking a button in the top-left portion of the window, and then choosing from a drop-down list box. Then, you can type a message in the text box at the bottom and click the **Send** button. You can also choose from a small selection of sounds ("Aaaah," "Joy," "Doh," and other such intellectual utterings).

So far I've heard mixed reactions to these graphical chat systems. Some people say they are awful; some say they're nothing special; some say it's just stuff to get in the way of the chat. Others really like them. Experiment and decide for yourself. Interestingly, MSN *used* to have avatar chat, in the form of something called Comic Chat—but the new version of the software does not have this feature. Maybe it will return in a later version, but I suspect that avatars are more of a gimmick than a really necessary feature.

Various other avatar chats are available on the Web although they seem to be less common today than a couple of years ago (which seems to indicate that the whole idea is a bit of a gimmick). Try one of these sites, which have links to a number of chat sites that use avatars:

Worlds (`http://www.worlds.com/index2.html`)

Virtual Places (`http://www.vplaces.net/`)

Excite Chat (`http://www.excite.com/communities/chat`)

Figure 8.6

Playing with avatars in Club Chat.

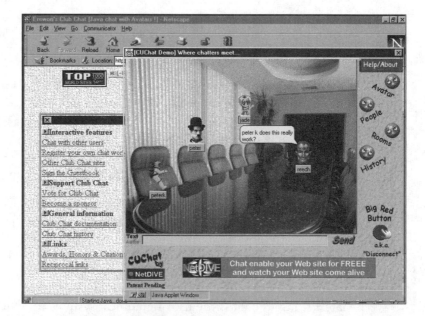

Web Chat's Coming Up Fast

Most chat participants are still using chat systems running on the online services, but it might not always be that way. Hundreds, perhaps thousands, of Web-based chat systems have sprung up and in some cases are quite good. There are chat sites set up for celebrity "visits," education-related issues, gay chat, skateboarding chat, and more.

If you're a chat fan and have been hiding out in the online service chat rooms, perhaps it's time to take a look at the World Wide Web and see what's available. (Here's a good place to start: `http://www.yahoo.com/Computers_and_Internet/Internet/World_Wide_Web/Chat/`.)

Web chat systems vary from the very clunky—your message is displayed within a Web page, which must be constantly rewritten to see the conversation—to the very good. The better sites, such as TalkCity (`http://www.talkcity.com/`), have their own chat programs that you must download before you enter the chat room—these days it's generally a pretty quick and easy installation of a browser plug-in (see Chapter 5, "Web Multimedia—From Flash to Napster," for a discussion of plug-ins). These are true chat systems, with the same sort of features as the chat rooms in the online services. You can see an example of the Talk City chat program in the Figure 8.7.

Chat Versus Discussion Group

There's a little confusion on the Web about the difference between chat rooms and discussion groups. Some Web sites advertising "chat" actually have Web forums (see Chapters 10 and 11). If the discussion isn't "real-time"—you type something, someone immediately responds, you type back—it's not chat.

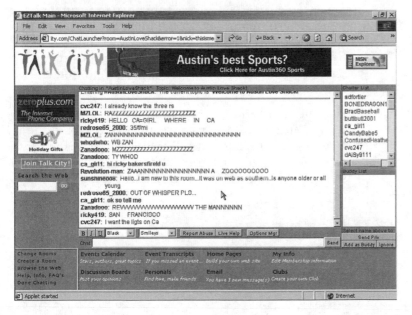

Figure 8.7

Talk City, one of the Web's more sophisticated chat sites.

Internet Relay Chat: Productivity Sinkhole?

I'll admit I haven't spent a lot of time in Internet Relay Chat (IRC). That's mainly because what few visits I have made have been so uninspiring that I can't think of a good reason to return. But there I go again, slamming a chat system. Many thousands of people really *do* like IRC, so let's take a look at how to use it.

Step 1: Get the Software

The first thing you'll need is an IRC *client program*. That's the program you'll use to send and receive IRC communications. If you are using a Macintosh, try Ircle, a well-known IRC program for that operating system. On Windows, you might try mIRC or PIRCH.

Go to the software archives I discuss in Appendix C, "All the Software You'll Ever Need," and download a copy of some kind of IRC program. Then follow the documentation's instructions to set up the program and spend some time reading everything there is to read. Unfortunately, IRC can be a little complicated, if only because it has so many features, so put in the time it takes to learn the program.

Nicknames

Your nickname is the name by which you will be identified in the chat sessions. Notice that you can remain anonymous in a chat session by entering incorrect information into the Real Name and Email Address boxes.

Step 2: Connect to a Server

The next thing you have to do is connect to an IRC server somewhere. IRC servers are programs run on someone's computer out on the Internet and act as "conduits," carrying information between IRC participants. These servers are the equivalent of the online services' chat forums. At a server, you'll find hundreds of IRC channels that you can choose from.

Find the command that you must use to connect to a server. With mIRC, for instance, the dialog box in the Figure 8.8 opens automatically when you start the program. You can get back to it later (to select a different server, for example) by choosing **File**, **Setup**.

Figure 8.8

Here's where you choose a server to connect to and enter your personal information in mIRC.

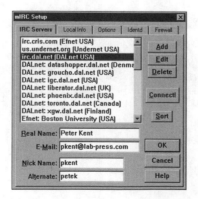

Select the server you want to use, click the **Connect** button, and away you go. You're connected to the server, and a dialog box appears, listing some of the channels (see Figure 8.9). This listing is by no means all the channels; most servers have hundreds. This box holds a list of the ones you are interested in (actually it's initially a list of channels that the programmer thought you might like to start with, but you can add more). To get into one of these channels, double-click it.

If you'd like to see a complete listing of all the channels, close the dialog box, type **/list** in the text box at the bottom of the main window (which is where you type your messages and any IRC commands), and press **Enter**.

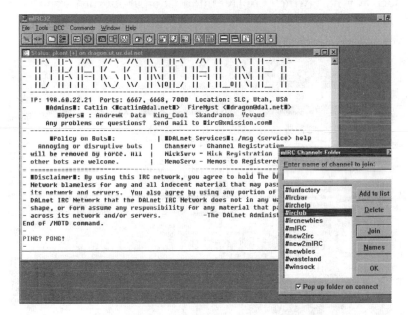

Figure 8.9

You've connected, and you're ready to join a channel.

Know the Commands

IRC commands begin with a slash (/), and there are loads of them. Most IRC programs hide the commands from you to some degree, providing menu commands instead, but they don't replace all of them. Some things can be done only by using the original typed IRC command.

139

In mIRC, the **/list** command opens a window in which all the channels are listed. This window might take a while to open because there are so many channels. As you can see in the title bar in the Figure 8.10, this server has 744 channels! If you want to enter one of these channels, all you have to do is double-click it.

After you are in a channel, just start typing; it's much like chatting in any other chat system. In the Figure 8.11, you can see a chat in progress. As usual, you type your message in the little box at the bottom, and you view what's going on in the big panel. The participants are listed on the right side. You can invite one to a private chat by double-clicking a name. You can right-click to see a pop-up menu with a series of commands such as Whois (which displays information about the user in another window).

Figure 8.10

mIRC's channel listing: Are 744 channels enough for you?

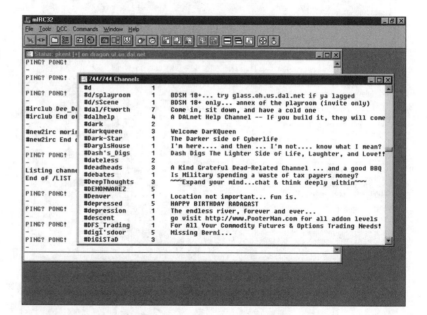

Figure 8.11

Here's where you chat in mIRC.

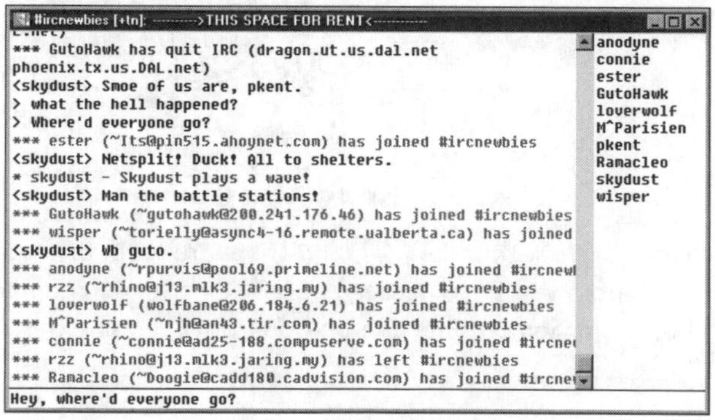

There's a lot to learn about IRC. IRC programs are a little complicated because IRC has so many features. For example, you can transmit computer files to other users; people often send pictures to one another. You can also add a special program that reads (with a voice, that is) incoming messages from other chat members, and you can ban, kick, and ignore users (if you open a channel, you have some control over who you let in) and plenty more.

Spend some time playing around with the program you choose to see what it can do, and read the documentation or help files carefully. It's complicated stuff, but after you learn what one program can do, you can pick up how to use one of the others very quickly.

How Many Conversations Can You Keep Going?

IRC is almost a game. People get into multiple chat sessions at once. They chat in the main window, and then they have a few private chat sessions in other windows. That's why it takes them so long to respond sometimes!

What Is It Good For? Real Uses for Chat

It could be argued that chat systems are a complete waste of perfectly good electrons. (*I* wouldn't claim that, of course, but I'm sure many people would.) The chat is often little better than gibberish. "Hey, dude, how goes it? ...Cool man, you?...Yeah, doing well; you chatted with that babe CoolChick, yet?...No, she cute?" Blah...blah...blah. This is neither educational nor particularly interesting.

I should note that not all chats are quite so inane. Chats allow people of like interests to get together in cyberspace, reaching across continents to discuss issues that interest them in a way that would be prohibitively expensive using any other technology. (I've proposed a stupidity tax to make the totally stupid chats prohibitively expensive once again.)

There are other worthwhile uses, too. This list points out a few such scenarios:

➤ Technical support can be given using chat rooms. This use will become more important as more software is distributed across the Internet. For instance, a small company that, in the past, might have provided support only within the United States can now provide support to the entire world by using chat.

➤ Companies can use chat systems for keeping in touch. An international company with salespeople throughout the world can arrange weekly "meetings" in a chat room. Families can do the same so that they can keep in touch even when they're separated by thousands of miles.

➤ Groups that are planning international trips might want to try chat rooms. For instance, if a scout group is traveling to another country to spend the summer with another group, a chat room could provide a way for the leaders to "get together" beforehand to iron out final details.

➤ Colleges can use chat. Many colleges already provide courses over the Internet, using the Web to post lessons and using email to send in completed assignments. In addition, teachers can use chat to talk with students, regardless of the geographic distance between them.

However, having said all that, chat might eventually be superseded by what's known as Voice on the Net, a system that allows you to place "phone calls" across the Internet and even have conference calls (see Chapter 12). But even Voice on the Net hasn't caught on; the adoption of both chat and Voice on the Net has been hurt by the fact that phone rates have dropped tremendously in the last few years, making connecting by typing less attractive than it used to be.

The Least You Need to Know

➤ A *chat* system allows participants to take part in public discussions or to move to private "rooms" if they prefer. A *talk* system is a direct link between participants in a conversation, without the need for a public chat room.

➤ Neither chat nor talk uses voices; you type messages and send them to and from.

➤ Chat sessions are often very crude and sexually orientated; if you're easily offended, pick your chat room carefully.

➤ All the online services have popular chat systems. Many Web sites have chat rooms, too.

➤ If you want to use Internet Relay Chat, you'll have to download an IRC program from a shareware site and then connect across the Internet to a server.

➤ You can use chat rooms to keep in touch with friends, family, or colleagues or to meet new people.

MESSAGE!

YO!

Chapter 9

Instant Messaging

In This Chapter

➤ What is Instant Messaging (IM)?

➤ Finding IM programs

➤ The IM War

➤ AOL Instant Messenger and MSN Messenger

➤ Using an IM system

➤ Using ICQ

In the last chapter, I talked briefly about *talk*, a system that's now known as *instant messaging*. This is a system that allows two people to get together and chat privately online; no need to go to a chat site, you just open your program, select whom you want to talk to, and begin typing.

There are a lot of instant messaging (IM) programs around, but almost all users are working with one of the following programs (and by far the most are using the first one):

AOL Instant Messenger: http://www.aol.com/aim/

Yahoo! Messenger: http://messenger.yahoo.com/

MSN Messenger: http://messenger.msn.com/

ICQ: http://web.icq.com/

PowWow: http://www.powwow.com/

You may run into various others:

Netscape Instant Messenger (http://home.netscape.com/aim/),
CompuServe Instant Messenger (http://www.compuserve.com/csim/),
Excite Messenger (http://messenger.excite.com/),
Lycos Messenger (http://www.messenger.lycos.com/),
Odigo (http://www.odigo.com/), **EveryBuddy** (http://www.everybuddy.com/),
Jabber (http://www.jabber.org/ and http://www.jabber.com/), and many more.
But in some cases these programs are merely branded versions of one of the others
(Lycos Messenger and CompuServe Instant Messengers, for instance, are actually AOL
Instant Messenger, and EveryBuddy is a special program that combines the AOL,
Yahoo!, ICQ, and MSN programs).

I used to recommend that people try out a few of these programs and see which they
prefer, and then tell their friends to download the same one. But it's probably a good
idea to work with one of the major systems, such as AOL Instant Messenger or Yahoo!
Messenger, because they're in such wide use.

How Many Users?

There are reportedly tens of millions of Instant Messenger users. Late in 2000, Jupiter Media Metrix estimated that AOL Instant Messenger had almost 22 million users; ICQ (actually owned by Yahoo!), had a little over 9 million users; Yahoo!'s program had almost 11 million users; and MSN Messenger had a little over 10 million users. A total of around 52 million instant-messaging users. (That's the theory; in fact, *far* fewer people actually use these programs regularly, and there's a lot of overlap, with many users working with several programs.) Other estimates put the total number of IM users at 130 million users, with 3 million new users each month (and if you believe that...).

The IM War and IM Interoperability

In 1999, Microsoft and AOL went to war over IM (Instant Messaging). In the summer Microsoft launched its own IM service, MSN Messenger...and made it compatible with the AOL IM service. That is, people using MSN Messenger could send messages to people using AOL Instant Messenger. At the same time Microsoft called for complete IM interoperability—all IM services should be able to communicate with each other, they said.

AOL didn't much like that. They had a monopoly in instant messaging, and decided to block access, so that other IM companies couldn't send messages into their system. So for months, a back-and-forth struggle went on, with AOL blocking access, other companies finding a way around the blocking, AOL blocking access again, other companies (including Microsoft and Yahoo!), complaining to the Federal Communications Commission, AOL blocking someone else, another group complaining to the Senate Commerce Committee.

I should note that AOL claims that it's blocking access for security and privacy reasons. On the other hand, these seem like excuses, buzzwords guaranteed to give people pause but actually nonissues. There's no reason that interoperability has to be insecure or require the release of private information.

At the time of writing, over a year after the beginning of the war and near the end of the year 2000, the war continues. It seems, however, that over the long term interoperability is inevitable, and that most IM systems will communicate with each other. With or without AOL Instant Messenger, the other guys will get together and make their programs talk to each other...and there's a very good chance that some court or government department will eventually force AOL to open its system up. (There's a chance that AOL may have to do so in order to complete its merger with Time Warner.)

For now, though, you may find that if you want to communicate with friends using different IMs, you'll have to install all those different systems (or perhaps use a program such as EveryBuddy).

FreeIM

A number of companies—including Microsoft and Tribal Voice (the publisher of PowWow)—launched an organization called Free IM (http://www.FreeIM.org/) to lobby the Federal Trade Commission and Federal Communications Commission. Their basic premise is that IM systems are like telephones—just as you should be able to pick up any phone to talk to any other phone, you should be able to use any IM to contact any other IM.

Using IM

So, make your choice. Pick a system; but how? I'd suggest that you check with the people whom you want to communicate with, to see which system they're using. Note, by the way, that just because you're *not* an AOL member doesn't mean you can't use AOL Instant Messenger. Even if you're not an MSN member, you can use that system. These companies are distributing their programs to anyone who wants one, so if you have AOL friends using AOL Instant Messenger, yet you're with some little Internet service provider, don't worry—you can still download and use that program.

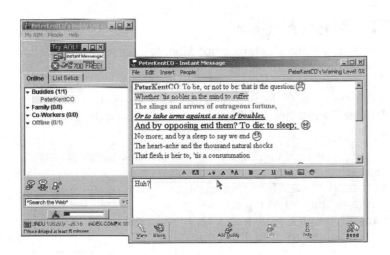

Figure 9.1

AOL Instant Messenger, the world's most popular IM program. On the left is the Buddy list, your own AOL IM directory.

So, what features does the world's most popular IM program have?

➤ Keep a list of people you commonly communicate with—your Buddy list. Then, double-click on a person to send that person a message. If the person's available, he can instantly reply.

➤ Change text color, size, text-background color, and style (bold, italic, underline).

➤ Create links in the messages; when the recipient clicks on a link, the referenced Web pages open in his Web browser.

➤ Place image "smileys" into messages.

➤ Insert text from a file into a message.

➤ Send "warnings" to people who have sent you obnoxious messages. If enough people send warnings, that person will be temporarily blocked from sending messages to *anyone*.

➤ Permanently block people from sending messages to you.

➤ View the person's profile.

➤ Select a "Buddy Icon," a picture to represent you, displayed when someone's viewing your messages (you can even use your own photograph).

➤ Create an "away message," displayed when someone tries to contact you and you are unable to respond.

➤ Transfer files to someone you're communicating with.

➤ Send pictures to people.

➤ Talk to people—yes, using your voice and a microphone.

➤ Play games with your IM buddies.

➤ All sorts of other configuration options: setting up the ticker displayed at the bottom of the Buddy list; modify alerts; set privacy options; and lots more.

The Enemy: MSN Messenger

It's not as widely used as AOL Instant Messenger, but MSN Messenger is preferred by many people, and has some interesting features. It has built-in voice-on-the-net that allows you to call from your computer to any telephone in the U.S. for free (we'll look at voice-on-the-net in more detail in Chapter 12, "More Ways to Communicate—Net Phones, Conferences, Videoconferences"). You can also call other countries at a very low rate.

It has built-in stock tracking, can send messages to pagers and cell phones, play games, and control whether your kids can use the program. Of course, it has instant messaging features, too—some unusual features such as an indicator showing when the person you're communicating with is typing, about to send something back to you, so that you can pause and wait for the response. It has more advanced text and messaging formatting, too. (Some very cute little smileys.)

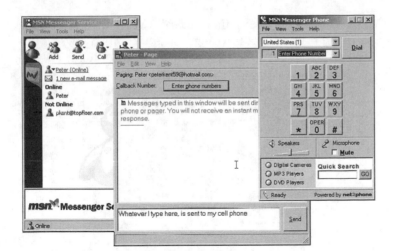

Figure 9.2

MSN Messenger, more than just IM. You can send pager or cell-phone messages, and even dial phone calls.

ICQ (Figure It Out)

ICQ is an instant messaging phenomenon in its own right. Started by a small group of Israeli programmers, in 1998 ICQ was bought by AOL for $287 million, with productivity bonuses that reportedly were potentially as much as $110 million or so.

It certainly is a great program, but it's far more than just an instant-messaging program. It allows both instant messaging and chat—you can have private or public communication sessions. But it also allows you to send notes that will pop up on people's screens, send files—simply drag a file and drop it onto the recipient's name, and away it goes—launch other programs when files arrive, tell people to telephone you, and so on.

It's a fantastic "collaboration tool," an ideal program for when you're working with people and need to be in constant contact, yet they're somewhere else. You can create a sort of virtual office, with people spread around the world, and constantly share information and ideas. You can even see whether your colleagues are available, as you can set an indicator to show whether you're out for lunch, currently at your computer, or whatever.

It works like this. When you get an ICQ account, you add other ICQ users to your list—you'll add the ICQ accounts of the other people you plan to work with, for instance. Then, you'll see little indicators in the ICQ window showing that status of these other ICQ accounts. Sally might have set her ICQ program to show that she's Away; Fred might have set his to show Extended Away; John might have set his to Occupied (Urgent Messages), so he doesn't want to be disturbed by trivia, but he's there if you really need him; Gill might not have logged on yet, so she's shown as Offline, and so on.

So, you can see exactly who's available, and what you can do. By clicking on their names and selecting procedures, you can send them messages, initiate a chat (or talk) session, transfer files to them, send notes asking them to call you, and various other things. In fact, there are so many features in this thing that the company even publishes a book explaining how to use it all—this is no dumb chat program.

Figure 9.3

ICQ can be complicated (right side), or not so complicated (left side); make your choice.

The product's free, too. (I haven't quite figured out what sort of productivity bonuses you can have when the product doesn't cost anything, and there's no advertising being sold on the system. That's Internet economics for you.) You can download it from `http://www.icq.com/`. A great system, well worth a look.

Oh, before we leave this chapter—have you figured out what ICQ stands for? Say the letters slowly, and then try them fast. Listen to the words that the letters seem to represent, and you'll figure it out.

The Least You Need to Know

➤ There are many IM systems, but only a handful of popular ones.

➤ Find out which IM systems your friends are using, and get the same.

➤ Right now, IM programs don't operate with each other—but may soon.

➤ IM programs have a wide range of features, from simple text messages to game playing and file transfers.

➤ ICQ is an IM system on steroids, a real collaboration tool.

Chapter 10

GOT ONE!

Finding and Using Newsgroups

In This Chapter

➤ What is a newsgroup?

➤ Existing newsgroups and what's in them

➤ Choosing and setting up a newsreader

➤ Reading and responding to messages

➤ Marking messages as read

➤ Rot13: encoded messages

➤ Sending and receiving computer files

➤ Special newsreader features

In this chapter, I'm going to introduce you to one of the Internet's most dangerous services: newsgroups. Many people find these discussion groups to be addictive. Get involved in a few groups and, if you have an addictive personality, you'll soon find that the rest of your life is falling apart as you spend hours each day swapping messages with people all over the world, on subjects such as bushwalking in Australia, soap operas, very tall women, or very short men.

If you don't have an addictive personality, newsgroups can be interesting, stimulating, and extremely useful. Anyway, being addicted to newsgroups is better than being addicted to booze or drugs. In this chapter, you'll find out what newsgroups are and how to use them.

What's a Newsgroup?

Let me answer the question, "What's a newsgroup?" with another question: Are you familiar with bulletin board systems (BBSs)? Electronic BBSs work much like the corkboard-and-thumbtack type of bulletin board. They're computerized systems for leaving both public and private messages. Other computer users can read your messages, and you can read theirs. There used to be tens of thousands of small BBSs around the world, each of which had its own area of interest, but they've been pretty much killed off by the Internet.

An information service such as CompuServe or America Online is essentially a collection of many bulletin boards (called *forums* in CompuServe-speak or *message boards* on AOL). Each of these services has literally thousands of these things.

As you've already seen, the Internet is a collection of networks hooked together. It's huge, and consequently it has an enormous number of discussion groups. In Internet-speak, these groups are called *newsgroups*, and there are thousands of them on all conceivable subjects. Each Internet service provider subscribes to a selection of newsgroups—perhaps just 5,000 or 10,000, but sometimes as many as 40,000, maybe even more. One service provider I've seen has more than 50,000 newsgroups available.

Newsgroups Dying Out?

As we went to press with this book, MSN announced that it would no longer carry newsgroups. If you are an MSN subscriber, you'll still be able to get to them through an independent service, as you'll learn later in this chapter,

But what does MSN's move signify? Perhaps that the days of the newsgroups are numbered, as the mailing-list discussion groups and Web-based discussion boards (see Chapter 11, "More Internet Discussions—Mailing Lists and Web Forums") take over their work.

What do I mean by *subscribe*? These newsgroups are distributed around the Internet by a service called Usenet. Consequently, they're often referred to as Usenet groups. Usenet distributes tens of thousands of groups (the number keeps changing), but not all service providers get all the groups. A service provider can choose which groups it wants to receive, in essence *subscribing* to just the ones it wants. Although more than 30,000 internationally distributed newsgroups exist (along with thousands more local groups), most providers get only a few thousand of them.

If your service provider subscribes to a newsgroup, you can read that group's messages and post your own messages to the group. In other words, you can work only with groups to which your service provider has subscribed. You read newsgroup messages by using a *newsreader*, a program that retrieves messages from your service provider's *news server*.

If you've never used a newsgroup (or another system's forum, BBS, or whatever), you might not be aware of the power of such communications. This sort of messaging system brings computer networking to life, and it's not all computer nerds sitting around with nothing better to do. (Check out the Internet's alt.sex newsgroups; these people are not your average introverted propeller-heads!) In my Internet travels, I've found work, made friends, found answers to research questions (much more quickly and cheaply than I could have by going to a library), and read people's "reviews" of tools I can use in my business. I've never found a lover or spouse online, but I know people who have (and, anyway, I'm already married). Just be careful not to get addicted and start spending all your time online.

Public News Servers

If your service provider doesn't subscribe to a newsgroup you want, ask the management to subscribe to it. If they won't, you *might* be able to find and read it at a public news server. Try looking at these sites for information about public servers:

http://dir.yahoo.com/Computers_and_Internet/Internet/Chats_and_Forums/Usenet/ Public_Access_Usenet_Sites/

Serverseekers.com: `http://www.serverseekers.com/`

Supernews: `http://www.supernews.com/`

So, What's Out There?

You can use newsgroups for fun or for work. You can use them to spend time talking with other people who share your interests—whether that happens to be algebra (see the alt.algebra.help group) or antique collecting (rec.antiques). You can even do serious work online, such as finding a job at a nuclear physics research site (hepnet.jobs), tracking down a piece of software for a biology project (bionet.software), or finding good stories about what's going on in South Africa for an article you are writing (za.events).

The following newsgroups represent just a tiny fraction of what is available:

alt.ascii-art. Pictures (such as Spock and the Simpsons) created using keyboard text characters.

alt.comedy.british.blackadder. Discussions about Mr. Bean's earlier life.

alt.missing-kids. Information about missing kids.

bit.listserv.down-syn. Discussions about Down's syndrome.

misc.forsale. Lists of goods for sale.

rec.skydiving. A group for skydivers.

sci.anthropology. A group for people interested in anthropology.

sci.military. Discussions on science and the military.

soc.couples.intercultural. A group for intercultural couples.

If you are looking for information on just about any subject, the question is not "Is there a newsgroup about this?" The questions you should ask are "What is the newsgroup's name?" and "Does my service provider subscribe to it?"

Can You Read It?

The many newsgroups out there take up a lot of room. A service provider getting the messages of just 3,000 newsgroups might have to set aside tens of megabytes of hard disk space to keep up with it all. So, service providers have to decide which ones they will subscribe to. Nobody subscribes to all the world's newsgroups because many are of no interest to most Internet users, and many are not widely distributed. (Some are of regional interest only; some are of interest only to a specific organization.) So, system administrators have to pick the ones they want and omit the ones they don't want. Undoubtedly, some system administrators censor newsgroups, omitting those they believe have no place online.

I've given you an idea of what is available in general, but I can't specify what is available to you. You'll have to check with your service provider to find out what they offer. If they don't have what you want, ask them to get it. They have no way of knowing what people want unless someone tells them.

News?

True to its UNIX heritage, the Internet uses the word *news* ambiguously. Often, when you see a reference to news in a message or an Internet document, it refers to the messages left in newsgroups (not, as most people imagine, to journalists' reports on current affairs).

Okay, Gimme a List!

The first thing you might want to do is find out which newsgroups your service provider subscribes to. You can do that by telling your newsreader to obtain a list of groups from the news server; I'll talk more about newsreaders later.

What if you don't find what you are looking for? How can you find out what's available that your provider does not subscribe to? There are lots of places to go these days to track down newsgroups. I like Liszt (`http://www.liszt.com/news/`), which currently lists more than 30,000 newsgroups, and Tile.Net (`http://www.tile.net/`), which you can see in the Figure 10.1. Both Liszt and Tile.Net also list thousands of mailing lists (see Chapter 11, "More Internet Discussions— Mailing Lists and Web Forums"). You can try the Usenet Info Center (`http://www.ibiblio.org/usenet-i/`) or the Finding Newsgroups and Mailing Lists page (`http://www.synapse.net/~radio/finding.htm`). You can also search at any Web search site (which you'll learn about in Chapter 15, "Finding What You Need Online"). For instance, try Yahoo! (`http://dir.yahoo.com/Computers_and_Internet/Internet/Usenet/Newsgroup_Directories/`).

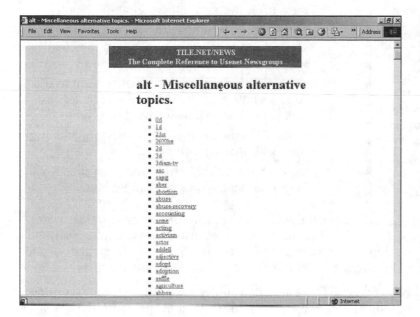

Figure 10.1

Tile.Net is a good place to find out what's available on Usenet.

Where Does It All Come From?

Where do all these newsgroups come from? People all over the world create newsgroups on their computers. Any system administrator can create a newsgroup, and many do. Each host has newsgroups of local interest that contain information about the service provider's services, local politics, local events, and so on.

A large number of newsgroups, although not all of them, are part of the Usenet system. Like the Internet, Usenet is a network of networks. No one owns it, and it doesn't own anything itself. It is independent of any network, including the Internet (in fact, it's older than the Internet). Usenet is simply a series of voluntary agreements to swap information.

What's in a Name?

Newsgroup names look much like host addresses: a series of words separated by periods. The reason for this format is that, like host names, newsgroup names are set up in a hierarchical system (although instead of going right-to-left, they go left-to-right). The first name is the top level. These are the primary top-level Usenet groups:

Moderated Groups

As you'll see when you refer to some of the directories of newsgroups, some newsgroups are *moderated*, which means someone reads all the messages and decides which ones to post. The purpose is to keep the newsgroup focused and to prevent the discussions from going astray. Of course, it might look a little like censorship, depending on what you want to say.

comp   Computer-related subjects.

news   Information about newsgroups, including software you can use to read newsgroup messages and information about finding and using newsgroups.

rec   Recreational topics, including hobbies, sports, the arts, and so on.

sci   Discussions about research in the "hard" sciences, as well as some social sciences.

soc   A wide range of social issues, such as discussions about different types of societies and subcultures, as well as sociopolitical subjects.

talk   Debates about politics, religion, and anything else that's controversial.

misc   Stuff. Job searches, things for sale, a forum for paramedics. You know, stuff.

Not all newsgroups are true Usenet groups. Many are local groups that Usenet distributes internationally (don't worry about the difference; it doesn't matter). Such newsgroups are part of the alternative newsgroup hierarchies. They have other top-level groups, such as

alt   "Alternative" subjects. These are often subjects that many people consider inappropriate, pornographic, or just weird. In some cases, however, the newsgroup is simply interesting reading, but someone created the newsgroup in an "unauthorized" manner to save time and hassle.

bionet   Biological subjects.

bit   A variety of newsgroups from BITnet.

clari   Clarinet's newsgroups from "official" and commercial sources; mainly UPI news stories and various syndicated columns.

courts   Newsgroups related to law and lawyers.

de   Various German-language newsgroups.

fj   Various Japanese-language newsgroups.

gnu   The Free Software Foundation's newsgroups.

hepnet   Discussions about high energy and nuclear physics.

k12   Discussions about kindergarten through 12th-grade education.

vmsnet   Subjects of interest to VAX/VMS computer users.

You'll see other groups, too, such as the following:

brasil   Groups from Brazil (Brazil is spelled with an "s" in Portuguese).

birmingham   Groups from Birmingham, England.

podunk   A local interest newsgroup for the town of Podunk.

thisu   This university's newsgroup.

Okay, I made up the last two, but you get the idea. You'll run into all sorts of different hierarchies, with new ones appearing all the time. To see a list of virtually all the top-level group names in both Usenet and alternative newsgroups, go to `http://www.magmacom.com/~leisen/mlnh/`.

Reaching the Next Level

The groups listed in the previous section make up the top-level groups. Below each of those groups are groups on another level. For instance, under the alt category is a newsgroup called alt.3d, which contains messages about three-dimensional imaging. It's part of the alt hierarchy because, presumably, it was put together in an unauthorized way. The people who started it didn't want to go through the hassle of setting up a Usenet group, so they created an alt group, where anything goes, instead.

Another alt group is `alt.animals`, where people gather to talk about their favorite beasties. This group serves as a good example of how newsgroups can have more levels. Because animals are such a diverse subject, one newsgroup isn't enough. Instead of posting messages to the `alt.animals` group, you can choose your particular interest. The specific areas include the following:

```
alt.animals.dolphins
alt.animals.felines.lions
alt.animals.felines.lynxes
alt.animals.felines.snowleopards
alt.animals.humans
```

These are just a few examples of the many newsgroups available. If you're into it, chances are good there's a newsgroup for it.

All areas use the same sort of hierarchical system. For example, under the bionet first level, you can find the genome level, with such newsgroups as `bionet.genome.arabidopsis` (information about the Arabidopsis genome project), `bionet.genome.chrom22` (a discussion of Chromosome 22), and `bionet.genome.chromosomes` (for those interested in the eucaryote chromosomes).

I'm Ready; Let's Read

Now that you know what newsgroups are, you'll probably want to get in and read a few. Newsgroup messages are stored in text files, saved on your service provider's computer system. You'll read the messages using a newsreader to help you filter through all the garbage.

If you are with an online service, you already have a built-in newsreader. These range from the good to the absolutely awful (CompuServe's was horrible last time I looked; maybe its next software upgrade will fix that). If you are with a service provider, they might give you a newsreader, or it might be already installed on your computer. For example, Netscape Navigator and some versions of Internet Explorer have built-in newsreaders, and Windows 98 comes with Outlook Express (see Figure 10.2), which includes a newsreader. Or you might have one of many other newsreaders, such as WinVN, Gravity, and Free Agent on Windows or NewsWatcher and Nuntius on the Macintosh. Note, though, that there are far fewer newsreaders available now than there used to be. As with other forms of Internet software—push programs and VRML viewers, for instance—there was a sudden "bloom" of software from 1994–1996, followed by a gradual die-off.

Figure 10.2

Outlook Express, which is included with Windows 98 and Windows 2000, displays the list of messages in the top pane and the selected message in the lower pane.

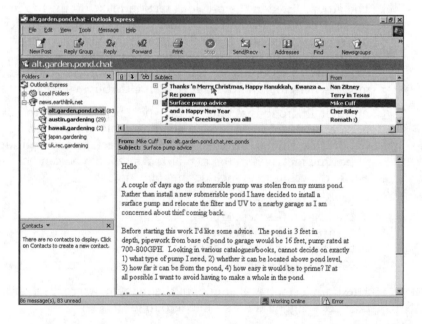

I'm going to use the Outlook Express newsreader for my examples in the following sections. If you have something different, the commands you use will vary, but the basic principles will remain the same. Of course, different programs have different features, so you might want to try out a few programs to see what you like (see Appendix C, "All the Software You'll Ever Need," for information about finding software).

Although each program is a little different, they all share certain characteristics. Check your program's documentation for the specific details and to learn about any extra features it includes. Even if you don't have Outlook Express, I suggest that you read this information because it provides a good overview of the functions available in most newsreaders.

If you are using an online service, you might be using that service's system to work in the newsgroups. In CompuServe, for instance, use **GO INTERNET** (or in the new CompuServe 2000, click the large **Internet** button in the toolbar and select **Newsgroups**); in AOL, use the keyword **Internet** to find more information about starting the newsreaders.

A Quick Word on Setup

I want to quickly discuss setup and subscribing. If you are with an online service, there's nothing to set up; it's all done for you. If you are with a service provider, though, you might have to set up the newsreader.

First, your newsreader must know the location of your news server. Ask your service provider for the hostname of the news server (the news server is the system the service provider uses to send messages to your newsreader); the hostname might be news.big.internet.service.com, or news.zip.com, or something like that. Then, check your newsreader's documentation to see where to enter this information.

The other thing you might have to do is subscribe to the newsgroups you are interested in. I've already said that your service provider has to subscribe to newsgroups; this means that the provider ensures the newsgroups are available to its members. However, the term *subscribe* has another meaning in relation to newsgroups. You might also have to subscribe to the newsgroup to ensure that the newsgroup you want to read is available to your newsreader. Not all newsreaders make you subscribe in order to read a newsgroup; and you don't have to worry about subscribing if you are reading newsgroup messages through a newsgroup "gateway" Web site such as Super-news (http://www.supernews.com/). Many newsreaders, however, require that you fetch a list of newsgroups from your service provider (the newsreader has a command you'll use to fetch and display the list and might even offer to do so the first time you start the program) and then subscribe to the ones you want to read. Subscribing is no big deal; you simply choose which ones you want. Until you subscribe, though, you can't see the messages.

Starting and Subscribing

Figure 10.2 shows the Outlook Express newsreader, which comes with Windows 98. The first time you use the program a dialog box opens, asking for all the configuration information. Then, the Newsgroups dialog box opens (shown in Figure 10.3) and begins grabbing a list of newsgroups from your service provider's news server.

Figure 10.3

The Outlook Express Newsgroup dialog box, where you can view a list of all the newsgroups your service provider has subscribed to; at the moment, the system is downloading a list of newsgroups from the server.

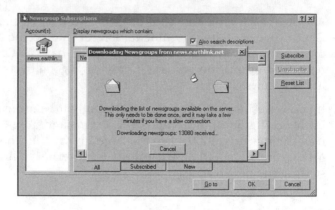

Where Are the alt. Groups?

If you are with an online service, you might find that you can't initially read the alt. groups and perhaps some others as well. Your online service might regard these groups as a trifle "naughty," in which case you have to apply for permission to read them. Go to your online service's Internet forum or BBS to find out how to activate these groups, or refer to the parental control information.

After you have the list, you can decide which newsgroups you want to read. (Remember that this is a list of only the newsgroups that your service provider has subscribed to, not a full list of all the groups distributed by Usenet. For information about finding newsgroups not included in this list, see the beginning of this chapter.) In Outlook Express, you click the group you want to read, and then click the **Subscribe** button, or simply double-click the name. (You can also use the text box at the top; type a name or part of a name to move to that part of the list.)

When you close the dialog box, you'll see a list of the newsgroups you subscribed to in a pane on the left side of the window. You can subscribe to more later by clicking the **Newsgroup** button or by selecting **Tools, Newsgroups** to see the dialog box again (to refresh the list, click the **Reset List** button). You can also open the dialog box, click the **New** tab, and then click the **Reset List** button to see a list of newsgroups that your service provider has added since you last collected the list.

Click one of the newsgroups you've subscribed to in the left pane, and the top pane will display a list of messages from that newsgroup (see Figure 10.4); it might take a little while for these messages to transfer.

Many newsgroups are empty—they rarely, if ever, contain messages—so you won't always see message headers in the top pane. Most newsreaders will have some kind of indicator showing how many messages are in the newsgroup (refer to the numbers in parentheses in Figure 10.4). If there are only a few messages, it's quite possible that all the messages are promotional messages completely unrelated to the subject of the newsgroup, perhaps advertising get-rich-quick schemes or pornographic Web sites.

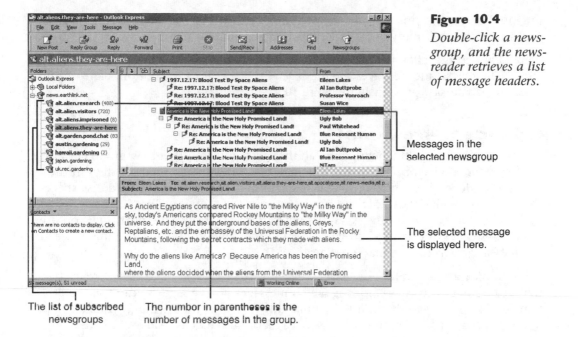

Figure 10.4
Double-click a newsgroup, and the newsreader retrieves a list of message headers.

The list of subscribed newsgroups

The number in parentheses is the number of messages in the group.

Taking a Look

Notice that some messages are indented below others (see Figure 10.5), and that there's a small - icon next to the top message; in other cases there's a + icon next to a message. These icons indicate that the message is part of a *thread* (known as a *conversation* in some newsreaders). Clicking the + icon opens the thread, clicking a – icon closes it.

So, what's a thread? Suppose you post a message to a newsgroup that isn't a response to anyone; it's just a new message. Then, a little later, someone else reads your message and replies. That message, because it's a reply, is part of the thread you began. Later, someone else sends a response to *that* message, and it becomes part of the thread. (Note, however, that there's generally a long lag time—a day or more—between the time someone sends a message to a newsgroup and the time that message turns up in everyone's newsreader.)

If you click the little - icon, the thread closes up, and you see only the message at the beginning of the thread. The icon changes to a + icon. Click the + icon to open up the thread again. (A message that has a - icon but does not have messages

Not All the Messages

You might not see all the messages listed at once. Some newsreaders enable you to specify a number to retrieve each time (in the program's Options or Preferences dialog box). So, if the newsgroup is very busy, only a portion of the messages will be listed; you'll have to use another command to retrieve the rest.

159

indented below it is not part of a message thread.) Most newsreaders (but not all) support threading and many other functions in a very similar manner.

To read a message, click the message's header (some newsreaders make you double-click). The newsreader retrieves the message and places it in the bottom pane of the window, as you saw previously in Figure 10.4.

The Messages Are Gone!

The first time you open a newsgroup, all the messages from that newsgroup currently held by your service provider are available to you. How long a message stays in the newsgroup depends on how busy that newsgroup is and how much hard disk space the service provider allows for the newsgroup messages. Eventually, all messages disappear. You don't necessarily see all the newsgroup's messages the next time you use your newsreader, though. When you return to the newsgroup later, you might see all the messages *except* those marked as read.

Why didn't I just say "all the messages except those that you have read"? Well, the newsreader has no way of knowing which messages you've read—it can't see what you are doing. Instead, it has a way of marking messages that it thinks you've read, and it generally provides you with a way to mark messages as read, even if you haven't read them (in effect, providing a way for you to tell the newsreader that you don't want to see the messages).

Marking Your Messages

Most newsreaders mark a message as read when you open the message. Some newsreaders enable you to quickly scan messages without marking them as read. Outlook Express, for instance, has a setting in the Options dialog box labeled **Message is read after being previewed for x second(s)**. So, you can set this option to, say, 10 seconds, allowing you to read a little bit of a message and move on, leaving the message marked as unread.

In addition, newsreaders often allow you to mark the messages as read even if you have not read them. This capability might come in handy to tell the newsreader that you don't want to see certain messages when you come back to the newsgroup in a later session. Suppose you get a couple of messages into a conversation and realize that it's pure rubbish (you'll find a lot of messages that have virtually no usefulness to anyone!). Mark the entire thread as read, and you won't see the rest of the messages the next time you open the newsgroup window. Or maybe the messages are worthwhile (to someone), but you quickly read all the messages' Subject lines and find that nothing interests you. Mark them all as read so you see only new messages the next time.

You can generally mark messages as read in several other ways as well. Here's what you can do in Outlook Express, for instance:

➤ Click a message header and select **Edit**, **Mark As Read**.

➤ Click a message header and select **Edit**, **Mark Conversation As Read** to mark the entire thread as read. (I recently noticed that Outlook Express 5.0 uses the term "conversation" in place of "thread.")

➤ Right-click a message header and select **Mark As Read** or **Mark Conversation As Read** from the shortcut menu.

➤ Choose **Edit**, **Mark All Read** to mark all the current newsgroup's messages as read.

Articles

In keeping with the "news" metaphor, newsgroup messages are often known as *articles*.

Different newsreaders handle read messages differently. Some newsreaders remove them from the list, so you see only the unread messages listed. Gravity, an excellent and popular Windows newsreader (http://www.microplanet.com/), does this. If you don't want the newsreader to remove the read messages, you can change the view by choosing **Newsgroup**, **Filter Display**, **Read Articles** to see just messages you've read, or **Newsgroup**, **Filter Display**, **All Articles** (or by selecting these from the drop-down list box in the toolbar) to make Gravity show the read message headers in gray text. Other newsreaders might use special icons or gray text to indicate messages that you've read.

I Want the Message Back!

If you need to bring a message back, your newsreader probably has some kind of command that enables you to do so. For example, Gravity has the **Newsgroup**, **Filter Display**, **Read Articles** command that I just mentioned. But if your service provider no longer holds the message you want to see—that is, if the message has been removed from the service provider's hard disk to make more space for new messages— you're out of luck. So, if you think there's a chance you might want a message later, save it using the **File**, **Save As** or equivalent command.

Outlook Express, on the other hand, displays all the messages, read and unread. But you can select **View**, **Current View**, and then choose an option. Choosing **Unread Messages**, for instance, would make Outlook Express work like Gravity; it would display only the messages you haven't yet read.

Many newsreaders even have commands for marking messages as unread. Perhaps you've read a message, but want to make sure it appears the next time you open the newsgroup. You can mark it as unread so that it will appear in the list the next time you open the newsgroup. In Outlook Express, for instance, select **Edit**, **Mark As Unread**.

Moving Among the Messages

You'll find a variety of ways to move around in your messages. As you already know, you can double-click the ones you want to view (some newsreaders use a single click). In addition, you'll find commands for moving to the next or previous message, the next or previous thread, and, perhaps, the next or previous unread message or thread. In Outlook Express, these commands are on the View, Next menu.

Many newsreaders also provide a way for you to search for a particular message. Outlook Express has several Find commands in the Edit menu, which enable you to search for a message by the contents of the From line or the Subject line. Outlook Express also enables you to search through the text of the currently selected message. Some other newsreaders have much more sophisticated utilities. In Gravity, for example, select **Search**, **Search** to access a dialog box in which you can search for text in the From or Subject lines or even within the text of the messages; you can also specify whether to search the selected newsgroup or all the subscribed newsgroups. You can even tell Gravity whether to search only those messages already transferred to the newsreader or to search messages still held by the news server.

Saving and Printing

If you run across a message that you think might be useful later, you can save it or print it. Simply marking it as unread isn't good enough because newsgroups eventually drop all messages. So, sooner or later it won't be available.

Most newsreaders have a File, Save As (or File, Save) command or toolbar button. Most also have a File, Print command or button. Of course, you can always highlight the text, copy it to the Clipboard, and then paste it into another application, such as a word processor or email program.

Your Turn: Sending and Responding

There are several ways to send messages or respond to messages. For example, you can use any of the techniques listed here in Outlook Express. (Although Outlook Express is typical, and many newsreaders use these same command names, some newsreaders might use different names.)

➤ You can send a message that isn't a response (that is, you can start a new thread). In Outlook Express, for instance, select **File**, **New**, **News Message** or click the **New Post** toolbar button, or select **Message**, **New Message**.

➤ You can reply to someone else's message. Choose **Message**, **Reply to Group** or click the **Reply Group** button.

➤ You can reply to someone privately via email (that is, send a message that *doesn't* appear in the newsgroup). Select **Message**, **Reply to Sender** or click the **Reply** button.

➤ Reply to both the author and the newsgroup at the same time. Select **Message**, **Reply to All**.

➤ You can send a copy of the message to someone else. Select **Message**, **Forward** or click the **Forward** button.

Sending messages to a newsgroup—or via email in response to a message—is much the same as working with an email window. You type the message and then click some kind of **Send** or **Post** button.

What's This Gibberish? Rot13

Now and again, especially in the more contentious newsgroups, you'll run into messages that seem to be gibberish. Everything's messed up, and each word seems to be a jumbled mix of characters, almost as if the message were encrypted. It is.

What you are seeing is *rot13*, a very simple substitution cipher (one in which a character is substituted for another). Rot13 means "rotated 13." In other words, each character in the alphabet is replaced by the character 13 places further along. Instead of A you see N, instead of B you see O, instead of C you see P, and so on. Got it? So, to read the message, all you need to do is substitute the correct characters. Easy. (Or *Rnfl*, as I should say.)

For those of you in a hurry, there is an easier way. Most newsreaders have a command that quickly does the rot13 for you. For instance, in Outlook Express, you can select **Message**, **Unscramble (rot13)**, and, like magic, the message changes into real words. If you don't run across rot13 messages and want to see what rot13 looks like, use the command to take a normal message and convert it to rot13 message (which is what I did for Figure 10.5). How do you create one of these messages to send to a newsgroup? You'll often find a rot13 command in the window in which you create a message. For instance, in Gravity's message composition window, there's an **Options**, **Scramble (rot13)** command. For some reason, Outlook Express, although it can unscramble messages, doesn't let you use rot13 when sending messages.

You might be wondering why a person would encode a message with a system that is so ridiculously easy to break. People don't rot13 (if you'll excuse my use of the term as a verb) their messages as a security measure that's intended to make them unreadable to anyone who doesn't have the secret key. After all, anyone with a decent newsreader has the key. No, using rot13 is a way of saying, "If you read this message, you might be offended; so if you are easily offended, *don't read it*!" Rot13 messages are often crude, lewd, or just plain rude. When a message is encoded with rot13, the reader can decide whether he wants to risk being offended.

Figure 10.5

An example of a rot13 message.

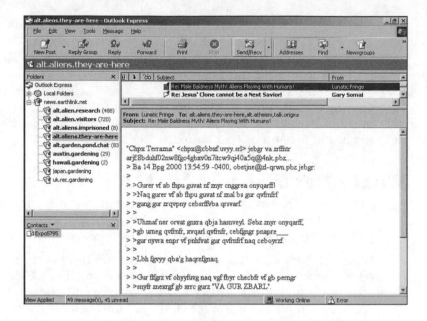

Pictures (and Sounds) from Words

The newsgroups contain simple text messages. You can't place a character into a message that is not in the standard text character set. So, if you want to send a computer file in a newsgroup message—maybe you want to send a picture, a sound, or a word processing document—you must convert it to text. Some of the newer newsreaders help you do this, either by automating the process of attaching *MIME*-formatted files to your messages or by *uuencoding* files and inserting them into your messages. Some newsreaders will even convert such files on-the-fly and display pictures inside the message when they read the newsgroup messages; others will automatically convert the file to its original format.

If you were using Outlook Express, for example, you could follow these steps to send a file:

1. Open the message composition window using the **Message**, **New Message** command or the **Message**, **Reply to Group** command.

2. Choose **Insert**, **File Attachment** or click the **Attach** toolbar button (the little paper clip). You'll see a typical File Open dialog box, from which you can choose the file you want to send.

3. Select the file and click **OK**. The name of the attached file appears in the bottom pane of the message composition window (see Figure 10.6).

4. Send the message (click the **Send** button or select **File**, **Send Message**). The name of the file appears in the message header when you view the messages in that particular newsgroup.

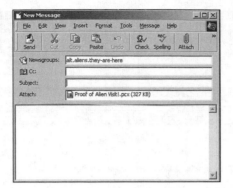

Figure 10.6

Most newsreaders let you send uuencoded or MIME files to a newsgroup. You can see the file at the bottom of this email composition window.

What method was used to send this message? MIME or uuencode? Outlook Express doesn't make this clear, and to be honest it doesn't matter much these days—most newsreaders these days can figure out which method has been used to post a message. Some newsreaders let you quickly specify which method to use; Gravity, for instance, enables you to select **uuencode** or **MIME** from a drop-down list box at the top of the window. In Outlook Express, the method of transmission is hidden away. By default, the program uses uuencode when sending to newsgroups (that's the standard method of sending files to newsgroups). If you want to use MIME, you have to go back to the main Outlook Express window, choose **Tools**, **Options**, click the **Send** tab, click the **Plain Text Settings** button, and click the **MIME** option button.

When a message with an attached file is posted to a newsgroup, what do participants of that newsgroup see? If the attached file is an image, as many are, most newsreaders will display the picture inside the message. Others might display a jumble of text (the image is actually transferred as text characters, which can then be converted back to the image by the newsreader), something like that shown in Figure 10.7

Net Tips

No Built-In Converter?

If you are using a newsreader that doesn't have a built-in conversion system, you can save the message on your hard disk and then use a conversion program such as Wincode (a Windows program that converts uuencode), munpack (a DOS program that converts MIME), or Yet Another Base64 Decoder (a Macintosh program that converts both uuencode and MIME). You can find conversion programs at the software libraries mentioned in Appendix C, "All the Software You'll Ever Need."

Figure 10.7

This message contains an attached file. The jumbled text is the file, converted to text. The text must be converted back before you can view the file.

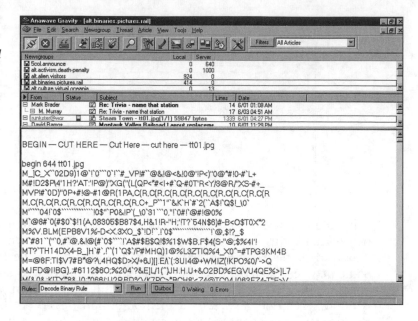

Even if your newsreader doesn't initially display the image within the message, it might be able to convert the image file. In particular, newsreaders can often convert GIF, JPEG, and perhaps BMP files to their original formats. In the case of Gravity, for instance, you can click the **View Image** button or select **Article**, **View**, and Gravity converts the file for you and then places it in a viewer window (as you can see in Figure 10.8). Outlook Express displays the image by default. (In some versions of Outlook Express, you can tell it *not* to display images by choosing **Tools**, **Options**, clicking the **Read** tab, and clearing the **Automatically Show Picture Attachments in Messages** check box; for some reason more recent versions don't provide this capability.)

A few newsreaders can even decode several messages together. If someone posts a large picture split into several pieces, for instance (as people often do), the newsreader might automatically retrieve all the pieces and paste them together.

The Fancy Stuff

Some newsreaders have extra features. For example, the newsreader might be able to automatically flag messages if the header contains a particular word. Or you might be able to set up the newsreader to automatically remove a message if the header contains a particular word. Outlook Express has a filtering system that you can use to automatically throw away some messages, depending on who sent the message or what the subject is, whether it's older than a specified time, or whether it's longer than a specified length (choose **Tools**, **Message Rules**, **News**). Some other newsreaders have much better filtering systems. Gravity, for instance, can throw the message away, display a special alert message, or save the message in a text file according to what appears in the header or body text.

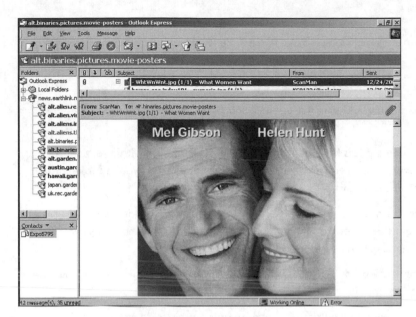

Many newsreaders display links in the newsgroup messages. You can click email addresses or Web URLs that appear in messages to automatically open the mail window or your browser. Outlook Express can set up a little slideshow, displaying one image after another in messages that contain multiple images.

Newsreaders can do a lot of different things, so you might want to experiment to find out what's available in the newsreader you have; if you spend a lot of time in newsgroups, you might want to go searching for the most capable newsreader. (Check out Appendix C for information about finding software.)

A Word of Warning

Newsgroups can be addictive. You can find messages about anything that interests you, angers you, or turns you on. If you are not careful, you can spend half your life in the newsgroups. You sit down in the morning to check your favorite newsgroups, and the next thing you know you haven't bathed, eaten, or picked up the kids from school.

Hang around the newsgroups, and you'll find people who are obviously spending a significant amount of time writing messages. These people are usually independently wealthy (that is, they work for large corporations who don't mind paying them to talk politics over the Internet or who don't know that they are paying them to do so). If you have a job, a family, and a life, be careful!

The Least You Need to Know

➤ A newsgroup is an area in which people with similar interests leave public messages, a sort of online public debate or discussion.

➤ Newsgroup names use a hierarchical system, and each group might have subgroups within it.

➤ Most major online services have built-in newsreaders. If you are with a service provider, it might have given you a newsreader. If for any reason you're looking for a newsreader, try the software "libraries" listed in Appendix C.

➤ To begin using the newsgroups, start your newsreader, and then download a list of newsgroups from the server. You might also have to subscribe to the groups you want to read; each newsreader does this a little differently.

➤ A good newsreader lets you view a "thread" or "conversation," which shows how messages relate to one another.

➤ Rot13 is a special encoding system that stops people from accidentally stumbling across offensive messages. Many newsreaders have a rot13 command that converts the message to normal text.

Chapter 11

More Internet Discussions— Mailing Lists and Web Forums

Are you getting enough sleep? Are you socializing, meeting with friends and family? Do you have time to eat and bathe? Yes? Then, you're clearly not spending enough time on the Internet. I've already shown you how to work with thousands of newsgroups, which are discussion groups on almost any subject (see Chapter 10, "Finding and Using Newsgroups"), but obviously that's not enough. So, here are thousands more discussion groups: the mailing lists and Web forums.

The difference between mailing lists and Web forums and newsgroups is simply the manner in which messages are distributed. Newsgroups are distributed through a system specifically set up for their distribution, but mailing lists are distributed via email, and Web forums make messages available at a Web site through the use of Web-page forms. How many of these discussion groups exist? Hundreds of thousands. L-Soft, the publisher of the well-known LISTSERV mailing-list program, claims there are over 190,000 LISTSERV mailing lists, and LISTSERV is just one of many programs used to run these lists. (Because there's no central distribution system, tracking them all is not easy.)

As for Web forums, anyone with a little time and money (or lots of time and a few geek genes) can set up a discussion group at his Web site, so there could be many thousands of these. Again, they're hard to track, but one directory, several years ago, estimated that there were about 25,000 Web forums. That's long before today's popularity of Web forums, so there are probably hundreds of thousands of these by now.

How Do Mailing Lists Work?

Each mailing list discussion group has an email address. You begin by subscribing to the group you are interested in. (I'll explain how in a moment.) The email address acts as a mail *reflector*, a system that receives mail and then sends it on to a list of addresses. Every time someone sends a message to a group of which you are a member, you get a copy of the mail. And every time you send a message to a group address, everyone else on the list gets a copy.

In Chapter 10, you learned that you read newsgroups using special programs called newsreaders. However, you don't need any special program to work with a mailing list; all you need is whatever program you use for reading your email. You send email messages to the list in the same way that you send messages to anyone else: You enter the mailing list's address in the To: box of your mail program's Compose window, type your message, and send it. Incoming messages from the mailing list are placed in your Inbox right along with messages from your friends and colleagues.

To find the mailing lists of interest to you, follow these suggestions:

➤ Use your Web browser to go to the Liszt site (`http://www.liszt.com/`), probably the best directory of mailing lists. You can also try Tile.Net (`http://www.tile.net/`). You can search these lists for a particular name or by subject.

➤ Go to `http://www.lsoft.com/catalist.html`, where you'll find the Catalist, the "official catalog of LISTSERV lists." They recently listed an index of more than 42,129 public lists, out of a total of 190,611 LISTSERV lists.

➤ Send an email message to `listserv@listserv.net`. In the message text, type **list global** *keyword*, where *keyword* is a word you want to search for within the mailing list names or subjects. For instance, you could type **list global geo** to find lists related to geography. You'll get an email message back listing the matches.

➤ Search for mailing lists at one of the Web search sites (covered in Chapter 15, "Finding What You Need Online"), or try the `http://dir.yahoo.com/ Computers_and_Internet/Internet/Chats_and_Forums/Mailing_Lists/` Web page.

➤ Go to the news.announce.newusers newsgroup. Sometimes you can find a list of mailing lists posted there. (See Chapter 10 for information about working with newsgroups.)

➤ Learn by word of mouth. Hang around in some newsgroups and mailing lists and you'll hear about private mailing lists that you might be able to join by invitation.

The Types of Lists

There are two basic types of mailing lists:

➤ Manually administered

➤ Automated

Peered Groups

Some LISTSERV mailing lists are *peered*. A peered LISTSERV group is the same as a *moderated* newsgroup: Someone is checking the mail and deciding what stays and what gets trashed.

Some very small mailing lists are set up to be administered by a person who will add your name to the list. Such lists are often private, with subscription by invitation only. Other lists use special mailing list programs to automatically add your name to the list when you subscribe. These are often, although not always, public lists that are open to anyone.

One of the most common and best-known forms of automated lists is the LISTSERV list. These lists are named after the LISTSERV mailing list program, which at one time was so common that the term LISTSERV has become almost synonymous with mailing-list discussion group; people often refer to these discussion groups as *listservs*, even if they're not managed using that program.

There are many other mailing list programs, too; Lyris and Majordomo are a couple of the most common. But you don't need any fancy mailing list software to set up a small mailing list; it's quite easy to set up a manually administered mailing list using a simple email program, or to use one of the free mailing-list services.

Free Services

Want to set up your own mailing list discussion group? There are services that make it very easy for you to do so. Check out eGroups (http://www.egroups.com/), Topica (http://www.topica.com/), and Coollist (http://www.coollist.com/), for instance.

Using a LISTSERV Group

There are almost 200,000 LISTSERV groups, covering subjects such as those listed in Table 11.1.

Table 11.1   A Sampling of LISTSERV Groups

Mailing List	Description
ACMEPET-L@ACMEPETMAIL.COM	AcmePet's Weekly Newsletter
AFNS@AFPRODUCTS.EASE.LSOFT.COM	Air Force News Service
AUSPGRIS@LISTS.DPI.QLD.GOV.AU	Australian Plant Genetic Resource Information System list
AUSSIE-AGTEACH-NET@LISTS.DPI.QLD.GOV.AU	The Aussie Agriculture Teacher's Discussion List
AUSTVGUIDE@YOUR.ABC.NET.AU	Australia TV Program Schedules
BIG@NETFINITY2.STOCKINVESTOR.COM	Stockinvestor Newsletter
BOSUENET@LISTSERV.HEANET.IE	Botswana Students Union Eire
BURPEENEWS@DISPATCH.GARDEN.ORG	A gardening newsletter from Burpee and the National Gardening Association
BVNEWSLETTER@MAILSERV.DIGITALCITY.COM	Black Voices Newsletter
CALIGUS@LISTSERV.HEANET.IE	Biology and management in the control of lice on fish farms' project
CELTIC-L@LISTSERV.HEANET.IE	CELTIC-L—The Celtic Culture List.
CHRISTIANITY-ONLINE@LISTSERV.AOL.COM	Christianity Online Connection newsletter
COLOCARD-FR@BLIZZARD.SNOW.COM	Colorado Card—Front Range
CSMS-G@CSMS.EDU.MN	Computer Science & Management School of Mongolia
CYBERGRRL-WEBNEWS@LISTS.CGIM.COM	CyberGRRL! Webnews
DIETCITY@PEACH.EASE.LSOFT.COM	The resource for diet and nutrition information on the Web!
DIX-NEUF@LISTSERV.LIV.AC.UK	19th Century French Studies
DOCOMO@ML.SOFTWARE.NE.JP	NTT DoCoMo Weekly news Magazine in Japanese
EDONLINE@TVISIONS.COM	The Journal of Electronic Defense Listserv
EMIGRANT@LISTSERV.IOL.IE	The Irish Emigrant—weekly newsletter for the Irish abroad
FBN@LISTSERV.AOL.COM	Fly-Fishing Broadcast Network
I-ADVERTISING@GUAVA.EASE.LSOFT.COM	The Internet Advertising Discussion List
IBN-L@LISTSERV.HEANET.IE	Irish Bird Network
KOSOVO-L@FIDO.ORG.YU	Kosovo crisis: discussions and articles (Yugoslavian list)

Table 11.1   A Sampling of LISTSERV Groups CONTINUED

Mailing List	Description
MAIG@LISTSERV.CYBERHQ.NET.MY	The Malaysian Astronomy Interest Group
MICRONLINK@MICRON.NET	The Micron Electronics, Inc. Product Announcement List
MOMSONLINE@LISTSERV.AOL.COM	Moms Online Main Mailing List
MSN-UK-NEWS@ANNOUNCE. MICROSOFT.COM	MSN Update: Your Guide to What's Happening on msn.co.uk
MW-WOD@LISTSERV.WEBSTER.M-W.COM	Merriam-Webster's Word of the Day
POSTMITA@LISTSERV.NIC.IT	Postmasters of Italian Domains
SCTB11@IDEFIX.SPC.ORG.NC	Eleventh Meeting of the Standing Committee on Tuna and Billfish
TASTING@PEACH.EASE.LSOFT.COM	Wine Tasting's List
TELECOMMAGAZINE@TVISIONS.COM	The Telecommunications Magazine Listserv
TVGUIDE@LISTSERV.TVGUIDE.COM	TV Guide Online Insider
VBHOWTO@LISTSERV.XTRAS.COM	The Weekly Source of Tips and Tools for the Visual Basic Developer
VOICES-L@ORACLE.WIZARDS.COM	Voices in My Head List
WWF-L@LISTSERV.AOL.COM	World Wrestling Federation Newsletter
YOUTH-TECH@LISTSERV.AOL.COM	A Weekly Newsletter for the Kids & Teens Technology Community

Does this list give you an idea of the wild, wacky, and well-worth-reading mailing lists available to you? (I'm planning to check out the Voices in My Head list.) And this tiny portion of what's out there just includes the LISTSERV groups; the many non-LISTSERV groups cover similarly eclectic subject matters.

The LISTSERV Address

A LISTSERV address consists of two parts: the group name and the LISTSERV hostname. For instance, the address of the Internet Tourbus group is `tourbus@listserv.aol.com`. Tourbus is the name of the group, and `listserv.aol.com` is the hostname, the name of the computer acting as the listserv server. A host is a computer that has the LISTSERV program, and it handles one or more LISTSERV groups. A site might have dozens of groups; the `listserv.aol.com`, for instance, also maintains the Netguide, AboutWorkNews, and Christianity-Online groups, among others.

Let's Do It: Subscribing

When you've found a LISTSERV group to which you want to subscribe, you must send an email message to the LISTSERV host computer (not to the discussion group itself) asking to subscribe to the list. Don't worry, you are not going to have to pay anything; the vast majority of mailing lists are completely free. Send a message with the following text in the body (not the subject) of the message:

> **SUBSCRIBE** *group firstname lastname*

For instance, if I wanted to subscribe to the Internet Tourbus list on AOL's Listserv server, I would send a message to **listserv@listserv.aol.com**, and in the body of the message, I'd write **subscribe tourbus Peter Kent**. (Many lists don't require that you include your name—I may be able to send the command SUBSCRIBE TOURBUS, without my name—but some do.) As you can see in Figure 11.1, you send the message to listserv@*sitename* (in this case, to listserv@listserv.aol.com), and the SUBSCRIBE message contains only the name of the group (not the entire group address).

Figure 11.1

This is all it takes to subscribe to a LISTSERV mailing list.

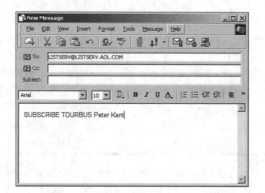

You might (or might not) receive some kind of confirmation message from the group. Such a message tells you that you have subscribed and provides background information about the group and the different commands you can use. You might receive a message telling you how to confirm your subscription. If so, follow the instructions in the message. You might also receive instructions about working with the mailing list; read these instructions carefully, as they will contain important information.

After you've subscribed, you can either sit back and wait for the messages to arrive, or you can send your own messages. To send messages, address mail to the full group address (to tourbus@listserv.aol.com, for example).

Enough Already! Unsubscribing

When you're tired of receiving all these messages (and the volume might be overwhelming), you'll have to unsubscribe, which you do by sending another message to the LISTSERV address. You still send the message to `listserv@`*`sitename`* (such as `listserv@listserv.aol.com`), but this time, type **SIGNOFF** *groupname* (**SIGNOFF tourbus**, for instance) in the body of the message.

Figure 11.2 shows the SIGNOFF message you use to unsubscribe. Again, make sure you address it to `listserv@`*`sitename`*, not to the group name. Make sure the group name—but not the entire group address—appears after SIGNOFF.

Don't Forget These Details

Note that you might have to put something in the Subject line; some email programs won't let you send email unless you include a subject. In such a case, just type something (a space or 1, for instance) in the Subject line. If your email program automatically inserts a signature (information such as your name, street address, and so on that is inserted at the end of the message), turn off the signature before sending the message, or you'll get error messages back from the LISTSERV site.

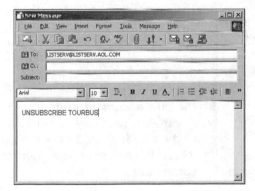

Figure 11.2

Unsubscribing from a LISTSERV mailing list is also easy.

Getting Fancy with LISTSERV

You can do a few neat things with LISTSERV. By sending email messages to the LISTSERV site, you can tell the LISTSERV software how you want to handle your messages. You can ask LISTSERV to send you an acknowledgment each time you send a message (by default, most groups won't do this). You can find information about another group member, or you can tell LISTSERV not to provide information about you to other users. You can tell LISTSERV to stop sending you messages temporarily (perhaps when you go on vacation), or you can tell it to send only the message subjects instead of the entire messages. You can request a specific message, and you can even search the archives for old messages.

When you first subscribe to a mailing list, it's a good idea to send the **info** command to the listserv@ *sitename* address (not the newsgroup). Put the word **info** in the body of the message. A document containing important information about working with the list will be returned to you.

You can also combine commands in one message. For instance, you can send an email message to listserv@ *sitename* with these lines in the body of the message:

list

query *groupname*

info ?

This message tells LISTSERV to send you a list of the groups handled by this site (**list**), to tell you which options you have set (**query** *groupname*), and to send you a list of information guides (**info ?**). It's a good idea to use this last command to find out about user documentation the list has available and then to use the **info** *documentname* command to have specific documents sent to you. (At some sites, sending email to the LISTSERV address with the message **INFO REFCARD** will get you a document outlining the commands.)

Message Digests

To make your mailing lists easier to handle, get message digests. With message digests, you'll receive one large message at the end of the day that contains all the messages the mailing list has received during the day instead of receiving dozens of messages throughout the day. To request message digests, send a message to the LISTSERV server at **listserv@***sitename* and type the message **set** *listname* **digest** (such as **set tourbus digest**).

The message you receive at the end of the day has a list of subjects at the top. You can use your email program's Find command (or save the message in a text file and use your word processor's Find command) to quickly get to the messages that interest you. If you want to turn off the digest, use the command **set** *listname* **nodig**. Note, however, that not all mailing lists can provide message digests.

Remember This!

Remember that when you want to send a message to be read by other group members, you must address it to the *groupname@sitename*. For all other purposes (to subscribe, unsubscribe, change user options, get more information, and so on), send the message to `listserv@sitename`. Send these messages to the group itself, and you might get complaints. But, hey, you wouldn't be alone. Many of us (me included, several times) forget to change the address and send these commands to the wrong address! These days, some LISTSERV servers can recognize a message that contains commands, intercept it before it gets to the mailing list group, and send it back to you.

Using Majordomo and Other Mailing-List Programs

Different mailing-list programs work in slightly different, yet similar, ways. Another very popular mailing-list program is Majordomo. Subscribing to a Majordomo list is similar to working with LISTSERV. To subscribe, send a message to `majordomo@sitename`. For instance, `majordomo@usa.net`, `majordomo@big.host.com`, and so on. In the body of the message, type **subscribe** *group firstname lastname*.

The same as with LISTSERV, eh? When you unsubscribe, though, you'll use a different command. Instead of SIGNOFF, use

unsubscribe group

Finally, when sending messages to the group, remember to send them to *group@sitename*.

Mailing-List Programs

There are many mailing-list programs. They all work in a similar manner, but with a few variations. In some cases, for instance, you don't have to provide your name, just enter a **subscribe** *group* command. Or maybe the command will be **join** *group*. Also, some mailing list programs require that you place the command in the Subject line, not the body of the message.

Majordomo might be set up differently, though. You might have to send your subscription message to *listname*-`request@hostname`. For instance, if the list is called goodbeer, and it's at the `bighost.com` hostname, you would send your subscription request to `goodbeer-request@bighost.com`. After you've subscribed, you can send your correspondence to the list to `goodbeer@bighost.com`.

The moral of this story is—read a mailing list's instructions carefully before subscribing and using the group.

Using Manually Administered Lists

Some lists are administered manually. That means there is no computer running the list; instead, some person reads the subscription requests and adds people to the list manually. Such a mailing list can be administered in many ways. You might send email to the person who administers the list and say, "Hey, add me to the list, please." Often, however, there's a special address associated with the list. You might have to send your subscription message to `listname-request@hostname` (just as you would for some of the Majordomo lists).

Beware of Replies

On the other hand, there's a very good reason to set up a mailing list so the reply automatically goes to the sender instead of the list. The single most common and embarrassing mistake made on mailing lists is to send a private message to the mailing list. This is not just a "newbie" mistake, by the way; even in mailing lists full of long-term Internet geeks, people accidentally post private messages publicly. If a mailing list is set up with a Reply To address that returns mail to the list, be very careful!

Handling Mailing List Correspondence

Working with a mailing list is quite simple. When a message arrives, you find it in your email inbox along with all your normal email. If you read a message to which you want to reply, use the reply function of your email program (see Chapter 6, "Sending and Receiving Email" for more information), and the new message is addressed to the correct place. At least, in most cases, it is addressed correctly. Check the return address that your email program enters for you. With some mailing lists, you'll find that the return address in the header of the message you received is not the address to which you are supposed to send messages—rather, it's the address of the person who sent the message to the group. I find this rather irritating, but many groups work this way. You might be able to use a **Reply to All** command (not all mail programs have this, but many do) to send a message to the originator *and* to the list. Otherwise, you'll have to type the list address into the To box in your mail composition window. To send a message about a new subject, write a new message, address it to the mailing list address, and send it.

In some ways, working with mailing lists is not as convenient as working with newsgroups. The newsgroup programs have a lot of features for dealing with discussions. Of course, your email program will almost certainly let you print and save messages just as a newsgroup program would. What's often missing, though, are the threading functions that you get in newsgroup messages (which enable you to quickly see which messages are part of a series of responses). Some mail programs have these—Netscape's Messenger, part of the Communicator suite of programs, does—but most do not. You might also find that messages are sent to you out of order, in which case you might end up reading a response to a message before you read the original message. This is another reason you might want to use the message digest (discussed earlier) to get the messages in the most convenient form possible.

Filtering Tools

Learn how to use your mail program's filtering tools. That way you can quickly direct incoming mail from mailing lists into the appropriate folders and even automatically delete messages that you're not interested in.

Using the Web Forums

Web forums are discussion groups associated with a particular Web site. They're often technical support forums, forums set up by a company to help provide information to their customers, but you might run into forums about many subjects and for many purposes.

Finding Web forums is a little difficult; they're the sort of thing you run into, rather than go looking for. Probably the best way to find them is at a search engine. I haven't yet been able to track down a good Web forum directory.

To use a Web forum, click the appropriate links at a Web site. You'll use forums to read messages and to respond to them; you can see an example in Figure 11.3.

Figure 11.3

A Jack-the-Ripper discussion, an example of a Discusware Web-based discussion forum.

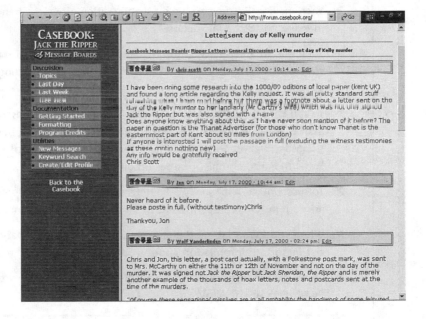

Discusware

Discusware is an excellent, and free, discussion-board system for Web sites. The publisher claims that 30,000 copies are in use around the world. You can find examples at `http://www.discusware.com/discus/`, and learn how to install the program at *your* Web site.

The Least You Need to Know

➤ A mailing list is a discussion group in which messages are exchanged through the email system.

➤ Mailing lists might be administered manually or run by a program such as LISTSERV, Lyris, Majordomo, or by a free service.

➤ Each mailing-list program uses a slightly different way to handle subscriptions and messages; read the instructions!

➤ Subscribe to a LISTSERV group by including the command **subscribe *groupname firstname lastname*** in the body of a message and sending the message to `listserv@sitename`.

➤ To subscribe to a Majordomo list, you normally send a message saying **SUBSCRIBE *groupname firstname lastname*** in the body. The message goes to the Majordomo address (such as `majordomo@bighost`), not the list name address. Some Majordomos might be set up differently, though.

➤ To subscribe to a manually administered list, write to the person running the list and ask to join. Or you might need to send an email to `listname-request@hostname`.

➤ When you join a list, send a message with the **info** command in the body to find out important information about working with the list.

➤ Thousands of Web forums are available, but they're hard to track down. Search for **"web forum"** at AltaVista.

More Ways to Communicate— Net Phones, Conferences, Videoconferences

In This Chapter

➤ Voice on the Net: the potential and problems

➤ Calling other computers

➤ Making PC-to-Phone calls, in the U.S. or worldwide

➤ Free phone calls within the U.S., and even overseas

➤ Text transmission, whiteboards, conferencing, and more

➤ Videoconferencing and other weird stuff

You've already seen a few ways that the Internet enables you to communicate with friends, family, and colleagues. You can use email, and you can use chat and instant messaging (Chapter 8, "Using Online Chat Rooms," and Chapter 9, "Instant Messaging"). But these systems are a little clunky. Most people alive today grew up in the telephone age; we're used to picking up a phone and *talking* to people. And although Internet programmers like to use cute names such as chat and talk, the fact is that these programs *don't* use real chat and don't use real talk; they use typing.

So, now I have some good news (and some bad news) for you. The good news is that there *is* a system that allows you to really talk across the Internet. The bad news? There's a good chance you'll never use it (at least not anytime soon) because of its disadvantages.

A year or two ago talking on the Internet—known as VON, or Voice on the Net— was set to be the Next Big Thing. But Next Big Things sometimes don't work out.

I'm embarrassed to admit that I called it the next big thing, even though I was aware of the problems. Still, VON *is* available, and some people do use it—and there's still a chance it will turn into something big—so, let's take a closer look.

The Incredible Potential of Voice on the Net

A few years ago, I wrote a book with my brother. Because he's in England and I'm in the U.S., I knew we'd be spending a lot of time on the phone—and that worried me. If I had to pay 80 cents a minute, my phone bill was going to skyrocket. So, I decided to look into Voice on the Net.

I figured that if I could communicate across the Internet rather than using the phone, I'd save a fortune. With an online service charging $19.95 for unlimited access, my calls would be essentially free. (Internet access in England was much more expensive at the time, but, hey, that's his problem.) Even if I used a service in which I was paying by the hour, it would probably, at that time, have been around $1.00 an hour, less than 2 cents a minute.

Can you see the potential now? Do you have relatives in Russia, Australia, or France? You can cut your costs to the bone, or you can spend the same amount of money but talk for a much longer time than you ever really wanted to. Similarly, if you run a business with offices around the world, you can connect the offices' networks to the Internet, get everyone a sound card and a mike, and spend the money you save on a new Mercedes.

But it gets even better. Imagine that someone created a special program that would allow phone calls across the Internet to be connected to real phone lines. A computer hooked up to the phone lines in, say, London could accept Internet calls from anywhere in the world, connect them to the phone system, and allow Internet users to make *domestic* calls within the United Kingdom. Such a system already exists, although perhaps the theory's better than the reality; we'll look at this sort of service a little later in this chapter.

Internet phones can carry more than just voice. They can also carry text and even doodles; some even enable you to transfer computer files at the same time you speak. So, while you are talking to someone, you can be transmitting the text of a memo or sketching something or sending a photograph. Internet phones are a very powerful tool you're going to be seeing a lot of very soon.

The Downside

That's the theory. Now for the facts. I never did use VON to communicate with my brother while working on that book; the disadvantages outweighed the advantages. The phone companies are in no imminent danger of going out of business.

First, many people don't have computers. Many don't have the sort of equipment required to use a VON system (you'll learn about the hardware requirements in a moment). Then, consider these other problems:

➤ The calls don't provide high-quality sound. You will *not* hear a pin dropping at the other end of one of these lines!

➤ They are inconvenient. Because few people spend all day connected to the Internet, you'd have to arrange a call in many cases. (Still, in the early days of the telephone, that's just what people did. They arranged a time to go to the drugstore and rent time on the phone, and their relatives on the other side of the country, or the world, did the same. In many parts of the world, that's still how people use telephones.)

➤ Currently, there are still a few compatibility problems; you have to make sure you're both using compatible software, and there are several different transmission systems.

Can You Hold Back Technology?

Although the phone companies will not be going out of business anytime soon, some were worried enough to try to ban Internet phones or force companies providing VON services to follow the same rules as true telecommunications companies. They reasoned, quite logically perhaps, that if a company provides international phone service, it doesn't matter whether it's over the Internet or through a phone company—the rules should be the same.

The phone companies have given up trying to ban the technology. Apart from the fact that this is similar to a group of horse-drawn carriage manufacturers trying to ban the new-fangled automobile, it's hard to see how you can ban this kind of technology. Even if you ban it in the United States, foreign companies will still sell it across the Internet. If we're going to do that, perhaps we should ban international credit card transactions or close our cyberborders.

Here's another problem for Internet phone calls. The price for long-distance telephone calls has been dropping precipitously for several years and seems likely to continue. I used to pay 80 cents a minute to call from the United States to the United Kingdom, but now I pay 12 cents, any time of day or night. And pressure seems to be lower still, with companies advertising rates around 10 cents or less a minute on weekends. With prices this low, VON systems are going to have to improve dramatically before many people will use them.

Web Savvy

Full-Duplex Versus Half-Duplex

If you have a full-duplex card, both you and the other person can talk at the same time. The card can record your voice at the same time it's playing incoming sounds. If you have only a half-duplex card, you'll have to take turns talking (like people talking over the radio in those old war movies: "Joe, you there? Over").

Do You Have the Hardware You Need?

The idea of working with VON might sound interesting, but there's a small hurdle you have to leap first. Do you have the right equipment?

To even consider using Internet phones, you'll need more than just some old computer. If you're still working with a 386 PC or a slow 486, VON probably won't work well. If you have a Macintosh, you'll probably need a Quadra, Performa, or Power PC (some of these programs run only on the Power PC). On any platform, you'll also need a reasonable amount of RAM—probably a bare minimum of 32MB, preferably 64MB or more. But as I always say, you can never have too much money, too much time off, or too much RAM.

Next, you'll need a connection to the Internet, of course, and it should ideally be some kind of fast connection; a cable modem, DSL, or something better. If you have a dial-in connection, you'll want at least a 28,800bps connection, but even that's a bare minimum, and your calls may sound pretty bad. (Remember, just because you have a fast modem doesn't mean you have a fast connection.)

You need a sound card, of course. Be sure that it's a 16-bit card or better and that it also allows you to record (some don't). Ideally, you need a *full-duplex* card. Check the card's specifications (on the box) when you buy it to see whether it's full-duplex. You also need a microphone and speakers or perhaps a headset. Most new computers come with all the required equipment (except, perhaps, a microphone, which you can buy pretty cheaply). But if your computer is three or four years old, you might not have what you need.

Finally, you need the software. That's easy enough to come by, but the big catch is that you have software that uses the same system for transmitting the voice signals as the software used by the person you want to call. That shouldn't be a problem anymore; early in 1998, the H.323 protocol was finally accepted as the industry standard for VON, so pretty much all VON programs should be able to communicate with all other VON programs.

Which Program Should I Use?

The most likely way you'll run into VON software is in conjunction with your Instant Messaging software. The three most popular systems—AOL Instant Messenger, Yahoo! Messenger, and AOL Messenger—all have VON built into them, as does PowWow, another very popular system (see Chapter 9, "Instant Messaging," for more information).

There are a couple of other significant systems: Net2Phone (`http://www.net2phone.com/`) and Microsoft's **NetMeeting**, which is built into some versions of Windows (`http://www.microsoft.com/netmeeting/`). And VocalTec's Internet Phone is very highly rated, although the company distributes the product only through third parties (not directly to consumers anymore—`http://www.vocaltec.com/`.) Netscape used to have a system called Netscape CoolTalk, and later on Netscape Communicator Conference, but they seem to have taken this product off the market. You can find other products by going to Yahoo! and searching for **internet voice** (see Chapter 15). Many such products are available as shareware, commercial products, and give-it-away-ware. You'll find WebPhone (NetSpeak), FreeTel, DigiPhone (Third Planet Publishing), and others. However, note that this is another area of Internet software that is actually shrinking, as companies stop developing products thanks to the overwhelming lack of interest in VON on the part of the general public, and the power of the top few products to grab what few users there are.

PC-to-Phone Connections

A variation of VON is what's become known as PC-to-Phone, the capability to make phone calls from your computer, across the Internet, and onto a local phone service. So, you might connect across the Internet from New York to Sydney and be connected to the Australian phone system, which means you can make international calls at very low rates.

The predominant company running PC-to-Phone services is Net2Phone, and in fact not only their own product but a number of other products use Net2Phone PC-to-Phone services. If you use MSN Messenger to talk through a microphone connected to your computer and connect to a phone somewhere, you'll be using Net2Phone's services. And there's even a system that lets you place free long-distance calls using your Web browser—dialpad.com (`http://www.Dialpad.com/`).

In some cases these calls are free. Call from MSN Messenger to any telephone in the United States, and there's no charge (they pop up a little browser window containing an advertisement, instead). AOL currently charges just one cent per minute for domestic calls.

Calls overseas are often very cheap. You can call London, England, for instance, at any time of the day or night, for just 4 cents a minute (compared with between 9 cents and 15 cents a minute through Sprint at the time of writing).

Such systems are on the borderline of being worthwhile. I can actually find rates to England of 6 or 7 cents, so the savings aren't great and perhaps won't be worth the hassle. On the other hand, if I had to call one of the areas of the world where telephone rates are very high, Net2Phones rates may be a real savings for me. I took a quick look at a discount phone plan, and discovered that in some cases Net2Phone would save me quite a bit. Afghanistan would cost $1.49 a minute through the discount plan, $1.13 through Net2Phone, and Belarus would cost 39 cents a minute for the discount plan but only 30 cents a minute through Net2Phone. Yet some countries are actually *more* expensive through Net2Phone—Belize, for instance, was 12 cents a minute more through Net2Phone than through the discount plan.

Free International PC-to-Phone

There may be a way to get free international phone calls. A number of services have been set up to enable you to call from your PC to particular countries. For instance, WowRing.com (`http://www.wowring.com/`) will let you call from the U.S. to Canada, France, Germany, Hong Kong, and the United Kingdom, at no charge, whereas MyFreeLD.com (`http://www.myfreeld.com/`) gets you to the United Kingdom, France, Switzerland, and the Netherlands.

You can find a list of such services at `http://www.pulver.com/fwd/`, and by searching at any major Internet search engine.

Internet Call Waiting

There's another interesting voice-related Internet service, something called *Internet Call Waiting*. If you use one phone line for both Internet connections and your telephone, an Internet Call Waiting service can let you know when someone is calling you.

Here's how it works. You find an Internet Call Waiting service; your phone company may be able to provide this service, or you can use an independent service such as BuzMe (`http://www.buzme.com/`) or WhoIsIt? (`http://www.whoisit.com/`). You add the Call Forwarding on Busy and Call Forwarding No Answer features to your phone line, forwarding the call to the Internet Call Waiting service. The service then checks to see whether you are online; if you are, it sends you a message, using Caller ID to even tell you *who* is calling. You can then decide whether to take the call, play a pre-recorded reply to the caller ("I'll Call You Back," or perhaps "Call Me Later"), reject the call, or send the call into a voice mail box.

Making PC-to-PC Calls

Let's take a look at how to work with one of these VON systems to call another PC. I'll assume that you have your sound card and microphone properly installed—that's one can of worms I'm *not* crawling into! I'll also assume that you've installed some sort of phone program and have run through the setup, whatever that may be (it will probably test your microphone, and may also ask for personal information such as your name, Internet email address, and so on). If you're using an instant messenger program, you may have to install some extra software to get the phone component to work.

What happens next depends on the system you're using, of course. To quote Ghostbusters, "Who ya gonna call?" Yes, I know, you were so excited about the idea of making phone calls on the Internet that you went ahead and installed everything you need. But you haven't quite persuaded your siblings or your mad Aunt Edna to do the same. So, you have nobody to call.

Most systems these days require that you know whom to call (in Figure 12.1 you can see how to place a call using Net2Phone). A year or two ago PC-to-PC calls were treated in some ways like chat rooms. For instance, if you were using VocalTec's Internet Phone, you would automatically connect to a server when you started the program. The server had hundreds of chat rooms—you could create your own room, so the actual number fluctuated—places where people could congregate and then choose to pair off in voice conversations. I think this concept is dying out, and you'll more likely need to provide the address of the person you want to contact.

Figure 12.1

With Net2Phone just enter the name of the person you want to talk to, and click the big CALL button.

When you are talking, you might find that the sound is a bit warbly. What do you want? Low cost *and* quality? If you are both using full-duplex modems, you can probably just talk as if you were on the phone. Otherwise, you might have to take turns speaking, clicking a button to turn your mike on and off. (The button is the equivalent of saying "over.")

Making PC-to-Phone Calls

Some of these systems allow both PC-to-PC and PC-to-Phone calls. Calling a phone is just as easy as calling another PC—easier in most cases; in fact, a phone is a phone whereas a computer is not—while computers may be offline, misconfigured, or not have the necessary hardware, at least if you're calling a phone number you know that there's probably a phone connected to it.

You can simply dial a number—type the number on your keypad or click on the buttons on the program—click the **Dial** or **Call** button or whatever, and then wait for the call to go through (you can see both AIM Phone and MSN Messenger Phone in Figure 12.2).

How Reliable?

I haven't used VON systems much, I'll admit, but if my limited experience is anything to go by you can assume that VON calls are *not* as reliable as real telephone calls. You'll see "all circuits are busy" and "technical difficulty" messages far more often than normal calls run into problems.

187

Figure 12.2

Both AOL Instant Messenger and MSN Messenger enable you to call from your computer to a telephone.

The Bells and Whistles

Some Internet phone products offer more than just voice connections. You might want to look for some of the following features in an Internet phone system:

➤ **An answering machine**   Some products, such as Conference, have built-in answering machines. If someone tries to contact you while you are not there, your answering machine takes a message. Of course, this feature works only if your computer is online. Although it's very useful for people with permanent network connections, it's not nearly as useful for people who dial into a service provider (although a lot of us these days leave our computers permanently connected to the Internet across the telephone line, which irritates the phone companies to no end).

➤ **Type-while-you-talk capability**   This feature can be very handy. You can send text messages at the same time you are talking. For example, you can send small memos or copy parts of an email message you're discussing. If you are working on a project with the other person, you might find it convenient to send to-do lists or schedules back and forth. Authors working together can send materials to each other, programmers can send bits of the code they are discussing, and so on. Figure 12.3 shows one system in which you can write as you talk.

➤ **Image transmission**   Related to the business-card feature and to the whiteboard feature (discussed in a moment) is the capability to send a picture while you're talking. If you haven't seen Aunt Natasha in Siberia for a while, she can send a picture of the kids while you are chatting.

➤ **Conferencing**   Why speak to just one person when you can talk to a whole crowd? Some of these programs let you set up conferences, so a whole bunch of you can gab at once. (If you think VON is clunky with one person talking, wait until you try talking to several people at the same time.)

➤ **Group Web surfing**   Only a few programs have this odd feature. The people connected via the program, in some cases a whole bunch of people, can go on group Web surfs together. When one person clicks a Web link, the other participants' Web browsers update to show the new page. This feature is in Netscape Conference and PowWow (http://www.tribal.com/).

➤ **Web-page indicator**   You can automatically add an icon to your Web page showing whether you are online and able to accept calls (another neat PowWow feature).

➤ **Whiteboards**   A whiteboard is one of those big white chalkboard-type things you see in conference rooms. A whiteboard feature functions similarly to the type-while-you-talk feature previously mentioned. Instead of typing something, though, you are using a sort of doodle pad. You can sketch something, and it's transmitted to the person at the other end. You can even use this feature to send pictures; you can open the file in the whiteboard so the person at the other end can see it. Conference's whiteboard appears in Figure 12.3.

➤ **Connecting voice to your Web page**   You can put links in your Web pages that, when clicked, open the user's Voice program so he can talk with you. This feature is for real geeks who rarely leave their computers. (You *do* have Web pages, don't you? See Chapters 13 and 14, to find out how to create them.)

Unfortunately, it's not a perfect world, so not all voice programs have all these neat features. In fact the programs in popular use today are actually much simpler than the ones widely used just two years ago; perhaps these features will revive. You'll just have to find the features that are most important to you and go with the program that has those features.

Figure 12.3

A whiteboard feature enables you to send a picture while talking.

Video and Other Weird Stuff

The next step is to add video to the "phone" conversations. The phone companies have been talking about a true video phone for 40 years, but it took the Internet to bring it about. Video has already been added to some VON products.

Mind you, this step is a much bigger one than putting voice on the Internet. Voice is fairly simple. There is not too much data involved in transmitting sounds, relatively speaking. The problem with video, though, is bandwidth. The term *bandwidth* refers to the amount of information that can be transmitted across a connection. A 28,800bps connection has greater bandwidth than does a 14,400bps connection, for instance. Video images contain a lot of information, and you want the information right away. After all, video makes sense only if it's in motion. So, a number of compromises have to be made. The pictures are small, are low-resolution, and have few individual images each second. Thus, video transmitted across the Internet can often be blurry and shaky. Unless you really need it, you might find that the novelty soon wears off.

Personally, I don't think video on the Internet will catch on for a few more years—not until very high-speed connections are cheap and widely available. You also need a fast computer, of course. For now, video is limited to companies with network connections or the relatively few individuals lucky enough to have cable or ADSL connections. However, that hasn't stopped a variety of companies from selling video software for use on the Internet. (And guess what's the real growth area for video on the Internet? Live sex shows and cybersex, of course!)

The best-known product is Cu-SeeMe ("see you, see me," get it? Yeah, yeah). This product is so well known in the computer business that it's becoming a generic term, in the same way that *Hoover* is a generic term for vacuum cleaners. You can find information about this product at http://www.cuseeme.com/ (where you can join video chats; see Figure 12.4). You can buy Cu-SeeMe cameras for under $40.

By the way, other weird and wonderful telecommunications systems are available on the Internet, too. How about getting your faxes and voice mail connected to your email system, for instance? If you live in the United States but do business in the United Kingdom, you can have a phone line set up in London, for example. Your customers can call and leave voice mail for you or can fax you at that number, and your messages can then be compressed and attached to an email message that is sent to you! You can have a number in New York, London, or Atlanta, or you can have a U.S. toll-free number.

Such systems are not just for people doing business in various locations, though. I use an email fax system for convenience; I get my faxes wherever I happen to be—as long as I have my laptop and am grabbing my email, I can get my faxes. I don't have a fax machine that runs out of paper or ink, it makes it very easy to store faxes—they're in a Fax folder in my email program—and I can forward them to other people with a click or two of the mouse. See **eFax** (http://www.efax.com/) or **Jconnect** (http://www.j2.com/) for more information. And keep your eyes open for other weird and wonderful telecommunications/Internet hybrid services.

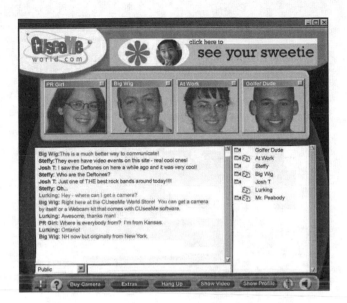

Figure 12.4

A video chat at the CU-SeeMe World.com (http://www.CUSeeMeWorld.com/), a video-chat community site.

The Least You Need to Know

➤ You can connect to other users and actually talk on the Internet at a fraction of the cost of normal long-distance or international calls.

➤ Internet-to-phone system servers are being set up that will enable you to connect across the world on the Internet, and then call someone using another country's domestic phone system.

➤ Phone software is plentiful and generally free. The instant messaging programs usually have some kind of Voice on the Net software built in.

➤ Many useful features are available in some products. You can send text or pictures while you talk, talk to a group of people, or even go on group Web trips.

➤ Video phones are available, but they require fast connections to the Internet to work well.

➤ Watch for other useful communications systems, such as fax and voice mail in your email.

191

Setting Up Your Own Web Site

A few years ago, I would never have considered putting a chapter about creating Web pages in an introduction to the Internet. But times change. Many newcomers to the Internet are setting up Web sites—in fact, many people get onto the Internet *so* they *can* set up a Web site.

Luckily, setting up a basic Web site is very easy. A Web site is just a collection of Web pages, and creating a single Web page is quite simple—so simple that I'm betting I can teach you to create a simple Web page in, oh, one chapter. No, I take that back! I'll bet you can create a very simple customized Web page in about 10 minutes. I'll cheat a little, though, by giving you a template, in which you can fill in the blanks.

My Fill-In-the-Blanks Web Page

I've created a Web page for you; you can get it from the email responder. Send an email message to ownweb@TopFloor.com. An email responder will automatically send you back a message. When you receive the response, save it as a text file with the HTM or HTML extension (for instance, save it as MYPAGE.HTM). Then, open the file in a text editor, such as SimpleText (on the Macintosh) or Notepad (in Windows). Or, instead of saving the message in a text file, copy the text from the email message and paste it into a text editor or word processing document. Remove all the text *before* the <HTML> text. (*Don't* remove the <HTML> part; just remove all the text prior to it.) Also, remove any text that appears after </HTML>, near the bottom of the message.

If you use a word processor instead of a text editor, you'll have to remember to save the file as a text file instead of as a normal word processing file when you finish working with it. As you'll learn later in this chapter, Web pages are simple text files. In many cases, using a word processor is not a great idea because word processors often automatically insert special characters such as curly quotation marks and em dashes, and other characters that can't be converted to plain text. Therefore, you're better off using a text editor.

For the impatient among you, those who don't want to wait for the mail to arrive (although it'll probably take only a few seconds), I've included the text from the sample file here. You can type the following lines into your text editor if you want, but you must be sure you type them exactly the same as they appear here:

```
<HTML>
<HEAD>
<TITLE>My Very Own Web Page--Replace if You Want</TITLE>
</HEAD>
<BODY>
<H1>Replace This Title With Whatever You Want</H1>
Put whatever text you want here.<P>
This is another paragraph; use whatever text you want.
<H2>First Subcategory: Replace this With Whatever Title You Want</H2>
<A HREF="http://www.mcp.com">The Macmillan Web Site</A><P>
<A HREF="url_here">Another link: replace this text</A><P>
<A HREF="url_here">Another link: replace this text</A><P>
<A HREF="url_here">Another link: replace this text</A><P>
<A HREF="url_here">Another link: replace this text</A>
<H2>Second Subcategory: Replace this With Whatever Title You Want</H2>
Put more text and links here.
<H2>Third Subcategory: Replace this With Whatever Title You Want</H2>
Put more text and links here.
<H2>Fourth Subcategory: Replace this With Whatever Title You Want</H2>
Put more text and links here.
</BODY>
</HTML>
```

Figure 13.1 shows you what this file looks like when displayed in a Web browser. For now, don't worry if you don't understand what is going on here; you're trying to break a speed record, not actually learn right now. In a few moments, I'll explain how this whole Web-creation thing works.

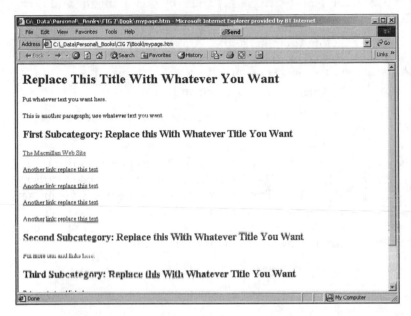

Figure 13.1

This is what the Web page template looks like in a Web browser.

First, I want you to replace some things. You can start with the text between the <TITLE> and </TITLE> tags. Whatever text you type between those tags will appear in the browser's title bar (refer to Figure 13.1), so replace the text that's there by typing your name, or **My Home Page**, or whatever you want. When you finish doing that, replace the text between the <H1> and </H1> tags. The text you type here will be a heading—the top-level heading, as a matter of fact. You can use the same text that you entered as the title if you want (that's what Web authors often do).

Now, save your work, but don't close the text file. Use your Web browser to open the file; you can double-click the file in Windows Explorer, or use the browser's **File**, **Open** command. You can now see the changes you've made.

Next, add some text to the file if you want. Replace the text immediately below the <H1></H1> heading, or remove it if you don't want it. (Notice, by the way, that you must end

What's a Tag?

Text that has a less-than symbol (<) in front of it and a greater-than symbol (>) after it is known as a *tag*. The tags tell your Web browser how to display the text in an HTML file.

195

each paragraph with the <P> tag.) After that, replace the next headings with names of categorics that describe the sort of links you want in your page. If you have favorite music sites that you visit, you might make the first heading Music. Another heading might be Financial, and another might be Goofing Around. It's your page. Use whatever categories you want. You can quickly see your changes by saving the file and clicking the browser's **Reload** (Netscape Navigator) or **Refresh** (Internet Explorer) button.

Be Careful

Be sure that you don't remove any of the < or > symbols. If you do, it can really mess up your page.

Before you change the "Another link…" lines, take a close look at the links I've created. The first one is a link to the Macmillan Web site. (This book is published by Que, a division of Macmillan.)

```
<A HREF="http://www.mcp.com">The Macmillan Web
Site</A><P>
```

The words *The Macmillan Web Site* appear on the Web page as the actual link text; you can see those words in Figure 13.1. The URL for the linked between the quotation marks, as in "`http://www.mcp.com/`". Keeping that in mind, go ahead and modify the links I've provided. For instance, you might change this:

```
<A HREF="url_here">Another link: replace this text</A><P>
```

to this:

```
<A HREF="http://www.napster.com">Napster</A><P>
```

Replace all the generic links with links to Web sites you like to visit. As a shortcut, you can copy a link, paste it a few times below each category heading, and then modify each of the copied links so that they point to more Web sites. When you finish making your changes, save the page and click the browser's **Reload** or **Refresh** button. Right before your very eyes, you'll see your brand-new 10-minute Web page. Didn't I tell you it was easy?

Making It Your Home Page

After you've created a home page, you need to tell your browser to use it as the home page. In Internet Explorer, begin by displaying your new page in the browser window. Then, select **Tools**, **Internet Options**, and then, under the **General** tab, click the **Use Current** button to set the page in the browser as the home page (see Figure 13.2).

To make your Web page the home page in Netscape Navigator (version 4 or 4.5 or thereabouts), load the page into the browser, and then choose **Edit**, **Preferences**, click the **Navigator** category, and click the **Use Current Page** button (see Figure 13.3).

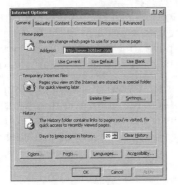

Figure 13.2
In Internet Explorer, you can click the Use Current button to select the currently displayed page as the home page.

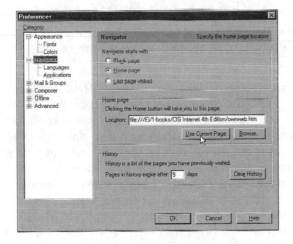

Figure 13.3
Setting the home page in Netscape Navigator 4.5 is similar to doing so in Internet Explorer.

The next time you start your browser, you'll see your very own home page. And the next time you click the **Home** button, up pops your home page.

Your Web Page: What's It Good For?

Why bother creating your own page? There are a few reasons. First, telling your browser to view a home page on your hard drive will speed up loading the program. Most browsers these days are configured to use a home page at the browser publisher's Web site, but it's much quicker to load from a "local" drive than to transfer a page from across the Internet. If that were the only reason, though, you could just copy an HTML document from the Web somewhere and put it on your hard drive.

The second reason has to do with the fact that everyone uses the Internet in a different way. The home page someone else has created won't have all the links you want and will contain plenty of links that you don't want. So, you might as well customize your home page to work the way you want it to work and include links to sites you want to go to. You can also create a home page that has a series of documents linked to it (such as one for work, one for music, one for newsgroups, and so on).

Another reason (if you still need coaxing) is that you might want to put information about yourself or your business on the World Wide Web. You're not limited to creating a Web page for your own use and saving it on your hard drive. You can create a Web page that the world can read by saving it on your service provider's system so that it's available to the Internet at large.

HTML Basics

You've already seen how simple Web authoring can be. Now you're going to learn a bit more theory about *HTML (Hypertext Markup Language)*. HTML is the language of the Web, and all those <xxx> tags you looked at are HTML tags.

HTML files are not very complicated. They're in a simple text format. The nice thing about a simple text file is that it's widely recognized by thousands of programs and many types of computers.

It's important to understand that although text editors (such as Notepad and SimpleText) create text files, word processors do not. A word processor is like an advanced text editor. It formats the text in many ways that simple text editors cannot. It adds character formatting (italic, bold, underline, and so on), special characters (curly quotation marks, copyright symbols, em and en dashes, and many others), and formats paragraph spacing, for example. That's why you have to be careful when creating HTML files in a word processor; you must save the file as text instead of in the word processor's file format. And in some cases, even if you do save in text format, the program may not convert some of these special characters properly. As I mentioned before, creating Web pages in word processors is, in general, not a good idea.

Rendering

This term is used to describe the action carried out by the browser when it looks at the HTML codes and formats the text according to the instructions within those codes. It strips the codes from the text and displays the resulting text in the browser.

HTML files are text files that have been specially designed to be read by Web browsers. They use the same characters as any other text file, but they use a special convention that all Web browsers understand. That convention is this: "If you see anything in brackets such as these < >, you know it's a special code." When Web browsers are rendering the HTML document into normal text so that they can display the document on the screen, they look for these brackets and follow the instructions inside them.

You've already created a Web page, so you know what tags look like. But take a minute to go back and examine the tags you used:

➤ <TITLE> </TITLE>   The text between these tags is the title of the document. You won't see this text in the document; it's simply an identifier that the browsers use. For instance, Netscape and Internet Explorer put the text in the title bar. In addition, this title is used in bookmark and history lists, and if you've put the page out on the Web, the title might be used by Web search sites (see Chapter 15, "Finding What You Need Online") to help them index or categorize your site.

➤ <H1> </H1>   These tags mark the first-level heading. You can include up to six levels using the tags <H2> </H2>, <H3> </H3>, <H4> </H4>, <H5> </H5>, and <H6> </H6>. Experiment with these tags in your own Web page.

➤ <P>   This tag is used at the end of a paragraph. Simply typing a carriage return in your HTML file will *not* create a new paragraph in the final document that appears in the browser. You must use the <P> tag instead. Without the tag, the paragraphs will run together.

Does It Have to Be Uppercase?

Don't worry about the case of the tags. You can type <title>, <TITLE>, <Title>, <TItlE>, or <TiTlE>—whatever tickles your fancy.

Anchors

The <A HREF="url"> tags are often called *anchors*. For this reason, many people refer to the actual links in the Web documents as anchors.

Notice that, in most cases, tags are paired. There's an opening and a closing tag, and the closing tag is the same as the opening tag with the exception of the forward slash after the left angle bracket. <H1> and </H1> form a pair, for instance. The <P> tag is one exception to this. You need only the <P> tag, and it appears after the paragraph.

Finally, there's an *anchor* tag, which is used to create a link:

<A HREF="http://www.mcp.com">The Macmillan Web Site</A><P>

Notice that the URL is included within the angle brackets and within quotation marks. A *link tag* (a tag that you use to create a hypertext link in your document) consists of <A, followed by a space, followed by HREF=". After that, you enter the URL. You've looked at URLs before; these are the same URLs that you can use to tell a browser to go to a particular Web site. At the end of the URL, you add ">, followed by

whatever text you want. (That text is going to appear on the finished Web page as the link text.) Following the text, you use the closing tag </A>. In the preceding example, I also used the <P> tag to start a new paragraph; I wanted to make sure that the link would appear on its own line.

A Word About Paragraphs

Web browsers don't deal with paragraphs in the same way that word processors do. If the browser finds several spaces, including blank lines, it will compress all the space into a single paragraph unless it sees the <P> tag somewhere. When it finds the <P> tag, it ends that paragraph and starts a new one below it, generally leaving a blank line between the two. If, for some reason, you want to move text down to the next line but you don't want a blank line between the two lines of text, you can use the <BR> tag instead of <P>. The <BR> tag inserts a line break without starting a new paragraph.

Don't Stop at One: Multiple Pages

You can easily create a hierarchy of documents. Why not have a document that appears when you open the browser, with a table of contents linked to several other documents? In each of those documents, you can then have links related to a particular subject.

Say you want to set up a document for the music sites you are interested in. Call it RNR.HTM, or MUSIC.HTM, or whatever you want. Create that document in the same way you did the first one, and put it in the same directory. You can then create a link from your home page to the rock 'n' roll document, like this:

```
<A HREF="RNR.HTM">Rock 'n' Roll</A>
```

Although RNR.HTM is a filename, you can use it in place of the URL. In fact, RNR.HTM is a URL: it's what's known as a *relative URL*. This link tells a Web browser to look for the RNR.HTM file. Although it doesn't tell the browser where to look for the file, the browser makes an assumption; because the URL doesn't include the hostname or directory, the only place the browser can look is in the same directory as the original file. (And that's just fine because you are going to place the RNR.HTM file in the same directory, right?)

This is really simple, isn't it? You create a home page (called HOME.HTM) with links to any number of other documents in the same directory. You might have links to sites for rock 'n' roll, art, music, conspiracy theories, or whatever sort of information you are interested in and can find on the Web. Then, you fill up those documents with more links to all those interesting sites. Whaddya know? You're a Web publisher!

Finding URLs

There are shortcuts to creating the links in your home page. Who wants to type all those URLs, after all? One way to grab the URLs is to visit the Web page you are interested in and copy the text from the Location or Address text box at the top of the browser window. To do that, you can highlight the text, and then press **Ctrl+C** or select **Edit, Copy**. (Most browsers have some method for copying the URL.) Then, you can just paste it into your home page.

You can also grab URLs from links on a document. Right-click a link to see a pop-up menu (if you're using a Macintosh, try clicking and holding the mouse button down for a second or two). Click the **Copy Shortcut** option in Internet Explorer, or click the **Copy Link Location** option in Netscape.

You can also grab information from the bookmark list or, in some cases, the history list. In Internet Explorer, you can open Favorites (that's the name it uses for its bookmark system). Choose **Favorites, Organize Favorites**, right-click an item, and choose **Properties**. Then, click the **Web Document** tab and copy the URL from the **URL** text box.

In Netscape, you can open the Bookmarks window (**Window, Bookmarks** or perhaps **Communicator, Bookmarks, Edit Bookmarks**) and do much the same thing. Right-click an item, select **Properties**, and then copy the URL from the box that appears. (Or click the item and select **Edit, Properties**.) You can also choose **File, Save As** to save the entire bookmark system in an HTML file. Then, you can open that file in a text editor and pick and choose which URLs you want.

Publishing on the Web

If you want to publish on the Web—that is, take the pages you have created and make them available to anyone on the Web—you have a two-step process to go through. First, you create the page. But then you have to place it somewhere that is accessible to the Internet. It has to be put on a Web server.

Most online services and Internet service providers allow their subscribers to post their own Web pages. Some of these services even allow each subscriber to post a megabyte or two—sometimes as much as 10MB—of Web pages, graphics, and so on. Check with your service to find out how much data you can post and where to put it. But a service provider isn't the only place to put a Web site. You have a variety of additional choices:

➤ **On your own Web server**   You can buy your own Web server (you need a computer, connection hardware, and Web-server software), connect it to the Internet, and place your Web site on that server. This is what I call the "open your wallet" method. It's expensive and complicated, and few people should try it. I'm not even going to explain how to go about doing this, based on the principle that "if you don't know how, you shouldn't be trying."

➤ **At a free-page Web site** There are organizations and individuals who provide free Web space to anyone who asks. Companies such as GeoCities (`http://GeoCities.com/`), Tripod (`http://Tripod.com/`), and Angelfire (`http://Angelfire.com/`). Go to Yahoo! (`http://Yahoo.com/`) and search for *free web pages* to find links to many different services.

Getting a Domain Name

To register a .com, .net, .org, or .edu domain name, go to Network Solutions (`http://www.networksolutions.com/`) or Register.com (`http://www.register.com`). For other domains, try a service such as AllDomains (`http://www.alldomains.com/`).

➤ **Your Internet service provider** Most ISPs provide some free Web space, too.

➤ **At a Web store** A number of stores allow companies to place pages in the Web store. For instance, a number of book sites sell space to small publishers.

➤ **At a Web host's site in a subdirectory or subdomain** A Web host is a company that sells space on its Web server to companies that want a Web site. The cheapest way to do this is to use the hosting company's URL and have your Web site as a subdirectory: `http://www.verybigwebhost.com/yoursite`, for instance.

➤ **At a Web host's site as a virtual host** You place your Web pages on a Web host's server, but you use your own domain name: `http://www.yoursite.com/`.

Finding a Web Host

A free Web site, or the space available at an online service or service provider, is fine for most people. But if you're serious about setting up a Web site for a small to medium company or for some kind of club or organization, you'll probably want to use a Web-hosting company, for several reasons:

➤ You need your own domain name. It will be easier for your clients or members to remember and easier to get listed at Yahoo! (the single most important search site on the Internet; they have a bias against sites placed in a subdirectory of an online service or service provider), and you won't have to change your Web site's URL each time you move your Web site. (Think about having to reprint all your business cards, letterhead, catalogs....) Most online services or service providers won't let you use your own domain name with your basic Internet access account.

➤ Most online services and service providers don't provide the sort of services that a Web site needs, such as the capability to run scripts (the things that make Web forms work).

Where can you find a low-cost hosting company? A good place to start is Budgetweb at `http://www.budgetweb.com/`. This large directory of Web-hosting companies has prices that start as low as $9 a month (I pay around $30 a month for my Web site; if you pay too little, you might end up with an unreliable service, of course).

There's a problem, though. Selecting a hosting company can be rather complicated. There are so many things to consider, you shouldn't choose one until you understand what you're looking for. I'll provide a little help, though. At my Web site, you'll find a free report called *20 Questions to Ask a Web-Hosting Company* (`http://PoorRichard.com/freeinfo/special_reports.htm`), which should give you enough information to get started.

Posting Your Web Pages

After you have a Web site, how do you get the pages from your computer to the Web site? Generally, you'll have to use FTP, which you'll learn about in Chapter 19, "Downloading Files (FTP, GoZilla, and CuteFTP)." This system enables you to transfer files from your computer to another computer on the Internet. Some of the online services use a different system, though; check with your online service for more information.

If you're using an HTML authoring program, though, you might have a transfer utility built in. These programs are like word processors for HTML. You type your text, format the text using normal word processing tools, and the programs create the HTML for you. Many of these tools are available, and they can greatly simplify Web creation. See `http://www.yahoo.com/Computers_and_Internet/Software/Internet/World_Wide_Web/HTML_Editors/` for links to some of these programs.

Using Web Templates

Now that you've learned a little about HTML, I guess I should tell you that you might not need to know anything about HTML. Many Internet service providers and hosting companies have templates you can use to create your Web pages. In other words, you can go to a hosting service's Web site and follow through a series of forms in which you enter your information, pick colors and backgrounds, upload images, and so on. All the HTML coding is done for you, and the page is automatically posted at the service's Web site. Most major services, such as the ones I mentioned earlier—GeoCities, Tripod, and Angelfire—have such utilities, for free.

The Least You Need to Know

➤ Creating a home page is very simple; you can use the template provided to create one in as few as 10 minutes.

➤ Enclose HTML tags within brackets < >.

➤ In most cases, you need an opening tag and a closing tag, such as `<TITLE>My Home Page</TITLE>`.

➤ You use tags to tell your browser which text you want displayed as titles, headings, links, and so on.

➤ To create a link, type `<A HREF="URL">Your Link Text</A>`, replacing *URL* and *Your Link Text* with those you want to use.

➤ If you use a filename in place of the URL in the link, the browser will look in the same directory as the current document.

➤ You can replace your browser's default home page with your new one.

➤ After you've created a page, you can post it at your service provider's site so the whole world can see it!

➤ There are other ways to post your site on the Web, though, from free sites to Web-hosting companies. Most businesses, clubs, and organizations should use a hosting company.

Chapter 14

Nifty Web Site Tricks

In This Chapter

➤ Be careful with the nifty stuff

➤ Inserting pictures into pages

➤ Using tables

➤ Working with frames

➤ Java applets and where to find them

➤ Images and sounds

The first thing people want to know after creating a few simple Web pages seems to be...How can I add cool stuff to my Web pages?

The answer is don't. Or, at least, think carefully before you do. Let me explain.

Don't Overdo It

Remember the days of "kidnap-note desktop publishing"? When desktop-publishing programs first became widely available, the standard of printed materials in the Western world plummeted, as millions of people with all the design skills of the average turnip suddenly realized they could create "professional-looking" printed documents cheaply and easily. They could select different fonts, different font sizes, and even different colors. They could place them left justified and right justified and centered. They could wrap words around pictures, and pictures around words. So, they did it all, often on the same page. The result was...a design disaster.

Well, we've reached a similar point on the Web. You can do all sorts of things to "spiff up" your Web pages. But should you? In most cases, not.

There's another problem. Unfortunately, a lot of people who *do* have design skills have led the way on the Web, creating beautiful and very cool Web sites. But these Web sites are often pointless, expensive, and don't serve any real purpose.

A few years ago, the mantra on the Web was "make it cool, and they will come." Make your Web site exciting and entertaining, and people would visit the site. This is complete nonsense. Sites need to be *useful*, not cool. Think about why someone would visit your site. Because of your "beautiful" design work? Probably not.

So, some of the information contained in this chapter is dangerous stuff. I'm going to explain how to add certain things to your Web site, but before you do so, consider whether you really should! We'll also look at some useful-if-not-abused stuff, too, such as pictures and frames. Oh, and we'd better not forget tables, a tool that is very handy for getting things to sit in the right place on a Web page.

Adding Pictures

Of all "multimedia" content placed into Web pages, pictures are the most innocuous (so much so that most people don't even think of them as coming under the multi-media umbrella). Don't be fooled, though—some of the most irritating content online is pictures. Don't simply create an image and upload it—check the size first! For instance, if you take a picture of the family with a digital camera, and then upload it right to your Web site, you may find that Aunt Edna, dialing in from Scotland, gets tired of waiting for the image to download.

Inserting an image into a page is very easy. Do it something like this:

```
<img height="51" width="187" src="logo.gif" alt="Company Logo">
```

Size *Does* Matter

How big should the images in your pages be? Assume that every 10K of image size is about 10 or 12 seconds of download time using a 28.8bps Internet connection. That doesn't mean using a 28.8bps modem, though, because actual connections are usually slower than the maximum modem speed.

It's a good idea to put the height and width attributes, although not essential. Doing so can speed up the loading of the page, though, because even if the image has not yet transferred, the browser knows how much space to leave for it. (How do you know the image size? Any good image-editing program should have a command somewhere that will display image "attributes" or "properties.")

The src attribute is the name of the file you want to appear in the Web page (or the path to the file, if it's not in the same directory as the page). And the alt attribute is another optional attribute; this is the text that pops up over the image when someone points at the image with the mouse pointer. (It's also displayed in place of the image if someone is viewing the page with images turned off in the browser.)

For the More Advanced Stuff...

I'm explaining the very simple stuff here. There are many more attributes that I'm not covering, things such as the ability to put borders around images or flow text around the image in a specific way. For the details, get a good HTML book (there are only about 100,000 in print, it seems), or visit one of the HTML reference sites online. One of my favorites is the **Index dot HTML** site, at http://www. blooberry.com/indexdot/.

Positioning Things with Tables

Tables are very handy tools. But let me tell you a secret; although I sometimes work in the raw code of a Web page—work directly on the HTML code in a text editor—I rarely do so for tables. Tables can be very confusing, so I generally use an HTML editor to create them for me.

Tables are created using a variety of HTML tags; the <table> and </table> tags enclose the entire table; the <tr> and </tr> tags are used to configure rows within the table, and the <td> and </td> tags enclose information in a particular table cell (the tag is td, not tc, meaning table data).

The following HTML code shows a table with two rows and two columns; I created this using Microsoft FrontPage.

```
<table border="1" width="100%">
  <tr>
    <td width="50%">Cell 1</td>
    <td width="50%">Cell 2</td>
  </tr>
  <tr>
    <td width="50%">Cell 3</td>
    <td width="50%">Cell 4</td>
  </tr>
</table>
```

Frames Are Okay (Sometimes)

A frame configuration is one in which two or more Web pages are displayed in a Web browser at the same time, each in its own portion of the browser window. Frames can be very useful, particularly to display a navigation panel in one frame—clicking on a link in the navigation panel in one frame can load a page into the other frame.

Frames should be used carefully, though. Some earlier browsers simply don't work well with frames. The first frame-enabled browser, Netscape Navigator 2, was only partly frame-enabled. It often crashed when encountering frames. And although newer browsers work well with frames, they can still be a nuisance, especially for users using screens with low video resolutions (not only people with old computers, but those with bad eyesight, too). I'd also recommend that you never use more than two frames in a window, three at the absolute maximum. The more frames in a window, the less room in each frame.

Don't Make This Frame Mistake

If you do create frames, don't make the mistake of omitting the scrollbars without checking to see whether the configuration works in low-resolution screens! (The advanced attributes let you configure various characteristics related to the scrollbars and border.) I often run across frame configurations without scrollbars that were created by Web authors using high-resolution monitors; but in low resolutions some of the text is not visible, and there's no way to scroll down to view it.

Frames are created using what is sometimes called a *frame-definition document*, or a *frames page*. Here's an example of the *frameset* inside such a document:

```
<frameset cols="150,*">
  <frame name="contents" target="main" src="contentspage.htm">
  <frame name="main" src="mainpage.htm">
  <noframes>
  <body>
  <p>This page uses frames, but your browser doesn't support them.</p>
  </body>
  </noframes>
</frameset>
```

The <frameset> tag defines the overall look of the browser and its internal frames. In this case, it's saying that there will be two columns, with the first one 150 pixels wide. (The second one will take up as much room as is left over after 150 pixels have been assigned to the first column.)

Each column, starting on the left side of the browser, has its own <frame> tag; each tag defines the frame name, and the source (src), which is a document that will be loaded into the frame. In this case, the frame named contents also has a target attribute, which is named the same as the name of the second frame. This means that if you put any links into the document loaded into that frame, when the user clicks on the link the referenced page will load not into the same frame, but into the target frame—the main frame.

What about the <noframes> and </noframes> tags? Everything between this text is displayed if the browser the page is loaded into is one that cannot handle frames.

Frames are actually quite easy to work with, but still, you may want to use an HTML editor to help you create them (if you can find one; most HTML editors do *not* create frame-definition documents).

Adding Java Applets

I'll explain this quickly, and then move on to something you're more likely to use! You can insert Java applets—little Java programs—into Web pages using the <applet> tag. Will you ever? Probably not, if the average Web-page author is anything to go by. Java applets are much hyped, but the average person will never install one (and very few will ever actually create their own Java applets; this is a realm for programmers, not computer neophytes). On the other hand, there are libraries of Java applets in which you can find applets you *may* want to install on your site, so perhaps you should take a look.

For instance, I found a simple little text scroller called DanScroller at JavaBoutique (http://javaboutique.internet.com/—see Figure 14.1). I simply downloaded the files to my computer, put them into the same directory as the page I wanted to place the scroller into, and then added this text (I copied the text from the library page at JavaBoutique):

```
<APPLET archive="Scroller.jar" code="Scroller.class" width=450 height=20>
    <PARAM name="copyright" value="(c) 1999 Dan MacFarlane.
http://www.dancity.com/">
    <PARAM name="text"
        value="This is the new scroller applet from DanCity.    You can
        easily specify your own scroll text and even incorporate hypertext
        links (mailto or http) and images into it!    You can also drag
        the text forwards or backwards for your viewing convenience!   ">
    <PARAM NAME="background" VALUE="#FFFFFF">
    <PARAM NAME="textcol"    VALUE="#330000">
</APPLET>
```

Figure 14.1

It took about five minutes to take this applet from the JavaBoutique library and install it in a Web page.

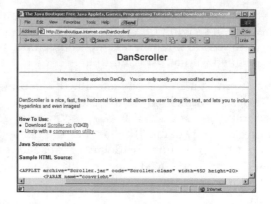

The <applet> tag is used to insert the applet into the page, but you'll notice that there are associated <param> (parameter) tags that pass information to the applet. In this case, you can change the second <param> tag to modify the text that appears in the scroller, and the last two change the background and text colors.

You can find more Java libraries by searching at Yahoo! for *java applets*.

Linking to Images and Sounds

You can very easily create links to images and sounds from your Web pages. Remember from the previous chapter, where I talked about linking from one page to another? Well, use the exact same type of tag, but simply provide the name of a mul-timedia file rather than a Web-page file.

What kinds of images? The two most common formats are GIF and JPG (sometimes using the JPEG extension). You may see PNG files mentioned here and there, but most browsers in use today do not work well with these types of images right now, so I'd limit myself to the GIF and JPG formats, if I were you. As for sounds...we'll look at them in more detail now.

Adding Background Sounds

Here's a truly obnoxious use of Web multimedia, adding background sounds to a Web page. Actually I *have* seen examples where it made sense, or was in some way funny or entertaining (see the HampsterDance site, at http://www.hampsterdance2.com/ hampsterdance.html, and http://www.NuttySites.com/, for a few examples).

Luckily, most people don't know how to add sounds to a Web page—at least, sounds that play automatically when the page loads. The competition between Microsoft and Netscape ensured that adding background sounds is not a simple matter—each browser handles background sounds in a different way, and not always correctly. (In fact, most authors of HTML books have given up in frustration and simply ignore this issue entirely, or cover it incompletely.)

So, in the interest of seeing a more diverse and obnoxious Web, I'm going to release this information into the Web community, and help you and your friends do what so many millions of other Web-page creators have had the sense *not* to do. Here's a simple way to add sounds to your Web pages. Add these two lines to the top of your Web page:

What Sound Files?

What types of sound files can you use? Common formats are .wav (Windows "wave" files), .snd (a Macintosh format), and .mid (MIDI—Musical Instrument Digital Interface—files). Most recent computers can also work with .mp3 (a CD-quality audio format) and .ram (RealAudio) files.

```
<embed src="filename" hidden autostart="true" loop="TRUE">
<noembed><bgsound src="filename" loop="infinite"></noembed>
```

This should cover both browsers; the sound should play in both early versions of Internet Explorer (using the `bgsound` tag) *and* Netscape Navigator or more recent versions of Internet Explorer (using the `embed` tag). Note that where I've put *filename*, you should put either the filename of the sound file (if the file is in the same directory as the Web page), or the full or relative path to the file. As for the other "attributes" in these tags, here's what they mean:

> hidden—The `embed` tag is really intended to place an object directly into the Web page. But for a background sound you don't really want anything visual to appear in the page, so place this word into the tag to make it hidden. (You can also put `hidden="true"`, as some HTML authors do.)

> autostart—You guessed it; this makes the sound start playing automatically.

> loop—Putting `"true"` after `loop` in the `embed` tag makes the sound play continuously; in the `bgsound` tag it should really be `"infinite"` (although `"true"` seems to work, too). Or put a number to specify how many times the file should play.

> `<noembed></noembed>`—If the page is loaded into Netscape Navigator, a recent version of Internet Explorer, or any other browser that works with the `<embed>` tag, everything between these two tags is ignored; that is, the `bgsound` tag will *not* be used. If it's loaded into an early version of Internet Explorer, or any other browser that *doesn't* use the `embed` tag, the text between these tags is *not* ignored. That is, the `bgsound` tag will be used. This avoids problems that may occur if a browser tries to play the sound using both methods.

The Least You Need to Know

➤ Be careful with multimedia in your Web pages—you generally don't need it.

➤ It's very easy to insert pictures into Web pages, using the <img> tag.

➤ The easiest way to work with tables is using an HTML editor, even if you like doing most things in a text editor.

➤ Frames are useful, but don't use more than two at a time.

➤ You'll probably never create your own Java applets, but may want to borrow them from Java libraries.

➤ It's easy to link to sounds, harder to create background sounds (unless you know this trick).

Part 3

Getting Things Done

Now that you've learned how to use the Internet's services, it's time to learn some important general information about working on the Net. This place is so huge, you might have trouble finding what you need; I'll show you where to look. You'll also need to learn how to stay safe on the Internet. You've heard about the problems that go along with using credit cards on the Internet, about kids finding pornography, and so on—we'll examine the truth and the lies.

I'll show you the best ways to download files from the Web—software, documents, music, whatever it is you want (there are a lot of choices), and we'll even discuss how to make money online.

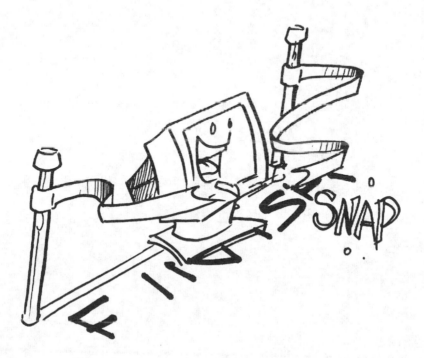

Finding What You Need Online

By now you must have realized that the Internet is rather large: tens, maybe hundreds, of millions of users, millions of files in FTP sites, millions and millions of Web pages, newsgroups, mailing lists—this thing is huge. How on earth are you ever going to find your way around?

Finding what you need on the Internet is surprisingly easy these days. Dozens of services are available to help you find your way around. That's what this chapter is about: finding what you need and where you need to go.

Finding People

The most complicated search task is finding people on the Internet. There are millions of Internet users and no single Internet directory. Unlike the online services, which have directories you can search to find someone you want to contact, there's no one place to search on the Internet. But that's not so surprising. After all, there's no single directory for the world's telephone system, and the Internet is comparable—it's thousands of connected networks that span the world. So, how are you going to find someone?

Quite frankly, the easiest way to find someone's email address is to talk to that person or talk to (or email) a mutual acquaintance. You can spend hours looking for someone in the Internet's various directories. If you know of someone else who might have the information, or know the person's telephone number, you can save yourself some time and trouble by tracking down the email address that way. If you can't contact the person directly, or can't think of someone else who knows the person you're after, you'll have to dig a little deeper.

Directories, Directories, and More Directories

There are a lot of directories on the Web. (No, I don't mean directories on a computer's hard disk this time; now when I say *directories*, I mean as in the telephone directory or directory assistance.) A good place to start is at your browser's people search page. For instance, if you're using Netscape Navigator 4.51, select the **People** button from the Personal toolbar (select **View**, **Show**, **Personal Toolbar**). In Netscape Navigator 4, click the **Guide** button and select **People** from the drop-down menu. In Navigator 3, click the **People** button in the Directory Buttons bar. If you're not using that browser, you can go directly to Netscape's People page (`http://home.netscape. com/netcenter/whitepages.html`). Each time you go to this page, Netscape displays the Netscape People Finder. Figure 15.1 shows the Netscape People Finder.

Figure 15.1

Netscape's People Finder form.

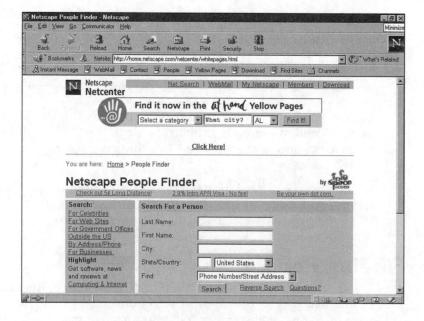

216

Another good directory to use is Yahoo! People Search (go to `http://people.yahoo.com/`), which you can see in Figure 15.2. This directory of people on the Internet is surprisingly good. I searched for my own name and found myself, along with about 90 other Peter Kents. (I hadn't realized there were so many of us.) You can search for a name and, using the advanced settings, narrow the search by including a city and state, or you can search for a telephone number. Note, however, that these directories are often quite out of date. I found a couple of old listings for myself; one of the email addresses had not worked for about three years.

If you don't find the person you need in Yahoo! People Search, don't worry; there's still a chance you'll find him. Yahoo!'s Phone Numbers and Addresses page (`http://dir.yahoo.com/Reference/Phone_Numbers_and_Addresses/Email_Addresses/`) has links to dozens more directories; when I looked a moment ago, I found links to over 100 directories, some of which had links to dozens more, including directories at colleges, celebrity directories, many regional directories, and so on.

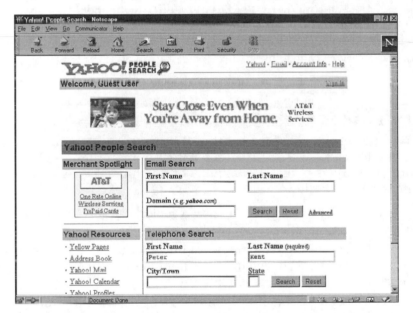

Figure 15.2

The Yahoo! People Search form.

I'm not going to go into more detail about these directories. A few years ago it was quite difficult to find people on the Internet (when I searched for myself for the first edition of this book, I had a lot of trouble finding myself—and I knew where I was!). These days there are so many directories of people that, with a bit of time and trouble, you have a good chance of finding the person you need (even if he doesn't have Internet access—you can often track down a phone number more easily than an email address).

Other Search Engines, Too

Yahoo! is not the only search engine you can use to find directories. We'll look at more search engines later in this chapter, and many of them will have links to directories you can use to find people, too.

Finding Businesses

If you want to find a business's phone number or address, you can often use the same directories you use to search for people. For instance, on the Netscape People Finder page (and Yahoo! People Search, for that matter) you'll find a link named Yellow Pages just below the personal search fields. You enter your geographic location, then the business name or type, and you'll receive a list of all the businesses in your area that fit the specified description. Most of them will even generate a map of the business's location that you can print out.

There are quite a few yellow-page services around, such as Yahoo! Yellow Pages (http://yp.yahoo.com/), Yell.com (http://www.Yell.com/), Switchboard (http://www.switchboard.com/), and Zip2 (http://www.zip2.com/). Your local phone company quite likely has a Yellow Pages site, too (Qwest has a service called Qwest Dex, for instance, at http://www.qwestdex.com/).

Using the Search Sites

You want to find information about something or other. Where do you start? The best place is probably at the Web search sites. There are dozens of these sites, and I'm always surprised what I can turn up in just a few minutes of searching. There are basically three ways to use these search sites:

➤ You can view a directory from which you can select a subject category and subcategories; then, you'll see a list of links to related pages.

➤ You can search an index of subjects; type a keyword into a form, and then click a **Search** button to carry out a search. You'll see a list of links to Web pages related to the subjects you typed into the search form.

➤ You can search an index of pages. Some search engines let you search for words within Web pages. AltaVista, for example, indexes hundreds of millions of words, in millions of Web sites! You'll see a list of pages that contain the words you typed into the form.

Which type of search should you use? The first or second method should normally be your first choice. Services such as AltaVista are very useful, but because they don't categorize the pages—they search for words within the pages instead of searching the subjects of the pages—they often give you more information than you can ever handle. The other services categorize pages (and sometimes even describe or review pages), so they are generally easier to use. Save places such as AltaVista for "plan B," when you can't find what you're looking for on your first attempt.

Finding the Search Sites

Getting started is easy. Most Web browsers these days have a button that takes you straight to a search page of some kind (generally a form that enables you to search a choice of search sites). For example, both Netscape and Internet Explorer have a Search button. In Internet Explorer 5.0, click the **Search** icon in the toolbar and a search engine form will appear on the left side of the screen. You can choose which search engine is used by clicking **Customize** at the top right of the search engine window. This will open another window where you'll see a list of search engines and directories. Choose one of the listed search sites as your default, and it will be used whenever you click the **Search** icon.

The Best?

Which is the best Web search site? There is no "best." Even though I really like Yahoo!, I sometimes use others. Each one is different and works in a different way, which means each one will give you a different result. Try a few and see which you like, or check to see how others rate them.

Here are a few search sites you can use. I've started with Yahoo! because that's where I prefer to start when I search, partly out of habit. Of course, after you've used a few search sites, you might find that you have a different preference.

➤ **Yahoo!** http://www.yahoo.com/

➤ **Lycos** http://www.lycos.com/

➤ **GO** http://www.go.com/

➤ **Google** http://www.google.com/

➤ **AltaVista** http://www.altavista.com/

➤ **Metacrawler** http://www.metacrawler.com/

➤ **Dogpile** http://www.dogpile.com/

What's the difference between a Web directory and a search engine? A directory provides categorized lists of Web pages from which you can select a category, and then a subcategory, and then another subcategory, and so on until you find the site you want. A search engine lets you use a program with which you'll search a database of Web pages. With a search engine, you type a keyword and click a **Search** button or press **Enter**. The search engine then searches the database for you. Some sites, such as Yahoo!, contain both directories and search engines. And some systems, such as Metacrawler, actually run a search on a number of different search engines and return the most relevant results to you. You can even choose which sites you want Metacrawler to search if you're not happy with your results using the default setting.

Browser Tip

Here's a quick way to search for something: Search directly from your browser's Location text box. If you're using Netscape Navigator, enter one or more words into the Location box. For instance, if you want to search for information about hiking in Iceland, type **iceland hiking**. Press **Enter**, and Netscape sends the search keywords to a search engine. If you're using Internet Explorer, type **find** followed by the word you want to search for: **find iceland**, for instance.

Note that if you're using an old browser you may find that typing a single word has a very different effect; it attaches .com to the word and searches for the resulting domain name.

How Do I Use the Search Engines?

Internet *search engines* enable you to search a database. Take a quick look at AltaVista (`http://www.altavista.com/`) in Figure 15.3 as an example. Start by typing a search term into the text box. You can type as little as a single word, but you might want to get fancy—in which case you should read the instructions. You'll find a link at AltaVista, probably labeled Help, that takes you to a document that describes exactly what you can type. Read this document; it gives you many suggestions and hints for using the search engine. (Most search engines have a link such as this to background information.)

As you will learn in the information document, you can enter these types of things at AltaVista:

➤ **Words between quotation marks (AltaVista calls these "phrases")** Entering words this way tells AltaVista to find the words in the exact order in which you type them: "the here and now."

➤ **Proper names** Be sure these names are capitalized correctly: Colorado, England, or Gore, for instance. (AltaVista will return both improperly and properly capitalized words if you enter the keyword entirely in lowercase.)

➤ **Plus or minus signs before words** Any word with a plus sign before it *must* be in the Web pages found; any word with a minus sign *must not* be in any Web pages found. So, if you enter **+madonna +pop +singer**, you'd receive only a list of Web sites that include all three of those words. If you enter **+scuba –Mexico**, you'd get a list of sites that include the word *scuba* but not the word *Mexico*.

➤ **Asterisks**   If you're not exactly sure how to spell your search term, replace the unknown portion with an asterisk. That is, if you want to look for information on Nantucket, but you're not sure how to spell it, just enter **Nantuck***. You can also use this feature to search for both singular and plural forms of a word (for example, **train***).

Figure 15.3

AltaVista, a Web search engine.

Each search engine is a little different and allows you to use different sorts of search terms. You can always search by entering a single word, but the more you know about each search engine, the more efficiently you can search.

When you first go to a search engine, look around for some kind of link to a Help document. When you finish reading the Help information, click the **Back** button to return to the page with the text box. Enter the word or phrase you want to search for, and then press **Enter** or click the **Search** button. Your browser sends the information too, and with a little luck you'll see a result page shortly thereafter (see Figure 15.4). Of course, you might see a message telling you that the search engine is busy. If so, try again in a few moments.

When I searched for "Iceland," AltaVista found seven related searches and 247,760 links to Web pages that contain information about Iceland. The document I'm viewing doesn't show me all the links, of course. It shows me the first 10 Web pages and provides a link at the bottom of the page that I can click to see the next 10. It also shows a variety of other ways to search for the term "Iceland," such as "Shop the Web for Iceland," which doesn't seem to make much sense but which actually does find products with the name "Iceland" in them (such as Orchestral Music of Iceland and "Selections recorded 1985–1990 by the Icelandic National Broadcasting Service").

Figure 15.4

AltaVista found a few links to Icelandic subjects for me.

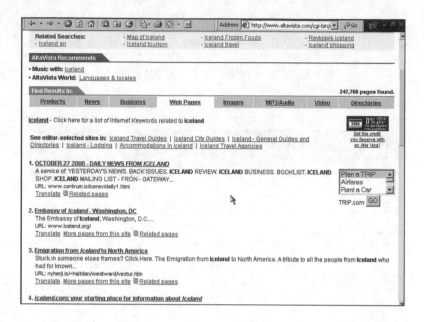

Browsing the Internet Directories

For an example of an Internet directory, take a look at Yahoo!, the single most popular search site on the Web. Go to `http://www.yahoo.com/`. Yahoo! has a search engine, so you can type a word into the text box if you want, but notice the category links: Arts & Humanities, Education, Health, Social Science, and so on. Each of these links points deeper into the Yahoo! system, a level lower in the hierarchical system of document categories. To see how this system works, click **Recreation & Sports**, and you see a document from Yahoo! with a list of more categories: Amusement and Theme Parks@, Aviation, Fitness@, Motorcycles@, and so on.

The @ sign at the end of some of these categories indicates that this entry is a sort of cross-reference: you will be crossing over to another category if you select this link. For instance, click **Fitness@**, and you'll see a page from the Health: Fitness category. This page also contains links to other fitness-related categories, from Aerobics to Health Clubs, and Organizations to Web Directories.

You'll also notice that some links are shown with bold text and numbers in parentheses after them, such as **Aerobics (9)**, and links that are not bolded, such as Just Move. The bold links take you farther down the hierarchy, displaying another document that contains more links. The number in parentheses after the link shows how many links you'll find in that document. The regular text links are links across the Internet to Web documents that contain the information you're looking for.

Finding Specific Stuff

Now that you've seen how to search for general stuff, you're ready to learn about searching for specific stuff. Instead of going to a general search site, you can go to one of many sites that help you find specific things. For example, you might want a site where you can search for Web pages related to animals (`http://www.animalworldwide.com/`), boat stuff (`http://boatingyellowpages.com/`), or kid stuff (`http://www.yahooligans.com/`). You can find scores of these specialized search sites, with information about everything from lawyers to pets. A good place to find them is at `http://dir.yahoo.com/Computers_and_Internet/Internet/World_Wide_Web/Searching_the_Web/Web_Directories/`. You can also find them at any of the other big search sites.

Just Tell Me in English

The latest thing in search engines is *natural-language searching*. The problem with most search engines is that they're not particularly friendly. They expect you to ask a question in just the right way. But hang on a minute—haven't we all seen *Star Trek* and *2001: A Space Odyssey*? Aren't we supposed to *talk* to these stupid computers in plain English?

In theory, a natural-language search engine enables you to ask a question in plain English: *Where can I find pictures of rabbits?*, for instance, or *How do I find cheap airline tickets?* In practice...well, they work pretty well although, as with most computer programs, far from perfectly. The best known of these systems is Ask Jeeves (`http://www.ask.com/`). This system responds with a number of things—first, it asks a number of questions, and if one of the questions is close to your question and you click on the Ask button next to it, you'll probably find the information you want. It also provides links to pages that it found through several other search systems—WebCrawler, Infoseek, Excite, Yahoo!, and AltaVista. When asked *Where can I find pictures of rabbits?*, it responded with, *Where can I see pictures of rabbits?*, *Where can I find a concise encyclopedia article on rabbits?*, *Where can I find information about rabbits as pets?*, *How can I determine the sex of my rabbit?*, and *Where can I search an online database of images?* All pretty good matches. Use common words (such as picture and rabbit) and there's a good chance you'll get some useful information. Sometimes with more obscure things, the search doesn't go quite as well. On the other hand, you never know. I tried *tell me the best way to employ a clinometer* and it actually found a page that explains how to build a clinometer for measuring tree heights, in addition to links to companies that make these instruments. There's another, newer search engine that supports natural language searches—it's called Northern Light (`http://northernlight.com/`).

Finding Out Where You're Going

Do you need directions to get to your aunt-in-law's house in Schenectady? And you've never even been to the state of New York? Don't worry—there are some very powerful tools on the Web that will make your life easy, or at least easier than calling Aunt Matilda and trying to interpret her instructions. Just go to MapQuest (http://www.mapquest.com/)—or Yahoo!, or almost any of the major search engines—and find a link that says **Maps** or **Driving Directions**. Then, you'll type in your home address and Matilda's address, and in a few seconds your monitor will display a map with text directions from your driveway to your dear auntie's doorstep. Or simply enter an address to see a map showing the location.

Figure 15.5

A MapQuest map, served up by Yahoo!'s map search service.

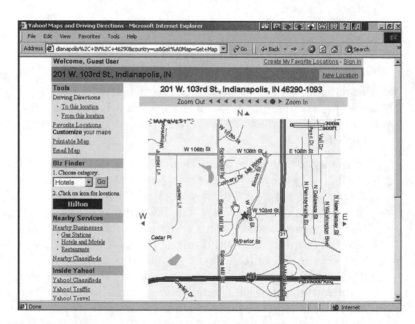

What to Do When You Get There

How about finding a movie to go to tonight? Try **Yahoo! Movies** (http://www. movies.yahoo.com/), **Moviefone** (http://www.moviefone.com/), **Now In Theaters** (http://www.nowintheaters.com/), or **Zap2it.com Movies** (http://www.zap2it.com/movies/). You'll be able to enter your ZIP code and find times and locations of movies playing close by. But you'll get more—descriptions, reviews, trailers, and far more information than you really need.

Prefer TV? Then, try **Zap2it.com TV Listings** (http://tvlistings.zap2it.com/), **Yahoo! TV Listings** (http://tv.yahoo.com/), **TV Guide** (http://www.tvguide.com/), or **TV Excite** (http://tv.excite.com). TV Excite will even let you create a list of favorite shows and episodes, and then search the airwaves to find them for you.

Finding Out What People Are Saying About You

Are people talking about you (do you hear voices in your head?)? If you want to know what people are saying about you on the Internet, you can search newsgroup messages for particular words. You can search for your own name to find out what your friends—or enemies—are saying about you, or you can search for a subject if you are researching a particular topic.

There are a number of places you can search newsgroups. One of the best is Deja.com (http://www.deja.com/usenet/). Or try Yahoo!; go to http://www.yahoo.com/. Select the **Advanced Search** link located to the right of the search button. Then, click the **Usenet** option but-

Search for Search Tools

You can use the search engines to help you find places to search for something else. For instance, typing **tv schedule** in a search engine will find Web sites that provide TV listings; typing **train schedule** would find sites that provide train schedules, and so on.

ton and enter your keywords. (Another alternative is to go to Metacrawler and select **Newsgroups** from the drop-down list box before you search.) When the search site carries out the search, it displays a page of links to the matching messages. Click a link to read the message.

Set a Bookmark to Repeat the Search Later

Here's a handy little trick. If you've just done a search about a subject that you think you'll want to check back on later—to see what new information has appeared on the Internet—bookmark the search. I don't mean the search site, but the search itself. Go to the search site, carry out the search, and when you get the page displaying the search results, bookmark that page. The next time you want to search, all you have to do is select that bookmark. Your browser automatically sends the search statement to the search engine, which carries out the search and displays the result. (This trick works on most, although not all, search sites.)

The Least You Need to Know

➤ There is no single directory of Internet users, so the easiest way to find someone is often to ask a mutual acquaintance.

➤ There are now lots of good directories. You might have to search a few, but there's a good chance that eventually you'll find the person you're looking for.

➤ There are lots of ways to find businesses, too, through yellow page search sites.

➤ A search engine is a program that searches for a word you enter.

➤ You can search indexes of keywords describing the contents of Web pages, or you can search the full text of the Web pages (millions of words in millions of pages).

➤ A directory is a categorized listing of Web links. Choose a category, then a subcategory, then another subcategory, and so on until you find what you want.

➤ Natural-language searches allow you to ask a plain-English question...and you'll often get a good answer, too.

➤ Services such as Deja.com, Yahoo!, and Metacrawler enable you to search newsgroup messages. The result is a list of matching messages. Click a link to read a message.

➤ You can set a bookmark on a page that displays search results; to repeat the search quickly at a later date, all you have to do is select that bookmark.

Shopping Online

Suppose you live in Waterloo, Iowa, and you wake up at 2 a.m. with the perfect gift idea for your spouse's rapidly approaching birthday. In the old days, you'd probably just roll over, go back to sleep, and forget about it the next morning. But in the world of the Internet, you can probably sneak out of bed, turn on your computer, and within minutes order those cleated rubber overshoes for next-day delivery.

Shopping on the World Wide Web used to be a hit-or-miss affair, but nowadays you can find practically anything you can imagine. Online shopping is especially well suited for durable goods such as books, CDs, electronics, software (which you can often download immediately after buying), sporting goods, toys, and so on. It's not quite as good for things such as clothing and furniture, because you can't try them out before you buy like you could in an actual store. And it may never be that popular for perishable items such as food (although there are, and will continue to be, companies that try to convince you otherwise).

How Do You Find What You Want?

There are various ways to find that product that will make your life complete. You may already know the name of a store. Several have become household names, or widely promote themselves offline and on. Companies such as Amazon.com (books), CDnow (CDs, of course), Lands' End (clothing), Victoria's Secret (small clothing), Pets.com (oops, they're out of business, despite their sock puppet spokesperson)... PetsMart.com (pet supplies), Furniture.com—oh, dear, that one's gone, too.

On the other hand, you may want to simply enter the name of the product you're searching for into a search engine (see Chapter 15, "Finding What You Need Online," for tips on searching). For instance, to generate a listing of sites that sell fruitcakes, just submit that term to your favorite search engine. Figure 16.6 shows what happened when I used Google to search for sites related to "fruitcakes." As you can see, Google found about 8,430 sites that have something to do with fruitcakes. And the first and fifth links on the search page are obviously to sites that sell fruitcakes.

Figure 16.1

Google shows several sites where I can buy a delicious fruitcake, along with recipe sites if I prefer to make it myself.

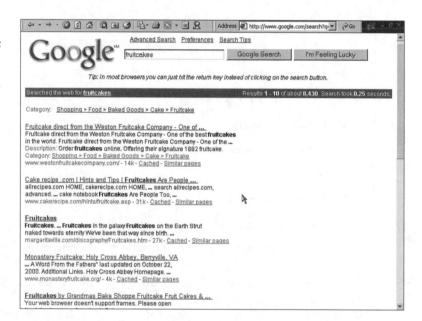

However, a note of caution. Some search engines may be biased. Both Yahoo! and Lycos sell e-commerce systems to small businesses, and both have special search functions that will do "shopping" searches. But, of course, those special searches search through their own clients' online stores, not the Web in general.

Comparison Shopping—Let Someone Else Shop for You

Before you jump in and shop, pause for a moment and consider using a service to help you find the best price. There are a number of comparison-shopping services, sometimes known as *shopping agents*.

In general, these services focus on specific product types, perhaps several types. For instance, **BarPoint.com** (http://www.barpoint.com/) checks prices on books, movies, music, computers, electronics, office products, pet supplies, and toys. **PriceScan** (http://www.pricescan.com/), one of the best known of these services, will help you find prices on a much wider range of goods: books, computers, digital cameras and supplies, household appliances, lawn mowers, sporting goods, watches, and many more categories.

Another well-known site, perhaps the best known thanks to a large marketing budget, is **mySimon** (http://www.mysimon.com/). When I wanted a new digital camera, I went to mySimon and clicked on **Consumer Electronics**, **Digital Cameras**. I knew I wanted a Kodak DC280, so I entered that in the search tool. MySimon returned 38 different online sellers of that model camera, with prices ranging from $344 to $749.95. As well as the normal goods—books, music, movies, and so on—mySimon can help you with a more varied range of products, such as food and wine, flowers, babies and kids (I think that category refers to goods for babies and kids, rather than the creatures themselves), and pet supplies.

Figure 16.2

Comparison shopping tools such as mySimon can save you hundreds of dollars; this camera ranges from $389 to $419.99.

If you're a compulsive shopper, you'll find plenty of choices in comparison services to keep you plenty busy online: services such as **BottomDollar** (`http://www.bottomdollar.com/`), **beHelpful** (`http://www.behelpful.com/`), **Metaprices** (`http://www.metaprices.com/`), and plenty of others. Search at any major search engine for **comparison shop** or **shopping agent**.

Be careful, though. Some comparison services are limited to a particular subset of stores. For instance, Yahoo! Shops (`http://shopping.yahoo.com/`) and Lycos Shop (`http://shops.lycos.com/`) both have comparison services, but only compare prices among stores hosted by Yahoo! and Lycos.

How Do You Pick?

Should you always take the lowest price? Perhaps not. In fact, surveys have found that buyers do *not* always pick the lowest price. They are more likely to pick the lowest price among the stores that they recognize, fearing to take a chance on an unknown merchant. On the other hand, remember that if you're buying with a credit card, you're well protected (we'll talk about this in the following section), so if you're looking for a product that is unlikely to require service or support, you may want to pick the cheapest.

Is It Safe?

Yes, if you use a credit card. That may surprise you, after all the nonsense we've heard over the last few years about the dangers of using your credit cards online. Here are the facts:

➤ Credit cards are rarely, if ever, stolen during transmission between a browser and a Web site.

➤ If you are charged for something you bought but have not received, complain to the credit card company. If the merchant cannot prove that it actually delivered the product to you (they'll need a Fedex delivery confirmation, certified mail receipt, or something similar), you will automatically be credited with the charge.

➤ If your card is stolen, the maximum you are liable for is $50. However, in many cases the credit card companies will not charge you even the $50. And some cards come with a guarantee that you will never be charged a fee for a stolen card or number. (All Visa cards, for instance, now have "zero liability.")

Online commerce is remarkably safe—for buyers. It's the merchants getting ripped off by people using stolen numbers; and those numbers are generally stolen out in the real world, not in cyberspace. (So, you want to know how to keep your credit-card numbers really safe? Use them *only* in cyberspace, never in restaurants, garages, the mall....)

Other Payment Methods

There are other ways to pay for products online:

➤ Offline methods through an online form—
Print a form, and then send a check or
credit-card number, or phone in the information.

➤ Checks—A few sites accept checks; pull a
check out of your checkbook, enter the rout-
ing number, account number, and check
number, and the store takes the money
directly from your bank account.

➤ Your telephone—You dial a number, and are
given a purchase or access code; your phone
number is then charged. This is a common
purchase method for pornography Web
sites.

➤ Online payment methods—The most common of these are systems such as PayPal and
Billpoint.

There are a variety of new "digital cash" systems,
of which only two are in wide use: PayPal
(http://www.PayPal.com/) and Billpoint
(http://www.Billpoint.com/). And of those two,
PayPal is by far the most common, with around
five million people holding accounts at the time
of writing. By the time this book is in print, it
could easily be millions more.

An Important Exception

There's an important exception in
credit-card safety—people who sign
up for memberships in pornography
sites report that overbilling is common. You might sign up for a single
month's membership, find that
you're being billed over and over,
and have trouble getting the site to
stop billing you. (If you have to subscribe to a porn site, you might find
that single-use credit-card numbers
are the way to go! See the information about American Express Private
Payments, Discover Deskshop Virtual
Credit Card, and the various reloadable credit cards under "Weird and
Wonderful New Cards," as follows.

Most eBay auction transactions are PayPal transactions (which must be very irritating
to eBay—Billpoint is owned by eBay). And Intuit is adding PayPal capabilities to their
Quicken and Quickbooks accounting programs.

How do PayPal and Billpoint work? You sign up for an account, providing a credit-
card number or bank account number (or, if you prefer, sending a check to "load" the
account with money). When you want to make a purchase, you use the system's control panel to specify whom you want to pay and how much. If the recipient already
has an account with the same system, the money is instantly transferred into his
account. If not, he receives an email telling him to come to the Web site and set up
an account, so the money can be placed into the account.

These payment types are great for informal and personal payments. Payments to
friends (someone lends you $10 at lunch, so you email him the money when you
get back to your office, for instance), and payments to people from whom you're

purchased goods in auctions. At the time of writing the vast majority of e-commerce systems did not accept these payment types. However, one at least does. BizBlast.com (http://BizBlast.com/) has a system that accepts PayPal payments, and others will probably accept them sometime soon.

Weird and Wonderful New Cards

A slew of new purchase cards is appearing on the scene, some of which are targeted toward online purchasers, at least partially. For instance...

➤ **VisaBuxx**—Targeting teenagers, this card has a set limit controlled by the card owner (generally the parent). The card is loaded with money, and after the money has been spent cannot be used until more money is loaded into it. http://www.visa.com/pd/buxx/

➤ **Visa Cash**—Similar to VisaBuxx, these cards can be reloadable or one-time disposable cards. http://www.visa.com/pd/cash/

➤ **Visa Smart Card**—This card has a chip embedded in it containing identifying information, and Visa will give you a free smart-card reader if you order one. The reader plugs into your computer and reads the card; the theory is that a merchant set up to use this technology can receive information transmitted by the reader, so your credit card is not transferred. The reality is that very few merchants are currently set up to use this system. http://www.ordersmartvisa.com/

➤ **American Express Cobalt Card**—Similar to the VisaBuxx and Visa Cash card, these are preloaded cards. http://www.americanexpress.com/

➤ **American Express Private Payments**—A system for the truly paranoid. When you want to buy something online, go to the American Express site and they'll issue you with a one-use number, and then make the charge against your account—you won't use your real American Express card number. http://www.americanexpress.com/privatepayments/

➤ **Discover Deskshop Virtual Credit Card**—Very similar to American Express Private Payments, this system uses a Windows-based program running on your computer to generate one-use credit-card numbers. http://www.discovercard.com/

"Name Your Own Price" Services

Sometimes known as *reverse auctions*, the most famous of the "name your own price" services is **Priceline** (http://www.Priceline.com/). They began with airline tickets, and currently sell home mortgages, cars, long-distance phone service, hotel rooms, and rental cars.

The basic concept is this. Figure out what you want to buy, and then go to Priceline and tell them how much you want to pay for it. For instance, want to fly from Denver to New York? Tell them when you want to go, and how much you want to pay, and Priceline will tell you whether they'll accept your offer. The weakness of the system is that they generally will *not* accept your offer, which has left a lot of potential clients who never came back (me for one). On the other hand, undoubtedly many people *have* got really good deals.

There are variations on this theme. You tell a system what you want and buyers bid on your business, pushing the price down over time (see **Pricemate**: http://www.pricemate.com/). Or as more people bid on something, the price goes down because they're buying in bulk (**ReverseAuction.com**: http://www.ReverseAuction.com/). But these systems are a bit of a gimmick, and some have been going out of business recently. Even Priceline, the king of "name your own price," has been closing down some of its divisions. (They figured out naming your own price for gas is just too much of a hassle for most people.)

Buying Items at Auction

Are you looking for a one-of-a-kind item, a collectible, or something that's so popular you can't find it in a store? Your best bet may be to check out the auction sites. These sites help individual buyers and sellers to get together and conduct personal transactions—the auction site charges a small fee for their trouble after a sale is made. The king of the auction sites is **eBay** (http://www.ebay.com/), where you can browse by category, geographic region, or theme. Click on the **Elvis** theme, and you'll find subcategories called **Elvis Buttons**, **Elvis Novelties**, **Elvis Belongings**, and more. When I looked, I found 27 items in the Elvis Belongings category, from a bed sheet with a current bid of $2.99 to an $8,500 gold-and-diamond necklace. If you take a fancy to Elvis's wool Army jacket, you simply register and make a bid that's higher than the current high bid. The seller sets a time limit on the bidding, and if your bid is the highest when time expires, you become the proud new owner of an itchy 1959 U.S. Army field coat.

There's a site called **Internet Auction List** (http://www.internetauctionlist.com/) where you can click on one of nearly 50 categories, and you'll see a list of auction sites that deal in products related to that category. It's a directory of auctions, and it's quite comprehensive.

Online Coupons and Discounts

The Internet is a goldmine for those seeking free stuff, discounts, and coupons. Coupon sites generally work in one of two ways: They provide a link to another Web site, where you'll automatically receive the stated discount when you buy online, or they display a coupon that you can print out and take to a local store.

Some of these sites are owned by well-known coupon companies, the same companies that send you coupons in the mail. For instance, at the Val-Pak site (http://www.valpak.com/), which you can see in Figure 16.3, you enter your ZIP code and email address and the system finds local coupons that you can then print. Other popular coupon sites are run by true dot-com companies, such as **Yahoo! Coupons** (http://coupons.yahoo.com/) and **H.O.T. Coupons** (http://www.hotcoupons.com/).

Figure 16.3

Print local coupons at the Val-Pak site.

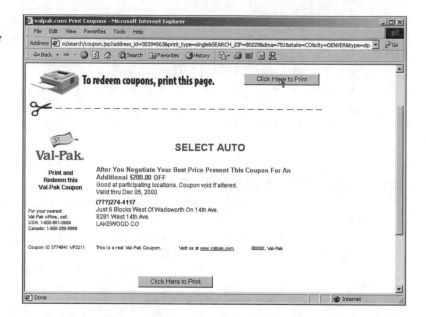

A number of sites produce coupons for online stores. For instance, I recently checked **InstantCoupons** (http://www.instantcoupons.com/) and found discounts at online stores for jewelry, office supplies, shoes, and many other items. Some of these discounts are at major stores, too, such as REI and Staples. Plenty of other sites have online coupons: **Daily eDeals** (http://www.dailyedeals.com/), **eCoupons** (http://www.dailyedeals.com/), **ShopLoop** (http://www.shoploop.com/), and many others you'll find at your favorite search engine.

One More Reason to Buy Online

The sooner you decide to take the plunge and start buying online, the more money you may save. Why? Because, at least at the time of writing, many commercial Web sites sell goods at close to cost, or even below cost in some cases. That's Internet economics for you. These business are trying to capture long-term customers—they're selling things at a loss in order to achieve that goal.

This can't go on forever. In fact, the Internet bubble is bursting. These companies can't continue losing money much longer. Late in 2000, Internet retailers are dropping like the proverbial flies, and the rest are losing money. It won't be long before investors pressure Internet retailers to stop losing money, and one thing they're going to have to do is increase prices. So, get it while the getting's good!

The Least You Need to Know

➤ You can buy almost anything on the Internet—and if you can't buy it now, you will likely be able to soon.

➤ Comparison shopping sites will save you lots of research time, and perhaps lots of money.

➤ Don't worry too much about thieves intercepting your credit-card information online; it's a rare occurrence, and you're protected by the credit-card company.

➤ There are other ways to pay online—checks, PayPal, phone.

➤ There's probably a discount or coupon for almost anything you want to buy.

➤ The best time to buy is now, before Internet businesses consolidate and raise their prices.

Making Money on the Internet

Want to make money on the Internet? That used to be easy. First, start a business selling some kind of Internet service or software. Run it for a few months on a shoestring, and then go public. It didn't appear to matter what the intrinsic value of the company was—as long as it has the word "Internet" attached to it somehow, you'd get rich.

Finally, the Internet-investment hype is dying out. During 2000, in particular in March of that year, and then to a greater degree in the fall, the bottom dropped out of the "dot com" investment market. Internet companies were dropping like flies (and maybe still are by the time you read this); if you'd really like to see how bad it got, go to http://f---edcompany.com/ (I've used the "sanitized" URL—you'll understand after you get to the site.)

The Internet bubble has burst. Some dot coms are even going out of business before their launch parties, in a matter of a few weeks rather than months or years. When I wrote the sixth edition of this book, Amazon.com was worth over $22 billion. (Barnes and Noble, on the other hand, a company that actually makes money, and sold many times more books than Amazon.com, was worth only $2.3 billion.) And today? Today, as I write this, Amazon.com's total market capitalization—the value of all its stock based on the current stock price—$7 billion. And it'll go further, I bet.

Andy Grove, the chairman of Intel, said a few years ago, "It remains to be seen whether the Internet companies that have essentially infinite access to capital will be able to grow up to be self-sufficient institutions and adjust to a future when money won't be free." Translation #1: These companies might not be worth what people are paying for them. Translation #2: When the investment money runs out, these companies might be in trouble. Well, it's finally happened, and a huge proportion of these companies are on the way out of business, or already history.

There's Another Way

But there *are* companies making money on the Internet, and doing *very* well.

Not so long ago, the only people making money on the Internet were people selling Internet services: software companies, service providers, hardware manufacturers, and so on. It seemed that almost nobody was making money on the Internet unless they were selling goods or services to people who wanted to make money on the Internet, sort of like an author making lots of money by selling get-rich-quick schemes to people who'd never get rich. In fact, the high failure rate of Internet businesses was a joke among Internet insiders. A few years ago, when I told an executive at a major Internet software company that I wanted to write a book about companies that have figured out how to make money on the Internet, he said, "Is anyone making money? I mean, we are, but is anyone else?"

These days it's easy to find companies that are succeeding. Many companies, including small one-person businesses, are taking orders online or using the Internet to successfully promote their business (Figure 17.1 has an example of a very successful small business that went online). I've spoken with a small publishing company selling $3,000 worth of books at their Web site each month, a small gaming-software publisher that finds a "significant" proportion of its new customers on the Web, and a two-man business selling toys online—and selling lots of them. *I* make money on the Internet, too. I sell enough books at my Web site (`http://TopFloor.com/`) to make far more than just pin money! I also know of a new business that started a mailing list discussion group. This business doesn't sell anything online, but the owner told me the mailing list became such a great promotional tool that it was the single most important factor in the business's growth and success.

I do a lot of radio interviews, and the most common question I hear is, "Can you really make money on the Internet?" My response is, "Yes, but you probably won't." Yes, because many people *are* doing it. You probably won't, because *most* people don't know how. To point you in the right direction, this chapter will give you a few guidelines for using the Internet as a business tool.

Figure 17.1

It is possible to make money online! HotHotHot was a small company that decided to put its products online in 1994—since then, it has been written up in the Wall Street Journal, Inc., Business Week, *and many other places.*

Do You Have a Product?

A lot of people have rushed into business on the Internet with the idea that as long as they have something—anything—to sell, they can make money. The Internet is paved with gold, so it's just a matter of kneeling down and digging it up. Many people who've never run a business before see the Internet as such a great opportunity that they'd better get in fast. Never mind that they don't know the first thing about selling, or filling orders, or managing a business. They want to get in, and they want to get in now.

But Internet users are not stupid—at least, no more stupid than anyone else. If you're selling garbage, you'll have a hard sell. The first step in going into business on the Internet is the same as going into business in real life: You've got to have a product or service people want to buy.

Can a Web Site Help Every Business?

There's so much hype on the Internet (remove the hype and it would collapse within hours) that many people now believe that every business should have, must have, a Web site. But in many cases a Web site won't do a lot of good. Don't expect a sudden rush of sales just because you have a couple of Web pages.

Take, for instance, the case of a small local plumbing business. Will merely setting up a Web site be worth the time and hassle (and believe me, it can take a lot of both), not to mention money (it doesn't have to take much money, though)? Probably not. Few people will search the Web looking for a plumbing company; they're more likely to look in the Yellow Pages (and even if they do look online, they'll probably use the online Yellow Page systems, such as Yahoo!'s Yellow Pages or Zip2, which won't take them to a company's Web site). Spending a lot of money on a Web site probably won't be cost-effective.

However, maybe a plumbing company *can* use a Web site. Let's say this company sells plumbing supplies and perhaps even has a plumbing supply catalog that it sends to independent plumbers. In this case, it makes sense for the company to have a Web site. The company's market might be nationwide, and the Web can become one more channel for reaching customers.

There's another very low-cost way that a Web site might help a small company. As radio-show host Tom King has suggested, a Web site can be used as what he called an "electronic business card" for businesses that are out and about providing services. The plumbing company could put its URL on the sides of the vans, in large letters: http://UnplugQuick.com/, or whatever. In effect, the vans become links to a little catalog of the company's services on the Web.

Some people will remember the URL they've seen on the side of the truck and might go to the site rather than look in the Yellow Pages. Such a business-card site isn't intended to attract visitors or do much more than provide a way for someone who's seen the URL to find the company's phone number, mailing address, information about services, perhaps a map showing where to find the company, and so on. Most people who see the URL won't visit the site, but a small Web site can be so cheap that it can still be affordable and worth using to catch the few who will. That's one of the nice things about the Web—you can experiment at a very low cost.

How Cheap?

Web sites can be very affordable, especially if you're willing to do the work yourself. Here's a quick breakdown of costs for a very basic "business-card" Web site:

Domain name registration	$15
Web site hosting	$9 to $20 per month
Good HTML-authoring program	$50 to $100, or perhaps free
Your time	???

Let's have a quick look at these items.

Domain Name Registration

To do any business Web site properly, you need your own domain name. That's the first part of a Web site. For instance, I have the domain name PoorRichard.com, so my Web-site domain is http://PoorRichard.com/ or http://www.PoorRichard.com/.

Your own domain name sounds better, more professional, and it's generally shorter and easier for your visitors to remember. If you move the Web site from one host to another, you can keep the domain name. It's also easier to get your own domain name registered on Yahoo!, the most important search system on the Web (it has a bias against Web sites that are subdomains of other domain names, such as `http://www.bigbiz.com/PoorRichard/`).

Registering a .com domain name—the .com is a commercial domain—can cost as little as $15 a year. There are lots of places you can register your domain name—some may charge as much as $70 for the first two years, others allow you to pay for just a single year, at a much lower cost; so shop around. Go to Yahoo! and search for *domain registration companies*.

The cost of your domain, then, could be as little as around $1.25 a month.

Web Site Hosting

We discussed Web hosting in Chapter 13, "Setting Up Your Own Web Site." You can host a very simple Web site, using your own domain name, for as little as $9 or $10 a month. You might pay more if you want extra services, perhaps $15 a month. I pay around $30 a month, but I have a big site with a lot of services, so I have to pay a little more.

HTML Authoring Program

In Chapter 13, you saw how to create Web pages. You can create a very simple "business-card" Web site doing the HTML yourself. But you can also buy an HTML-authoring program, or even use shareware or freeware, and very quickly create things that would be quite complicated if you had to learn all the HTML. A good HTML-authoring program costs around $50 to $100. That's $4.17 to $8.33 a month over the first year.

You might even be able to get away with paying nothing. If you use Netscape Communicator, for example, you have a program called Netscape Composer. It's not a full-featured authoring program, but it will do all the basics. There are many other free HTML programs around, too.

Your Time

This one's tricky. It depends on how you value your time. You'll have to spend some time finding a hosting company and learning how to use the HTML program. How long? Hard to say. You might end up spending five hours looking for a hosting company, perhaps less if you're not very choosy (remember to see my free report, *20 Things to Ask a Web-Hosting Company,* at `http://PoorRichard.com/freeinfo/special_report.htm`). Then, perhaps another five hours really getting to know your HTML-authoring program. Within 10 hours, perhaps a lot less, you could have a decent little site up and running.

So, what's the total cost? Depending on your choices, around $5 to $10 a month for the domain and authoring program over the first two years, plus whatever you decide to pay for hosting, which probably is $9 to $20 a month. Not a huge investment. Note, however, that this amount is for a simple business-card-type site. The more complicated you get, the more you'll end up paying, although the real cost might be in terms of the time you put into the site.

There's No Such Thing As an Internet Business

There's no such thing as an Internet business; there is, however, such a thing as a business that uses the Internet as a business tool. It's important to remember this, because ultimately, if you're in business on the Internet, you're still in business. And that can be lots of hard work. If you're selling products on the Internet, most of the work might be done *off* the Internet, for example. Creating the products, processing orders (which, for many small businesses, might be done offline), fulfilling orders, and addressing customer service problems are all issues that you must deal with. It's important to remember that if you're going to set up a business on the Internet, you are still setting up a real business, and you need to understand all the real-world concerns that entails.

Search Engines Are Not Enough

You've probably heard that a Web site is a billboard on the information superhighway. This Internet mantra has been kept alive by the Web design companies that want your business. Guess what? It's not true.

You can see a billboard as you drive by on the freeway. A Web site just sits there in the darkness of cyberspace, waiting for someone to visit. It's not a matter of "build it and they will come." If you don't *bring* visitors to the site somehow, nobody will see it. There are many ways to bring visitors to the site; the most obvious is using search engines. But there are problems with that method.

There are millions of Web sites on the Internet, all vying for business. And there seem to be thousands of businesses claiming that they can put you right at the top of the search engines' lists. These companies create special coding, which will be read by any search engines that look at the Web pages in your site. This coding, known as META tags, is designed to push your Web site to the top of its category at the search engines. Be a little wary of these claims, though.

First, it's going to cost you, perhaps 25 cents or more for every person who comes to your Web site thanks to a listing created by a search optimization company. But cost might not be too much of a problem, because the company might not send much traffic your way; one company told me that on average it sends around 25 people a day to a Web site using its service—not exactly a flood.

Results from search engine optimization don't work well for a few reasons. First, you can't fool Yahoo!, the single most important search site; entries are added to Yahoo! by real human beings, not a computer program, so they don't care about META tags. As for the other search sites, they're constantly modifying the way they index pages, trying to stop these companies from fooling them into putting Web pages high into their lists. Finally, there's an awful lot of competition; we can't all be at the top of a list.

It's important to get your Web site registered at the major search sites: Yahoo!, Excite, AltaVista, HotBot, Netscape's new Netsite, Lycos, and so on. Visit each site and find a registration link. The number one tip for good site registrations is to be sure the title tag in the page you are registering is descriptive of the page, including keywords that people are likely to use when looking for pages like yours. But relying on search sites is not enough; you need more ways to bring people to your site.

Why Would Anyone Come to Your Site?

First, consider why anyone would want to come to your site. The billboard idea doesn't work; setting up a Web site and waiting for people to arrive doesn't work. But "make it useful, let people know about it, and then they'll come" really does work. If your site is useful, and you do your best to let people know about it, they will visit.

Think about your Web site. Ask yourself, "Why would anyone come to my site? If it wasn't *my* site, would I visit?" If you can't answer the first question, and the answer to the second is no, then you've got a problem.

Common Sense Advice

Remember this basic concept when creating a Web site: *Forget cool—think useful!* Don't get carried away with all the hype about multimedia and "cool" Web sites, but think carefully about why people would come to your site.

Don't Forget the Real World

If you're already in business, you already have ways to tell people about your Web site: your business cards; the side of your car, van, or truck; your letterhead; your print, radio, and TV ads. Let people know about your Web site and give them a reason to visit. If you're not in business yet, but plan to launch an Internet business, you'll ignore the real world at your peril. Notice that all the large Web businesses advertise in the real world. They do that because they know they can't ignore the real world and focus solely on Internet promotions. (Yahoo!, by the way, doesn't place its own banner ads on the Web, but it does spend a lot of money on TV and print ads. Yahoo! sells banner ads...so they know they don't work.)

Don't forget to use the press, too. If you have a Web site of interest to horse lovers, be sure the horse magazines know about it; if your site is aimed at sailors, send a press release to the sailing magazines, and so on.

Look for Partnerships

Here's something else all the large Internet companies already do. They look for partnerships with other Web sites. For instance, do a search for some kind of music subject at Yahoo!, and you'll see the logo of a music retailer pop up along with the list of Web sites. The retailer paid a lot of money for that partnership, of course, but partnerships can start at a very low level. Ask people to link to your Web site; if someone has a list of links, a directory to useful resources, perhaps your site should be in the directory.

Offer to give away products at someone's Web site. I've done book giveaways to promote new books. Web site owners are often happy to do this, because they feel it adds value to their site. You'll need a form at your Web site (which is a little out of the scope of this chapter, but simple feedback forms are often easy to install, or at least cheap to have installed for you). People who want to win the product can then register their email address with you. You can then use the list to announce the winners and gently plug the product, too. I've used this method to build my Poor Richard's Web Site News newsletter (`http://PoorRichard.com/newsltr/`). When people signed up for a free copy of one of my books, I asked whether they wanted a free subscription to my newsletter, too—and most did. Look carefully for ways to work with other sites; they're often very powerful ways to bring people to your site.

Use Mailing Lists and Newsgroups (Carefully!)

You can also promote your site in discussion groups, but do so very carefully. Don't go into these groups and simply advertise your site. But if group members would find your site interesting, you can mention that. For instance, a law site might mention articles of interest to writers and publishers in the writing and publishing discussion groups; a horse site might announce schedules of competitions in horse show groups; and so on. The discussion groups provide a great way to reach people, as long as you're careful not to annoy them with obnoxious advertising.

Don't Forget Email

It's easy, with all the hype about the Web, to forget the power of email. But email publishing is very popular and very effective. Even many successful Web sites use email as a promotion. For instance, the CDnow site (`http://www.cdnow.com/`) has a periodic, customizable newsletter that's free for the asking—and hundreds of thousands of people have asked! You can select particular types of music, and CDnow will send you announcements about those genres. This fantastic marketing tool is really low cost, next to nothing when compared to the cost of doing a real-world mailing to that many people.

Your mailing list is unlikely to be that large, at least for a while. But it's still worth building. Consider creating bulletins, newsletters, and product announcements. Don't turn every one into an ad; be sure there's something of value in every message you send out. But don't ignore the value of contacting people via email, either.

Read My Special Reports

I've barely scratched the surface here; there's an awful lot to learn if you want to set up business on the Internet. Visit my site for free reports on the subject, and hey, why not sign up for my free newsletter, too? You can find details at `http://PoorRichard.com/`.

The Least You Need to Know

➤ Thousands of people are making money on the Internet; you can too, perhaps, but only if you know the ropes.

➤ Think carefully about if and how a Web site can help your business. Depending on what you're trying to do, you might find the cost doesn't outweigh the benefits.

➤ Web sites can be very cheap. A simple "business-card" site might cost between $14 and $30 a month.

➤ A Web site is not a billboard. You have to bring people to your site somehow, and that takes work.

➤ Register with the search engines, but don't get hung up about them; you can't rely on them to bring in all your business.

➤ Look for other ways to bring in visitors. Give people a reason to visit your site, and then get the word out about the site every way you can think of.

➤ Don't forget to use email; it's an essential marketing tool.

Chapter 18

Staying Safe on the Internet

In This Chapter

➤ Keeping kids "safe"

➤ Protecting your email

➤ The identity problem

➤ Internet addiction

➤ Protecting your credit card

➤ Keeping out of trouble with your boss or spouse

There are many dangers on the Internet—most of them imagined or exaggerated. We're led to believe that our children will become corrupted or be kidnapped, our credit cards will be stolen, and we'll be arrested for copyright infringement. Although some of these dangers are real, keep in mind that you're sitting in front of a computer at the end of a long cable. Just how dangerous can that be? If you use a little common sense, it's not dangerous at all.

Your Kid Is Learning About Sex from Strangers

Sex, sex, sex. That's all some people can think of. The media's so obsessed with sex that sometimes the only thing that our journalists seem to notice are stories with a little spice in them. Consequently, the press has spent a lot of time over the past few years talking about how the Internet is awash in pornography. The funny thing is that when they first started talking about it, there really wasn't much of a problem. Sure, the pornography was there, but you weren't likely to find it unless you went looking for it.

You Can Do Your Own Research

Because this is a family book, I'm not going to go much further on this topic. If you care to research the subject of sex on the Internet further, just go to the search engines (see Chapter 15, "Finding What You Need Online") and search for "sex" or "69" or some other such term. (But don't carry out this experiment and then blame me if you're offended by something you find!)

These days the situation's different. You can easily run into pornography online—or, more to the point, your kids can easily stumble across it. Porn sites send out a lot of junk email, so your kids may eventually see invitations to visit Web sites, such as "ANYTHING YOU WANT AND CAN IMAGINE! WATCH HOT WOMEN FROM ALL OVER THE WORLD DO IT LIVE!!"

In 1996, the Computer Decency Act was holding porn sites back—much of the really explicit stuff was hidden away on private Web sites. To get in you had to subscribe by providing a credit-card number. Since then, the Computer Decency Act has been struck down by the courts. There are still many private sites, but quite a lot of very explicit stuff is available at the free Web sites.

There's something a little odd going on in the world of pornography. It's becoming "respectable." Celebrities are getting involved—movie stars and rock stars. Porn companies are being traded on the stock market. And, in fact, the world's largest purveyors of pornography are well-known, respectable institutions such as AT&T, which makes more money selling porn (through its @Home cable service) than Larry Flynt of *Hustler* fame. The trend is definitely toward pornography becoming more available.

In fact, you can now stumble across pornography by merely mistyping something into your Web browser. Some pornpreneurs have registered domain names that are similar to other more popular domain names. For instance, type **whitehouse.com** into a Web browser instead of **whitehouse.gov**, and you'll end up at a porn site. So, when you make your fingers do the walking, walk slowly and carefully.

Don't Expect the Government to Help

If you have kids, you already know that they can be a big bundle of problems. The Internet is just one more thing to be concerned about. Still, you signed up for the job, and it's your responsibility.

Many people have suggested that somehow it's the government's responsibility to look after kids. (These are often the same people who talk about "getting the government off our backs" when it comes to other issues.) A few years ago, the U.S. Congress passed the Computer Decency Act (CDA), which bans certain forms of talk and images from the Internet. This law definitely had an effect, and pornography was, for a while, harder to find on the Internet. But the CDA was a sloppily written piece of overreaction; it could be construed to ban all sorts of genuine public discourse, such as discussions about abortion. Consequently, the law was judged unconstitutional by a federal court in Philadelphia and later overturned by the U.S. Supreme Court.

The court in Philadelphia wrote that "those responsible for minors undertake the primary obligation to prevent their exposure to such material." Hey, isn't that what I said? (I originally wrote most of this, in an earlier edition, *before* the law was struck down. Looks like there could be a judicial career waiting for me!)

The bottom line is that the Computer Decency Act is history. Even if it's replaced by something else (various U.S. states are trying a variety of clumsy experiments), remember that the Internet is an international system. How is the U.S. government going to regulate Swedish, Finnish, Dutch, or Japanese Web sites? It's not. So, what are you going to do to keep your kids safe?

It's Up to You; Get a Nanny

If you want to protect your kids, I suggest you spend more time with them at the computer or get a nanny. You can't afford a nanny, you say? Of course, you can. Lots of programs are available to help you restrict access to "inappropriate" sites. Programs such as Net Nanny (I'm not endorsing this one in particular; I just used it so I could put "Nanny" in the heading) contain a list of sites that are to be blocked; you can add sites from your own hate-that-site list, or you can periodically download updates from the Internet. Using these programs, you can block anything you want, not just pornography. As the Net Nanny site says, you can "screen and block anything you don't want running on your PC, such as bomb-making formulas, designer drugs, hate literature, Neo-Nazi teachings, car-theft tips—whatever you're concerned about."

You can find Net Nanny at http://NetNanny.com/. To find other such programs, search for the word **"blocking"** at Yahoo! or some other Web search site (or go directly to http://www.yahoo.com/Business_and_Economy/Companies/Computers/ Software/Internet/Blocking_and_Filtering/Titles/). You'll find programs such as SurfWatch, CyberPatrol, CYBERSitter, NetShepherd, TattleTale, Bess the Internet Retriever, ChatNANNY (which tracks activity in chat rooms), and Snag. (I'm serious, all these are names of real programs!) If you use an online service, you'll also find that it probably offers some way of filtering out areas you don't want your kids to get to. America Online has had such filtering tools for a long time. MSN enables you to block the Internet's alt. newsgroups and other "adult" areas.

Both major browsers have blocking tools built into them. In Internet Explorer, select **Tools, Internet Options**, click the **Content** tab, and then the **Settings** button. In Netscape Navigator, select **Help, NetWatch**.

However, you should be aware that *these systems don't work!* The theory is that Web sites will rate themselves, by entering special descriptive information into the HTML source of the Web pages. The browsers will read this information and decide whether or not the sites can be viewed. So, you, as a parent, can specify that your kids cannot see sites with sexual or violent content, for instance.

The Internet Content Rating Association (ICRA)

In May of 1999, a group of major Internet companies met in London to form an international organization to protect children (and, note, free speech) on the Internet. The companies included Microsoft, AOL Europe, Bertelsmann Foundation, British Telecom, Cable & Wireless, Demon Internet (UK), EuroISPA, IBM, Internet Watch Foundation, Software & Information Industry Association, and T-Online Germany. These companies have decided to push a Web-site rating system based on the RSACi (Recreational Software Advisory Council on the Internet) system that is embedded into Internet Explorer and Netscape Navigator. Almost two years later, though, the system is still not working well.

However, *very few Web sites use these ratings!* This gives you two options. You can tell the system not to display any sites that do not contain the rating information. But that's most sites on the Web; your browser will display very few Web sites, even, at the time of writing, blocking CNN, the White House, and the BBC (although you *can* get through to Disney.com). Or you tell it to block only sites that contain rating information indicating that the site contains sex or violence. And as most sex- and violence-related sites *don't* specify this information, a lot of bad stuff will be accessible.

I'd suggest that if you want to block information, you use one of the commercial systems, and do not rely on the browsers' absurdly weak systems.

By the way, you'll hear people criticize these blocking programs for two reasons: 1) because they're not perfect (of course, they're not) and 2) because they're an affront to the concept of free speech. Personally, I believe they are very useful and reasonably effective. I believe in supervising my kids, and these programs provide a supervision tool for a new era. They also provide a way for concerned parents to keep their kids away from sites they object to without locking people up and forcing adults to read nothing more than sixth-grade materials on the Web.

From a personal viewpoint (it's *my* book, after all), this whole sex-on-the-Internet is a whole lot of fuss about almost nothing. Sure, clean up the Internet—but what are you going to do about the schoolyard? Schools are hotbeds of filthy language and talk about sex, sprinkled with the occasional pornographic magazine and actual sex. I have the perfect solution, though. I call it "chemical supervision," and it entails giving kids drugs to reduce certain hormonal levels. Remember, you heard it here first.

Your Private Email Turned Up in the *National Enquirer*

Email can get you in a lot of trouble. It got Oliver North in hot water, and ordinary people have lost their jobs or been sued over things they've said in email. Several things can go wrong when you use email:

➤ The recipient might pass the email on to someone else.

➤ The message can be saved on a backup system and read by someone other than the recipient later.

➤ Someone could spy on you and read your email looking for incriminating comments.

The most likely scenario is that the recipient intentionally or thoughtlessly passes on your message to someone whom you didn't count on seeing it. The second problem—that the message could be copied to a backup system—is what got Oliver North (and others) into trouble. Okay, you can't expect Oliver North to understand this stuff. But it's even got Microsoft in trouble! Microsoft email messages have been used in their recent problems with the Justice Department. Even if you delete a message and the recipient deletes the message, it might still exist somewhere on the network if the system administrator happened to do a backup before it was deleted.

Digital Signatures

You can also use public-key encryption systems to digitally sign documents. When you encrypt a message with the private key, it can be decrypted only with your public key. After all, your public key is public. But if it can be decrypted with your public key, it *must* have come from your private key. Therefore, it must have come from you.

So, if you are ever the subject of some kind of investigation, that message could be revived. A message goes from your computer, to your service provider's computer, to the recipient's service provider's computer, to the recipient's computer—at least four places from which it could be copied.

Finally, someone might be out to get you. Internet email is basic text, and a knowledgeable hacker with access to your service provider's system (or the recipient's service provider's system) can grab your messages and read them.

What do you do, then? The simplest solution is to avoid putting things in email that you would be embarrassed to have others read. The more complicated solution is to encrypt your email. A number of encryption programs are available that scramble your message using a public-key encryption system, and, as discussed in Chapter 7, "Advanced Email—HTML Mail, Voice, and Encryption," encryption systems are now being incorporated into email programs. Figure out how they work, and use them.

If you don't have an email program with built-in encryption, you can find an add-on system. A good way to start is to search for the **encryption software** at any of the Web search sites. There's a problem with these systems, though. Right now, they're complicated to use (the systems built into email programs are generally much simpler). PGP, for instance, can be very complicated; if you want to use it, I suggest that you get one of the "front-end" programs that make it easier to use, such as WinPGP. In addition, because few people use encryption anyway, if you want to use it, you'll have to arrange to use it first. Remember also that even if you encrypt your mail messages, they're not completely secure; you're still trusting the recipient not to pass on the decrypted message to someone else.

Prince Charming Is a Toad!

I'm not sure why I should have to explain this, but when you meet someone online, *you don't know who that person is!* Something about electronic communications makes people quickly feel as though they know the person with whom they are communicating, but they don't!

There are two problems here. First, cyberspace is not the real world. People communicate in a different way online. As another author told me recently, "I know people who seem to be real jerks online, but who are really nice people offline. And I've met people who seemed to be great online, but were complete jerks offline."

Then, there's the misrepresentation problem. Some people flat out lie. A man who claims to be single might be married. A woman who claims to look like Michelle Pfeiffer might really look like Roseanne Barr. A 35-year-old movie executive who graduated from Harvard might actually be a 21-year-old unemployed graduate of Podunk Bartending School. It's easy to lie online when nobody can see you. Couple that with a natural tendency to feel like you know the people you meet online, and you have trouble.

Internet Stalkers

Internet stalkers are for real. People have been murdered, raped, and variously assaulted by people they've met online. But remember, they can't get to you unless you provide them the information to reach you. Getting into trouble is unlikely, but it can happen, so use some common sense. If you really have to meet someone you've run into online, for instance, do so in a way that you can leave if you decide your offline impression of the person doesn't match your online impression. Arrange that first meeting for a public place, for example.

Not everyone lies online, though. As my friend Phyllis Phlegar wrote in *Love Online* (Addison Wesley), "Even though some individuals choose to be deceptive, many others see the online world as the ultimate place in which to be totally honest, because they feel safe enough to do so." (Phyllis met her husband online, by the way.) She also recognizes the dangers: "As long as the person or people you are talking to can't trace you, free-flowing communication between strangers is very safe." But if you're not careful and you give out information that can be used to trace you, Prince Charming might turn out to be the Prince of Darkness. And if you do choose to meet someone in person after meeting that person online, be cautious.

She's a He, and I'm Embarrassed!

Chapter 8, "Using Online Chat Rooms," covers chat systems, which are great places to meet people. For many, they're a great place to meet people of the opposite sex (or of whichever sex you are interested in meeting). But keep in mind that sometimes people are not of the sex that they claim to be. I don't pretend to understand this, but some people evidently get a kick out of masquerading as a member of the opposite sex. Usually, men masquerade as women, which could be construed as the ultimate compliment to womanhood or could simply be blamed on the perversity of men. Either way, there's a lot of it around, as the saying goes. (I recently heard chat systems described as being full of "14-year-old boys chatting with other 14-year-old boys claiming to be 21-year-old women." True, it's an exaggeration, but it illustrates the point well.) So, if you hook up with someone online, bear in mind that she (or he) might not be quite who he (or she) says (s)he is.

You Logged On Last Night, and You're Still Online This Morning

The Internet can be addictive. I think three particular danger areas stand out: the chat systems, the Web, and the discussion groups (mailing lists and newsgroups). Apparently, chat is extremely addictive for some people. I've heard stories of people getting stuck online for hours at a time, until early in the morning—or early in the morning after that. I know of people who've met people online, spent hundreds of hours chatting, and finally abandoned their spouses for their new "loves."

The Web is not quite so compelling, but it's a distraction, nonetheless. There's just so much out there. If you go on a voyage of discovery, you *will* find something interesting. Start following the links, and next thing you know you've been online for hours. Discussion groups are also a problem. You can get so involved in the ongoing "conversations" that you can end up spending half your day just reading and responding.

Other problem areas: addictions to gambling, pornography, stock trading, and auctions. (Evidently, many people are getting sucked into the online auctions, and are unable to think of anything beyond that next great deal they're going to find in eBay.)

What's the answer to Net addiction? The same as it is for any other addiction: self-discipline, along with some support. It also helps if you have a life in the real world that you enjoy. Fear probably helps, too (such as the fear of losing your job or kids). If you need help, why not spend a bit more time online? Do a search for "**addiction**," and you'll find Web sites set up to help you beat your addiction. Visit, for instance, the The Center for On-Line Addiction (http://NetAddiction.com/), where you can ponder important questions such as "Is CyberSex Cheating?" and "Do you spend too much time online?"

Profiles

If you are a member of an online service, be careful about what you put in your profile. Most services allow you to list information about yourself—information that is available to other members. Omit your address, phone number, and any other identifying information!

Just Because You're Paranoid Doesn't Mean Someone Isn't Saying Nasty Things About You

A little while ago, someone started saying rather unpleasant things about me in a mailing list. What she didn't tell people was that she had a sort of vendetta going against me and had for some time. (No, I'm not getting into details.) Anyway, I saw her comments in one mailing list and was struck by a thought: There are tens of thousands of internationally distributed newsgroups and thousands more mailing lists! What else is she saying? And where?!

There's a way to find out what's being said about you (or someone or something else) in newsgroups and Web pages. This is something that might be very useful for anyone who is in the public eye in any way (or for people involved in feuds).

To see what's being said about you in a Web page, search AltaVista; this service lets you use a search engine that indexes all the words in a page, instead of just categorizing Web pages (Chapter 15 explains how to use search engines). To search a newsgroup, though, you'll need a program such as Deja (`http://www.Deja.com/`). In Deja, you type a name or word you want to search for, and the service searches thousands of newsgroups at once and shows you a list of matches (see Figure 18.1). Click the message you are interested in to find out exactly what people are saying about you. (You can also search Deja from some of the other search engines, which have links to it.)

Figure 18.1

Deja provides a great way to search newsgroup messages. (Looks like Elvis has been busy.)

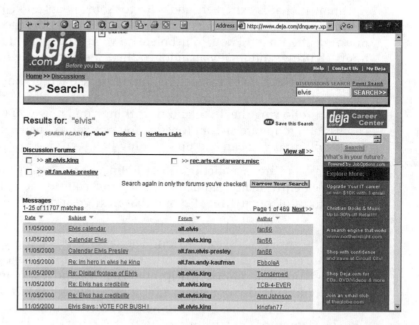

When I did this little search on my own name, I was surprised at what I found. I discovered information about a science-fiction conference at which I was to speak (funny thing is, I'd forgotten I was supposed to attend, so it was lucky I did the search!), and I found messages in which people recommended a book I'd written about PGP. I also discovered that there's a stunt man called Peter Kent (I found that in alt.cult-movies).

Deja is not the only such service; you can find a list of these services by going to Yahoo! and searching for **usenet searching**.

I Was "Researching" at Hustler Online, and Now I'm Unemployed

This title is more than a joke. Some people really have been fired for viewing "inappropriate" Web sites during work hours. This seems quite unfair to me; companies give people Web browsers, often unnecessarily. They provide a temptation, and then fire the people who succumb!

Of course, you can avoid such problems by staying away from the sites in the first place. But if you must go there, practice safe surfing by clearing the cache when you finish! (I discussed the cache in Chapter 3, "More Web Basics—Searching, Saving, and More.") When you visit a site, a copy of the Web page is saved on your hard disk in case you want to view it again at a later time. In effect, this creates a history of where you've been. And speaking of history, most browsers these days have excellent multi-session history lists, which will also list every Web page you've seen for the past few weeks!

To cover your tracks, clear the cache to remove the offending pages. Then, clear the history list (either clear it completely, or remove just the offending entries). Netscape Navigator and Internet Explorer also keep a list of URLs you've typed into the Location bar, so if someone starts typing, say, www.4work.com at your computer, before the URL is completed the browser might automatically finish it for you by typing www.4adultsonly.com! (In any case, you might not want your boss to know that you've been visiting 4work.com, either—it's a job search site.)

It's Bugged!

Your boss can spy on your Internet activities using special software programs, regardless of whether you clear the cache and history list. So, maybe you'd better just get back to work.

Someone Bought Tires with My Credit Card!

Not so long ago, somebody went on a buying spree with one of my credit cards. He bought tires, a computer, some jewelry, and various other goodies. (He was caught and had the goods confiscated, but a week or two later had the nerve to go to the police and ask for the jewelry back, claiming he'd used a different card to buy it.) Now, was my credit card stolen online? No, it was stolen in a restaurant.

But for some reason people think that shopping on the Internet is dangerous. If you're going to avoid using your card online, it only makes sense to stop using it in grocery stores and gas stations, which are hotbeds of criminal activity compared to the Internet.

The Real Fraud

There is credit-card fraud online, but it's the merchants getting hit, not the buyers. The use of stolen credit-card numbers to make online purchases is very common, ranging from a percent or two of transactions in some businesses up to major proportions of all sales. Pornography sites, in particular, are hit hard by online fraud!

How can it be safe online? First, credit-card number theft is quite rare on the Internet. It can be done, but only by a computer geek who really knows what he's doing. But why bother? Credit-card numbers are not very valuable because it's so easy to steal them in the real world. A little while ago I handed over my credit card to a supermarket clerk; the clerk returned the card, putting it down on the counter. The woman behind me set her bag down on the card, and from the look on her face when I asked her to move her bag, I'm sure she knew it was there. Stealing cards is easy offline, hard online. In fact Internet-business author Jill Ellsworth found that credit-card companies regard Internet transactions as *safer* than real-world transactions.

The second reason that online transactions are safe is that both Netscape and Internet Explorer, the two most used browsers, have built-in data encryption. Many Web sites now use special Web servers that also have built-in encryption. When a credit-card number is sent from one of these browsers to one of these secure servers, the data is encrypted and is therefore unusable. Figure 18.2 shows how several Web browsers indicate a secure Web site. Notice the little padlock in the lower-right or lower-left corner of the window? Internet Explorer versions 4 and 5, and Netscape Navigator 4 use a locked padlock to indicate that a site is secure. Netscape 2 and 3 display a key image in the lower-left corner for the same purpose; if the key is broken, the site is not secure. Navigator 4 also puts a yellow line around the padlock toolbar icon.

But aren't credit cards stolen online? There have been a number of highly publicized cases in which people broke into systems and stole information en masse. No matter how you pass your credit-card number to a vendor, the most dangerous time is *after* they've received the number—and there's little you can do about that. (Your number could be taken in an offline transaction and stored on a company's Internet-accessible computers.)

Look for the padlock icons.

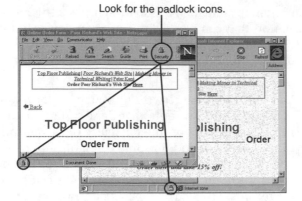

Figure 18.2

When you see a locked padlock or a key in the status bar, you can send your credit card without worry.

My Wife Found My Messages in alt.sex.wanted

A lot of people are saying a lot of odd things on the Internet. Undoubtedly, each day thousands of people with very poor judgment make millions of statements that could get them in trouble. This little problem has long been recognized. And for some time now there's been an (almost) perfect way around it: You post messages anonymously.

One way to do that is to configure your email or newsgroup program with incorrect information (with another name and email address, for instance). When you send the message, the header contains that incorrect information instead of the true data. That tactic will fool most list members, but it's not completely safe; the header also contains information that allows the message to be tracked by a system administrator (or the police), and in any case falsifying the header in your email is likely to upset people and might even be illegal soon.

A better method is to sign up for a free email account on the Web. A lot of companies now provide such email accounts (search for **free email** at a search site). Why do they do this? So they can sell advertising. Anyway, many of these systems allow you to sign up for an account anonymously. Sure, you have to provide information about yourself, but it doesn't have to be real.

To use email, you log on to your Internet account through whichever service provider or online service you happen to use. Then, you go to the free-mail system's Web site and log on to your mail account. You can now send and read your email. Each message that goes out is sent from the Web site, not from your service provider or online service. So, there's nothing in the header that directly identifies you.

How safe is this email service? Someone reading your message won't be able to find you without the help of the system administrators at the email service and your service provider or online service. So, this service is pretty safe for day-to-day anonymity, but perhaps not so safe if you are doing something that might offend the government or police of the country in which those services are found.

Another method is to use an anonymous remailer, a system that posts the messages for you, stripping out all information that can be used to track you down. In other words, you send the message to the remailer with information about which newsgroup or person it should be posted to, and the remailer sends the message on, sans identity.

Another Problem

Who runs the anonymous remailers? If you were a smart computer cop, wouldn't it occur to you to set up your own anonymous remailer? It already has occurred to various police forces, so you can't be absolutely sure that the anonymous remailer you are using isn't merely a trick to track down people saying things that they shouldn't say.

Can I Take It for Personal Use?

In most cases, you probably can. When you connect to a Web site, all the things that are transferred to your computer end up in the cache anyway. However, some enthusiastic copyright lawyers claim that the use of a cache is in itself illegal, that even storing images and text on your hard drive goes against copyright law.

You can find these services by searching for **remailers** at a search site. But note that these systems are not perfect. They depend on the reliability of the person running the service and, in some cases, on that person's willingness to go to prison. If the police come knocking at his door, the administrator might just hand over his records. (This has happened; at least one anonymous remailer has handed over information.) Another problem with remailers is that they go one way only. You can send, but not receive.

Nothing's completely safe. Even using a genuine anonymous remailer can leave you at risk; your email could be intercepted between your computer and the remailer, for instance. As the *Frequently Asked Questions About Anonymous Remailers* document says, "Hard-core privacy people do not trust individual remailers… [they] write programs that send their messages through several remailers…only the first remailer knows their real address, and the first remailer cannot know the final destination of the email message." One such program is Mixmaster, which you'll find if you search for **mixmaster remailer** at a search site.

I "Borrowed" a Picture, and Now They're Suing Me!

As you've seen throughout this book, grabbing things from the Internet is as easy as stealing from a baby—but there's none of the guilt. It's so easy and so guilt-free that many Internet users have come to believe in a sort of "finder's keepers" copyright morality. If it's there, and if you can take it, you can use it.

The law says otherwise, though. Here's a quick summary of copyright law: If you created it, it belongs to you (or to your boss if he paid you to create it). You can put it anywhere you want, but unless you sign a contract giving away rights to it, you still own the copyright. You don't have to register copyright, either.

Copyright law is quite complicated, however, and this summary misses many essential details. The important thing to understand is that it *doesn't* belong to you if you didn't create it! Unless something has been placed on the Internet with a notice explicitly stating that you can take and use it, you can take it for personal use, but you can't use it publicly. You can't steal pictures to use at your Web site, for instance. (Even if there is a notice stating that the item is in the public domain, it might not be. After all, how do you know that the person giving it away created it?)

Copyright law even extends to newsgroups and mailing lists. You can't just steal someone's poetry, story, ruminations, or whatever from a message and distribute it in any way you want. It doesn't belong to you. Of course, if you are concerned that your work will be taken from a newsgroup or mailing list and distributed, don't put it there!

I Downloaded a File, and Now My Computer's Queasy

Yes, you know what I'm talking about: computer viruses. These nasty little programs get loose in your computer and do things they shouldn't, like wipe out your hard drive or destroy the directory information that allows your computer to find files on the drive.

First, my role as contrarian dictates that I inform you that much of the fuss about viruses is greatly exaggerated. When something goes wrong with a computer, a virus usually gets the blame. An example of how the virus threat is exaggerated is the famous Good Times virus. This virus never existed; it was a myth from the start. The story was that an email message containing a virus was being passed around the Internet. The story was obviously wrong because a plain email message without a file attached cannot contain a virus.

Only files that "do things" can contain viruses. That includes program files, as well as document files created by programs that have macro languages. For instance, a variety of Word for Windows and Excel macro viruses just appeared in the past few years (what took them so long?). If a file can do nothing by itself—if it has to have another program to do something to it—it can't carry a virus. A plain text file (including text messages) can't do anything, and GIF or JPG image files cannot cause harm. (I'm just waiting for the next big hoax: Someone will start a rumor that there's an image file used at many Web sites that contains a virus and that all you have to do is load the page with the image to infect your computer.)

Yes, viruses do exist. Yes, you should protect yourself. There are many good antivirus programs around, so if you plan to download software from the Web (not just images and documents from applications other than advanced word processors), you should get one.

I've Been Browsing, and Now They're Coming to Get Me

If you browse around on the Web, can you be identified? Well, not easily. In most cases, a Web-site owner cannot track a visitor back to a particular computer. But still, a lot of people are very concerned about privacy and the fact that perhaps, just perhaps, they are identifiable.

One problem is trust. To a great degree, the Internet is based on trust, although perhaps misguided. For instance, let's consider cookies for a moment. These are little bits of information saved in text files on your computer's hard drive. Your account name at a Web site might be saved in a cookie, for instance, so the next time you arrive at the site your account name is automatically entered into a log-in form. Now, there's a lot of nonsense spoken about cookies, and about how Web sites can steal information from them. They can't—a site can retrieve only a cookie that it set on your hard drive itself. But consider this. If you download a piece of shareware, that program could, without your ever realizing it, read your cookies, and transmit the information across the Internet. Of course, it could read much more—it could look for Quicken and Microsoft Money files and transmit them, too (although Microsoft has the perfect solution—make their files so huge it would take forever to transfer them).

Web Sites Sharing Cookies

You may have heard in the press about Web sites sharing cookies. Here's how it happened. An advertising company placed banner ads on many thousands of different Web sites. The advertising company was setting cookies—when a banner was displayed, it came from the advertising company's servers, and at the same point a cookie was set—not the individual Web sites' servers. In this way, the company could combine information from many different Web sites, building profiles of an individual user's activities at those different sites.

So, a lot of what we do on the Internet is based on trust, trust that the programs we're using aren't out to steal information, for instance. We also assume that we won't be tracked back from a Web site to our computer. But such tracking is possible. Not by most Web-site owners, but certainly by governments and police agencies. There is a digital trail left when you wander around the Internet. It's a trail that's split into pieces, and parts of the trail are available to different people and companies. But if you have enough influence, you might be able to persuade everyone along the trail to provide you with the information you need.

There are people, of course, who don't have such a high degree of trust, and so there are now a number of systems in development that will make it possible to surf the Web anonymously. For instance, there's a program called Freedom, from a Canadian company called Zer0-Knowledge Systems (http://www.ZeroKnowledge.com/). This system allows you to create various different "digital identities," and to transmit information through their server. The system works with the Web, and with newsgroups. "For example," they say, "if you like to debate politics online you can designate one pseudonym as your 'politics' pseudonym. Use it when you post in political newsgroups, surf activist Web sites, email your political contacts, and chat in political chat rooms. No one can trace it back to your real self."

There's also a service called Anonymizer (`http://www.Anonymizer.com`). Visit this site, enter a URL into a form at the site, and the service will grab the page for you and forward it to you. Is there really a call for such services? Well, Anonymizer claims to have "anonymized" over three-quarters of a billion Web pages since 1996!

The Least You Need to Know

➤ Yes, there's sex on the Internet, and your kids can find it. Get a filtering and blocking program if you want to keep the kids away.

➤ Email can easily be stolen or forwarded. Don't write anything that you could be embarrassed by later.

➤ People on the Internet sometimes lie (just like in the real world). They might not be who they say they are (or even the sex they claim to be).

➤ Internet addiction? Snap out of it! (Or go online and get some help.)

➤ You can search thousands of newsgroups at once, with systems such as Deja, to see what people are saying about you.

➤ Your boss can find out which Web sites you are visiting, so watch out!

➤ Credit-card transactions made on the Internet are safer than those made in the real world.

➤ Anonymous email accounts can protect your identity in email and newsgroups.

➤ You don't own what you find on the Internet; it's copyright protected.

➤ Viruses are relatively few and far between; but it's a good idea to protect yourself with an antivirus program.

Chapter 19

HERE THEY COME!!

Downloading Files (FTP, Go!Zilla, and CuteFTP)

In This Chapter

➤ What is FTP?

➤ FTPing with your Web browser

➤ Clues that will help you find files

➤ FTPing with true FTP programs

➤ Dealing with compressed files

➤ Protecting yourself from viruses

➤ Using download utilities (SmartDownload and Go!Zilla)

The Internet is a vast computer library. Virtually any type of computer file imaginable is available somewhere on the Internet. You'll find *freeware* (programs you can use free) and *shareware* (programs you must pay a small fee to use) and *open source* programs (programs that belong to nobody and everybody—nobody claims copyright) and almost all types of media files: music, pictures, video, 3D images, and many types of hypertext documents. Where are these files? They are stored in two different types of "libraries," on Web sites and in FTP sites.

It used to be, even in the early days of the Web, that virtually all files intended for download were stored in FTP sites. FTP is a quaint old UNIX-geek term; it stands for *file transfer protocol,* and it's an old UNIX system for transferring files from one computer to another. FTP is the original core of the Internet: The whole purpose of the Internet was to allow the transfer of computer files between research institutions.

Even email came later; it was reportedly slipped into the Internet by geeks who didn't keep the bureaucrats fully apprised. (The geeks feared that the managers would think email would be misused; from what I've seen of electronic communications, the managers would have been right!)

In this chapter I'm going to explain two things. First, you'll learn about how and why to use FTP. But I'll also come back to the subject of downloading files from Web sites, and explain a little more detail than we covered in Chapter 3, "More Web Basics—Searching, Saving, and More."

What Is FTP?

The FTP sites spread all over the Internet contain tens of millions of computer files. Although some of these sites are private, many are open to the public. With FTP, you might discover a fascinating file on a computer in Austria (or Australia, or Alabama, or Anywhere). You might have checked it out because someone told you where it was, because you saw it mentioned in an Internet directory of some kind, or because you saw a message in a newsgroup about it. You might have even found the file at a Web site and chosen to use FTP to transfer it—I'll explain why you might want to do that under "It's the Real Thing: Using a Genuine FTP Program," later in this chapter. The file could be a public domain or shareware program, a document containing information you want for some research you're working on, a picture, a book you want to read, or just about anything else.

FTP's Still Widely Used

Many Internet users will never use FTP, and have no idea what it is. But that doesn't mean FTP isn't still in wide use. Particular "communities" on the Web still use FTP libraries. For instance, there are millions of MP3 files (see Chapter 5) stored in FTP libraries, and people involved in pirating software often use them, too.

Suppose then that you're searching for a certain file. You might be told to "FTP to such and such a computer to find this file." That simply means "use the FTP system to grab the file." In some cases, you might have specific permission to get onto another computer and grab files. A researcher, for instance, might have been given permission to access files on a computer owned by an organization involved in the same sort of research—another university or government department, perhaps. (I have private FTP directories on various publishers' FTP sites, so I can upload Web pages, or chapters for a book, or whatever.) To get into a directory that requires special permission, you need to use a login name and a password.

In other cases, though, you'll just be rooting around on other systems without specific permission. Some systems are open to the public; anyone can get on and grab files that the system administrator has decided should be publicly accessible. This type of access is known as *anonymous FTP* because you don't need a unique login name to get onto the computer; you log in as anonymous and enter your email address for the password. If you are working at the UNIX command line, as many unfortunate people still do, you have to type this information. If you use anything else, you are using a program that will enter this information for you.

Different Flavors of FTP

FTP was originally a command-line program in which you had to type commands at a prompt and press the Enter key. Information would then scroll past on your screen, perhaps too fast for you to read (unless you knew the secret command to make it slow down or stop). You'd have to read this information and then type another command. Although UNIX geeks get some sort of strange masochistic pleasure out of that sort of thing, real people found early FTP to be a painful experience—and most people avoided it.

However, for about seven or eight years now there have been graphical FTP programs, Windows and Macintosh programs using familiar point-and-click, and even drag-and-drop, tools. Most of these graphical FTP programs enable you to see lists of files and use your mouse to carry out the operations. Using FTP with these systems was a pleasure; all of a sudden FTP became easy.

Of the many graphical FTP programs available, the best I've seen are CuteFTP and WS_FTP (Windows shareware programs) and Fetch and NetFinder (Macintosh shareware programs); see Appendix C, "All the Software You'll Ever Need," for information about finding all these programs. Another Macintosh FTP program is Anarchie, a shareware program that melds FTP with Archie (which I'll mention later). But many others are available, particularly for Windows.

Finally, FTP was incorporated into Web browsers. You can now go to an FTP site using your Web browser. Because the FTP site appears as a document with links in it, you can click a link to view the contents of a directory, to read a text file, or to transfer a computer file to your computer.

We'll look first at running FTP sessions with a Web browser, for a couple of reasons. First, it's a very easy way to work with FTP. Second, you probably already have a Web browser. However, there are some very good reasons for getting a hold of a true FTP program; I'll discuss this issue a little later in the chapter.

Hitting the FTP Trail

To work through an FTP example, let's go to `ftp://ftp.dartmouth.edu/`. This site is where you can find the Macintosh Fetch FTP program. (If you prefer to visit another FTP site, you can follow along and do so; the principles are the same. You can find a list of FTP sites to play with at `http://tile.net/ftp-list/`.)

265

What's in a Name?

Take a minute to analyze a site name. The `ftp://` part tells your browser that you want to go to an FTP site. The FTP site name (or hostname), `ftp.dartmouth.edu`, identifies the computer that contains the files you are after. That name might be followed by a directory name. I haven't given you a directory name in this example, but I could have told you to go to `ftp.dartmouth.edu/pub/software/mac/`. The `/pub/software/mac/` bit tells the browser which directory it must change to find the files you want.

To start, open your Web browser, then click inside the **Address** or **Location** text box, type `ftp://ftp.dartmouth.edu` (or `ftp://` and the address of another site you want to visit), and press **Enter**. In most browsers these days, you can omit `ftp://` as long as the FTP site name begins with ftp. In other words, instead of typing `ftp://ftp.dartmouth.edu`, you can generally get away with typing only `ftp.dartmouth.edu`.

In a few moments, with luck, you'll see something like the screen shown in Figure 19.1. Without luck, you'll probably get a message telling you that you cannot connect to the FTP site. If that happens, check to see whether you typed the name correctly. If you did, you'll have to wait and try again later; the site might be closed, or it might be very busy.

Name or Number

The FTP site or hostname could be a name (such as `leo.nmc.edu`) or a number (such as `192.88.242.239`). If it's a number, or if the name doesn't begin with `ftp.`, you *must* precede it with `ftp://`.

Incidentally, there's another way to get to an FTP site. Many Web authors create links from their Web pages to FTP sites. Click the link, and you'll go to that site. Try visiting `http://tile.net/ftp-list/`, and you'll see what I mean.

Files and Links: What's All This?

What can you see at the FTP site? Each file and directory is shown as a link. Depending on the browser you are using, you might see information about the file or directory (see Figure 19.1). You might see a description of each item (*file* or *directory*, for instance) and the file size, so you'll know how big a file is before you transfer it. You'll often see the file date and little icons that represent the directory or file type. Figure 19.1 shows both files and directories.

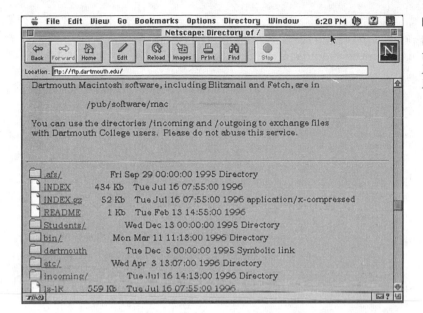

Figure 19.1

Using FTP in a browser is very simple. This is the Macintosh version of Netscape Navigator.

Private FTP Sites

To enter a private FTP site, you have to enter a login ID and a password. You can often enter the FTP site information in the format `ftp://`***username*:*password*@*hostname*/*directory*/**. For example, if you enter `ftp://`**joeb:1234tyu@ftp.sherwoodforest.com/ t1/home/joeb**, your browser connects to the `ftp. sherwoodforest.com` FTP site and displays the /t1/home/joeb directory; it uses the username **joeb** and the password **1234tyu** to gain access. However, in some browsers, using that method causes the browser to save your password in a drop-down list box associated with the Location text box—anyone else using your computer can see the ID and password if they know how. So, to be really safe, use the format `ftp://`***username*@*hostname*/*directory***. When the browser connects to the FTP site, it opens a dialog box into which you can type your password.

Click a directory link to make the browser display another Web document that shows the contents of that directory. In most browsers, you'll also find a link back to the parent directory: In Netscape, you'll see an "Up to a higher level directory" link, for instance. Figure 19.2 shows what you will find if you click the **pub** link at the ftp.dartmouth.edu site. Why pub? Because that's the name commonly used for the directory that holds publicly available files. You can see that there are a couple of files in this directory and many more subdirectories (the subdirectories are the little folders).

Figure 19.2

The contents of the pub directory at the FTP site. This time you're looking at a Windows version of Netscape.

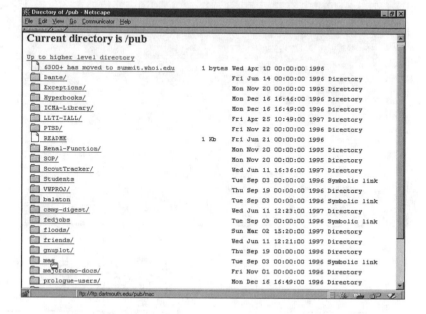

What happens when you click a link to a file? The same thing that would happen if you did so from a true Web document. If the browser can display or play the file type, it will. If it can't, it will try to send it to the associated application. If there is no associated application, it will ask you what to do with it, allowing you to save it on the hard disk. This process all works in the same way as it does when you are at a Web site—the browser looks at the file type and acts accordingly. (See Chapter 5, "Web Multimedia—From Flash to Napster," for more information.)

Finding the Pot o' Gold

Now that you're in, you want to find the file that you know is somewhere on this system. (In my example, you're looking for Fetch, the Macintosh FTP program.) Finding files at an FTP site is often a little difficult. There are no conventions for how such sites should be set up, so you often have to dig through directories that look like they might contain what you want, until you find what you want.

When you first get to an FTP site, look for files called INDEX, OO-INDEX, README, DIRECTORY, and so on. These files often contain information that will help you find what you need. The more organized sites even contain text files with full indexes of their contents or at least lists of the directories and the types of files you'll find.

Click one of these files to transfer the document to your Web browser, read the file (all Web browsers can display text files), and then click the **Back** button to return to the directory.

You'll often find that directories have names that describe their contents: mac will have Macintosh software, xwindow will have X Window software, windows will have Microsoft Windows software, gif will contain GIF-format graphics, and so on. If you know what you are looking for, you can often figure out what the directory names mean. In the example, you knew where to go because when you first arrived at the site you saw a message saying that Fetch was in /pub/software/mac. So, you clicked **pub**, and then **software**, and then **mac**.

Getting the File

When you find the file you want, click it, and save it in the same way you would save a file from a Web document (see Chapter 3, "More Web Basics—Searching, Saving, and More"). The following figure shows Fetch being saved from FTP.

Many files on FTP sites are *compressed*. That is, a special program has been used to "squeeze" the information into a smaller area. You can't use a file in its compressed state, but if you store it and transmit it in that state, you'll save disk space and transmission time. You can read more about these compressed formats in Chapter 4, "Understanding Web Programs and File Types." In this example (see Figure 19.3), you are transferring an HQX file that contains a SIT file. A program such as StuffIt Expander can extract the SIT file (a compressed file) from within the BinHex HQX file (a common format for transferring Macintosh files across the Internet).

Figure 19.3

You can save files from FTP sites with a few clicks.

It's the Real Thing: Using a Genuine FTP Program

There are some very good reasons for using a genuine FTP program instead of making do with your Web browser. First, you might run into FTP sites that don't work well through a Web browser. Some browsers simply don't like some FTP servers. Also, if you need to *upload* files to an FTP site—transfer files from your computer to the FTP site—it's much easier to do so using an FTP program than a Web browser. Some browsers may allow you to drag and drop—drag files from Windows Explorer and drop them into an FTP directory in the browser. But many browsers simply do not allow you to upload at all.

Why would you ever want to upload files? The most likely reason is that you have a Web site hosted on a server somewhere, and need to transfer Web pages, created on your computer, to the Web site (see Chapter 13, "Setting Up Your Own Web Site").

Another reason for getting hold of a true FTP program—a reason that's little understood yet very important—is that some good FTP programs (such as CuteFTP) can resume interrupted transfers. For instance, suppose you've almost finished transferring the latest version of your favorite Web browser, which could easily be 15MB or more, when the transfer stops. Why it stops is not important; perhaps your two-year-old rugrat just reached up and pressed that big red button on the front of your computer. Perhaps your service provider's system just died. Maybe lightning struck the power lines somewhere, and the power went out. Whatever the reason, if you're using a Web browser to transfer that file, you'll probably have to start all over again. If you were using a good FTP program, though, you could reconnect, go back to the FTP site, and begin the transfer again, but all that the program would need to do would be to transfer the missing part of the file, not all the stuff that had already transferred.

Now, I've heard it said that the Internet represents in some ways a giant step *backward* in technology. Well, okay, I've said it myself a few times. Resumed transfers is one of those cases in which the technology being used on the Internet is way behind what has been used *off* the Internet for years. (Online help is another case.) "Resumed download" technology is slowly finding its way to the Internet, but for the moment your Web browser probably *cannot* resume interrupted downloads. (We'll look at some cases in which your browser can resume downloads a little later.)

Some FTP programs, although not all, can. (Note that not all FTP *servers* can resume interrupted transfers, so even if your FTP program *can*, this feature won't work at all FTP sites.)

Same Name, Different Extension

While digging around in an FTP site, you might notice that files often have the same name except for the last few characters; you might find THISDOC.TXT and THISDOC.ZIP, for instance. The first file is a simple ASCII text file, and the second is a ZIP file, which (you'll probably notice) is much smaller than the first. If you know you can decompress the file after you have it, download the compressed version; doing so will save you transfer time.

If you transfer a lot of files across the Internet—in particular, large files—you should use a true FTP program. Not only can you use the FTP program when you are working in an actual FTP site, you can also use it at other times. In many cases, when you think you're transferring from a Web site, the file is really coming from an FTP site. For example, Figure 19.4 shows Shareware.com, a large shareware library. Notice that underneath the links to the download files you can see little labels that tell you where each file is stored—ftp.tas.gov.au, for instance. In this case, you can quickly see that the file is coming from an FTP site. However, most Web pages won't be this convenient. You can still figure out if the file is coming from an FTP site, though; point at the link, and in the status bar you'll see the URL of the file—in this case, ftp://ftp.tas.gov.au/pub/simtelnet/win95/music/cd2mp31u.zip.

You can quickly copy this information from the link by using the browser's pop-up menu (in a Windows browser, right-click on the link and choose something such as **Copy Shortcut**, or **Copy Link Location**; in a Macintosh browser, you'll probably be able to hold the mouse button down for a moment to open the pop-up menu). Then, you can paste the information into your FTP program and use that program to download the file.

If that's not enough, here are two more reasons to use a real FTP program. It's often quicker and easier to connect to a site using an FTP program than a Web browser, and you can also set an FTP program to keep trying automatically every few minutes. So, if the site's busy, the FTP program can keep trying until it gets through. You also might run into cases in which the browser FTP features are not enough. For those times, you need to get a real FTP program. For instance, CuteFTP has a very good bookmark system that allows you to quickly jump from one area of an FTP site to another; and it even allows you to edit text and HTML files directly on the FTP site.

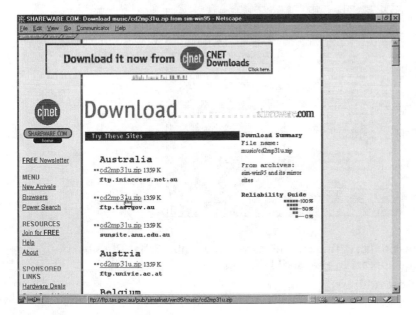

Figure 19.4

Yes, it's a Web page, but the files the page links to are stored at an FTP site, as you can see by pointing at a link and looking at the status bar.

Which and Where

There are lots of good FTP programs. If you use the Macintosh, try Fetch or Anarchie. For Windows, try WS_FTP or CuteFTP (my personal favorite). Many good Windows FTP programs are available as freeware or shareware on the Internet. See Appendix C for ideas on where to look for the software you want. (Remember, you need a program that will allow you to resume interrupted downloads, which means you'll probably have to pay the registration fee!)

When you get an FTP program, go through that old familiar routine: Read the documentation carefully to be sure you understand how to use it. (FTP programs are generally fairly easy to deal with.) To give you an idea of how FTP programs work, let's take a quick look at CuteFTP. CuteFTP is very easy to use. If you've ever used UNIX FTP, you know that using it is like eating soup with a fork—not particularly satisfying. CuteFTP, on the other hand, is what FTP should be. You have all the commands at your fingertips, plus a library of FTP sites to select from. No more mistyping FTP host-names!

Installing CuteFTP is simple. Just run the installation program. Then, start CuteFTP by going through the Windows Start menu or double-clicking CuteFTP's Program Manager icon. CuteFTP has two ways to connect to an FTP site: You can add an entry to the Site Manager (press **F4** to open it, and then click **Add Site**) or use Quick Connect (**Ctrl+C**). Use the Site Manager for FTP sites you expect to visit again (they'll be stored in the Site Manager); use Quick Connect if you *don't* expect to be back.

For instance, in Figure 19.5 you can see the FTP Site Edit box, the one that opens when you add a site to Site Manager. Enter the following information:

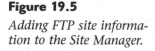

Figure 19.5

Adding FTP site information to the Site Manager.

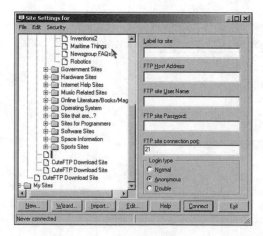

1. Type a **Label for site** (anything that helps you remember what the site contains). This name appears in the Site Manager's list on the left side.
2. Enter the **FTP Host Address**.

3. If you are going to an "anonymous" FTP site, leave the **FTP site User Name** and **FTP site Password** boxes empty, and leave the **Anonymous** option button selected at the bottom of the dialog box. You need to enter only a **User Name** and **Password** if you're going to a private FTP site.

4. You can generally ignore the **FTP site connection port** setting, unless you've been told by the site administrator to use something different.

5. Click the **OK** button to save the information.

6. In the Site Manager's list on the left, click the new entry, and then click **Connect** to begin the session.

When you click **Connect**, CuteFTP tries to connect to the FTP site. After it connects, you'll see the FTP site's directories listed on the right and the directories on your computer's hard disk listed on the left (see Figure 19.6). You can move around in the directories by double-clicking folders or by right-clicking somewhere in the right pane and selecting **Change Directory** from the pop-up menu (that feature is handy, because if you know where you want to go it's a lot quicker to type it in than to go through each directory in the path to get there).

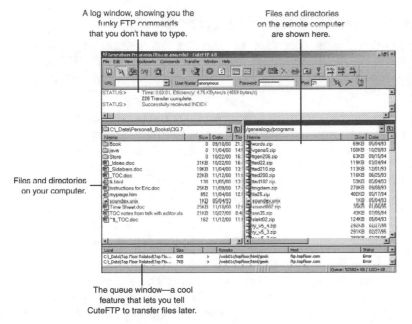

A log window, showing you the funky FTP commands that you don't have to type.

Files and directories on the remote computer are shown here.

Files and directories on your computer.

The queue window—a cool feature that lets you tell CuteFTP to transfer files later.

Figure 19.6

FTP transfers made easy: Just drag the files you want onto the directory on your hard disk.

To read an index file, right-click the file and select **View**. To transfer a file to your system, just drag it from one side to the other (or if you prefer using menus, right-click and choose **Download**).

ASCII Versus Binary

Notice the little **a/01**, **010**, and **ab** buttons on the right side of the toolbar? These buttons control whether the files are transferred as ASCII (the ab button), as Binary (the 010 button), or whether the program should decide the better way to transfer them (the a/01 button). Make sure you select the correct one before transferring a file. Select **ASCII** for files you know to be ASCII text files; select **Binary** for anything else. Remember, word-processing files are not ASCII; they're binary; they contain special codes that are used to define the character formatting. You can tell the program to automatically determine a file's transfer type by selecting **Edit**, **Settings**, and then clicking on the **ASCII/Binary** menu option and configuring specific file extensions.

It's Alive! Viruses and Other Nasties

If you haven't been in a cave for the past six or seven years, you've probably heard about computer viruses. A *virus* is a computer program that can reproduce itself and even convince unknowing users to help spread it. It spreads far and wide and can do incredible amounts of damage.

As is true of biological viruses, the effects of a virus on your system can range from nearly unnoticeable to fatal. A virus can do something as harmless as display a Christmas tree on your screen, or it can destroy everything on your hard disk. Viruses are real, but the threat is overstated. It's wise to take certain precautions, though, to ensure that you don't transfer viruses from FTP sites—or Web sites, for that matter—to your computer system. We'll be talking more about viruses in Chapter 18, "Staying Safe on the Internet."

Searching FTP Sites

Let's say you're looking for a particular file. You know it's out there somewhere, and you're pretty sure you know the name of the file. You haven't been able to track it down on the Web, but you also know it's probably something that's been around for a few years and is almost certain to be lurking somewhere in an FTP site. How do you find it?

Start with the Lycos search system (a Web-search system that we saw in Chapter 15, "Finding What You Need Online."). It has a database of more than 100 million FTP files. Visit `http://ftpsearch.lycos.com/`. You'll find four different ways to search for

FTP files. You can simply enter a word into a very simple search form. You can use the Advanced form or the Normal form (which seems to be somewhere between the basic and Advanced forms). And then there's the "original" form, which is more complicated, and seems to be similar to an *Archie* search.

Archie is the original FTP search system. (I won't go into detail, because Lycos' FTP Search is much easier.) The name comes from the word *archive* (as in file archive). Remove the *v* and what do you have? Archie.

There are Archie programs for both Windows and the Macintosh (one Mac FTP program, Anarchie, has a built-in Archie utility). But there are also Archie "gateways," Web sites that will help you search Archie. There aren't many left, though; if you want to find one, I suggest you search for **archie** or "**archie gateway**" at a Web search engine such as Yahoo!.

Finding FTP Sites

If you'd like to explore the Internet's FTP sites, visit the TILE.NET/FTP Reference to Anonymous Sites (`http://tile.net/ftp-list/`), or perhaps the Monster FTP Sites list (`http://hoohoo.ncsa.uiuc.edu/ftp/`).

Download Utilities

There's another way to handle Internet downloads—using various download utilities. The two most popular are probably Netscape's SmartDownload (`http://home.netscape.com/download/smartdownload.html`), and a Windows program called Go!Zilla (`http://www.GoZilla.com/`).

SmartDownload's main advantage is that it allows you to resume interrupted downloads, or even to interrupt them yourself and continue later. For instance, you could begin a download, and then decide you need to make a phone call; pick up the phone and make the call—stopping the download—and then complete the download later.

Go!Zilla is a much more advanced download utility. In fact, I found it took quite some getting used to. (I've no doubt it's many features are very useful, but I'm set in my ways and found it irritating to have Go!Zilla continually taking over downloads for me.)

Go!Zilla sits quietly in the background waiting for you to begin downloading a file. When you click on a link in your browser to download a file it grabs the information and, depending on your choice, either downloads it right away or saves it for download later (see Figure 19.7).

You can quickly gather together files that you want to download; click on a link, hold the mouse button down, drag the link to the Go!Zilla window (or to a little Go!Zilla "drop" icon), and release the mouse button. The file is listed in the Go!Zilla window, where you can quickly type a description of the file. Then, do the same for more

275

links, as many as you want, from as many different Web sites as you want. When you're ready to download files, click **Download Now** and it'll transfer them all, while you go for lunch.

Figure 19.7

Go!Zilla knows when you're trying to transfer a file; it can do so right away, or later if you prefer.

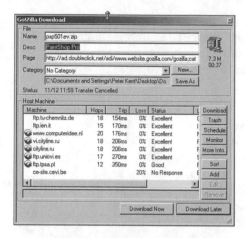

Figure 19.8

Go!Zilla transfers the files for you while you find something better to do.

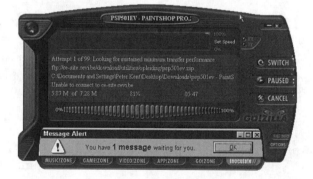

Go!Zilla has lots of neat features, such as a built-in unzip utility, a file library that helps you categorize and find files you've downloaded, and a "leech" mode that gathers together files from a Web site or FTP site for you; you then choose the ones you want to download.

It's definitely a useful little download utility, although I have one caveat; running in Windows 2000 (and perhaps some other versions of Windows?) it's a little buggy, with the Go!Zilla window disappearing when you need it! (Quite likely a bug that will be fixed soon, though.)

The Least You Need to Know

➤ FTP stands for file transfer protocol and refers to a system of file libraries.

➤ Anonymous FTP refers to a system that allows the public to transfer files.

➤ Start an FTP session in your Web browser using the format `ftp://hostname` in the Address text box (replacing *hostname* with the appropriate URL) and pressing **Enter**.

➤ Each directory and file at an FTP site is represented by a link; click the link to view the directory or transfer the file.

➤ If your browser can't connect to a particular site, or if you want the capability to resume interrupted downloads, get a true FTP program, such as CuteFTP (Windows) or Fetch (Macintosh).

➤ Protect yourself against viruses, but don't be paranoid. They're not as common as the antivirus companies want you to think.

➤ Download utilities such as SmartDownload and Go!Zilla can make downloading from Web sites easier.

Chapter 20

Accessing the Internet with Cool New Devices

In This Chapter

➤ Why other Internet-connection devices are needed

➤ Web-enabled cell phones

➤ Handheld computers, telephones, and TVs

➤ Email devices and Internet computers

➤ Receiving email on your pager

➤ Telephones, printers, and faxes

➤ Connecting elephants and other pets

The growth of the Internet is slowing because so many people who had computer hardware and computer *wetware* (a geek term for brainpower) are already on the Internet. For more people to get onto the Internet, two things must happen:

➤ More people need to begin using computers, so those computers can be connected to the Internet.

➤ Internet capabilities must be built into other devices, so people can connect to the Internet even if they don't have a computer.

Of course, the question is: Why would anyone want to connect to the Internet if he didn't have a computer? The answer is: He probably wouldn't. So, don't expect a huge rush of non–computer-literate people trying to get onto the Internet. There are plenty of people who don't care about the Internet, so however easy it becomes to access the Internet, they won't.

Nonetheless, things will change. Email, for instance, will become pervasive, and eventually even people without Internet access will feel the pressure to use email. A number of Internet services will become so useful that nonusers will envy users. For instance, the Internet provides so many ways to get information when planning a trip, it's hard to beat. You can look up businesses in Internet Yellow Pages around the world and even print out maps and directions to those businesses (check to see that the hotel really is "just a short walk to the beach"). Need to meet someone at a local restaurant? Using the Web, you can get step-by-step directions from your hotel to the restaurant, along with a map. (For this type of information, by the way, visit Zip2— http://www.Zip2.com/—or MapQuest—http://www.MapQuest.com/.) You can see photographs of hotels, check airline schedules and prices, view information about the local climate and bar scene, and so much more.

Eventually, even non–computer-owning non-Internet users will want these services. Some will buy computers. Others will use some other kind of Internet device. This chapter takes a quick look at alternatives to computers for accessing the Internet.

Before we start, Kent's First Law of Internet Connectivity:

> If it *can* be connected, it *will* be connected.

What sorts of things can be connected to the Internet (and therefore *will* be connected to the Internet)? There are basically two types of devices: devices used to access information over the Internet and devices used to feed information to the Internet (some devices do both). Here are a few of the wonderful things that are already hooked up to the Internet or will be soon:

➤ Televisions
➤ Pagers
➤ Telephones
➤ Cars
➤ CD Players
➤ Printers and fax machines
➤ Pets
➤ Parking meters
➤ Police scanners
➤ Your house
➤ Clothing
➤ Hot tubs
➤ Ant farms
➤ Elephants

If you want to see a huge sampling of the weird and wonderful things already connected, visit this Yahoo! page: `http://dir.yahoo.com/Computers_and_Internet/Internet/Devices_Connected_to_the_Internet/`. You'll find categories for Audio Equipment, Coffee Machines, Clocks, Calculators, Pagers, Robots, and Soda Machines.

So, let's take a look at a variety of interesting ways to access the Internet, and finish with a few odd examples of data being fed into the Internet.

Cell Phone Access

If you think your ear is stuck to your cell phone a little too much, move it around to the front of your face and *look* at it. If you've got one of the new Internet-enabled phones, you'll be able to get online to...

➤ Get your email

➤ View news, stock quotes, weather, and more

➤ Find information about restaurants, and get directions

➤ Buy music online (CDnow, for instance, is phone enabled)

➤ Use Instant Messaging (see Chapter 9, "Instant Messaging")

➤ Get stock quotes

These phones have what are known as *microbrowsers*, simple Web browsers that display text but not graphics. These devices are not intended for accessing normal Web pages, but are designed to get to information that has been specially formatted for them. There's something called HDML—Handheld Device Markup Language—that is derived from HTML and intended for creating Web pages that can be used by microbrowser-enabled phones.

There are many Web-enabled cell phones around; most companies make them, in fact. Note, though, that you'll pay extra to use the Web through a cell phone, perhaps $5–$10 a month.

By the way, even if your cell phone isn't Web-enabled, it can probably still receive email messages. You can mail short messages to most cell phones by emailing to *phonenumber@company*.com; for instance, `5555551212@att.com`.

WAP Pages

Want to see an example of a WAP-enabled page? (WAP means Wireless Application Protocol, the system used by wireless devices to access the Internet.) See `http://wap.cdnow.com/` for what the CDnow music store looks like when accessed through a wireless device. (See `http://www.CDnow.com/` for what it looks like in a normal Web browser.)

Handheld Email Devices

There are a number of handheld email devices coming onto the market, the most popular of which will probably be the Blackberry (http://www.blackberry.net/). You'll run into this in various places; AOL sells it as the AOL Mobile Communicator, for instance.

These resemble large pagers, with lots of buttons. They send and receive email messages, and come in various configurations: They can work with Microsoft Outlook, with the Microsoft Exchange email server, or with a provided Internet email account; and the AOL version even works with AOL Instant Messenger (see Chapter 9). They have a built-in personal organizer, too, for contacts, appointments, and tasks.

These might seem like a good idea—I certainly like the idea of being able to check my email at any time by pulling a little box out of my pocket and pressing one or two buttons. However, many people will be deterred by the price. They start at around $399, and the monthly fees range from around $40 to $75.

Telephone Access

Here's a weird one. I don't know why anyone would use this, but undoubtedly someone out there has found a purpose for it. AOL has a service called AOL by Phone (http://www.aol.com/), which allows you to dial in and access email, news, restaurant reviews, movie listings, and various other forms of information. The system uses voice recognition, so you can, in theory at least, merely speak into the telephone and ask for the information you want. The service is $4.95 a month.

Intercast PC/TV

TV and the Web are being slowly joined, through *intercast PC/TV*. That's the merging of Web pages into TV signals. There's a lot of empty space in a TV signal, and it's possible to transmit extra information, information that the TV doesn't need. For instance, closed captions for the deaf are transmitted in this way, as is the information used in teletext systems in Europe.

So, a TV show can carry a Web page that is related to the show. A cooking show, for instance, could carry a Web page containing recipes. If you like what they're cooking, change to the Web page, read the recipe, and print it out on the printer connected to the TV. This is not the same as WebTV, by the way. WebTV grabs Web pages off the Web along the phone line the WebTV box is connected to. An intercast TV grabs the Web page from the TV signal, so it needs no Internet connection.

Of course, right now there are few intercast shows, and intercast TVs are not available, but they will be soon. On the other hand, Intercast PCs are available; Windows 98 comes with WebTV software built into it, so if you have the right sort of TV tuner card in your computer you can work with intercast broadcasts. Or you can install a program such as Intel's Intercast Viewer, which runs in Windows 95 or 98 (and is bundled with a number of PC tuner cards).

Net Tips

Not Quite Here

A number of broadcasters have experimented with transmitting intercast data: CNN, CNBC, MTV, NBC, QVC, Lifetime, and so on. For example, while watching a CNN program, you can browse through story summaries in your Web browser, and use links to other resources on the CNN Web site.

However, this is a technology whose time has not yet arrived—and may not for some time to come.

Handhelds

So-called *handheld* computers, or *PDAs (Personal Digital Assistants)*, are gaining in popularity as businesspeople grow tired of lugging around laptops. If all you need while traveling is basic computing capabilities, handhelds might be enough. Some of these machines even have modems, email programs, and, yes, Web browsers.

For instance, for $99 you can buy an OmniSky (http://www.omnisky.com/) wireless modem to fit a Palm, HP Jornada, or Visor PDA. Then, for $39.95 you get unlimited Internet access.

What can you do with these things? Well, you can get to your email, downloading messages from multiple POP accounts if you want. You can view Web pages—as with a cell phone's microbrowser, PDAs work with Web pages designed for them. You can bookmark Web sites, buy products, trade stocks, and save information from Web sites directly into PDA applications.

Internet Computers

Several years ago, a number of prominent people in the computer business promised $500 Internet PCs—computers designed for Internet use, at a very low cost. Well, it took five years, and a reduction in price across the board in the computer industry, but the $500 Internet PC is finally here.

Compaq recently began selling the iPAQ Home Internet Appliance, starting at $499. In fact if you sign up for three years of MSN Internet service, they'll even give you one. (The only way to use the product is through MSN.)

These are not your normal computers. They are instant on—no wait while the computer boots. There's no hard disk, either, so you can't install new software—what you get is what you stick with. (The system itself can upgrade itself, but you can't install programs yourself.) They come with Internet Explorer and a variety of browser plug-ins, plus you can get email through a Hotmail account accessed through the browser. And here's an unusual feature. One of the models comes with a computer screen that, when not in use, works as a digital photo frame. (That is, it will display one of your photos.)

Another example of an Internet computer is the Apple iMac. The iMac is a low-cost Internet version of the Macintosh (it starts around $800). Just plug it into a phone line and into power, and away you go. I should note, however, that iMacs are real computers—they *do* have hard disks, and you *can* install software.

Mail Devices

A number of simple devices, intended for email and little else, are turning up on the market. They are very easy to install; plug them into a phone line and follow a simple configuration program, and you're up and running.

For instance, there's the MailStation (`http://www.mailstation.com/`). This product costs $99.95, and $9.95 a month. It has a simple email program with a spell checker, the ability to store around 400 email messages, and a 1,000-entry address book. You can even get some information from Yahoo!—news stories and astrology reports, for instance. The device *cannot* handle pictures and other email attachments, though. These are stored at a special Web site, for which you'll need a computer.

Who would use a MailStation? It's clearly targeted at older users, probably the parents and grandparents of active Internet users who want to get them onto the Internet— "Reduce the generation gap to milliseconds" is their motto.

Net Tips

Mivo 300

Early in 2001, the manufacturer of MailStation will release a new product, Mivo 300, a sort of MailStation on steroids. It *will* accept pictures in emails, and also has some limited World Wide Web functions.

Then, there's Audrey, from 3Com (`http://www.3com.com/ergo/`). This is an Internet-connected home organizer. You can create emails (I say create, because you can type them, write them with a stylus, or speak them). There's a Web browser, with a bookmark system based on a dial—select Web "channels" at the twist of a knob. And it has a variety of non-Internet features, such as a datebook that can be synchronized with a PalmPilot.

Audrey starts at $499 ($549 if you want a color other than "linen"), although accessories such as printers are extra, of course.

Pagers

Do you have an alphanumeric pager? Did you know you can receive email on it? A number of services will receive your email, and then forward it to your pager number. Some services even allow someone to enter a message into a Web page, and then click a button to send that message to a pager.

Some pager companies can set you up with an email address, so you can receive your messages. But even if your pager company doesn't do this, you can always get an account with a paging-service company, which might have better features than the pager company. For instance, you might be able to exceed the message limit. If your pager accepts, say, only 100 characters, you can use a service that will break your email messages into several pages, so you can exceed the limit. A service might also allow you to set filters to send some messages to the pager, but forward all others (for instance, pages from your spouse get sent to the pager and pages from your boss get forwarded to your email account, or vice versa depending on your relationships).

Some services will also send news, weather, or stock reports at predetermined times and can retrieve email from your normal email account so you don't need a special email account just for your pager. If you'd like to track down these services, go to a search engine and search for pager email.

Refrigerators

Yep, that's right, you'll soon be able to buy a fridge that's Internet connectable. Why? The fridge should be able to keep an eye on food quantities, and order more from your grocer across the Internet. (The fridge is, apparently, to be released in Britain, where supermarkets are jumping into online commerce much more quickly than in North America.) It might also be able to connect to recipe databases and, er, online banking. Whether it can determine the age and digestibility of various things that have been sitting in the back of your fridge for a while before it reorders, I'm not sure. The Electrolux Screenfridge was supposed to be in production already, but Electrolux is now saying that it doesn't know when it will release it. You can check it out at http://www.electrolux.co.uk/screenfridge/.

Printers and Faxes

Need to send a fax to the corporate office in Kuala Lumpur? Why not send it over the Internet? If both offices have fax machines connected to the Internet, the fax can go over the Net for free. If the office in Kuala Lumpur has a printer connected to the Internet, your computer can send a file directly to the printer; the printer is, in effect, an Internet fax machine. Such devices will probably become commonplace not too long from now.

Cash Registers

Many fast-food store cash registers are already connected to the Internet. These *Point of Sale (POS)* terminals are mostly based on Windows PCs these days, so it's pretty easy to connect them. But why bother? Well, it allows a restaurant owner to sit at home and view the day's takings, across the Internet, in all his restaurants. It also, with an optional video camera, allows him to look in on the store and check up on the kids running it! Be sure they're wearing their hats the right way around, and so on.

It's a Wired, Wired, Wired World

Imagine a world in which everything that can be connected is connected. We're going to see all sorts of things connected to the Internet over the next few years. For instance, you probably know that Bill Gates has wired his house—it's what's sometimes called an *intelligent* house. (Bill Gates might not be scared by the thought of Microsoft software controlling his living space, but it would scare the hell out of me.) I don't know whether his house is connected to the Internet, but there's no reason it couldn't be. And that's reason enough to think that eventually many houses *will* be connected to the Internet.

If you go on a vacation and forget to turn down the heat, don't worry; just connect to your house's heating interface on the Web, and set the heat to whatever you want. Want to check your phone messages? Get them over the Net. After houses are connected to the Internet, of course, new devices will be created—or old devices used in a new way—to provide reasons to connect over the Internet. For instance, you'll be able to view a snapshot of everyone who's rung your doorbell while you've been away, or view a picture of the front yard to see whether the kid next door kept his promise and mowed the lawn.

Some weird connections to the Internet are closer than you might think. Have you heard that parking meters will be networked soon? Networking meters provide all sorts of benefits (in general, not to the parkers, of course, but to the cities that own the meters). For instance, meter monitors (or whatever they're called now; I understand the term *meter maid* is no longer politically correct) will be able to see exactly which meters are just about to run out of money and rush to get there before the person who parked the car. If you network something, you can connect that network to the Internet. So, some people have been suggesting that cities might connect their parking-meter networks to the Internet, so parkers could feed the meters through a Web page. Of course, there are disadvantages to this, because it makes meter feeding way too easy and might cut down on meter availability, but I wouldn't be surprised if some cities try it.

How about elephants? Sound ridiculous? I've heard about a dairy research farm that considered networking its cows, and it's not so far from cows to elephants. Imagine a research project tracking the movement of Indian elephants. Many such projects already use radio trackers. It's not such a leap of imagination to consider connecting the radio signals to the Web, so people all over the world could watch the movement of the elephants. (It might not be a good idea in areas rife with ivory poachers, of course.) You heard it here first; elephants *will* be connected to the Internet.

In fact, we're not so far off. Check out Elephant.net, the Malaysian Elephant Tracking Project: `http://www.boh.com.my/elephantnet/`. They use Java maps to show the movement of the elephants they're tracking. It's not real-time—that is, you're not seeing the signal directly from the elephant—but it could be one day.

Now we come to Kent's Second Law of Internet Connectivity:

> The degree of usefulness is no predictor of connectivity.

In other words, just because something is useful doesn't mean it will be connected before something that isn't useful. Remember this: Some of the first noncomputer devices connected to the Internet were drink machines. That's right, some bright computer-science undergraduates figured out that if they connected the department's drink machines to the Internet, they could view information about the machines over the Internet; no more arriving at the machine to discover that one's favorite drink was out of stock! Not too long after drink machines came hot tubs (as if anyone really cares about the temperature of a hot tub in someone's home on the other side of the world). So, no matter how ridiculous or seemingly pointless the connection—it *will* be made! All sorts of useless stuff will be connected—and is connected—to the Internet. Luckily, plenty of useful stuff will be connected, too.

The Least You Need to Know

➤ Pretty much *everything* that's electronic can be connected to the Internet. If something's not electronic, an electronic device can be added. So, elephants will soon be connected to the Net.

➤ Many cell phones contain microbrowsers for Web access.

➤ You can now get your email through handheld devices (such as Blackberry), or desktop email devices.

➤ PDAs can access the Internet through wireless connections for around $40 a month.

➤ Intercast PC/TV is the transmission of Web pages within TV signals. A number of broadcasters are already intercasting Web pages within their transmissions.

➤ It's very easy to send email and other information, such as news and weather, to a pager.

➤ Telephones, printers, and faxes will soon be connected to the Internet. Fridges, too.

THAT'S NOT AN INTERNET HAT!

Chapter 21

Ideas

In This Chapter

➤ What use is the Internet?

➤ Using the Internet for business and pleasure

➤ Finding information online

➤ Music and culture

➤ What else do you want to do?

Throughout this book, I've explained many of the services the Internet can provide. But you might now be wondering, "What good are these things?" Unfortunately, until you get onto the Internet, get hooked, and forget that you have responsibilities out in the "real" world, it's difficult to understand what the Internet can do for you. (Imagine, for a moment, the Neanderthal thawed out of the ice and introduced to modern technology: "Okay, so I can use this soap stuff to remove the smell from my armpits, right? Why?") This chapter gives you a quick rundown on just a few of the ways in which ordinary (and some not-so-ordinary) people are incorporating cyberspace into their daily lives.

Keeping in Touch

The world has shrunk over the past few years—at least for those of us in cyberspace. I hadn't spoken with my sister in a decade or two, but now that she's online I hear from her every week or two (every day or two if her computer's acting up). My brother lives a continent away, but I hear from him frequently via email. An old school friend and I planned a trip to Iceland, using email to swap lists of things we'll need. Just recently I've received email from several people I'd worked with a decade ago in another life. Email is a wonderful system—sort of like the U.S. mail on amphetamines.

Meeting Your Peers

Many people use the Internet as a way to keep in touch with their peers. They can find out about job opportunities, new techniques and tools used in their business, or problems they've run into that they think *surely* someone else has experienced. The mailing lists, chats, and discussion groups provide a fantastic way to meet other people in your business field.

Business Communications

As I write this book, every now and then I have a question for the editor. I simply write the message and click a button, and off it flies. Later, when I finish this chapter, I'll send the document file via email, too. Then, later still, after the chapter's been edited, the editor can send it back via email. I'll change the edits back to what I originally wrote and then send it back yet again.

Many businesses have discovered that the Internet provides a rapid communications tool. Why type a letter, memo, or report into a word processor, print it out, put it in an envelope, take it to a mailbox (or call FedEx), and wait a day or five for it to arrive when you can send the same word processing document and have it arrive a minute or two—even a few seconds—later?

Vacations and Flights

There are many places to help you with your travel plans—from picking a vacation spot to buying an airline ticket. Some services, such as Microsoft's Expedia (http://www.expedia.com), will even email you periodically to let you know about the lowest available rates to destinations you're particularly interested in.

Net Tips

Lower Than Low?

Warning: "Lowest available rate" is airline jargon that does not actually mean the "lowest available rate" in the airline industry. It means "the lowest rate from the list of rates we're looking at." Discount-ticket sites such as Cheap Tickets—http://www.cheaptickets.com/—will get you lower prices still.

Product Information

We live in an instant-gratification society, the entire purpose of which is to get toys into your hands faster and faster. Do you need information about that new car you want to buy, for instance? If so, go to `http://www.edmunds.com/` to check it out (you learned about Web addresses like this in Chapter 2, "Working on the World Wide Web"). As you can see in Figure 21.1, the page contains the car's specifications as well as a picture of it. You can drool over it—and even find out just how much the dealer paid for it.

Figure 21.1

With what you'll save on this baby, you'll be able to buy Internet access for the rest of your life!

Product Support

There's a downside to the Internet, of course: It's run by computers, which, as we all know, are the work of Satan. Still, the next time your computer does something weird or you need a new print driver, go online and find the fix or software you need. Many computer and software companies, perhaps most, now have an online technical support site. Although it would be nice if all these sites were well designed, some of them are as easy to use as ice skates on a sand dune.

Getting Software

We're back to instant gratification. You know that program you just saw advertised in *Internet Windows Computing World* magazine? Want to try it out? Go online and download a demo right now! There's no more waiting. Pretty soon everybody will be buying software and transferring it straight to their computers...or not, perhaps. It's been a tremendous frustration for Internet pundits who think it's just so *obvious* that all software should be sold online to see that the adoption of online software sales has been incredibly slow. Most software is still sold in boxes, and will continue to be for some time.

You can use one of the Internet's great shareware libraries, too. (See Appendix C, "All the Software You'll Ever Need," for more information.) Figure 21.2 shows the TUCOWS site. TUCOWS, The Ultimate Collection of Winsock Software, is a library of shareware Internet programs for all flavors of Microsoft Windows, and even Macintosh and OS/2 software, programs for PalmPilots and Visors, and so on. You can find it on the Web at http://www.tucows.com/.

Figure 21.2

TUCOWS: The Ultimate Collection of Winsock Software (Windows, the Macintosh, OS2, PalmPilots, and plenty more).

Researching Stuff

If you are writing a school paper, researching a book, or planning a vacation, the Internet contains a cornucopia of illuminating tidbits. It's *not* a library (contrary to the nonsense of those in the Internet community who got a little carried away with their predictions), and it will be a long time before it can replace one. Still, it does give you access to huge amounts of useful information that's just waiting to be used.

Suppose you are planning to visit, oh, I don't know, how about Iceland? Get onto the World Wide Web and search for Iceland (you learned how to search for stuff in Chapter 15, "Finding What You Need Online"). What do you find? A hundred or more sites with information about Icelandic travel, sports, culture, media, real estate (there's no way *I'm* moving there), news, and more.

Visiting Museums

I suppose you can't afford to visit the Louvre *and* the Smithsonian this year. What a shame. Still, you can get online and see what you are missing (see Figure 21.3). The potential here is greater than the reality. Maybe someday most of the masterpieces in the world's great museums will be online; but right now, many museums just provide one or two pictures and information about which subway to take to get there.

Figure 21.3

Visit the Louvre this summer from the comfort of your own home (`http://www.louvre.fr/`).

Keeping Your Driver's License Up to Date

Moved recently? Need to update your driver's license's address information? If you're lucky, your state's Bureau of Motor Vehicles has a Web site from which you can download the necessary forms, along with forms to apply for special plates, order temporary tags, apply for a hearing-impaired ID card, or report a crash with an uninsured motorist. Start by searching for bureau of motor vehicles at a major search site.

Finding Financial Information

Want stock quotes? Want to invest online? Want to do your taxes online? How about information about competitors or about online banking services? You'll find it on the Internet. You can find links to great financial services at the search sites discussed in Chapter 15. Or try Yahoo! Finance (`http://quote.yahoo.com/`) or InvestorGuide (`http://www.investorguide.com/`). There are plenty of online investment services, too. All the major investment houses have online sites—Charles Schwab, Fidelity, Dreyfus, and so on. But there's also a new breed of broker-age house that grew up on the Internet, sites such as E*TRADE, which now has over a million accounts (`http://www.etrade.com/`).

Listening to Music

If music is your passion, you'll be happy to know that you can hear some of the latest from the music world when you find it on the Internet. You'll want an MP3 player and RealPlayer (see Chapter 5, "Web Multimedia—From Flash to Napster"), and then visit Internet Underground Music Archive (`http://www.iuma.com/`), Napster (`http://www.Napster.com/`), or MP3.com (`http://www.MP3.com/`). Would you prefer bagpipe music or film scores, or maybe you want to buy some CDs—try CDnow (`http://cdnow.com/`). Whatever you're looking for, you can find it on the Internet.

Reading Magazines and 'Zines

You'll find thousands of magazines and 'zines online. (For the not-quite-so-hip among you, a *'zine* is a small magazine, usually published on a shoestring by some-one with three or more pierced body parts.) You'll find underground books and comics, as well as newsletters on almost anything you can imagine (and probably a few things you can't imagine). A good place to start is Liszt (`http://www.liszt.com/`).

Hiding from the Real World

There's a wonderful cartoon that is legendary in the computer world. It shows a dog in front of a computer terminal, and it has the caption "Nobody knows you're a dog on the Internet." It's unfortunate that the need exists, but quite frankly, there are people who use the Internet to hide from the real world. For one reason or another, they have trouble with face-to-face relationships, yet on the Internet they can feel safe and part of a community.

If You *Can't* Get Out

Some people would love to have more face-to-face relationships but for some reason can't get out to meet people. Perhaps they are elderly or disabled or have been posted to the Antarctic. Or maybe they're not leaving their apartment for fear of being served a subpoena. Regardless of the reason, the Internet provides a link to the rest of the world for those times when you can't physically get somewhere.

Shakespeare on the Net

A little while ago I met a fellow computer book writer who stages Shakespeare's plays in IRC (Internet Relay Chat). This chap (he's English) takes a play, modifies it slightly to his taste (he recently staged an updated version of *Macbeth*), and breaks it down into its individual character parts. He sends each "actor" his lines only, no more. Each line has a cue number, so the person playing the character will know when to type the lines. Then, they start, each person typing his or her lines at the appropriate cue position. It's an act of discovery for all the "actors" because they don't know what the other characters will say until they say it. Strange, but strangely fascinating.

Joining a Community of People with Common Interests

Suppose you have some, er, let's say unusual interests. You believe the U.S. government has been chopping up aliens for years—or maybe that it's in cahoots with aliens. Or suppose that, by chance, you are consumed with a hatred of purple dinosaurs (one in particular, anyway) or that you feel compelled to tell others of your latest, um, erotic experience in the air or under water.

Now suppose that, in your neighborhood, there are few people who share your interests. With whom do you share your thoughts? Where can you find a sense of community? On the Internet, of course, in the newsgroups and mailing lists (see Chapters 10 and 11). (And yes, the examples previously suggested are real examples.) You might be surprised at the sort of people you find online. It's not all techno-chat. I have a friend who's a member of a discussion group on the subject of renovating antique tractors, for instance!

Remember Your Old Friend, Chat?

As you learned in Chapter 8, "Using Online Chat Rooms," IRC is a chat system. You type a message, and it's immediately transmitted to all the other people involved in the chat session. They respond, and you immediately see what they have typed.

You Don't Trust Your Doctor

I must admit I don't have a lot of faith in doctors. Grandma was right: Stay away from hospitals—they're dangerous! Many people go to the Internet in search of the answers their doctors can't provide. Whether you have a repetitive-stress injury, cancer, or AIDS, you'll find information about it on the Internet. Want to try homeopathy, acupuncture, or just figure out what leeches can do for you? Try the Internet.

Be careful, though; the Internet's ability to provide you with health-related information is a double-edged sword. Although you'll find a lot of useful information, you'll also run into some pretty strange ideas, many of which have as much relation to reality as Charles Manson does.

Shopping

Much of the press seems to think that the raison d'être for the Internet is for K-Mart and Sears to find another way to sell merchandise. Internet shopping has been grotesquely overrated for several years—but recently it's taken off. It's not living up to its potential yet, but nonetheless, millions of people are making purchases on the Internet. In particular, they're buying books, CDs, and software. But they're also buying telescope lenses, clothing, and even groceries.

Cybersex

The Internet provides a wonderful form of communication for those who seem to have trouble finding others with similar sexual proclivities. This is by no means a minor part of cyberspace; some commentators even claim that the sexual use of online services played a major part in their growth. (That's probably not as far-fetched an idea to anyone familiar with America Online's tremendously popular chat rooms.) You can get online and talk about things that your parents or spouse might consider *very* weird, with people who consider them quite normal.

Political Activism

As they say, political activism infects every form of human communication—or was that pornography? Anyway, the Internet is the latest frontier for political activities, providing militia groups a means of keeping in touch and providing Democrans and Republicats a place to seek votes.

Subversion

The Internet provides a great way to subvert the political system in which you live. That's right, you, too, can publish information that your government doesn't want published—whether it's information about how NutraSweet was created as part of a plot to take over our minds or what was going on during the latest coup (see Figure 21.4). The Internet has played a role in just about every major and minor political upheaval in the last few years, from the last coup in Moscow to recent fighting in Palestine. Closer to home, the Internet has become a thorn in the side of the U.S. government as it makes the distribution of encryption software so easy.

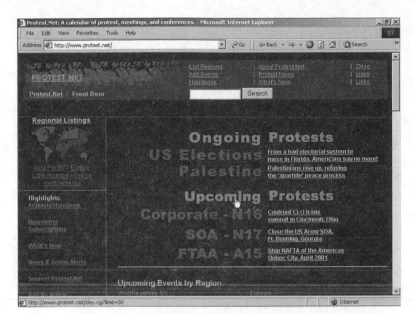

Figure 21.4
Looking for a protest this weekend? Try Protest.net.

Looking for Work (and Help)

Thousands of people are looking for work on the Internet, and thousands more are offering both full-time and contract positions. Many professional associations have special mailing lists used for transmitting job leads. Do a little research, and you could have dozens of leads arriving at your home every day.

Job hunting online is an area that has, for certain professions, almost completely taken over from newspapers, an example in which Internet tools have already become the primary tools. If a company is trying to hire a Java programmer or HTML designer these days, they generally won't bother advertising in local papers anymore. (The ads for Java programmers you may see in your local papers were posted by companies that have no idea what they're doing, or are desperate.) The first place people in these types of technical professions look these days is online, at Web sites such as Monster (`http://www.Monster.com/`), Techies.com (`http://www.techies.com/`), and HotJobs (`http://www.HotJobs.com/`). But just about any job seeker can find leads online these days.

Clubs and Professional–Association Information Sources

Are you running a large club or professional association? Why not set up a Web site? Your members can then check the Web site to find out when the next meeting is being held, search a database of fellow members, find out about the association's services, and more. Potential members can find out how to join, too.

Mating and Dating

Do people *really* meet online and get involved in romantic relationships of various kinds? Yes, they really do. I'd be inclined to make a joke about it, except that I have a friend who met a man online who eventually became her husband and the father of her child.

Long-Distance Computing

Being a computer geek comes with a real disadvantage: You always seem to be working. If you find yourself wishing you could get to the programs on your desktop computer while you are on vacation or are visiting relatives or clients, for example, you might have considered buying one of those remote control programs. You install the program on your laptop and then dial into your desktop machine. The program enables you to copy files between the computers and even run programs across the connection.

As you might guess, however, the long-distance phone calls can get very expensive, but now there's a new way to do it. Some of these programs let you make the connection across the Internet. So, if you use a national service provider that has phone numbers throughout the United States (or even an international provider or an online service that has numbers throughout the world), you can dial into a local number and connect to your computer across the Internet and pay only a fraction of the long-distance charge. Even if you don't want to go to quite these lengths, you can still log in and pick up your email wherever you happen to be.

File Sharing

Here's another simple tool for long-distance computing: file sharing. Services such as XDrive (http://www.xdrive.com/) and DriveWay (http://www.DriveWay.com/) let you place files on their computers. Anyone with access to the World Wide Web, along with your account name and password, can download the files to their computers. You can share files with colleagues in other cities, or place files online before you go on a business trip—you'll be able to download them to another computer when you arrive at your destination.

Take the Family on Vacation Without Paying for Tickets

"Wish you were here!" is a platitude as old as vacation postcards. Of course, you don't really mean it, or you would have taken them with you. But now you can take one step closer to taking them with you, yet still not have to put up with them.

Here's what I'm getting at. Take a video camera and the upload software. Now and then during your trip visit an Internet café or library with Internet access. Upload your photos, and email them. Or use a photo-album service to post the photos online—services such as ClubPhoto (http://www.clubphoto.com/), MyFamily (http://www.MyFamily.com/), and Ofoto (http://www.ofoto.com/). Your friends and family will be able to see what you're up to with minimal delay.

Keeping the Kids Busy

There's a lot of fuss about nasty stuff on the Internet that kids shouldn't see...but there's plenty of really good stuff out there, from sites that help them with science experiments, to sites that make history and geography fun. One of the best places to get started finding good kids' sites is Yahooligan! (http://www.yahooligans.com/).

News on Demand

It's hard for the news media to compete with the Internet. Want to know how much of a lead George Bush has over Al Gore in Florida? You could wait for tomorrow's paper, and get an out-of-date number. You could turn on the TV, but you might have to wait through Sports News and the cute news-staff banter before you get to the information you need. Or you could go online and get a number that was updated just five minutes ago.

There are so many news sites that you'll be spoiled for choice. CNN is online, of course (http://www.cnn.com/), but then so is your local paper, probably. You can get to ABC (http://www.abcnews.go.com/), MSNBC (http://www.msnbc.com/), and NBC (http://www.nbc.com/). But even more useful than finding your local news source online is the ability to view news from other places; see what's happening in the old country; hear a different perspective on an international news event (you might wonder whether the U.S. press is even covering the same event, the perspective is often so different); or get a feel for a country you'll be visiting soon (and many of the sites are in English). You can find news from Britain (from the BBC: http://news.bbc.co.uk), Mexico (Excelsior: http://www.excelsior.com.mx/), Australia (The Sydney Morning Herald: http://www.smh.com.au/), Cambodia (Phnom Penh Daily: http://www.phnompenhdaily.com/), Eire (The Irish Times: http://www.ireland.com/), and just about any other country in the world.

What Did I Miss?

In addition to the ideas I've listed in this chapter, you could probably find a few thousand or more other uses. The Internet is huge and it's diverse; it's whatever you make of it.

The beauty of the Internet is that although people begin as observers, they end up being participants. They become active in discussion groups and perhaps even start their own groups. They often create their own Web sites (it's surprisingly easy, as you saw in Chapters 13 and 14).

Take a look at the Internet to see what's out there and how other people are using it. Who knows? You might soon find that it becomes part of your life. (Don't say I didn't warn you!)

The Least You Need to Know

➤ You can use the Internet for personal and business correspondence.

➤ Web sites provide product information, support, and purchasing options.

➤ You can access all kinds of online information, from research, to museums, to financial services, to medical information, to job searches.

➤ Listen to your favorite music group, or read your favorite author.

➤ Read the news, find a job, find a date...whatever you want to do, the Internet can probably help you.

Chapter 22

21 Questions— The Complete Internet FAQ

In This Chapter

➤ Basic computer skills

➤ What's online?

➤ Can you sell fish on the Internet?

➤ Slowdowns and connection problems

➤ Forged emails

➤ Staying anonymous and much more

In this chapter, you will find answers to some questions you might have and a few problems you might run into—everything from the meaning of certain terms to solutions for certain problems.

1. How Do I Use This Mouse Thing to Open That Window Thing?

Please, please, please...do yourself a favor. Learn how to use your computer. Many people bought computers specifically so that they could use the Internet, so they jumped into the Web right away. They're stumbling around trying to figure out how to get here or there or do this or that, but they're handicapped by the fact that they've *no* idea how to use their computer. Take a course on basic computer skills. Read *The Complete Idiot's Guide to PCs*. Do *something*. Your time online will be so much easier and more productive.

Here's a little tip to get you going, for Windows users. Two tips, in fact.

A: You don't have to close a program when you open another one.

B: To change from one program to another, hold down the **Alt** key and press the **Tab** key once—keep the **Alt** key held down. You'll see a box showing you all the programs you have open. Each time you press **Tab** you'll highlight another program. When you've highlighted the one you want, let go of the **Alt** key.

2. Why Won't My Browser Display This, That, or the Other?

When you buy a TV, you expect to be able to use it to watch any program on any channel you have available. You don't expect to see error messages telling you something in a program can't be displayed or messages saying that if you want to see a particular program you'll have to install the *Jerry Springer* plug-in.

That's not the way it works on the Web. Browsers behave differently. Some browsers won't work with JavaScript or Java (or you might have turned off these things in your program preferences). Old browsers can't display frames and can't work with plug-ins—or if you have a recent browser, maybe you haven't installed the plug-in that a particular site requires.

You can avoid some of these problems, but by no means all, by working with the most up-to-date version of Netscape Navigator or Internet Explorer. Whichever browser you choose, there will *always* be certain features that won't work properly.

3. Is the Internet a Good Resource for Homework?

Definitely. So good, in fact, that many schools and colleges are seeing the same information over and over again, as their students take, um, shortcuts and copy information verbatim, directly from Web sites.

If a student can withstand the temptation to cheat, they'll find that there are Web sites related to just about any subject you can imagine, and certainly any that are covered in a typical school curriculum.

4. Is Everything Online Now?

No, but I'm constantly surprised by just how much you *can* find on the Internet, and, after you have a little practice in online searches, how quickly you can find it. Have you heard the joke about the agnostic dyslexic something or other? This is a joke I heard a year or two ago, and just couldn't remember how it all hung together, or what the punch line was.

I went to AltaVista (http://www.AltaVista.com/) and searched for **+agnostic +dyslexic +dog** (I remembered there was a dog in the joke). The first link returned by the search engine led to a missing page. I returned to AltaVista, and looked down the list. The third link caught my eye, as the first line of the entry started with "Did you hear about the dyslexic, agnostic, insomniac?" I went to the page, and there it was, within about two minutes of searching I found the joke:

> *Did you hear about the dyslexic, agnostic, insomniac?*
>
> *He lay awake all night wondering if there really is a dog.*

Okay, so it's just a joke. (Although, isn't that what the Internet's *really* for, to save fax paper by allowing jokes to circulate between offices via email?) But you can play this same trick with just about any subject. Somehow, someway, you can track down all sorts of obscure and interesting information, from hotels in Iceland, to lines from Shakespeare's plays, to battle plans from Civil War battles. It's all there, somewhere.

5. Is the Internet Any Good for Anyone but Geeks?

Not so long ago the Internet really was the province of the geeks. The information online tended to be technical, and you needed to be a bit of a geek to use the Internet, anyway.

These days there's something for everyone. Here's an example. You've heard the fuss about MP3, probably, about how the music industry is up in arms about the theft of music online? Well, take a guess at another form of theft of intellectual property that's become common online: embroidery.

Perhaps you haven't seen these fancy sewing machines that will embroider designs automatically. Insert a floppy disk with an embroidery design file on it, insert the material you want embroidered, and the machine will do it for you. Well, there are thousands of people online buying, selling, and trading these designs; and stealing them, too. I'd hate to perpetuate a stereotype of these people as just little old ladies, but they're not your average computer geeks, either!

Another example. I have a friend whose hobby is restoring old tractors. He spends a lot of time online talking to other tractor restorers, too.

Pick a subject. Technical or not, there's a community around it somewhere on the Internet.

6. Can You Sell Fish on the Internet?

This is a real question that someone asked me during a radio-show interview. (The question came from a fisherman in Alaska who was looking for new markets.) And I don't have the definitive answer. All I can say is, "maybe." But you'd better have a really good plan!

I don't know how you can go about selling fish (to see a site that tries see Figure 22.1), but I do know that you can sell various kinds of stuff—real stuff, not other Internet services. The editors took a poll and told me they'd seen salad dressing, teddy bears, model horses, live horses, legal services, picture-scanning devices, Internet tutoring, and real estate for sale. There are also books, CDs, and videos—as well as hot sauce, pizza, and a newsletter for writers of children's stories, and all sorts of other stuff. Of course, all these people are not necessarily making money doing this, but some most certainly are.

CDnow sold 16 million dollars' worth of music CDs in 1997, around $50 million in 1998, for instance, and that company was started by 24-year-old twin brothers (see *The CDnow Story: Rags to Riches on the Internet*, by Jason Olim, Matthew Olim, and Peter Kent, Top Floor Publishing). CDnow is still selling many millions of dollars' worth of CDs, although its stock price dropped dramatically and it was sold to Bertelsmann, a large German publisher.

More modest successes abound. I know a small publisher selling more than $30,000 worth of books a year through his Web site; a company that sells a remote control "flying saucer" (it's actually a helium balloon) gets a significant portion of its income from the Web; and a fantasy-sports software company finds many new customers on the Internet. My own Web site (`http://PoorRichard.com/`) is most definitely making a profit, and sales are growing. If you want to know more about making money on the Internet, see Chapter 17, "Making Money on the Internet."

Figure 22.1

Maybe you can sell fish on the Internet.

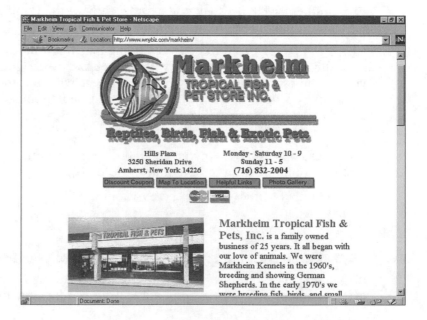

7. If I Have a Fast Connection, Why Are Transfers So Slow?

You've just installed a fancy new Internet connection, perhaps a DSL line or a cable modem, the very latest in technology you've been told, and still some Web sites are about as speedy as molasses on a cool day in Iceland. What's going on here? Your information has to pass through many computer systems, along lots of lines; hey, it might be coming from halfway across the world, after all.

Think of this transfer across the Internet as a relay race. The information you want is passed from person to person, maybe dozens of times, between the Web site and you. The last person in the chain is that speedy 56Kbps modem you bought. But when you look at the others involved in the race, you see that some are as athletic as Roseanne, and others are as fast as your grandmother. Still others might be very fast, but they've got other jobs to do, too. They are involved in hundreds of relay races at the same time! If you are at a very popular Web site, for instance, hundreds of other people just like you are trying to get information at the same time, and that relay runner might be having serious problems keeping up. (In any case, your 56Kbps modem isn't operating at 56Kbps; phone lines can't handle rates that fast.) I know I've told you that the Internet is a bunch of telephone wires connected to one another, but the truth is that it often operates like millions of bottlenecks strung together on a long piece of string.

If it's any consolation (and it probably isn't), it's not just you having problems; millions of other people are sitting at their computers in Alberta, Arizona, Austria, and other places beginning with different letters, saying, "I just bought this 56Kbps modem. Why did I bother wasting my money?" Why would anyone bother to get a fast modem? Because with a slow one, you'll be even slower. The Internet isn't slow all the time, so the faster your modem, the faster data transfers will be.

Another reason that your traffic might be slow is something called *differentiated service levels* or *preferential packets*. Information sent across the Internet is sent in small packets of data, each packet containing the address that's needed to get it to where it has to go. The packet can also include priority information. There are reports that the companies owning the Internet backbones are now selling priority service to major corporations. (A backbone is a major line on the Internet; you might think of the line from your computer to your service provider as a path, the line from your service provider to the backbone as a road, and the backbone as a major freeway.)

If a backbone company sells preferential treatment, it means that information going to or from the preferred site goes through right away. Any other packets of information have to wait in a queue. Each time a preferred packet arrives, that packet goes to the front of the queue. Mid-afternoon in North America is often a very busy time on the Internet anyway; corporate employees come back from lunch and log onto the Dilbert site or perhaps even do some work. But if those employees are getting preferential treatment, it's even slower for the rest of us. So, if your packet is sitting in a queue on a backbone on the other side of the country, it doesn't matter how fast your modem is—the packet can't get to you!

305

8. What's the Difference Between Yahoo! and Netscape Navigator?

If you've read this far, you should understand the difference. But I've heard this question a few times now—or rather, I've heard statements that made it clear that the speaker didn't understand the difference—so I thought I should cover it. Statements such as "Oh, you've got Yahoo! on your computer, too." Or "I know how to start Yahoo!, but I'm not sure how to get to my company's Web site."

Netscape Navigator (or Internet Explorer) is a program running on your computer. Yahoo! is a Web page. The confusion arises because many people have Yahoo! (or Netcenter, or some other search page) set as their home page—the page that is displayed whenever the browser starts.

What appears in the center of the browser is not part of the browser; it's something that somebody has published on the Web. It's available to anyone who has access to the Internet, so don't think you're special because you've got it.

9. Why Isn't Anyone Reading My Web Page?

I guess you heard the nonsense that "A Web page is a billboard that can be seen by millions," and you believed it. Let me put it this way: There are 250 million people in the United States, but if you put up a *real* billboard somewhere, will 250 million people see it? I won't bother answering that.

The Web is not a highway, and your page is not a billboard. If you want people to come to your Web page, you have to promote it. Don't believe all that "If you want people to come to your Web site, it has to be compelling" nonsense, either. A Web page has to serve a purpose; if it serves its purpose well and is well promoted, it can do well (even if it doesn't use Java to display some pointless animation).

10. How Can I Remain Anonymous on the Internet?

Many people are concerned with keeping their privacy and anonymity on the Internet. In particular, women who like to spend time in chat rooms often feel the need to put up a protective wall between themselves and other members. If a relationship develops with someone online, they want to be in control of how much information about themselves they allow others to discover.

There are some basic strategies you can use to maintain your anonymity on the Internet:

➤ Get an account with an online service or service provider and obtain an account name that is nothing like your own name. If your name is Jane Doe, use an account name such as *HipChick* or *SusanSmith*.

➤ Many online services enable you to enter information about yourself, also known as a profile, that others can view (in chat rooms, for instance). If you are with an online service, be sure your profile is empty.

➤ After you are on the Internet, be careful not to leave identifying information when you're leaving messages in newsgroups, working with mailing lists, and so on.

Although these strategies won't ensure full anonymity, they work pretty well in most cases. To find out who HipChick or SusanSmith is, someone would have to persuade your service provider to divulge information. That's not impossible, but in most cases, it's unlikely (unless you're doing something to incite the interest of the police or the FBI).

You can also get a free email account from Juno, Yahoo!, Hotmail, or many other companies. When you fill in the form identifying yourself, dissemble (the word used to be lie, I believe, but politicians thought that word too coarse). See Chapter 18, "Staying Safe on the Internet," for more information on staying safe and anonymous.

11. Can People Find Information About Me Online?

Yes. Whether you're online or not, they can find all sorts of information about you, more every day. In 1995, I used a variety of online databases to track down the friend of the wife of an old army friend of my father's. (Read it slowly.) The wife had lost track of her old school friend in the late 1940s. All she knew was the friend's maiden name, her married name, and that she had lived in Denver at that time. With only that information I was able to track the friend down—she was living in New York—within a few hours.

And I'm no expert. The people who know what they're doing can find all sorts of information—Social Security numbers, vehicle registrations, credit records, and plenty more. And there's nothing you can do about it.

12. Can Someone Forge My Email?

A year or two ago I saw a message in a mailing list from someone complaining that an email message to the list was forged. Someone else had sent a message using this person's email address. Another member of the list wrote a message telling her that she should be more careful. He said (a little bluntly) that if she left her computer unattended, she should expect trouble. Thinking I'd play a little game, I sent a forged message to the list in *his* name. (No, I didn't know him, and I definitely didn't have access to his computer.) "That'll teach him," I thought, "He should be more careful."

It's very easy to forge email messages—so easy, in fact, that I'm surprised it doesn't happen more often. (It probably happens more often to people who spend a lot of time in newsgroups, mailing lists, and chat rooms—where it's easy to get into fights—than to people who use other services.) A person can forge a message simply by entering incorrect configuration information into a mail program or, better still, the mail program of a public Web browser. However, before you run out and play tricks on people, I should warn you that this mail can still be traced to some degree. (It might be difficult, though, for anyone other than someone with a warrant to get the service providers to do the tracing for him.)

How can you avoid this problem? There's not much you can do except keep your head down and stay out of "flame wars" (which I'll discuss next). You *could* digitally sign all your messages, as discussed in Chapter 7, "Advanced Email—HTML Mail, Voice, and Encryption," although that might be overkill.

13. What's a Flame?

I've heard it said that the Internet will lead to world peace. As people use the Net to communicate with others around the world, a new era of understanding will come to pass…blah, blah, blah. The same was said about the telegraph and the television, but so far, there hasn't been much of a peace spinoff from those technologies! But what makes me sure that the Internet will not lead to world peace (and might lead to world war) is the prevalence of flame wars in mailing lists and newsgroups.

A *flame* is a message that is intended as an assault on another person, an *ad hominem* attack. Such messages are common and lead to flame wars, as the victim responds and others get in on the act. In some discussion groups, flame wars are almost the purpose of the group. You'll find that the Internet is no haven of peace and good-will—and I haven't even mentioned the obnoxious behavior of many in chat rooms.

14. I'm Leaving My Service Provider. How Can I Keep My Email Address?

I currently have three Internet accounts. Over the past few years, I've had dozens of accounts, and that means I've had dozens of email addresses. Although this is unusual, it's certainly not unusual for people to have a handful of accounts as they search for the best one. Unfortunately, keeping your friends and colleagues up to date on your email address is a real hassle. If only there were a way to keep the same address, even when you changed providers.

There just might be. You can register your own domain name. You can do this through a number of places (search for **domain registration** at a search engine). At the time of writing, it costs as little as $15 a year. Many service providers will register a domain for you, but they might charge you an additional fee to do so.

After you have your own domain name, you can set up a mail service (search for **email service** at a search site such as Yahoo!) and assign the domain name to that service. Then, all your email addressed to that domain will be sent to the service, which will store it in your POP (Post Office Protocol) account. You'll use a mail program to download your mail from there. If you plan to set up a Web site with a Web-hosting company, you can register the domain to that company's servers, and you'll get your email there (see Chapter 13, "Setting Up Your Own Web Site").

After you've set up an email service, or are getting email through a Web-hosting company, it doesn't matter which service provider or online service you use to get onto the Internet. You can change from one company to another as many times as you like, and you'll still be able to get to your mail through the email provider or hosting company. Email services start at around $5 a month, and even Web-hosting accounts are available for less than $10 a month.

Another way to keep your email address is to sign up with a free or low-cost email service. A number of these are around now (search at http://www.yahoo.com/ for **free email service**). These services are usually free because they sell advertising that is shown when you get your mail. If you don't mind that, though, this is a good way to get and keep an email address, regardless of how many times you change your service provider. One of these companies (MailBank: http://MailBank.com/) has bought up thousands of domain names based on people's last names, so for $3 a year you can have an address that uses your last name as the domain name: john@kent.org, fred@smithmail.com, and so on.

15. Why Can't I Get Through to That Site?

You'll often find that you cannot connect to sites that you've used before or that you've seen or heard mentioned somewhere. You might find Web pages that you can't connect to, FTP sites that don't seem to work, and Telnet sites that seem to be out of commission. Why?

The first thing you should check is your spelling and case; if you type one wrong character or type something uppercase when it should be lowercase (or vice versa), you won't connect. (Figure 22.2 shows the dialog box Netscape Navigator displays when you've typed the name incorrectly.) Another possibility is that the service you are trying to connect to might just be very busy, with hundreds of other people trying to connect. Depending on the software you are using, you might see a message to that effect. Or it could be that the service is temporarily disconnected; the computer that holds the service might have broken or might have been disconnected for service. Finally, the service might not be there anymore.

Trying again a few times often helps; you'll be surprised just how often you can get through to an apparently dead site just by trying again a few moments later. Also, note that some software is a little buggy. For instance, some browsers seem to hang up and appear unable to transfer data from a site at times; but canceling the transfer and starting again often jump-starts the process.

Figure 22.2

Oops! I mistyped the URL, and my browser can't find the host.

Don't Place the Blame Too Quickly

Often, it's your service provider, not the site you are trying to connect to, that's having problems. Try connecting to a variety of sites, and if you can't get through to any, it's probably a problem with your connection to the service provider or with the provider's system. Try disconnecting and logging back on.

Remove the Period

When you type a URL, don't type a period at the end. You might find URLs in books and magazines that appear to end with a period because they are used at the ends of sentences. But real URLs don't end with periods.

16. Why Won't This URL Work?

URLs are a special case because even if they don't seem to work, you might be able to modify them and get them to work. First, be sure you are using the correct case. If a word in the URL was shown as uppercase, don't type lowercase (if the URL doesn't work with some words uppercase, though, you might try lowercase).

Second, be sure you are using the correct file extension if there is one. If the URL ends in .htm, make sure you are not typing .html, for instance. If the URL still doesn't work, start removing portions of the URL. Suppose you have this URL:

```
http://www.big.net/public/software/macintosh/
internet/listing.html
```

You've tried using both `listing.html` and `listing.htm` at the end, and neither seems to work. Drop `listing.html` and try again. You might get a document with links to something you can use. If you still don't get anything, remove the `internet/` part (in other words, you are now typing just `http://www.big.net/public/software/macintosh/`). If that doesn't work, remove the next part, `macintosh/`. Continue in this manner, removing piece after piece, and in many cases you'll eventually find something useful.

17. Why Do So Many People Hate AOL?

It's an unfortunate truth that America Online members have a bad reputation on the Internet. You might run across rude messages in which people insult AOL members or treat them as if they are the scum of the earth.

310

Here's what happened. AOL, like all the online services, decided that it had better get Internet access in a hurry. So, it started adding Internet services, and it added news-group access quite early. All of a sudden, about a gazillion AOL members flooded onto the Internet in a rush that would have had the bulls at Pamplona running in the opposite direction. Millions of AOL members overwhelmed these discussion groups with questions such as "How do you download files from this group?" and "Where are the pornographic pictures?" Of all the online services' members, AOL's members were probably the least computer-literate. (AOL had targeted the family market, whereas CompuServe, for instance, had been a geek service for years.)

The Internet had been, until just a few months before, a secret kept from most of the world. All of a sudden, it was as busy as a shopping mall on a Saturday afternoon, and every bit as cultured. And there was an obvious scapegoat: all those people with @aol.com email addresses! Unfortunately, you might still run across anti-AOL bias on the Internet.

18. My Download Crashed, So I Have to Start Again. Why?

Most online services use file-transfer systems that can "recover" if the transfer is inter-rupted. For instance, if you are halfway through downloading a file from CompuServe when your three-year-old kid decides he wants to see what happens when he presses the big red button on the front of your computer, all is not lost. After you reboot the computer and reconnect to CompuServe, you can begin the file transfer again. But you don't have to transfer the whole thing; instead the transfer begins in the middle.

However, that usually won't work on the World Wide Web. (In some cases it will work—in most cases it won't. It all depends on the type of utility the site is using for transferring files.) You often can resume interrupted downloads at FTP sites, though, with some FTP programs and download utilities such as Go!Zilla (see Chapter 19, "Downloading Files (FTP, Go!Zilla, and CuteFTP"). If you prefer to use your Web browser for transferring files, though, you'll have to keep your kid away from the computer (or try covering the button with a piece of card).

19. Where Do I Find...?

You're in the wrong chapter; see Chapter 15, "Finding What You Need Online."

20. Are .com and .net Interchangeable?

What's the difference between .com, .net, and .org? Often not much, except that .com is often assumed. These are known as TLDs, Top Level Domains. A .com domain is supposed to be a commercial domain. A .net domain is in some way Internet-related—Internet service providers often have .net domains—and an

.org domain is supposed to be some kind of organization, such as a charity or professional organization. But partly because at one time browsers were set up to work with .com as the default, .com has become the domain to get. (A few years ago, typing a single word into a browser would make the browser try to go to *thatword*.com—type **cat**, for instance, and it would try to go to `http://www.cat.com/`).

So, even if a service provider has a .net domain, it probably also has a .com domain, too. `http://www.earthlink.com/` and `http://www.earthlink.net/` will both get you to the same place.

That's not to say you can interchange .com and .net, or .org for that matter. If you're given a URL that ends in .net, you need to use .net, because .com might not work. However, more and more companies are registering matching domain names—.com, .net, and .org. The registration authorities are encouraging this, perhaps as a way to make more money. It certainly negates the whole purpose of having different TLDs.

Things will change soon, though. In 2001, we're going to see scores more TLDs, such as .ads, .air, .antiques, .cool, .factory, .kids, .men, .sex, .travel, .writer, and many more. The days of .com dominance is coming to an end.

21. How Can Companies Sell So Cheaply Online?

Two words: investment capital. In many cases companies are selling products for less than they are paying for them. And in many more cases they may charge more than the wholesale price, but they're still charging less than the cost of the product and customer acquisition combined.

Someone has to pay the difference, of course, and until now that's been done by investors. The idea was that these companies were "grabbing real estate," getting as many customers as possible with the hope that at the end of the day they'd have more than the competition and eventually be able to make a profit. (Perhaps you've heard the old joke about Internet pricing: "We lose money on each product, but we make up for it on volume.")

It can't continue. The bubble burst in 2000, hundreds of e-businesses are going e-out of business, and the rest of the survivors will eventually push prices back up to rational levels. Investors will want to see actual profits now. It's been fun for buyers, but the party's coming to an end.

Just One More Question...

You're going to come away from this book with lots of questions because the Internet is big, there are many different ways to connect to it, and there's a huge amount of strange stuff out there. I hope this book has helped you start, but I know you'll have many more questions.

After you are on your own, what do you do? Try these suggestions:

➤ **Get the FAQs** FAQ means "frequently asked questions," and it refers to a document with questions and answers about a particular subject. Many newsgroups and mailing lists have FAQs explaining how to use them, for example, and Web sites often have FAQ pages. Look for these FAQs and read them!

➤ **Continue your reading** I've written about a dozen Internet books and need to sell them, so continue buying (and reading) them. Well, okay, there are other writers putting out Internet books, too (you might have noticed a few). To become a real cybergeek, you'll need to learn much more. So, check out a few of these books.

➤ **Read the documentation** There are literally thousands of Internet programs, and each is a little different. Be sure you read all the documentation that comes with your programs so you know how to get the most out of them.

➤ **Ask your service provider!** I've said it before, and I'll say it again: If your service provider won't help you, get another service provider! The Internet is too complicated to travel around without help. Now and again you'll have to ask your service provider's staff for information. Don't be scared to ask—and don't be scared to find another provider if the first one won't or can't answer your questions.

The Least You Need to Know

➤ Learn how to use your computer properly; it will make life online far easier.

➤ Getting rich on the Internet is a lot harder than it's been made out to be.

➤ You might have a fast modem, but if the Internet is busy, things will still move slowly.

➤ Use an email service if you want to be able to switch between service providers without changing your email address each time.

➤ You can be anonymous on the Internet if you are careful.

➤ Buy now while prices are cheap—it won't last!

➤ If your service provider won't answer your questions, you need another service provider!

Part 4
Resources

You'll find reference information in this part of the book. There's a glossary of Internet terms, many covered in this book and a few that you'll run into elsewhere. I've also provided a quick look at the new Internet tools built into Windows 98 and ME. And I'll tell you where to find the software you need: programs to help you on your travels around the Internet, games, print drivers, and unlimited other things.

Speak Like a Geek—The Complete Archive

ActiveX A multimedia authoring system for the World Wide Web from Microsoft.

ADSL Asynchronous Data Subscriber Line; more commonly referred to as *DSL*.

alias A name that is substituted for a more complicated name, usually in an email program. For example, you can use a simple alias (pkent) instead of a more complicated mailing address (pkent@topfloor.com) for a mailing list.

America Online (AOL) A popular online information service and one-time generous donator of floppy disks to just about every North American household. These days they donate colorful coasters in the form of CDs.

anchor A techie word for an *HTML* tag used as a link from one document to another.

anonymous FTP A system by which members of the Internet "public" can access files at certain *FTP* sites without needing a login name; they simply log in as anonymous.

Archie An index system that helps you find files in more than 1,000 *FTP* sites. Rarely used these days.

archive file A file that contains other files (usually compressed files). It is used to store files that are not used often or files that might be downloaded from a file library by Internet users.

ARPANET The Advanced Research Projects Agency (of the U.S. Department of Defense) computer network, which was the forerunner of the Internet.

article   A message in an Internet newsgroup.

ASCII   American Standard Code for Information Interchange, a standard system used by computers to recognize text. An ASCII text file can contain the letters of the alphabet, the punctuation characters, and a few special characters. The nice thing about ASCII is that it's recognized by thousands of programs and many different types of computers.

attribute   A characteristic of something. In *HTML*, a *tag* attribute is a characteristic of that tag, a little piece of information inside the tag that modifies the way in which the tag works.

B2B   A geek business term meaning Business to Business; a mode of operation in which a business sells products or services to other businesses. See also *B2C* and *P2P*.

B2C   A geek business term meaning Business to Consumer; a mode of operation in which a business sells products or services directly to consumers. See also *B2B* and *P2P*.

backbone   A network through which other networks connect.

bandwidth   Widely used to mean the amount of information that can be sent through a particular communications channel. A 14.4bps *modem* is a low-bandwidth channel, whereas a *cable modem* is a high-bandwidth channel.

baud rate   A measurement of how quickly a modem transfers data. Although, strictly speaking, this is not the same as bps (*bits per second*), the two terms are often used interchangeably.

BBS   See *bulletin board system*.

beta test   A program test based on the premise, "This program is virtually finished, but because we need a little help smoothing out the rough edges, we'll give it to a few more people."

BITNET   The "Because It's Time" network (really!). A large network connected to the Internet. Before the Internet became affordable to learning institutions, BITNET was the network of choice for communicating.

bits per second (bps)   A measure of the speed of data transmission; the number of bits of data that can be transmitted each second.

bookmark   A URL that has been saved in some way so that you can quickly and easily return to a particular Web document. See also *Favorites*.

bounce   The action of an email message being returned because of some kind of error.

bps   See *bits per second*.

browser, Web   A program that lets you read *HTML* documents and navigate the Web.

BTW   An abbreviation for "by the way"; it's commonly used in email and news-group messages.

bug   A malfunction in a computer program. Internet software seems to have led the software business to new levels of bug inclusion.

buglike feature   When a programmer or technical support person, talking about the stupid way in which a program handles a particular procedure, says, "That's not a bug, that's the way we designed it"—that's a buglike feature. This term was used by the *Mosaic* programmers at the *NCSA*, who understood that just because you designed something one way doesn't mean you *should have* designed it that way.

bulletin board system (BBS)   A computer system to which other computers can connect so their users can read and leave messages or retrieve and leave files. The Web pretty much put the BBS community/industry out of business, as Web communities are much easier to run and join than BBS systems.

cable modem   A device that connects a network card in your computer to a cable TV line, to provide Internet access. Some of these systems are very fast, at a very good price—probably the best value in Internet connectivity that you can find. If you can get one of these (it might not be available in your area yet), you should do it!

cache   A place where a browser stores Web documents and images that have been retrieved. The cache might be on the hard disk, in memory, or a combination of the two. Documents you "return to" are retrieved from the cache, which saves transmission time.

CDF   Channel Data Format, a system used to prepare information for *Webcasting*.

CERN   The European Particle Physics Laboratory in Switzerland, the original home of the World Wide Web.

CGI (Common Gateway Interface)   A program running on a Web server using information submitted from a Web page.

chat   A system in which people can communicate by typing messages. Unlike email messages, chat messages are sent and received as you type (like a real chat—only without the voice). The most popular pure Internet chat system is Internet Relay Chat. There are a number of Web-site–based chat systems, too. The best and most popular of all the chat systems, however, are on the online services—in particular, *AOL*'s chat rooms. See also *talk*.

CIX   The Commercial Internet Exchange, an organization of commercial Internet service providers.

client   A program or computer that is "serviced" by another program or computer (the *server*). For instance, a Web client—that is, a Web *browser*—requests Web pages from a Web server.

compressed files   Computer files that have been reduced in size by a compression program. Such programs are available for all computer systems (for example, PKZIP in DOS and Windows, tar and compress in UNIX, and StuffIt and PackIt for the Macintosh). Sometimes known as *archive* files, although the terms are not really synonymous, an archive file is not necessarily compressed (although many are).

CompuServe   A large online information service, owned by AOL.

cracker   Someone who tries to enter a computer system without permission. Cracker is the correct term, although the term *hacker* is often mistakenly used in its place.

CSLIP (Compressed SLIP)   See *Serial Line Internet Protocol (SLIP)*.

cyberspace   The area in which computer users travel when navigating a network or the Internet.

DARPANET   The Defense Advanced Research Projects Agency network, which was created by combining *ARPANET* and *MILNET*. The forerunner of the Internet.

DDN   The Defense Data Network is a U.S. military network that is part of the Internet. *MILNET* is part of the DDN.

dedicated line   A telephone line that is leased from the telephone company and is used for one purpose only. On the Internet, dedicated lines connect organizations to service providers' computers, providing dedicated service.

dedicated service   See *permanent connection*.

dial-in direct connection   An Internet connection that you access by dialing into a computer through a telephone line. Once connected, your computer acts as if it were an Internet host. You can run *client* software (such as Web *browsers* and *FTP* programs). Compare to *dial-in terminal connection*.

dial-in service   A networking service that you can use by dialing into a computer through a telephone line.

dial-in terminal connection   An Internet connection that you can access by dialing into a computer through a telephone line. Once connected, your computer acts as if it were a terminal connected to the service provider's computer. Prior to 1994/1995 this was the most common form of Internet access, although these days it's rare. (Most users are working with *dial-in direct connections*.) This type of service is often called *interactive* or *dial-up*.

dial-up service   A common Internet term for a *dial-in terminal connection*.

direct connection   See *permanent connection*.

DNS   See *Domain Name System*.

domain name   A name given to a host computer on the Internet.

Domain Name System (DNS)   A system by which one Internet host can find another so it can send email, connect *FTP* sessions, and so on. The hierarchical system of Internet host domain names use the Domain Name System. The DNS, in effect, translates words into numbers that the Internet's computers can understand. For instance, if you use the domain name poorrichard.com, DNS translates it into 207.33.11.236.

dot address   An informal term used for an *IP address*, which is in the form *n.n.n.n*, where each *n* is a number. For instance, 192.17.3.3.

download   The process of transferring information from one computer to another. You download a file from another computer to yours. See also *upload*.

DSL   Data Subscriber Line (see also *ADSL*), a very fast digital line provided by the phone company if you're very lucky. (It's not yet available everywhere.)

e-book   An electronic book. We're entering the era of the e-book; by the end of the first decade of this century e-books will be very common, quite possibly rivaling paper books.

EARN   The European network associated with BITNET.

EFF   See *Electronic Frontier Foundation*.

EFLA   Extended Four-Letter Acronym. Acronyms are essential to the well being of the Internet. See *TLA*.

Electronic Frontier Foundation (EFF)   An organization interested in social, legal, and political issues related to the use of computers. The EFF is particularly interested in fighting government restrictions on the use of computer technology.

email   Short for electronic mail, the system that lets people send and receive messages with their computers. The system might be on a large network (such as the Internet), on a bulletin board or online service (such as CompuServe), or over a company's own office network.

emoticon   The techie name for small symbols created using typed characters, such as *smileys* :)

encryption   The modification of data so that unauthorized recipients cannot use or understand it. See also *public-key encryption*.

321

etext   Electronic text, a book or other document in electronic form, often simple ASCII text. See also *e-book*.

Ethernet   A protocol, or standard, by which computers might be connected to one another to exchange information and messages.

FAQ (Frequently Asked Questions)   A document containing a list of common questions and corresponding answers. You'll often find FAQs at *Web sites*, in *newsgroups*, and at *FTP* and *Gopher* sites.

Favorites   The term used by Internet Explorer for its *bookmark* list.

Fidonet   An important network that is also connected to the Internet. Well known in geek circles.

file transfer   The copying of files from one computer to another over a network or telephone line. See *File Transfer Protocol*.

File Transfer Protocol   A *protocol* defining how files transfer from one computer to another; generally abbreviated as *FTP*. FTP programs transfer files across the Internet. You can also use FTP as a verb to describe the procedure of using FTP, as in, "FTP to ftp.demon.co.uk," or "I FTPed to their system and grabbed the file."

Finger   A program used to find information about a user on a host computer. Often used in the early days of the Internet boom, this system has now been largely forgotten.

flame   An abusive newsgroup or mailing list message. Things you can do to earn a flame are to ask dumb questions, offend people, not read the FAQ, or simply get on the wrong side of someone with an attitude. When these things get out of control, a flame war erupts. Sometimes also used to refer to an abusive email message.

flamer   Someone who wrote a flame.

Flash   A popular animation format used in many Web sites, created by Macromedia.

form   A *Web* form is a sort of interactive document. The document can contain fields into which readers can type information. This information might be used as part of a survey, to purchase an item, to search a database, and so on.

forms support   A Web *browser* that has forms support can work with a Web *form*. Very old Web browsers don't work with forms.

forum   The term used by CompuServe for its individual bulletin boards or discussion groups (similar to Internet *newsgroups*).

frames   Some Web pages are split into different frames (or panes); in effect, these frames create two or more independent subwindows within the main browser window.

Free-Net A community computer network, often based at a local library or college, which provides Internet access to citizens from the library or college or (sometimes) from their home computers. Free-Nets also have many local services, such as information about local events, local message areas, connections to local government departments, and so on. There aren't many of these around anymore. You can visit a Free-Net at `http://www.prairienet.org/`

freeware Software provided free by its creator. (It's not the same as *public domain software*, as the author retains copyright in freeware.) See also *shareware*.

FTP See *File Transfer Protocol*.

gateway A system by which two incompatible networks or applications can communicate with each other.

geek Someone who knows a lot about computers. Sometimes used disparagingly, to refer to someone who knows much about computers, but very little about communicating with his fellow man—and, perhaps more importantly, with his fellow woman. (Vice versa if the geek happens to be a woman, although the majority of geeks are men.) Geeks may spend more time in front of their computers than talking with real people. The term "geek" might have begun as a derogatory term, but many geeks are proud of their geekness—and many have become very rich because of it. As Dave Barry (who got rich before becoming a computer geek) once said, "I'm a happy geek in cyberspace, where nobody can see my haircut."

Gopher An old Internet system, predating the Web, using Gopher *clients* and *servers* to provide a menu system for navigating the Internet. (Most Web browsers can act as Gopher clients.) Gopher was started at the University of Minnesota, which has a gopher as its mascot. Gopher is pretty much dead, although it's possible to find Gopher servers if you look hard.

Gopherspace Anywhere and everywhere you can get to using *Gopher* is known as Gopherspace.

GUI (Graphical User Interface) Pronounced *goo-ey*, this is a program that provides a user with onscreen tools such as menus, buttons, dialog boxes, a mouse pointer, and so on.

hacker Someone who enjoys spending most of his life with his head stuck inside a computer, either literally or metaphorically. See also *geek* and *cracker*.

Helper See *viewer*.

history list A list of Web documents that you've seen in the current session (some browsers' history lists also show documents from previous sessions). You can return to a document by selecting it in the history list.

home page   1. The Web document your browser displays when you start the program or when you use the browser's Home command. 2. The main page at a Web site. (Personally, I don't like this second definition—because the first definition predates the second, so the second just confused things—but there's not much I can do about it.)

host   A computer connected directly to the Internet. A service provider's computer is a host, as are computers with permanent connections. Computers with *dial-in terminal connections* are not; they are terminals connected to the service provider's host. Computers with *dial-in direct connections* can be thought of as "sort of" hosts: They act like hosts while connected.

host address   See *IP address*.

host number   See *IP address*.

hostname   The name given to a *host*. Computers connected to the Internet really have *host numbers*, but hostnames are easier to remember and work with. A hostname provides a simpler way to address a host than using a number. See also *domain name*.

hotlist   An old term for a list of URLs of Web documents you want to save for future use. You can return to a particular document by selecting its *bookmark* from the hotlist.

HTML (Hypertext Markup Language)   The basic coding system used to create Web documents.

HTTP (Hypertext Transfer Protocol)   The data-transmission *protocol* used to transfer Web documents across the Internet.

hyperlink   See *link*.

hypermedia   Loosely used to mean a *hypertext* document that contains, or has links to, other types of media such as pictures, sound, video, and so on.

hypertext   A system in which documents contain links that allow readers to move between areas of the document, following subjects of interest in a variety of different paths. With most browsers, you use the mouse to click a link to follow the link. The *World Wide Web* is a hypertext system.

IAB   See *Internet Architecture Board*.

IAP   Internet Access Provider, another term for *service provider*.

ICANN   The Internet Corporation for Assigned Names and Numbers, the organization that is responsible for managing *domain names* and *IP* numbers.

IE   A common abbreviation for *Internet Explorer*.

IETF   See *Internet Engineering Task Force*.

IMAP   Internet Message Access Protocol, a system used to provide access to Internet email. Although this system is often used by corporations that link their networks to the Internet, most Internet service providers use a system called *POP*. Unlike POP, the messages remain on a host computer; they are not transferred to the user's computer except when he is reading the message.

IMHO   An abbreviation for In My Humble Opinion, which is often used in email and newsgroup messages.

index document   A *Web* document that lets you search some kind of database. This term and *index server* is not used much these days; you'll hear the simple term "search page" instead.

index server   A special program, accessed through an *index document*, that enables you to search some kind of database.

inline images   A picture inside a Web document. These graphics must be GIF, JPG, XBM, or PNG format files because those are the formats browsers can display. (XBM is very rarely used, and PNG, although more common, is not supported properly by many browsers.)

Integrated Services Digital Network (ISDN)   ISDN allows voice and data to be transmitted on the same line in a digital format—instead of the normal analog format—and at a relatively high speed. ISDN is an Albanian acronym for "Yesterday's Technology Tomorrow." Despite the fact that ISDN was invented around the time of the Spanish-American War, the telephone companies just couldn't seem to figure out how to install this technology—and now ISDN's days are numbered, because it's rapidly being superceded by *DSL*.

interactive service   See *dial-in terminal connection*.

internal loop   See *loop, internal*.

internet   Spelled with a small i, this term refers to networks connected to one another. "The Internet" is not the only internet.

Internet II   The Internet used to be a nice little secret, a special toy for members of academia and the military-industrial complex. But since all you plebes got onto the Internet, it's been pretty crowded and slow. So, a new network, called Internet II, is being created just for academia and military research. Don't expect them to make the same mistake twice and invite you to join!

Internet address   See *IP address*.

Internet Architecture Board (IAB)   The council of elders elected by *ISOC*; they get and figure out how the different components of the Internet will all connect.

Internet Engineering Task Force (IETF)   A group of engineers that makes technical recommendations concerning the Internet to the IAB.

Internet Explorer   A Web browser from Microsoft. It's generally accepted as the best browser available, having beaten Netscape Navigator some time ago (through methods fair or foul; you decide).

Internet Protocol (IP)   The standard protocol used by systems communicating across the Internet. Other protocols are used, but the Internet Protocol is the most important one.

Internet Relay Chat (IRC)   A popular *chat* program. Internet users around the world can chat with other users in their choice of IRC channels.

Internet Society   The society that, to some degree, governs the Internet; it elects the *Internet Architecture Board*, which decides on technical issues related to how the Internet works.

InterNIC   The Internet *Network Information Center*. Run by Network Solutions, Inc., InterNIC manages the *domain name* database.

IP   See *Internet Protocol*.

IP address   An address that defines the location of a host on the Internet. Such addresses are normally shown as four bytes, each one separated by a period (for example, 192.156.196.1). See *dot address* and *hostname*.

IRC   See *Internet Relay Chat*.

ISDN   See *Integrated Services Digital Network*.

ISOC   See *Internet Society*.

ISP   An abbreviation for Internet Service Provider that's much loved in geekdom. See also *service provider*.

Java   A programming language from Sun Microsystems. Programmers can create programs that will run in any Java "interpreter," so a single program can run in multiple operating systems. (That's the theory at least; in practice, the programs often malfunction.) Netscape Navigator and Internet Explorer both have built-in Java interpreters.

JavaScript   A sort of subset of Java, JavaScript is a scripting language that's simpler to use than Java (the scripts are actually inserted into Web pages, they are not separate programs). Both Netscape Navigator and Internet Explorer can run JavaScripts at least some of the time.

JPEG   A compressed graphic format often found on the World Wide Web. These files use the .jpg or .jpeg extension.

JScript   Microsoft's version of *JavaScript*; it contains as much of JavaScript as Microsoft can manage to add (Netscape develops JavaScript, so they're always ahead of Microsoft), plus some JScript-specific commands.

Jughead   Jonzy's Universal Gopher Hierarchy Excavation And Display tool. A *Gopher* search tool that's similar to *Veronica*. The main difference between Veronica and Jughead is that Jughead searches a specific Gopher server whereas Veronica searches all of *Gopherspace*.

KIS   See *Knowbot Information Service*.

Knowbot   An old term for a program that can search the Internet for requested information.

LAN   See *local area network*.

leased line   See *dedicated line*.

link   A connection between two *Web* documents. Links are generally pieces of text or pictures that, when clicked, make the browser request and display another Web document.

linked image   An image that is not in a *Web* document (that's an *inline image*), but is connected to a document by a *link*. Clicking the link displays the image. Often known as an external image.

LINUX   A very popular version of *UNIX*, created by Linus Torvalds (the name is a contraction of Linus Unix). The correct pronunciation is "linix," not "lie-nix"!

LISTSERV list   A *mailing list* discussion group that is handled by the popular LISTSERV mailing list program.

local area network (LAN)   A computer network that covers only a small area (often a single office or building).

log in   The procedure of *logging on* or logging in. Also sometimes used as a noun (and often spelled *login*) to mean the ID and password you use to log on.

logging off   The opposite of *logging on* or logging in; telling the computer that you've finished work and no longer need to use its services. The procedure usually involves typing a simple command, such as **exit** or **bye**, or, in more recent days, clicking a **Disconnect** or **Log Off** button.

logging on   Computer jargon for getting permission from a computer to use its services. A logon procedure usually involves typing a username (also known as an account name or user ID) and a password. This procedure makes sure that only authorized people can use the computer. Also known as logging in.

loop, internal   See *internal loop*.

lurker   Someone involved in *lurking*.

lurking   Reading newsgroup or mailing list messages without responding to them. Nobody knows you are there.

mail reflector   A mail program that accepts email messages and then sends them on to a predefined list of other email addresses. Such systems provide a convenient way to distribute information to people.

mail responder   A system that automatically responds to a received email message. For instance, many companies use `info@hostname` addresses to automatically send back an email message containing product and company information. Email `ownweb@TopFloor.com` for an example.

mail robot   An email system that automatically carries out some sort of email-related procedure for you.

mail server   1. A program that distributes computer files or information in response to email requests. 2. A program that handles incoming email for a host.

mailing list   1. A list of email addresses to which a single message can be sent by entering just one name as the To address. 2. Discussion groups based on a mailing list. Each message sent to the group is sent out to everyone on the list. (*LISTSERV lists* are mailing-list groups.)

MB   Abbreviation for *megabyte*.

MCImail   An email system owned by MCI.

megabyte   A measure of the quantity of data. A megabyte is a lot when you are talking about files containing simple text messages, but not much when you are talking about files containing color photographs.

meta-search site   A search site that allows you to search many other search sites. For instance, enter a question into Ask Jeeves (`http://www.askjeeves.com/`), and the system will search WebCrawler, Yahoo!, Infoseek, Excite, and AltaVista all at once.

The Microsoft Network   A major online service (at one point the fastest growing service in history) that was launched in 1995 when Windows 95 was released. Also known as MSN.

MILNET   A U.S. Department of Defense network connected to the Internet.

MIME (Multipurpose Internet Mail Extensions)   A system that lets you send computer files "attached" to email. Also, used to identify file types on the Web.

mirror site   A copy of another site, such as an *FTP* or *Web* site. Every so often the contents of the main site are copied to the mirror site. The mirror sites provide alternative locations so that if you can't get into the original site, you can go to one of the mirror sites.

modem   A device that converts digital signals from your computer into analog signals for transmission through a phone line (modulation) and converts the phone line's analog signals into digital signals your computer can use (demodulation). (So-called ISDN modems are not true modems; they don't modulate and demodulate.)

Mosaic   The first popular *GUI Web browser*, created by *NCSA*. This was the first graphical browser; some of the original Mosaic programmers helped to found Netscape Communications, the publisher of *Netscape Navigator*.

MP3   Short for *MPEG* Layer-3, an audio format that can hold one minute of CD-quality music in a single MB, along with pictures (album art, for instance), and notes (such as lyrics and contact information for the musician or band); good MP3 players can not only play the music but display the text and images. See also *Napster*.

MPEG   A file format, created by the Moving Picture Experts Group, that can carry sound and video.

MUD   A type of game popular on the Internet. MUD means Multiple User Dimensions, Multiple User Dungeons, or Multiple User Dialogue. MUDs are text games. Each player has a character; characters communicate with one another when the users type messages.

Napster   A controversial *P2P* system that makes sharing *MP3* files among users very easy. The music business is worried because using Napster you can download any music you want without buying it. http://www.napster.com/

navigate   Refers to moving around on the Web using a *browser*. When you jump to a Web document, you are navigating.

NCSA   National Center for Supercomputing Applications, the people who made the *Mosaic* Web *browser*.

netiquette   Internet etiquette, the correct form of behavior to use while working on the Internet and in *Usenet* newsgroups. These guidelines used to be summarized as "Don't waste computer resources, and don't be rude," although these days netiquette refers more to politeness than thrifty use of *bandwidth*.

Netnews   See *Usenet*.

Netscape Communicator   A suite of programs based on *Netscape Navigator*; it contains Navigator (a *Web browser*), Messenger (*email* and newsgroups—the newsgroups portion is called *Collabra* in some versions), AOL Instant Messenger (*talk*), and

Composer (a *Web*-page editing program). Some versions also include Netcaster (a *push* program), Conference (a *chat* and *VON* program), IBM-Host-on-Demand (*tn3270*), and Calendar (a scheduling program), although Netscape seems to have lost interest in these programs.

Netscape Navigator   At one time the Web's most popular browser, created by some old *NCSA* programmers who started a company called Netscape Communications. Recently dropped down to second position, after *Internet Explorer*.

Network Information Center (NIC)   A system providing support and information for a network. See also *InterNIC*.

Network News Transfer Protocol (NNTP)   A system used for the distribution of *Usenet newsgroup* messages.

newbie   A new user. The term might be used to refer to a new Internet user or a user who is new to a particular area of the Internet. Because everyone and his dog is getting onto the Internet, these loathsome creatures have brought the general tone of the Internet down a notch or two, upsetting long-term Internet users who thought the Internet was their own personal secret.

news server   A computer that collects newsgroup data and makes it available to *newsreaders*.

newsgroup   The Internet equivalent of a *BBS* or discussion group (or *forum* in CompuServe-speak) in which people leave messages for others to read. See also *LISTSERV list*.

newsreader   A program that helps you find your way through a *newsgroup*'s messages.

NIC   See *Network Information Center*.

NNTP   See *Network News Transfer Protocol*.

NOC   Network Operations Center, a group that administers a network.

node   A computer device connected to a computer network. That device might be a computer, a printer, a router, or something else.

NREN   The National Research and Education Network.

NSF   National Science Foundation; the U.S. government agency that runs the *NSFnet*.

NSFnet   The National Science Foundation network, a large network connected to the Internet.

offline   The opposite of *online*; not connected.

offline browser   A program that automatically collects pages from Web sites and then makes them available for viewing *offline*.

online   Connected. You are online if you are working on your computer while it is connected to another computer. Your printer is online if it is connected to your computer and ready to accept data. (Online is often written "on-line," although the non-hyphenated version seems to be the most common form these days.)

online service   A commercial service (such as *CompuServe, The Microsoft Network,* and *America Online*) that provides electronic communication services. Users can join discussion groups, exchange email, download files, and so on. These services now have Internet access, too, so they might also be considered *Internet service providers (ISPs).*

P2P   A geek term meaning "Peer to Peer," a networking configuration in which computers communicate directly with each other, as opposed to communicating via *servers.* See also *B2B* and *B2C. Napster* uses a P2P method of operation.

packet   A collection of data. See *packet switching.*

packet switching   A system that breaks transmitted data into small *packets* and transmits each packet (or package) independently. Each packet is individually addressed and might even travel over a route different from that of other packets. The packets are combined by the receiving computer.

PayPal   Finally, a digital payment system that actually works. PayPal lets you send money safely through email. http://PayPal.com/

permanent connection   A connection to the Internet using a *leased line, DSL* line, or cable connection. The computer with a permanent connection acts as a host on the Internet. This type of service is often called *direct, permanent direct,* or *dedicated service* and is very expensive to set up and run. However, it provides a very fast, high *bandwidth* connection. A company or organization can lease a single line and then allow multiple employees or members to use it to access the Internet at the same time.

permanent direct   See *permanent connection.*

personal certificate   An electronic certificate containing *encryption* data used to encrypt and sign email or computer files or to identify the owner to a *Web site.* See also *public-key encryption.*

plug-in   A special type of *viewer* for a *Web browser.* A plug-in plays or displays a particular file type within the browser's window. (A viewer is a completely separate program.)

point of presence   Jargon meaning a method of connecting to a service locally (without dialing long distance), often abbreviated *POP.* If a service provider has a *POP* in, say, Podunk, Ohio, people in that city can connect to the service provider by making a local call.

Point-to-Point Protocol (PPP)   · A method for connecting computers to the Internet via telephone lines; similar to *SLIP,* although a preferred, and these days more common, method.

331

POP   See *point of presence* and *Post Office Protocol*.

port   Generally, port refers to the hardware through which computer data is transmitted; the plugs on the back of your computer are ports. On the Internet, port often refers to a particular application. For instance, you might *Telnet* to a particular port on a particular host.

Post Office Protocol (POP)   A system for letting hosts get email from a server. This system is typically used when a dial-in direct host (which might have only one user and might be connected to the Internet only periodically) gets its email from a service provider. The latest version of POP is POP3. Do not confuse this with another type of POP, *point of presence*. Unlike *IMAP*, POP mail is transferred to the user's computer.

posting   A message (article) sent to a newsgroup or the act of sending such a message.

postmaster   The person at a host who is responsible for managing the mail system. If you need information about a user at a particular host, you can send email to postmaster@*hostname*.

PPP   See *Point-to-Point Protocol*.

private key   The code used in a *public-key encryption* system that must be kept secure (unlike the *public key*, which might be freely distributed).

Prodigy   An online service founded by Sears.

protocol   A set of rules that defines how computers transmit information to one another, allowing different types of computers and software to communicate with one another.

public domain software   Software that does not belong to anyone. You can use it without payment and even modify it if the source code is available. See also *shareware* and *freeware*.

public key   The code used in a *public-key encryption* system that might be freely distributed (unlike the *private key*, which must be kept secure).

public-key encryption   A system that uses two mathematically related keys: a *private key* and a *public key*. Information that has been encrypted using one key can be decrypted only by using the associated key. The private key is used to digitally sign an electronic document or decrypt files that were encrypted using the public key.

push   A push program periodically retrieves data from the Internet and displays it on the user's computer screen. A push program is a sort of automated *Web browser*. See also *Webcasting*.

RealAudio   A well-known streaming audio format.

332

reflector, mail   Messages sent to a mail reflector's address are sent automatically to a list of other addresses.

reload (or **refresh**)   A command that tells your browser to retrieve a Web document even though you have it in the cache. Microsoft uses the term refresh for this command in its Internet Explorer browser. (In Netscape Navigator, the Refresh command simply redisplays the Web page to clear up any display problems.)

remote login   A BSD (Berkeley) UNIX command (rlogin) that is similar to *Telnet*.

rendered   An *HTML* document has been rendered when it is displayed in a Web browser. The browser renders it into a normal text document by removing all the HTML codes, so you see just the text that the author wants you to see. An unrendered document is the *source HTML* document (with codes and all).

rlogin   See *remote login*.

rot13   Rotation 13, a method used to scramble messages in *newsgroups* so that you can't stumble across an offensive message. If you want to read an offensive message, you'll have to decide to do so and go out of your way to decode it.

router   A system used to transmit data between two computer systems or networks using the same *protocol*. For instance, a company that has a permanent connection to the Internet will use a router to connect its computer to a leased line. At the other end of the leased line, a router is used to connect it to the service provider's network.

RTFM   Abbreviation for (Read the F***ing Manual), which is often used in reaction to a stupid question (or in response to a question which, in the hierarchy of *newbies* and long-term Internet users, is determined to be a stupid question).

server   A program or computer that services another program or computer (the *client*). For instance, a *Gopher* server program sends information from its indexes to a Gopher client program, and *Web servers* send Web pages to Web browsers (which are Web clients).

service provider   A company that provides a connection to the Internet. *Online services*, although generally regarded as different from service providers, are in fact also service providers because in addition to having their own services, they provide access to the Internet.

SGML   Standard Generalized Markup Language. *HTML* grew out of SGML.

shareware   Software that is freely distributed, but for which the author expects payment from people who decide to keep and use it. See also *freeware* and *public domain software*.

shell account   Another name for a simple *dial-in terminal* account.

Shockwave   A popular multimedia format used in many Web sites, created by Macromedia.

shopping cart   A program that enables visitors to a Web site to place orders and purchase products.

signature   A short piece of text transmitted with an email or newsgroup message. Some systems can attach text from a file to the end of a message automatically. Signature files typically contain detailed information on how to contact someone: name and address, telephone numbers, Internet address, CompuServe ID, and so on—or some strange little quote or poem.

Simple Mail Transfer Protocol (SMTP)   A *protocol* used to transfer email between computers on a network.

SLIP   See *Serial Line Internet Protocol*.

smiley   A symbol in email and newsgroup messages used to convey emotion or provide amusement. Originally, the term referred to a symbol that seems to smile, but the term now seems to refer to just about any small symbol created with text characters. You create smileys by typing various keyboard characters. For example, :-(means *sad*. Smileys are usually sideways: Turn your head to view the smiley. The more technical term for a smiley is *emoticon*.

SMTP   See *Simple Mail Transfer Protocol*.

snarf   To grab something off the Web and copy it to your computer's hard disk for future use. Snarfing is often illegal if done without permission (a copyright contravention).

source document   An *HTML* document, the basic ASCII file that is *rendered* by a browser.

spam   The term given to unsolicited email sent to large numbers of people without any regard to whether those people want to receive the mail. Originally, the term referred specifically to a single message sent to large numbers of newsgroups. The term comes from the Monty Python Spam song, which contains the refrain, "Spam, Spam, Spam, Spam, Spam, Spam, Spam, Spam."

stack   See *TCP/IP stack*.

start page   A term used by Microsoft in early versions of its Internet Explorer browser to refer to the *home page* (the page displayed when you start your browser). Just to confuse users, more recent versions of Internet Explorer refer to the home page as Home Page.

streaming   In the old days, if you transferred an audio or video file, you had to wait for it to be transferred to your computer completely before you could play it. Streaming audio and video formats allow the file to play while it's being transferred.

tags   The codes inside an *HTML* file. Web *browsers* read the tags to find out how they should *render* the document.

talk   A program that lets two or more Internet users type messages to each other. As a user types a character or paragraph, that text is immediately transmitted to the other user. There are several common talk programs: talk, ntalk, and Ytalk are old UNIX systems, but these days AOL Instant Messenger and ICQ are becoming very popular. Talk is similar to *chat*, although chat systems are intended as meeting places, whereas talk programs are private. See also *chat*.

tar files   Files *compressed* using the UNIX tape archive program. Such files usually have filenames ending in .tar.

TCP/IP (Transmission Control Protocol/Internet Protocol)   A set of *protocols* (communications rules) that control how data transfers between computers on the Internet.

Telnet   A program that lets Internet users log in to computers other than their own host computers, often on the other side of the world. Telnet is also used as a verb, as in "Telnet to debra.doc.ca." However, while still used in many special situations, the average Internet user has no idea what Telnet is and will never need to know.

Telneting   Internet-speak for using Telnet to access a computer on the network.

TLA   Three-Letter Acronym. An acronym for an acronym. What would we do without them? See also *EFLA*.

tn3270   A *Telnet*-like program used for *remote logins* to IBM mainframes.

trojan horse   A computer program that appears to carry out a useful function but which is actually designed to do harm to the system on which it runs. See also *virus*.

troll   Someone who posts unsolicited, inflammatory messages on a newsgroup or mailing list and is merely looking to get a rise out of people. He is "trolling" for people to bite on his bait. Don't flame a troll—that's just what they want you to do.

UNIX   A computer operating system. Many—probably most—host computers connected to the Internet run UNIX.

upload   The process of transferring information from one computer to another. You upload a file from your computer to another. See also *download*.

URL (Universal Resource Locator)   A Web address.

Usenet   The "User's Network," a large network connected to the Internet. The term also refers to the *newsgroups* distributed by this network.

UUCP network   A network of UNIX computers connected to the Internet.

uudecode   If you use *uuencode* to convert a file to ASCII and transmit it, you'll use uudecode to convert the ASCII file back to its original format.

uuencode   The name given a program used to convert a computer file of any kind (sound, spreadsheet, word processing, or whatever) into an ASCII file so that it can be transmitted as a text message. The term is also used as a verb, as in "uuencode this file." Most email programs handle *MIME* transmissions properly these days, so uuencoding files is rare.

VBScript   A scripting language from Microsoft, which is similar in concept to *JavaScript*.

Veronica   The Very Easy Rodent-Oriented Netwide Index to Computerized Archives, a very useful program for finding things in *Gopherspace*.

viewer   A program that displays or plays computer files that you find on the Web. For instance, you need a viewer to play video files you find. These programs are sometimes known as *helpers* or *plug-ins*.

virus   A program that uses various techniques for duplicating itself and traveling between computers. Viruses vary from simple nuisances (they might display an unexpected message on your screen) to serious problems that can cause millions of dollars' worth of damage (such as crashing a computer system and erasing important data).

Voice on the Net (VON)   A service through which you can talk to other Internet users. You need a sound card, microphone, speakers, and the right software; then, you can make Internet phone calls. They're warbly, but very cheap.

VON   See *Voice on the Net*.

VRML   Virtual Reality Modeling Language, a system used to create three-dimensional images. In 1995, Internet pundits claimed that most Web sites would be using VRML by now and lots of it, but the pundits forgot that VRML doesn't run well on most people's computers. Since then, people have lost interest in VRML, despite the fact that now many people's computers do run VRML well. VRML's time has not yet arrived.

W3   See *World Wide Web*.

WAIS   See *Wide area information server*.

WAP   Wireless Application Protocol, the technology used to transmit information from the World Wide Web to that stupid little screen on your cell phone. Also used to transmit to Personal Digital Assistants (such as the PalmPilot). Expect many of the early WAP companies to go out of business (there's more hype in WAP than reality right now).

Web   Pertaining to the *World Wide Web*.

Web forum   A discussion group running on a Web site.

Web server   A computer system—a computer running special server software—that makes *Web* documents available to Web browsers. The browser asks the server for the document, and the server transmits it to the browser.

Web site   A collection of *Web* documents about a particular subject on a *host*.

Web-hosting company   A company that sells space on a Web server to people who want to set up Web sites.

Webcasting   Distributing information via *push* programs.

Webspace   The area of cyberspace in which you are traveling when working on the *Web*.

WebTV   A system used to display Web sites on a television. A box containing a *modem* is connected to a TV; the signals from the Internet are transmitted on the phone lines (not along the TV *cable* line) and displayed on the TV screen. The WebTV service is owned by Microsoft (the boxes are manufactured by Sony and Philips/Magnavox, although the term is also widely used to describe the technology in generic terms. If you're excited about getting onto the Internet, a good way to dissipate some of that excitement is to buy WebTV. On the other hand, some people love it. Takes all kinds.

White Pages   Lists of Internet users.

Whois   A UNIX program used for searching for information about Internet users.

Wide area information server (WAIS)   A system that can search particular databases on the Internet.

World Wide Web   A *hypertext* system that allows users to travel through linked doc uments, following any chosen route. World Wide Web documents contain topics that, when selected, lead to other documents.

WWW   See *World Wide Web*.

XML   Extensible Markup Language, a subset of SGML. *HTML*-like tags that extend HTML by allowing designers to create their own tags. Particular industry groups could then create programs that would recognize those tags. For instance, the medical industry could create special programs that recognize tags such as <MD>, <RX>, <WHINER>, and <VERYSICK>.

Windows
Internet Features

Microsoft has integrated the Windows operating system more closely with the Internet, and Windows 98 and Windows ME have a plethora of Internet-related tools. Tight integration of the operating system and the Internet enables Microsoft to update the operating system frequently. This is a real boon for all Windows users, ensuring that we can all work with the very latest bugs available.

The U.S. Justice Department claimed that Microsoft uses unfair practices to destroy competition (which it probably did), and that one of those practices is adding features to the operating system—in other words, by adding various utilities to the operating system, Microsoft is harming the companies that would otherwise be creating and selling similar software. That might be so, but do we need a government department overseeing the development of Microsoft Windows? The operating system presents enough problems as it is without lawyers and bureaucrats helping design it! (This strikes me as akin to letting lawyers design a kid's playground—"You can have any structure you want, as long as it's not more than six inches off the ground.") At the time of writing, this case was not settled, and probably won't be for some time. In the meantime, you'll find that Windows contains plenty of Internet features...including a free browser.

Justice Department Versus Microsoft

I'm no cheerleader for Microsoft. But on the other hand, I'm not sure I want the Justice Department designing software, either. Consider, in relation to the fuss about Microsoft adding its browser to the operating system, the following:

➤ Microsoft is not the only operating-system publisher to believe that people buying an operating system should get a free browser; IBM provides one with OS2, and the current version of the Apple operating system includes two browsers!

➤ Microsoft was not the first company to bundle a Web browser with an operating system; IBM included a browser in OS2 in mid to late 1994, long before Microsoft had even released the beta of Internet Explorer.

➤ Web browsers were traditionally free; in 1994, there were dozens of Web browsers available, and most were available at no cost.

➤ Netscape claims that Microsoft hurt it by giving away a browser in the operating system, but if Netscape's executives really believed they could build a multibillion dollar business based on a simple utility such as a Web browser, a utility that had a history of being free, they must have been smoking something pretty strong. (In fact, Netscape knew quite well that most users of Netscape Navigator did not and would not pay for it.)

Anyway, this appendix is a quick summary of the features included in Windows 98 and Windows ME at the time of writing, with information on how to find each program. Note that some of the Internet features might not be installed on your computer yet—it all depends on the choices made by the person who installed Windows onto your computer. You can add any missing programs by running Windows Setup (assuming you have the installation disk, that is). If the item you want has not been installed, select **Start**, **Settings**, **Control Panel**, and then open the **Add/Remove Programs** icon, and click the **Windows Setup** tab. In the list box that you'll see, click the category, the **Details** button, and then select the item you want to install.

Windows 98 and ME Features

Let's begin with Windows 98 and Windows ME (then, you'll look at the new ME features). Table B.1 shows the Internet related features, sorted by category (the category you'll see in the **Add/Remove Programs** dialog box).

Table B.1 The Optional Internet Features in Windows 98

Category	Feature
Communications	Dial-Up Networking
	Microsoft Chat
	Virtual Private Networking
Internet Tools	MS FrontPage Express
	Microsoft VRML Viewer
	Microsoft Wallet
	Personal Web Server
	RealAudio Player
	Web Publishing Wizard
	Web Based Enterprise Management
Microsoft Outlook Express	(Email, newsreader, and address book; this is a category by itself)
Multimedia	Macromedia Shockwave Director
	Macromedia Shockwave Flash
	Microsoft Media Player
	Online Services America Online
	AT&T WorldNet Service
	CompuServe
	Prodigy Internet
	The Microsoft Network
WebTV for Windows	(Category by itself)

To further complicate the issue, Microsoft has online upgrades (**Start**, **Windows Update**). If you upgrade your system, it might not match exactly what's shown here. You should be able to find the latest programs in this Windows Update area, though.

Online Services

Thanks to Bill Gates' battle with the U.S. Justice Department, America Online, and Netscape, Windows 98 includes software for several online services. In other words, America Online will be able to save millions of dollars by not including a free disk in all its junk mail to American homes. Instead, Windows 98 users can simply select AOL or one of several other online services and log right in. To find these online service programs, select **Start**, **Program Files**, **Online Services** (see Figure B.1). Windows 98 currently includes software for America Online, CompuServe, AT&T WorldNet, Prodigy Internet, and, of course, The Microsoft Network.

Figure B.1

Thanks to the Justice Department, choosing an online service is easier than ever (which is bad news for thousands of small Internet service providers, of course).

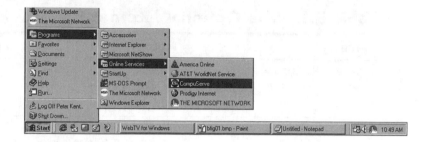

System Setup Tools

Windows 98 has several tools to help you set up your Internet connection:

➤ **Dial-Up Networking**   This utility creates connections to Internet service providers, so you can get onto the Internet. In theory, it provides a simple point-and-click configuration system. In practice, it doesn't. Note, however, that in many cases you don't need to use this utility at all. For instance, if you use one of the online services already built into Windows 98; the connection will be configured for you automatically. You can use the Connection Wizard to help you set up Dial-Up Networking. You can open Dial-Up Networking by selecting **Start**, **Programs**, **Accessories**, **Communications**, **Dial-Up Networking**, but you'll probably want to use the Connection Wizard instead.

➤ **Connection Wizard**   This program leads you through the process of setting up Dial-Up Networking. In theory, it "automatically handles the software configuration steps necessary for gaining access to the Internet." Although I almost let my cynicism get away with me (having seen, in Windows 95, what phrases such as "automatically handles" really mean), I must say that the Connection Wizard is quite good, a great improvement (why wasn't this in Windows 95?). It even has a referral service that helps you find a service provider in your area. Select **Start**, **Programs**, **Internet Explorer**, **Connection Wizard**.

➤ **ISDN Configuration Wizard**   Dial-Up Networking is designed to work with ordinary phone lines, but this program helps you set up a connection to an ISDN line. To open this program, select **Start**, **Programs**, **Accessories**, **Communications**, **ISDN Configuration Wizard** (if you haven't installed an ISDN device, this option won't appear).

Email and Newsgroups

Microsoft Outlook Express combines an email program (see Chapter 6, "Sending and Receiving Email," and Chapter 7, "Advanced Email—HTML Mail, Voice, and Encryption"), a newsreader (see Chapter 10, "Finding and Using Newsgroups"), and an address book. If you're working on a computer set up by your corporate employer and are connected to the corporate network, there's a good chance you'll be using Outlook Express. If you get to pick your own software, you might want to find something else.

Microsoft often creates software based on the principle "It might not be the best, but at least it's the biggest." I've used Microsoft Exchange, the clunky forerunner to Outlook Express, so I just can't bring myself to use this new incarnation (although admittedly it looks, at first glance, like a bit of an improvement). Much better programs are available. (I like Gravity for newsgroups and Eudora for email, but you might find something that suits you better.)

To start Outlook Express, use the **Outlook Express** icon on the desktop or on the taskbar, or select **Start**, **Programs**, **Internet Explorer**, **Outlook Express.** You can get to the Address book directly using **Start**, **Programs**, **Internet Explorer**, **Address Book**.

Internet Explorer Web Browser

Internet Explorer is the Web browser that the Justice Department (and Netscape) is so upset about. Explorer is a very good browser, although I'm not convinced it's a great one; I currently prefer Netscape Navigator, although there have been times when I thought Explorer was better; these programs seem to leapfrog each other. To start Internet Explorer, click the Explorer icon in the taskbar, or select **Start**, **Programs**, **Internet Explorer**, **Internet Explorer**.

Browser Plug-Ins

You learned about browser plug-ins and viewers in Chapter 5, "Web Multimedia— From Flash to Napster," and Windows 98 and ME provide several. Do you really need all these? I'd say no (the Web could really do with a little less multimedia, and a little more good writing), but who knows, perhaps you feel you have to experience the best that the Web has to offer. Now and again even I, the Internet Curmudgeon, feel that I just *have* to see *why* a Web author feels that I just *must* view his site using the Shockwave plug-in (when it's all over I rarely find myself in agreement with him). The most useful plug-ins are the RealPlayer and Windows Media Players plug-in.

These are the Windows 98 plug-ins:

> ➤ **Microsoft VRML Viewer**   This program is a Virtual Reality viewer. If you find any 3D images on the Web, this plug-in can probably handle them. You won't find many, though.

➤ **Microsoft Wallet**   You can use this special commerce plug-in to pay for purchases at Web sites. It provides a convenient way to store and transfer your
credit-card information. (You can protect the credit-card numbers by providing
a password.) It will also store your address and other contact information. The
only problem is that few Web sites are set up to work with the Wallet. It still
keeps useful information close at hand, though (no more running off to find
your credit cards before buying something). To add your information, open the
Internet Properties dialog box by using the **Internet** icon in the Control Panel
or by selecting **View**, **Internet Options** inside Internet Explorer. Then, click the
Content tab to find the Wallet settings.

➤ **NetShow Player**   This program plays streaming video and audio. (*Streaming*,
you'll remember from Chapter 5, means that the information plays at the same
time it's being transferred across the Internet; a nonstreaming data file has to
transfer completely before it can begin playing.) For instance, the MSNBC news
Web site (`http://www.msnbc.com/`) uses data that plays through NetShow Player.
However, although you'll find Netshow in some Windows 95 versions, the program has really been replaced by Windows Media Player.

➤ **RealPlayer**   This program plays sounds and video; it's often used at music and
news Web sites.

➤ **Shockwave Director**   This program plays Macromedia Director files, which are
animation files that you'll sometimes run across.

➤ **Shockwave Flash**   This program plays another form of smaller and "lighter"
animation file.

➤ **Windows Media Player**   This is a complete, easy-to-use, all-in-one player. You
can use the Media Player to locate, download, and play back audio and video,
including the popular MP3 files.

When Internet Explorer needs to run one of these plug-ins, it will automatically open
the right one.

Microsoft Chat

Microsoft Chat, which you saw in Chapter 8, "Using Online Chat Rooms," is built
into Windows 98 and Windows ME. To open the program, select **Start**, **Programs**,
Internet Explorer, **Microsoft Chat**.

Web Publishing Tools

Windows 98 provides several Web publishing tools. You can find all these items in
the Internet Explorer folder; select **Start**, **Programs**, **Internet Explorer**.

➤ **MS FrontPage Express**   This editor from Microsoft FrontPage creates Web
pages for you, as you can see in Figure B.2). It's a sort of Web-page word

processor; you type the text and select formats, font types, colors, and so on, and FrontPage Express adds all the HTML codes for you (see Chapter 13, "Setting Up Your Own Web Site").

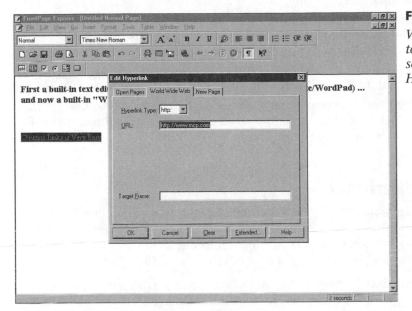

Figure B.2

Windows has a text editor, a simple word processor, and now it has an HTML editor, too.

➤ **Web Publishing Wizard** This program simplifies the process of transferring pages from your computer to the computer that will host your Web pages.

➤ **Personal Web Server** You can set up a Web site on your own computer and make it available to other people on your corporate network (if the network is running the TCP/IP protocol, ask your system administrator) or even on the Internet (if people on the Internet have access to your computer). You can also use it to test a Web site on your own computer before publishing it on the Internet. The Personal Web Server is a very simple Web server that you configure by filling in forms in your Web browser. (Remember, the server is the program that receives browsers' requests for Web pages and transmits those pages to them.)

"Corporate" Tools

Windows 98 has several tools that I think of as "corporate" tools—that is, programs that you're unlikely to use at home, but might work with if you are employed by a medium-to-large corporation.

➤ **Microsoft NetMeeting** This "conference" program enables you to communicate with people across the Internet instantly by typing messages, drawing on a whiteboard, or transferring files (see Chapter 12, "More Ways to Communicate—Net Phones, Conferences, Videoconferences"). You might even be able to include voice and video. Open this program by using **Start, Programs, Internet Explorer, Microsoft Netmeeting**.

➤ **Virtual Private Networking**   This system can be used to build a private network on the World Wide Web. Authorized people can use a "tunnel" through the World Wide Web to access the corporate network. So, wherever you happen to be traveling, as long as you can access the Internet you can get to the network. This system is something that the network administrator must set up.

➤ **Web-Based Enterprise Management**   This tool is used for managing various corporate and network tasks through a series of Web pages on the network. It's another toy for the network administrator.

WebTV for Windows

This system is *not* the same as the WebTV product discussed in Chapter 1 ("Your Connection to the Online Universe"), although it was created in conjunction with that product. Rather, it's a system that enables you to display TV information and Web pages carried by TV signals on your computer.

WebTV for Windows likes to have a TV tuner card available, which is a card installed in your computer that allows the computer to display TV signals, but it can still do a few things even if your computer can't display TV. Without a TV tuner, it can display television schedules, downloaded from the Web, for you. If you have a TV tuner installed in your computer, you can quickly select a program in the schedule and watch the program on your computer (see Figure B.3). If that program is carrying Web pages embedded in the signal, those pages can be displayed.

How can a TV signal carry a Web page? There's a lot of empty space in a TV signal, and because a Web page doesn't take up much room, relatively speaking, it's possible to cram the page into the dead space in the TV signal (into the vertical blanking interval). A TV with some kind of processor in it can then pull the Web page out and display it separately. This technology is nothing particularly new; such systems have been used for years in Europe to transmit data on television screens. In Great Britain, for instance, TV viewers can switch from the normal TV broadcasts to a special TeleText menu, from which they can select news articles, weather reports, and so on.

The main problem with using WebTV to view Web pages carried by TV signals is that very few TV signals carry Web pages, although that will probably change over the next year or so. You can start WebTV by clicking the **WebTV** taskbar icon or by selecting **Start, Programs, Accessories, Entertainment, WebTV for Windows**.

346

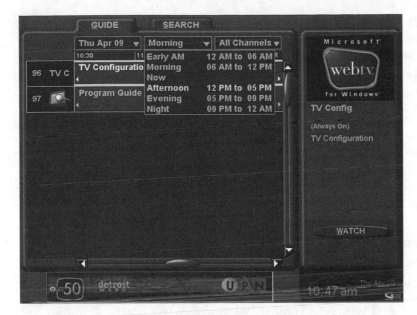

Figure B.3

If you don't get enough TV already, now you can watch it when you should be working or at least figure out what you'll watch when you escape from your cubicle this evening.

Windows ME's New Internet Features

Windows ME, like Windows 98 before it, strives to further integrate your computer with the Internet. However, Windows ME seems to place more emphasis on multimedia and ease of use. The following are the Internet-related features you'll find in the latest Windows operating system:

Additional Internet Features in Windows ME

➤ **Windows Movie Maker**   This new feature allows you to edit, catalog, and email your home movies or video files you have obtained from the Web. Movie Maker digitizes your videos so that you can take out the bumps and glitches and save the edited files to CD (so long as you have a Writable CD hardware) or your hard disk. Once digitized, shorter videos can be attached as an email attachment. To access Movie Maker in Windows ME, select **Start**, **Programs**, **Accessories**, and **Windows Movie Maker**.

➤ **My Pictures Folder**   This is more than just a Folder. In Windows ME, you can view your images as thumbnails, sort them, and present them as a full-screen slide show. You can also configure the My Pictures folder (or any folder containing images) with a previewer that allows you to zoom in and out, print, and even rotate. To show pictures in Thumbnail view, open the appropriate folder in Windows Explorer or My Computer, and select **View**, **Thumbnails**. Graphic images from your digital camera, from scanning, or those you have downloaded from the Web will be shown in miniature. To configure the folder with a previewer, select **View**, **Customize This Folder**. The Customize This Folder Wizard will open. Click **Next**, select **Choose or Edit an HTML Template for This Folder**, and then click **Next**, again. Click **Image Preview** and follow the instructions on your screen to complete the Wizard.

➤ **Internet Connection Sharing**   If you have more than one computer, you can easily create a home network using Windows ME. And, one big advantage of a home network is that multiple computers can use the same Internet connection simultaneously. This could put a stop to some of those "My turn to use the Internet!" arguments. Select **Start**, **Programs**, **Accessories**, **Communications** and **Home Networking Wizard**.

➤ **Internet Security**   Windows Me features a greatly improved version of TCP/IP that provides enhanced security and reliability when you are connected to the Internet. Microsoft also promises faster data transfer rates while using the Internet.

➤ **MSN Messenger Service**   These days, instant messages are all the rage and now there is another service to choose from. Windows ME comes with MSN Messenger which allows you to keep track of your friends that are online and have real-time chats with as many as three of them at the same time.

➤ **Multiplayer Internet Games**   Windows ME comes with five new multiplayer Internet games that you can play with online opponents around the globe. There are no Web sites to access or software to download. Windows ME will help you locate other players from around the world who match your skill level and speak your language—or not. You can even choose from a list of standard chat messages that can be automatically translated if your opponent is from another country or speaks a different language.

Web Integration

Both Windows 98 and Windows ME attempt to integrate the computer desktop with the Web and even provide Weblike features on the desktop. (Of course, it would work a little better if we all had fast, permanent connections to the Internet, which is what Bill Gates and various telecommunications companies promised we'd have by Christmas of 1998. By the time you read this, it'll be 2001, perhaps much later...and most of the nation *still* won't have fast, permanent connections to the Internet.)

➤ **Active Desktop**   This feature makes your Windows desktop work like a Web page. Instead of double-clicking an icon, you can just single click (and the icon labels look like Web links). Windows Explorer looks like a browser and works like a browser to some degree; click a file, and Explorer displays the file, for instance. To set up Active Desktop, select **Start**, **Settings**, **Active Desktop**.

➤ **Push**   Windows 98 and Windows ME have built-in "push" systems. You can embed Web pages into the desktop. Want the latest sports news every morning? Find a good sports Web site, and then embed the page into your desktop so it's always there. Windows 98 also provides a variety of preconfigured push *channels*, which are essentially Web pages specially configured to work with the push system. Eventually, you'll be able to receive push channels via satellite transmissions. (Don't you love the word "eventually"? Writers use it to mean "I've no idea when.") There's a View Channels icon on the taskbar, and when you first start Windows, you'll see a special Channel box on the right side of the window.

Maintenance and Configuration

Look in the Control Panel (**Start**, **Settings**, **Control Panel**), and you'll find an Internet Properties icon. The Internet Properties dialog box provides all sorts of Internet-related settings, from how to automatically dial the Internet to how to keep your kids away from "bad" Web sites. You can also open this dialog box from inside Internet Explorer; select **View**, **Internet Options** inside Internet Explorer.

You'll also find a number of Help Troubleshooters for Internet-related subjects: The Modem, Microsoft Network, and Dial-Up Networking. These little interactive programs try to help you figure out why something isn't working (if you're lucky, they might even succeed). Choose **Start**, **Help**. On the **Contents** tab, click **Troubleshooting** and then **Windows 98 Troubleshooters**.

Finally, you can update Windows 98 across the Internet. Open the **Start** menu, and you'll see a **Windows Update** option. This option opens your browser, connects to a Microsoft upgrade Web site, and runs the Windows Upgrade Wizard. If there are any bug fixes waiting for you—ahem, I mean "system enhancements"—the Wizard will automatically transfer and install them.

Windows Update

The Windows Update area of the Microsoft Web site has lots of goodies you can download free. Microsoft knows its Web site is as easy to navigate as the London docks during a heavy fog, so it has kindly added a menu option to your Start menu. Simply select **Start**, **Windows Update**, and Internet Explorer will open and connect to the appropriate page. Perhaps. Sometimes it doesn't work too well.

In Windows ME, or if you've updated Windows 98, you can set the Windows update to automatically update your system, periodically.

Whichever way you choose to access Windows Update, after you *do* get through, you'll find toys such as those on the following list. (Most of these have been included in Windows ME already.)

➤ The latest and greatest updates to all your favorite Windows utilities.

➤ **Agent 2.0**   Used to display "characters used in interactive guides and entertainment features on some Web sites," an invaluable business tool. If you hate those little characters that tell you how to use Word or Excel, you won't want this.

➤ **AOL ART Image Format Support**   Download America Online art now...so you don't have to later.

➤ **DirectAnimation**   Speed up animations.

➤ **Web Folders Internet Publishing Utility**   Work with files on your Web server in the same way you work with files on your computer.

➤ **Web Publishing Wizard**   A tool for posting Web pages to a Web server.

➤ **Language Support**   View Web pages in languages such as Arabic, Japanese, Hebrew, Korean, and many others.

Bug-Fix Watch!

It can be fun to visit the Windows Update area. See whether you can spot the bug fixes cleverly disguised as product improvements! Here's a tip. If you can't understand exactly what the file is supposed to do, yet Microsoft says it's a critical or recommended update, it's probably a bug fix. Or if you download it and find the new features are so minimal as to be almost worthless, it's probably a bug fix.

All the Software You'll Ever Need

You've read about a lot of software in this book, and there's much more that hasn't been mentioned. Thousands of shareware, freeware, and demoware programs for the Macintosh, Windows 3.1, Windows 95, Windows 98, Windows ME, Windows NT, Windows 2000, and all flavors of UNIX are available for you to download and use. "How do I find all these programs?" you ask. It's easy to find software after you know where to look.

The Search Starts at Home

You can always begin looking at home. If you use one of the online services, you'll find stacks of software within the service—no need to go out onto the Internet. All the online services have Internet-related forums (or BBSs, or areas, or whatever they call them). These are good places to begin, and you can usually download the software more quickly from there than from the Internet. In addition, many online services have forums set up by software vendors and shareware publishers. These are good places to get to know, too.

If you are with a true Internet service provider, you'll often find that your service has a file library somewhere. The library will have a smaller selection than the online services do, but it might be a good place to start, nonetheless. On the other hand, you might want to go straight to the major Internet software sites, which will have a much greater range of programs.

Different Types of Software

Shareware is software that is given away free, but which you are supposed to register (for a fee) if you decide to continue using it. *Freeware* is software that is given away with no fee required. *Demoware* is software that is generally free, but is intended to get you interested in buying the "full" program. There are many other related terms, such as *crippleware* (shareware that will stop working in some way—perhaps the entire program stops working, or maybe just one or two features—after the trial period is over).

Finding a Browser

In this book, I've mentioned two programs in particular—Netscape Navigator and Internet Explorer—that you need to know how to find. You might already have one or the other of these. Many online services and service providers already provide one of them in the software package you get when you sign up. If you want to get the latest version or try the competing program, go to one of these sites:

> Netscape Navigator: http://www.netscape.com/
>
> Internet Explorer: http://www.microsoft.com/ie/

I've mentioned dozens of other programs throughout this book. You can find most of those programs at the sites I discuss next.

The Internet's Software Libraries

The Internet is full of wonderful software libraries. Check out some of the following sites, but remember that there are more, which you can find using the links mentioned in the section "Finding More," later in this appendix.

> ➤ **TUCOWS (Windows)** (http://www.tucows.com/)   TUCOWS (shown in Figure C.1) originally stood for "The Ultimate Collection of Winsock Software" (meaning Windows-related Internet software), but these days it has software for the Macintosh, OS2, and even for *PDAs (Personal Digital Assistants)* such as the PalmPilot and Visor.
>
> ➤ **Stroud's Consummate Winsock Applications Page (Windows)** (http://cws.internet.com/)   Another excellent Windows software archive.

Figure C.1

The TUCOWS site is an excellent place to find all sorts of useful Windows software. (The more cows a program's been awarded, the better it is.)

➤ **Winsite (Windows)** (http://www.winsite.com/ or ftp.winsite.com)   Another good Windows archive. Winsite claims to be the "Planet's Largest Software Archive for Windows." It now has a special section, Casino Winsite, containing gambling software. Note that it's often difficult to get to the FTP site.

➤ **TopSoft (Windows, Macintosh, UNIX)** (http://www.topsoft.com/)   This relatively small site has a nice selection of useful programs, and you'll find a detailed description for each one (many other sites have very simple descriptions, or none at all, for the programs they store).

➤ **ZDNet Downloads** (http://www.zdnet.com/downloads/)   This site contains many Windows programs (more than 10,000 files). It's well organized, with detailed descriptions of the files.

➤ **ZDNet MacDownload.com (Macintosh)** (http://www.MacDownload.com) Go to this site to find a large Macintosh software archive.

➤ **Nonags (Windows)** (http://www.nonags.com/)   This site is dedicated to software that has "no nags, no time limits, no disabled features, or any other tricks. Most are really free, a few are shareware..."

➤ **Shareware.com (Windows, Macintosh, UNIX, OS2, Atari, Amiga, DOS)** (http://www.shareware.com/)   This site contains a huge collection of software for all major operating systems. You can search for a keyword and come up with all sorts of interesting things here. Shareware.com claims to have more than 250,000 files.

➤ **Jumbo (Windows, DOS, Macintosh, UNIX)** (http://www.jumbo.com/)
Another excellent site, Jumbo contains thousands of programs (it claims to have
more than 300,000) for a variety of operating systems. It also provides a variety
of "starter kits," collections of programs for decompressing files and checking
them for viruses.

➤ **Keyscreen (Windows)** (http://www.keyscreen.com/ or http://www.
screenshot.com/)   This unusual site (see Figure C.2) doesn't have many
programs—around 470 shareware and freeware applications—but it provides
pictures of programs (more than 2,100), so you can see whether you might like
them before bothering to download them.

Figure C.2

*Keyscreen lets you see
what you're downloading
before you do so.*

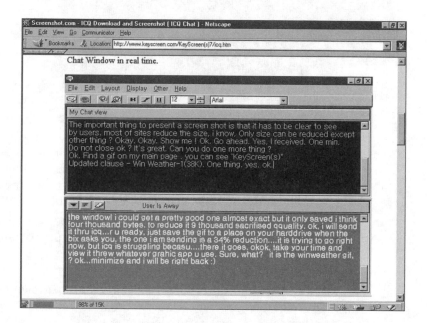

➤ **Info-Mac HyperArchive (Macintosh)**
(http://hyperarchive.lcs.mit.edu/HyperArchive.html)   This large collection of Macintosh software contains lots of files, but it's not very easy to work
with.

➤ **The Ultimate Macintosh Site (Macintosh and Apple)** (http://www.
ultimatemac.com/ or http://www.flashpaper.com/umac/)   You'll find lots of
information about the Macintosh, along with software, at this Web site. You'll
find links to Apple shareware sites, too.

➤ **WUGNET (Windows User's Group Network)** (http://www.wugnet.com/
shareware/)   You'll find hundreds of handpicked Windows shareware programs
at this site (many of them Internet-related applications). WUGNET picks a great
program each week, and the archives store previous weeks' choices going back
a couple of years.

354

➤ **Browsers.com** (http://www.browsers.com/) This site has links to all sorts of browser-related software and information.

Finding More

New software archives appear online all the time, and many are specialized sites, providing software for particular purposes. You can search for more at the search sites discussed in Chapter 15, "Finding What You Need Online." For example, you can go to Yahoo!'s http://www.yahoo.com/Computers_and_Internet/Software/ page and find links to all sorts of software sites—software for amateur radio, CAD (Computer Aided Design), astronomy, and just about everything else. Also try Pass The Shareware (http://www.passtheshareware.com/), a site with loads of links to shareware sites.

Don't Forget Demos and Drivers

Thanks to the Internet, the distribution of demo software has increased greatly. Commercial software publishers often create versions of their software that they give away. Some of these programs are full working versions that just stop working after a while; others are "crippled" in some way from the very beginning (perhaps a few important features don't work). These demos offer a good way to find out whether the company's product is worth buying, and in some cases they even have enough features to make the demo worth keeping. You'll often see these demos advertised in the computer magazines with the URL of the company's Web page.

Looks Can Be Deceiving

Many demos are created by companies that think the way to make sales is to create a totally worthless demo that doesn't even show what the full product could do. Sometimes you're better off working with shareware or freeware than a demo.

Many companies also give away software such as drivers, a fact that came in handy for me when I wanted to print something on a color printer at a local copy store. The store had an Apple printer, so I went to the Apple Web site, dug around a little, and found the Windows driver for that printer. I was then able to print the page to a file using that print driver and take it to the copy shop.

Looking for Something Strange?

If you're looking for a program that you can't find at the popular software libraries, remember that you can always search for it using the techniques discussed in Chapter 15, "Finding What You Need Online." It's amazing what those search sites can turn up sometimes! So, if you're looking for something really obscure that the average library doesn't hold, don't give up too soon.

Index

Visit our Web site at
www.quepublishing.com

- New releases

- Links to deep
  discounts

- Full catalog of hot
  computer books

- Source code

- Author links
  and web sites

- Customer support